SELECTED LETTERS OF
MARGARET LAURENCE AND ADELE WISEMAN

Over a period of forty years, from 1947 to 1986, Margaret Laurence and Adele Wiseman wrote to each other constantly. The topics they wrote about were as wide-ranging as their interests and experiences, and their correspondence encompassed many of the varied events of their lives. Laurence's letters – of which far more are extant than Wiseman's – reveal much about the impact of her years in Africa, motherhood, her anxieties and insecurities, and her development as a writer. Wiseman, whose literary success came early in her career, provided a sympathetic ear and constant encouragement to Laurence.

The editors' selection has been directed by an interest in these women as friends and writers. Their experiences in the publishing world offer an engaging perspective on literary apprenticeship, rejection, and success. The letters reveal the important role both women played in the buoyant cultural nationalism of the 1960s and 1970s.

This valuable collection of previously unpublished primary material will be essential to scholars working in Canadian literature and of great interest to the general reading public. The introduction contextualizes the correspondence, and the annotations to the letters help to clarify the text. The Laurence–Wiseman letters, written with verve, compassion, and wit, offer a fascinating glimpse into the lives and friendship of two remarkable women.

JOHN LENNOX is a member of the Department of English and Associate Dean of the Faculty of Graduate Studies at York University. He is co-author of *William Arthur Deacon: A Canadian Literary Life* and co-editor of *Dear Bill: The Correspondence of William Arthur Deacon*.

RUTH PANOFSKY currently teaches at Ryerson Polytechnic University, and is author of *Adele Wiseman: An Annotated Bibliography*.

EDITED BY JOHN LENNOX
AND RUTH PANOFSKY

Selected Letters of Margaret Laurence and Adele Wiseman

UNIVERSITY OF TORONTO PRESS
Toronto Buffalo London

Published by University of Toronto Press Incorporated 1997
Toronto Buffalo London

Introduction © John Lennox and Ruth Panofsky 1997
Margaret Laurence's Letters © Jocelyn and David Laurence 1997
Adele Wiseman's Letters © Tamara Stone 1997

Printed in Canada

ISBN 0-8020-4247-3 (cloth)
ISBN 0-8020-8090-1 (paper)

Printed on acid-free paper

Canadian Cataloguing in Publication Data

Laurence, Margaret, 1926–1987
Selected letters of Margaret Laurence and Adele Wiseman

Includes index.
ISBN 0-8020-4247-3 (bound) ISBN 0-8020-8090-1 (pbk.)

1. Laurence, Margaret, 1926–1987 – Correspondence.
2. Wiseman, Adele, 1928–1992 – Correspondence.
3. Novelists, Canadian (English) – 20th century –
Correspondence.* I. Wiseman, Adele, 1928–1992. II. Lennox,
John, 1945– . III. Panofsky, Ruth. IV. Title.

PS8523.A86Z547 1997   C813'.54   C97-931364-3
PR9199.3.L38Z547 1997

Frontispiece: Margaret Laurence and Adele Wiseman looking at a copy of Laurence's *A Jest of God*. From the *Montreal Star*, 27 August 1966. Reproduced by permission of the National Archives of Canada (photographer: Blackham, PA 198128).

This book has been published with the help of a grant from the Humanities and Social Sciences Federation of Canada, using funds provided by the Social Sciences and Humanities Research Council of Canada.
University of Toronto Press acknowledges the financial assistance to its publishing program of the Canada Council for the Arts and the Ontario Arts Council.

For Bram and Liza
and in praise of friendship

Contents

ACKNOWLEDGMENTS ix

Introduction 3

A Note on the Text 28

The Letters 31

INDEX 409

Acknowledgments

Any undertaking of this kind is the result of invaluable cooperation. We would like first to express our sincere gratitude for the support that has come from Jocelyn and David Laurence and from Tamara Stone, who have given us permission to publish this edition of their mothers' correspondence.

Others have offered their constant cooperation. Kent Haworth, York University Archivist, and his predecessor, Barbara Craig, were our allies from the beginning. We were admirably served by York librarians Phyllis Platnick, who has worked the longest on the Wiseman papers, and Mary Lehane, who assisted with research and inter-library loans. Others in the archives were of very important assistance, among them Laurel Parsons, who helped in numerous ways, and Jennifer Harris, who has come to know the Wiseman papers very well. Edwidge Munn of the National Archives of Canada also lent us her expertise. In England, we were assisted by Barbara Rosenbaum, who searched the nooks of the British Library at Colindale trying to locate obscure Laurence materials. Linda Greenlick of the *Jewish Chronicle* in London was speedy and efficient.

We are also, as always, very grateful to friends and colleagues – Clara Thomas encouraged us from the beginning and Donez Xiques and Peggy Wigmore worked alongside us on their own Laurence projects and engaged in lively conversations about lives and letters.

Within York's Academic Technology Support Group we thank Patricia Cates and her colleagues for their long-standing support. We also remember with great affection and admiration Patricia Humenyk, whose interest, patience, and unfailing good humour accompanied the manuscript from the very beginning. John Dawson of the Instructional Technology Centre was instrumental in helping us to provide illustrations.

We thank Gerald Hallowell, our editor at the University of Toronto Press, for his interest and confidence in our project. We are appreciative of the careful attention that Emily Andrew, Darlene Zeleney, and copy-editor Barbara Tessman brought to our manuscript.

We acknowledge also the generous support of the Humanities and Social Sciences Federation of Canada, which provided the grant in aid of the publication of this volume.

SELECTED LETTERS OF
MARGARET LAURENCE AND ADELE WISEMAN

CORAGGIO AVANTI

> a bravery given to you long ago
> by strange beloved people
> and passed on
> our slogan through the years

And it's not easy
but we will

sister   friend

From 'For Adele Wiseman on Her Fiftieth Birthday ... 1978,' a poem by
Margaret Laurence, published in *Dance on the Earth: A Memoir*

Introduction

Margaret Laurence wrote to Adele Wiseman on 21 July 1963: 'Your letters make me feel I actually exist.' Almost two years later, on 23 February 1965, Wiseman requested Laurence to 'Please write, to me and at your work. There are few other satisfactions.' The most often repeated phrase in their correspondence was 'Please write.' Letters were a lifeline that allowed them to talk about the world they inhabited in all its complexity, anxiety, triumph, and variety; they articulated in the course of their long correspondence a core identity as writers and women. As importantly, each also expressed her need for and trust in the other. This was the bedrock of their relationship.

Their letters limn themes that are of enduring interest: creative obsession and exhausting tensions between specifically female responsibilities of family and the demands of their vocation. The early letters illuminate the situation of women writers in an era – in Canada at least – long before the women's liberation movement, and they underscore very real apprehensions about making a living. Above all, their correspondence is a testament to what Wiseman and Laurence learned over time – that female friendship could help sustain their commitment to writing. In response to feelings and realities of isolation and exile, their letters affirmed and constantly renewed a sense of community and solidarity with each other. Over a period of almost forty years and across several continents they wrote each other constantly, recognizing from the start the centrality of a shared sense of literary vocation that was eventually to bring them public recognition.

Their lives and careers were characterized by different patterns. Wiseman (1928–92) came to prominence early with the resounding popular and critical success of *The Sacrifice* (1956), which won the

Governor General's Award and other literary prizes. Then followed a long silence of almost twenty years, during which she worked on a number of literary projects, chief among them being her play *The Lovebound*. She had fixed many hopes on the play, but ultimately it had to be privately printed. It was not until almost twenty years after the publication of *The Sacrifice* that her second novel, *Crackpot* (1974), appeared. *Old Woman at Play* (1978) was a moving autobiographical exploration and celebration of the creative impulse through a meditation on her mother and the dolls that her mother made. Her last work, *Memoirs of a Book-Molesting Childhood and Other Essays* (1987), contained autobiographical and critical pieces.

Apart from Henry Kreisel's *The Rich Man* (1948) and Mordecai Richler's *Son of a Smaller Hero* (1955), *The Sacrifice* was the first Canadian novel to explore Jewish life in Canada, and Wiseman returned to this theme in *Crackpot*. Imbued with the immense learning of her culture, and writing in the shadow of the Holocaust, Wiseman brought to the attention of Canadian readers the dynamics of a cultural reality that most did not know. In the 1950s, she was among the cultural and literary heralds of the creative flowering that was to characterize the cultural nationalism of the 1960s, but she was never to re-experience the recognition that her first success had brought to her.

One of the most prominent participants in that flowering, Margaret Laurence (1926–87) achieved recognition after an important literary apprenticeship that included the publication of *A Tree for Poverty* (1954), her translation of Somali poetry; *This Side Jordan* (1960), her first novel, which was set in pre-independence Ghana; and *The Prophet's Camel Bell* (1962), a memoir of her year in Somaliland with her husband, Jack. None of these had the impact of *The Sacrifice*, but with the appearance of *The Stone Angel* (1964) and the subsequent works in the Manawaka cycle, Laurence steadily became the best-known and most successful Canadian novelist of her generation. Like Wiseman, she had an intuitive understanding of the power of myth. To this she brought a distinctively Canadian sense of history, place, and idiom, and above all a gathering of unforgettable characters. One could say that Wiseman had participated in preparing the ground in which writers like Laurence would flourish.

Today, when these women's works are read in the context of widespread assumptions about distinctive female traditions and cultures, the letters between Laurence and Wiseman serve to remind us of the extent to which they lived within – if not always in agreement with – the parameters of a solidly patriarchal world. Wiseman's splendid first novel is rooted in the conflicts among three generations of men in an immigrant Jewish family. Laurence's first works and many of her short stories focused on male figures in a male-dominated culture and were submitted for approval to Jack Laurence, whom his wife regarded for years as her best critic. The 1940s, 1950s, and much of the 1960s were dominated by male writers. Laurence had a lifelong admiration for the fiction of Joyce Cary, and Wiseman was very aware of the work of contemporary American writers such as Saul Bellow, William Styron, and Norman Mailer. Publishers were men, and so were agents. For Laurence her first publishers were Lovat Dickson and Alan Maclean in England, then Jack McClelland in Canada and Alfred Knopf in New York. For Wiseman it was Kildare Dobbs who accepted her manuscript at Macmillan in Toronto and then sent it to Viking Press in New York. She successfully approached Victor Gollancz in London about British publication. For a brief while, Wiseman used Laurence's New York agent, Willis Wing. When Wing's agency closed, it was John Cushman who became Laurence's trusted and respected representative until his sudden death in 1984.

In this climate and during the years before either was known, the two women shared a common goal of staking out a territory for themselves as women writers. In this enterprise they – and especially Margaret Laurence – required the kind of emotional and psychological support that sprang from the trust and respect of a 'sister friend.' They were a community of two, anticipating and forging a future in which creative achievement and ambition could be discussed without embarrassment. In those early years, it was only to Wiseman that Laurence could reveal most fully the extent of her creative obsession. While they moved easily in the world of men, there were unspoken conventions beyond which a woman writer of their generation could not go. For Laurence especially, the social and domestic obligations attached to marriage and motherhood were such that she would write only after everyone else was in bed. She could write to Wiseman in the comforting knowledge that they shared with each other the uniqueness of being both female and creative. Pregnancy, birth, and babies were as natural subjects as ideas, drafts, and books. This made them allies in ways and on levels that were unknowable to men.

Laurence's letters to and from the Canadian poet Al Purdy constitute the other sustained writerly correspondence of her career. It began when Laurence was living in England and had come to public prominence, and it crackles with the energy of two strong-minded people who admired each other. Although their exchange is candid and reflective of much of what Laurence discussed with Wiseman – sometimes even the phrases are the same – there is a tension of need in Laurence and of expectation in Purdy that provides a fascinating edge to what they have to say. Laurence always required support, and Purdy expected her to do more writing and eventually to return to Canada. Both were highly strung, anxious, and joined by a common small-town, Scots-Irish heritage. For all the self-deprecation evident in the correspondence, each had, by the time their letters began, a firmly entrenched and publicly recognized identity as 'writer.'

The Laurence–Wiseman letters articulate the stages and price of becoming a writer. To literary historians and scholars they uncover details about Laurence's experiences in Somaliland, the Gold Coast, and Vancouver that allow us a far greater understanding of the writer's life and her creative emergence. The power of observation, the sensitivity to indigenous peoples, the awareness of the politics of power, and her anti-nuclear stance were all to play a part in Laurence's fiction. The letters also lead us to early literary publications such as Laurence's poem in the *Canadian Tribune*. Because none of Wiseman's letters to Laurence before 1962 survives, it is Laurence's half of the correspondence that supplies us with details about Wiseman's life in the 1950s and early 1960s, and reveals in Wiseman a level of adventurousness and curiosity that is fascinating to discover. Over the years the communications of both women reflect high spirits, enterprise, joy in marriage and children, anguish in the face of personal and emotional unhappiness, and always the driving sense of creative vocation. The dominant characteristic of the Laurence–Wiseman friendship was reciprocation without the tension of self-interest or intimidating expectation. This trust was possible because their friendship had begun so early and with such a meeting of minds. Their closeness was also made possible, paradoxically, by their physical distance from each other. And their letters reflected the extent to which, for them – as for many creative women – work and life had to come together because they could not be separated.

In its continuity and candour, this correspondence is remarkable in the Canadian literary community. In the letters' long-standing demonstration of sustained friendship between creative women in this country, they may well be unique. To understand the context in which that friendship was situated, it is useful to recall the fact that Margaret Laurence and Adele Wiseman were proud to call themselves prairie writers and prairie women. Much of their friendship was celebrated under this banner. For all that such an affinity suggested, they were very different people in character and background. Unlike Wiseman, Laurence had known traumatic personal loss from a very early age and did not have in her adult life the comforting and reassuring presence of immediate family that had been, and always would be, Wiseman's great support. The kinship bond was extremely meaningful to Laurence and she became profoundly attached to Wiseman's family and especially to her mother. The effects of this bond were compounded by the differences between Wiseman's and Laurence's personalities. Where Laurence was anxious, Wiseman was often unperturbed; where Laurence was vulnerable, Wiseman was resolute; where Laurence was confessional, Wiseman was reticent; where Laurence spoke from the heart, Wiseman was more likely to be circumspect. Wiseman always felt secure whereas, for many reasons, Laurence did not. So much of what Laurence poured into her letters – and the energy is palpable – Wiseman was able to dissipate in conversation and interaction with her family and friends.

Laurence's Manitoba roots were steeped in Scots-Irish ethnicity. Her family had been residents of Neepawa since its founding: her paternal grandfather, John Wemyss, was a lawyer who had incorporated the town in 1883. Her father, Robert Harrison Wemyss, was also a lawyer. Her maternal grandfather, John Simpson, a cabinet maker from Milton, Ontario, had moved with his wife and young family to Neepawa in 1895 and established a cabinet making and undertaking business. As a thriving agricultural town, Neepawa reflected the economic growth of rural Manitoba and the Scots-Irish virtues of hard work, thrift, and social probity.

The Wemyss and Simpson families were an integral part of the small Neepawa establishment, and Margaret, in turn, was one of the privileged daughters of the town. As she put it, she came from a family of 'determined women, intelligent and talented women'[1] who had opportunities of which they took full advantage. Her mother, Verna, had been a pianist; her stepmother, Margaret – her mother's sister – had been a high school teacher who had spent a year in Bermuda on a teaching exchange. Her two other maternal aunts, Velma and Ruby, were nurses, one a public health nurse in British Columbia and the other the first head of nursing in Saskatchewan's Public Health Department, the first woman in Canada to hold such a post.

The traumas of Laurence's childhood and youth – the deaths of her mother and her father before she was ten, the effects of the Great Depression of the 1930s, and her family's reluctant removal to the home of her dictatorial grandfather – cannot be underestimated, but they were played against the social and cultural bulwark of an extended family and the security of its rooted position among the founders of Neepawa. As a cherished child, Margaret was given stimulation and encouragement by her stepmother – whom she called her 'mother' – who also was sympathetic to the need for women to be self-sufficient and to Margaret's particular literary bent. As Laurence grew older, she inevitably came to resent the stultifying conventions and restrictions of Neepawa and longed to leave it. When she did move away at the age of eighteen to attend United College in Winnipeg, she resolved never to return to live in Neepawa, and she never did. But Laurence's sense of who she was remained forever deeply connected to the place of her birth.

Shortly after the incorporation of Neepawa, Manitoba experienced its boom years between 1897 and 1912. They were characterized by record demand and prices for wheat, land, and real estate. Relatively inexpensive steamship and railway transport, combined with an aggressive advertising campaign in Europe on the part of Clifford Sifton, the federal Minister of the Interior, brought to the province 'a ployglot mosaic of diverse peoples.'[2]

One of the most striking results of this influx of thousands of immigrants was the consolidation of North Winnipeg as the centre of the Manitoba Jewish community. It was to the North End that the Wiseman family came in 1925, after spending their first two years in Canada living in Montreal. As a young boy in Russia, her father, Pesach Waisman, had wanted to be a cantor, but on his father's death he had been apprenticed at the age of nine to his uncle, who was a tailor. Adele's mother, Chaika Rosenberg, had trained as a dressmaker. Both had experienced the anti-Semitic oppression of the Tsarist era, had known famine, and had lived through the First World War and the Russian Revolution. As socialists and Jews, they were sympathetic to the revolution, but they were looking for a better life for their children and escaped from Ukraine with their baby daughter, Miriam.

By the time the Wisemans arrived in Winnipeg, where Adele was born in 1928, the boom years were past, the Great War had left its mark, and the General Strike of 1919 had shown both labour militancy and state retaliation. The city was still relatively prosperous, however, and the Wisemans opened a tailoring business and were eventually able to purchase a house. When the Great Depression came, their lives changed and were thereafter marked by the need to scrape together a living from the hardscrabble circumstances of the 1930s. The parents' business demanded ceaseless work. The house was rented out and the family leased a working space that they divided into a shop and living quarters. Mr and Mrs Wiseman kept the family together and educated their children by working themselves to the point of exhaustion.

As increasingly secularized Jews whose socialist sympathies were deepened by their Canadian experience, the Wisemans lived among the debates and issues of the North End. Distant from the religious, orthodox community, the Wiseman children were high achievers and attended the secular and left-leaning I.L. Peretz School rather than the traditional Talmud Torah. They were later enrolled in the Liberty Temple School when I.L. Peretz seemed to be losing its working-class and progressive character. To a bookish child like Adele, scepticism about entrenched authority was balanced by respect for learning and achievement – above all, by esteem for the printed word.

The differences in character and background between Laurence and Wiseman were bridged by what they had in common. Each was bright, intellectually gifted, and drawn to literature. Both were restless and intense, although Wiseman's background tended to make her as fascinated with ideas as with issues, whereas Laurence was more drawn to issues. Each had been touched visibly by the Depression, although it was the Second World War that most powerfully affected their growing up: Laurence in terms of the deaths of boys she had known and by the cataclysm of the atomic bomb; Wiseman by the cultural and familial horror of the Holocaust. It could be said that each lived her life thereafter in the shadow of the war. In terms of vocation, both knew very early that they wanted to be writers. Both were also profoundly affected by their sense of the individual's responsibility to society, Laurence through the principles of the Social Gospel and Wiseman through the traditional expectation, based on Talmudic injunction, that each Jew contribute to the community. In addition – and this had a profound effect on Laurence – Wiseman was part of a large, disputatious, and loving family that seemed to live at the crossroads of the world.

University represented a different experience for each woman. For Wiseman, it was a natural extension of the debate and enquiry that she knew first-hand from her own background, and she took it in her stride. For Laurence, it was a revelation and revolution on all levels – intellectual, personal, and political. Laurence and Wiseman did not know each other at university, although they did share some common instructors, pre-eminent among them being the English professor Malcolm Ross, who was to establish his reputation as a critic of Canadian literature, the editor of *Queen's Quarterly*, and the first editor of McClelland and Stewart's New Canadian Library series.

According to Wiseman, she and Laurence met in the summer of 1947, soon after Margaret's graduation and just prior to her marriage to Jack Laurence in September of that year. The two women had first encountered each other at the Ukrainian Labour Temple in Winnipeg's North End when each was trying to get newspaper work. Margaret had met Jack Laurence in a rooming house where she and her friend Mary Turnbull had shared accommodation. He was a war veteran, ten years her senior, who had served with the Royal Air Force as a sergeant and mechanic in Burma. His benefits as a returned veteran provided the opportunity for him to undertake an engineering degree at the University of Manitoba.

After their marriage, the Laurences moved into an apartment on Burrows Avenue in North Winnipeg opposite the Wisemans' home, and the friendship between the two families – and especially between Margaret and Adele – grew and deepened. For Margaret, university, marriage to an older, travelled man, friendship with Adele and the Wiseman family, and living in North Winnipeg constituted an entrée to a much wider and more exciting world than the one in which she had been raised. It was a change that was to mark her whole life.

The first letter from Margaret to Adele dates from shortly after the Laurences' marriage, when Margaret was visiting her mother in Neepawa and Jack was on a surveying project in St Norbert, Manitoba. Margaret's youthful antipathy to her home town is palpable as is her guilt at feeling so superior. The letter's tone also indicates her relief at having left the town for a wider world. As she saw less of her mother and Neepawa over the next two years, she became closer to the Wiseman family and more involved in the life of North Winnipeg. While Jack worked to finish his engineering degree and Adele her courses in psychology and English, Margaret entered the workforce. She found employment as a journalist with the *Westerner*, a publication with communist sympathies, and then with the *Winnipeg Citizen*, a cooperative daily. Her broadly social democratic sympathies were complemented by her affiliation with these periodicals. They were to be fully activated in Africa.

Spring 1949 was marked by the graduation of both Adele and Jack, with Adele being awarded the Chancellor's Prize for her short story 'Nor Youth Nor Age.' She stayed in Winnipeg, working as a tutor and essay marker for the University of Manitoba and as a playground supervisor in the summer. As an inveterate traveller, Jack Laurence wanted to work abroad, and Margaret was ready for new sights: they left in July for London, England, and soon Jack was hired by Sir William Halcrow and Partners while Margaret found work in an employment agency. They were to spend eighteen months in London.

In spite of inferior living conditions and postwar food rationing, Margaret's and Jack's letters of the time reflect high spirits, happiness, and the excitement of living in a very large city. For her part, Wiseman had not found a full-time job after graduation and the Laurences' example prompted her to ask them to make enquiries on her behalf about teaching positions in London. In late May or early June 1950, Margaret told Adele to get in touch with Jewish Social Work Agencies. Soon Adele was in correspondence with Phyllis Gerson, warden of the Stepney Jewish Girls Club in London's East End. Gerson, an English social worker and graduate of the London School of Economics, was a remarkable woman. She had been a leader of the Stepney Club from 1929 to 1944, had spent two years with the First Jewish Relief Unit, and then had returned to the club as its warden, a position she was to hold until her retirement in 1973. She was also a justice of the peace in Hackney Juvenile Court and had been made a Member of the Order of the British Empire.

At Adele's request, Margaret went to meet Phyllis Gerson. Gerson outlined what the club was prepared to offer Adele. In return for room and board at the club and some pocket money, Adele would be put in charge of group activities. Any discussion about full-time work would come after her arrival. Margaret was enthusiastic about the project and urged Adele to accept the offer. She listed the advantages and concluded by appealing to Adele's North End sympathies, arguing that the position would provide 'interesting work with East End London youngsters' as well as furnishing 'a really fine way of getting to know that side of London (the East End, as you know, is the workingclass area). Honestly, Adele, at the distance which you are still from England, you couldn't do any better about a job' (19 July 1950). Margaret had also admitted to Phyllis Gerson that Adele's primary goal was to be a writer.

Wiseman found herself at a decisive point that summer. She was employed as a playground supervisor, had no prospects of a permanent job, and had been accepted at the University of Iowa for admission to their creative writing program. Now she had the chance to live for a time in England. She declined Iowa's offer and in late summer set out for England.

The Laurences were also on the point of a new adventure. In June, Jack Laurence had applied for a job in the Somaliland British Protectorate, where engineers were wanted to construct irrigation reservoirs to help fight long periods of drought. His application was successful, and the couple made plans for their departure. The Laurences were in London only long enough after Adele's arrival to see her safely established at the Stepney Club before they themselves left at the end of November for Rotterdam, where they were to catch the boat that would take them to Aden. Just prior to the Laurences' departure, Margaret wrote to the Wisemans in Winnipeg: 'I was over at Adele's the other afternoon, and we read each other's scripts and told each other that we were going to write the two great novels of the century! In actual fact, however, if she gets this novel of hers finished the way she wants it to be, it will be infinitely better than anything I shall ever write. She has got a tremendous amount of talent' (17 November 1950).

If North Winnipeg and London had been a revelation to Margaret, the voyage by boat to Aden was the sea change that anticipated the transformative effect of Africa on her over the next six years until the Laurences' return to Canada. By the same token, though less dramatic, Adele's experience in London and then in Italy, where she went in the summer of 1951 to teach at the Overseas School of Rome, was also crucial to her development as a writer. The patterns of their writing reflected this pattern of continuity and change.

In 1949 Wiseman had begun working on the short story that would eventually become her celebrated first novel, *The Sacrifice*. Wherever she went in those years and whatever changes of circumstance she experienced, her core creative activity – work on her novel – was constant, and Wiseman had a single-minded and obsessive commitment to it. For Laurence, caught up by the events of moving, culture shock, getting settled, her husband's change of jobs, and the birth of her children, Wiseman's assiduity and single-mindedness were astonishing and intimidating. Laurence had worked in fits and starts for several months on a novel about a love affair between a young woman and a Ukrainian boy in a small prairie town, but she had abandoned it before the change and sweep of Somaliland. She felt profoundly unsettled by her African experience and realized that her creative energies were being confounded, challenged, and rechannelled by this new circumstance. She seemed to be casting about while Wiseman moved resolutely ahead to the completion of a powerful story about her own culture that was to earn kudos and prizes upon its publication.

Convinced of her vocation but unsure of its expression, Laurence was thoroughly caught up in learning a new personal, cultural, and linguistic geography. For her part, Wiseman was immersed more deeply than ever in giving voice to her own. This dynamic defined a characteristic of their friendship that emerged and endured in their sisterly relationship. Though Laurence was older by two years, she always felt a palpable measure of deference to Wiseman that originated in her admiration for Wiseman's intellect and her outsider's love of the dynamics of the Wiseman household. Above all, this deference resulted from Laurence's sustained admiration of Wiseman's unflinching dedication to writing her first novel and Laurence's awe at the resounding critical and popular success of *The Sacrifice* upon its publication in Canada and – most especially – in England.

Almost as if by some principle of imaginative primogeniture, Wiseman became the senior writer; it was the position that she implicitly occupied from then on in their friendship. When, in later years, Laurence's own writing carried her to unprecedented prominence as the Manawaka works appeared in steady and prolific succession, while Wiseman's voice seemed silent, Laurence felt protective of Wiseman. The protectiveness reinforced and was another manifestation of the sense of deference that had always been part of their friendship and always would be.

The extant letters written during the years when the Laurences were in Africa and Wiseman lived in England, Italy, and Canada are all Margaret's. They underscore how one cannot overestimate Africa's effect on her. The letters are a fascinating record of daily living, orchestrated by the rhythms of the mail, that also are a window on impression, process, and new creative direction. For Margaret, letters were, in the first instance, an invaluable means of orienting herself to a new and highly charged environment. A beneficial corollary to this was the way in which the new world before her eyes challenged her as a writer to describe it simply and evocatively and, in so doing, to practise her craft. Some of these early descriptions were composed almost as set pieces and anticipate the painterly quality of many descriptions of setting in the Manawaka cycle. In a way, as Laurence and others have pointed out, Africa was the making of her as a writer because it effectively delayed the appearance in her writing of the prairie background that was to propel her to prominence. She later reflected on how fortunate she had been that her first real challenge as a writer was to translate and describe a land and culture totally different from her own. That exercise began in her letters, which are fascinating in their charting of the artistic and personal growth of Margaret Laurence.

The African experience was also significant because it made her aware as never before of the politics of imperialism and of the individual's responsibility to combat abuses of power and privilege. Laurence's political sympathies, rooted in the Social Gospel tenets of her prairie Methodism, her work as a journalist, and in the Winnipeg Old Left, took on flesh in Africa and turned her into an activist who encountered the colonial system at first hand and – unlike her husband – despised it, idealizing what she projected as Africa's independent future. It is also important to remember that her initial reputation rested on her being recognized as a Commonwealth writer. In fact, as late as 1968, she was to be included among the writers of Africa in a proposed series of Twayne handbooks on the literatures of the Commonwealth to be edited by Joseph Jones of the University of Texas.[3] These facts mark the extent to which the 1950s brought revelations and experiences that were to be the agents of metamorphosis. Her outspoken views were not welcome in her social circle. Progressively, and more and more decisively, these years were unfitting Margaret for her and Jack's return to Vancouver. In becoming a very different person from the woman who had left Canada, Margaret was also changing in ways that would eventually make her marriage untenable.

These were also exciting years for Wiseman. While Margaret and Jack were experiencing the challenges of living in Somaliland, Adele was busy in Rome with her teaching and further work on her novel. She came to know some of the members of the expatriate North American community, including the rising Jewish-American literary and cultural critic Leslie Fiedler and his wife. It was in Rome in early June 1952 that Wiseman saw the Laurences again. They were travelling to London on leave to await the birth of their first baby. In the fall, they would be returning to Africa, but this time to the British colony of Gold Coast, the future republic of Ghana. There Jack was to take up a new job with his old firm, Sir William Halcrow and Partners, as an engineer involved in building the new port of Tema. Margaret and Adele discussed many things during their visit and predominant among them was their writing – Margaret her Somali stories and translations of Somali poetry and Adele her novel. They met again in London in late summer after the birth of the Laurences' daughter, Jocelyn, when Adele stopped over on her return to Winnipeg.

During the next three years, while the Laurences were in Gold Coast. Wiseman held a number of jobs – as tutor and essay marker at the University of Manitoba, technical assistant in a Winnipeg entomological laboratory, and executive secretary with the Royal Winnipeg Ballet. She also sold scripts for broadcast to the CBC. By March 1954 the manuscript of her novel was finished. For her part, Laurence had also been busy with her writing. Her Somali short story 'Uncertain Flowering' had been accepted by *Story* magazine in New York, she continued to work on her translations of Somali poetry, which were published as *A Tree for Poverty* in 1954, and she was writing a novel set in Somaliland, although this work was ultimately abandoned.

After an absence of five years, the Laurences were ready for an extended Canadian vacation in 1954. Margaret and Adele saw each other twice in Winnipeg, in May and then in July. As always, they were anxious to talk about their work. As Margaret had written to Adele just prior to leaving for Canada, 'You know, except for Jack – who is always a very helpful critic – I never talk to anyone about writing – in fact, most people here don't know how I spend all my time, and probably think I'm lazy as hell. It's a relief to be able to write to you about it – I expect that you sometimes feel, too, that it's odd that such an important area of one's life is shared with so few people, in fact, hardly any' (7 April 1954). Wiseman gave Laurence her novel manuscript to read during the vacation, and Laurence was enthusiastic, arguing vehemently against criticisms levelled at it by Margaret and John Stobie, both members of the English department at the University of Manitoba. Adele found their objections initially discouraging, but she began revisions on the novel in the fall and they continued well into 1955.

A new stage was emerging for Margaret after her and Jack's return to Africa in September 1954. She sent to Malcolm Ross, now editor of *Queen's Quarterly*, her first story to be set in West Africa – 'Drummer of All the World' – which he eventually accepted for publication. Although she continued to labour at her Somaliland novel, progress was slow and was interrupted by the birth of her son, David, in August 1955.

July 1955 had been eventful for Wiseman. She had submitted her finished manuscript to Kildare Dobbs of Macmillan in Toronto and had accepted an invitation to be a delegate at the Canadian Writers' Conference at Queen's University in Kingston, Ontario. From Kingston, Wiseman continued on to Montreal to visit her sister before leaving for London and the Stepney Club. She knew that Macmillan was enthusiastic about *The Sacrifice* and that they had secured a contract with Viking Press in New York, whose readers required minor revisions. She spent the fall on these and, in a very buoyant mood, met Margaret in October when the Laurences arrived in London for a three-month leave. On their return to Africa, Margaret set aside her Somaliland novel and undertook a new short story, 'mainly about an African schoolteacher who's lost the old life and not yet firmly grasped the new' (3 April 1956). By the summer it had grown to 350 pages and had 'a good title. "This Side Jordan"' (10 July 1956). Laurence's new-found sense of creative direction complemented Wiseman's success of that year, which included a contract for the novel with Victor Gollancz in England and publication, to very favourable reviews, in Canada and the United States in September and in the United Kingdom in October.

By this time, Margaret and Jack had decided that they would return to Canada. Their decision was accelerated by the news that Margaret's mother, who was now living in Victoria, had terminal cancer. The Laurences determined that Margaret and the children should return home in early January 1957 and that Jack would join them as soon as possible. By the beginning of December she had finished the first draft of *This Side Jordan* and gave it to Wiseman to read during their three-day layover in London. Then, in Victoria, temporarily settled in her mother's house, Laurence entered an exhausting round of caring for her children, agonizing about her mother, waiting for Jack's return, and – her salvation – bearing down on revisions to her novel, some of which had been suggested by Adele. In the midst of all this activity, she caught sight of what was to be her next project: 'Someday I would like to write a novel about an old woman. Old age is something which interests me more and more ... I picture a very old woman who knows she is dying and who despises her family's sympathy and solicitude and also pities it, because she knows they think her mind has partly gone – and they will never realize that she is moving with tremendous excitement – part fear and part eagerness – towards a great and inevitable happening, just as years before she experienced birth' (17 March 1957).

Laurence's overwhelming responsibilities, worries, and sadness of this time contrasted sharply with Wiseman's sudden and resounding good fortune. *The Sacrifice* was the recipient of several important honours in 1957: the Governor General's Award for fiction, the National Conference of Christians and Jews Brotherhood Award, and the Beta Sigma Phi Award for the best first Canadian novel. In addition, *The Sacrifice* was published in Dutch and Italian translations. Wiseman was also the recipient of two fellowships – a Canada Council Arts Fellowship and a Guggenheim Fellowship – which allowed her to plan for an extended stay in New York, where she intended to work on her new project, a play entitled *The Lovebound*. Subtitled *A Tragi-Comedy*, the story was set in late summer 1939 aboard an ancient freighter crowded with Jews fleeing Europe who try without success to find refuge in North and South America. Never published, it was privately printed for Wiseman in 1960.

By November 1957 Wiseman was living in New York, where she shared an apartment with Amy Zahl, a British photographer whom she had met in London. Wiseman remained in New York for four years and became affiliated with the Yaddo and MacDowell artists' retreats in New York and New Hampshire. Zahl and Wiseman had plans to go to China and then collaborate on a book about the trip. They got advances from Macmillan of Canada and advertised for financial support in newspapers in Winnipeg, Toronto, Montreal, and New York. In June 1961, Wiseman set out from Norfolk, Virginia, by coal freighter to Japan, where she was to meet Zahl. During the voyage she completed revisions to *The Lovebound* and on her arrival in Japan mailed it to her New York agent, Willis Wing. He was also Laurence's agent, and Wiseman had retained his services just prior to her departure. Ultimately, the trip was a major disappointment for Wiseman. The authorities refused the two women admission to China when they reached Hong Kong. Zahl returned to England to prepare for her marriage to David Gottlieb, an American scientist whom she had met while waiting for Wiseman in Tokyo. Wiseman spent several weeks in Hong Kong, gathering material for some articles and coping with her disappointment over Wing's negative assessment of *The Lovebound*. She flew to London in October to attend Amy Zahl's wedding. While she was there, Wiseman became very ill, underwent surgery, and did not return to Canada until the following April.

This five-year period of Wiseman's wide public recognition and personal adventure coincided with the years of Laurence's growing unhappiness in Vancouver. It was almost as if, from the moment of her return to face the trauma of her mother's terminal illness, Laurence recognized in that dissolution a foreshadowing of what was to follow in her own life. Coming back to Canada in 1957 was for her in creative terms what the African experience had been in cultural terms – a shock, exacerbated by her mother's prolonged suffering, followed by wracking doubt, slow and painful transformation, and then rebellion and a measure of independence. This confluence of factors found its catalyst in what she came to call her 'old lady novel.'

Margaret Laurence had come back to a culture of entrenched domestic patterns and expectations that were at real variance with the person she had become. For all her uneasiness with the colonial world of Africa, her writing had benefited from the presence of a household staff, however modest. Now the burden of running a house – meals, cleaning, laundry, childrearing – fell completely on her shoulders. In addition, she was never at ease in Vancouver, did not like the house they were living in, and was always intimidated by the area's mountainous topography.

She coped constantly with a sense of being torn between the demands of her writing and the claims of her family. Jack himself was also restless, never completely happy with his work, on the lookout for new opportunities, and soon hankering to leave Canada again. He was a traveller and a man who enjoyed expatriate life; his longing for another overseas posting, prompted by his professional dissatisfaction, was becoming progressively stronger. Once Margaret had admired his taste for life in exotic climes; it was now to prove critical to their increasing incompatibility. In spite of the trappings of marriage and motherhood, Margaret had become a very different person from the woman who had left Canada ten years earlier. The transformation and her obsessive commitment to her writing were new forces in her marriage. Her and Jack's priorities and interests had diverged; ultimately their personal and professional differences were to prove intractable.

The torment of those years was apparent soon after they returned to Canada. Margaret completed the first draft of *This Side Jordan* while her mother was dying; she marked essays for the University of British Columbia to earn extra income for the family, but felt alienated from the academic community; the book that she was to write out of her Somaliland diaries, *The Prophet's Camel Bell*, occupied her towards the end of her years in Vancouver. The goals that beckoned and the depression she experienced were in constant conflict.

Nevertheless, there were significant and heartening successes, among them, the publication of *This Side Jordan* in Canada, the United States, and Britain; the Beta Sigma Phi Award for the novel; the publication of short stories in *Prism International* in Vancouver and in the annual anthology published by Macmillan (London), *Winter's Tales*; and the successful completion and acceptance for publication of *The Prophet's Camel Bell*. These gave Laurence a sense of achievement despite the enormous unease she was experiencing.

She was also acquiring her own circle of friends through her writing. Jack McClelland was her Canadian publisher, a contemporary who had an appreciation and understanding of her and a deep-rooted respect for writers and writing. It was through McClelland that she retained Willis Wing and came to know John Cushman, who was a member of Wing's firm. Eventually, she became a client and fast friend of Cushman and his wife, Jane. Lovat Dickson, a director of Macmillan in London, had agreed to publish *This Side Jordan* and became for Laurence a benevolent senior literary statesman. Another director of Macmillan, Alan Maclean, editor of *Winter's Tales*, became her most trusted literary adviser in England. Also a contemporary, he became a close personal friend, and it was his family's country home, Elm Cottage, Laurence's beloved 'Elmcot,' that she rented and eventually bought. Laurence also counted greatly on the example, interest, and good will of the highly respected Vancouver novelist Ethel Wilson who wrote Laurence in praise of her early publications in *Prism International* and whom Laurence visited on several occasions. In the welter of domestic responsibilities, creative ambitions, and general restlessness, Laurence saw in Ethel Wilson an indispensable example of a serious and successful writer who took time to be generous about the work of others.

In her writerly relationship with her husband, Margaret had experienced an ambivalent combination of gratitude and malaise. In her isolation in Africa and then in Vancouver, she asked Jack for his opinion, and he offered criticism and encouragement. She was grateful, but by stages she became less and less content with her compliance. Yet she was not ready to trust her own sense of what was right for her stories. As the years passed, malaise turned gradually and inevitably into restiveness and finally into rebellion when she insisted, in the case of her 'old lady' novel – which became *The Stone Angel* – on the integrity of her own creative instincts, even at the price of her marriage.

By the spring of 1962, just as Wiseman returned to Canada, Laurence was close to the point of crisis. More than ever, she felt the pull between her family and her writing. Rumblings of the change to come had been evident the previous year when, just after the publication of *This Side Jordan*, she had written to Wiseman to say that she had changed her name. The force of her language identified her restive state of mind: 'I've always detested my name, and only you and Jack and one other very close friend now call me "Peg," which I don't mind so much – it was Peggy I hated, so I have killed her off (I hope)' (22 January 1961). At the same time she was incubating a new project that had overwhelmed her half-hearted attempt to begin a second African novel, and by September 1961 the first draft of her old lady novel was nearly completed. Then, as was her custom, she gave the manuscript to Jack to read. He told her that he did not like it. Although her letters to Wiseman spoke forcefully about the writer's need to write as the work demanded, Laurence herself was still dependent on her husband's judgment. She was shaken, put the manuscript away, and turned her hand to another project, the book on her and Jack's experiences in Somaliland, which she began in earnest in January 1962 and which, she said later, was her 'farewell' to Jack.[4]

Despite her own resolution to leave the old lady manuscript for six months, she reread it and decided that it was, in fact, terrible and in need of wholesale revision. As she coped with this frustration, she was experiencing difficulty with the Somaliland book, and Jack was again restless in his job and wanting the family to leave Canada. For all Margaret's apparent disparagement of the old lady novel, it was a force that connected her with deep and powerful aspects of her own background as inexorably as it was pushing and pulling her to her future.

The pressure intensified, and Margaret was showing signs of excessive anxiety – bad headaches and the physical sensation of pins and needles. She finished *The Prophet's Camel Bell* and sent it off to her agent, but the fraught circumstances of its composition caused her always to disparage it. She took diet pills in an effort to lose weight, resumed work on the old lady novel, revised *The Prophet's Camel Bell* when it was accepted for publication, and coped with a houseful of guests. Her normally high-strung temperament was stretched to its limit, and she was in a particularly volatile state as she found herself caught up in an exhausting cycle of frustration and anxiety. Her feelings towards her novel indicated how alienated she had become and how much she was misreading her own talents and instincts. Buried deeper still were corrosive resentment and rage, which could not be suppressed much longer, and her feeling that she was going crazy.

When it looked as if Jack would receive a job offer in Pakistan, the crisis boiled over. Still struggling with her confusion over her manuscript, resentful of her dependence on Jack, touchy from her dissatisfaction with the Somaliland memoir, and anxious about her children's education away from Canada, Margaret confronted her husband in a jarring and explosive exchange. She informed him that she and the children would not be going with him to Pakistan but would be leaving instead for England where she intended to try and make a living as a writer.

Margaret acted with a decisiveness that she had never shown before. Her eruption was particularly gut-wrenching since she had always dreaded Jack's disapproval and would go to any lengths to avoid confrontation with him. It was also inevitable, the only means by which she could hope to dislodge the despair that had claimed more and more of her sense of herself as a person and a writer during her years in Vancouver. Jack Laurence had been for her an example of maturity, self-confidence, and unruffled competence that she had, at some level, found intimidating. Now that her confrontation with him had taken place, she realized that he had also been a kind of father figure and that their separation would allow her to move from an extended, dependent adolescence into true adulthood.

It is at this crisis point that we first hear Wiseman's voice in the Laurence–Wiseman correspondence. She speaks as a friend would speak – concerned, supportive, careful, and anxious to be fair to both sides at the same time. In its contrast to the intensity of Laurence's letters of the time and in keeping with the exchanges between them, it also demonstrates another aspect of their friendship – Laurence's great need for communication.

Margaret finished final revisions to *The Prophet's Camel Bell* during the first two weeks of September 1962, made arrangements for her and the children's flight to London, coped with the vocal misgivings of her and Jack's families, and asked Jack to look after the rental of the Vancouver house which, she later admitted, she had hated from the moment she moved into it. On 12 October she, Jocelyn, and David left Vancouver for Winnipeg, where they spent a few days with Adele and her family. There, learning that her baggage was overweight, Laurence packaged the only copy of her old lady novel, some of her children's books and toys, and some tennis shoes and sent the parcel by sea mail to London. Then they flew on to Toronto, where she saw Robert Weaver, editor and radio producer, John Gray, president of Macmillan Canada, and her McClelland and Stewart editor, Claire Pratt. The family's arrival in London on 22 October was followed by a flurry of activity and, within days, Laurence had taken a flat in Hampstead and was prepared to begin a new life.

The next twelve months were to prove a period of major adjustment for both women. For her part, Adele Wiseman was still trying without success to place her play for publication. Since her return to Winnipeg the previous spring, she had been writing children's stories and selling scripts for broadcast on the CBC. She had not, however, found a job and so returned to marking essays for the English department at the University of Manitoba. Her prospects changed radically when she was hired in the summer of 1963 as a part-time instructor by Sir George Williams University and by Macdonald College of McGill University. Although she taught at Sir George Williams for only one year, she was to remain at Macdonald College until the end of August 1969. The move to Montreal was to mark her definitive departure from Winnipeg.

After the excitement of leaving Canada and settling in London, Margaret Laurence experienced exhaustion and sheer terror as she pondered her future in England. Her first task, after finding a place to live and enrolling the children in school, was to finish the revisions to her novel that she had provisionally entitled 'Hagar.' Her apprehensions were allayed when Macmillan accepted it for publication four months after her arrival in London. Next to the well-being of her children and the demands of her writing, Margaret's priority was to earn enough money to be self-sufficient. Jack Laurence provided her with a monthly allowance and, after his return from Pakistan in June 1964, he made Elm Cottage his home base during the intervals when he was not working abroad. The arrangement lasted until January 1967, when Jack took a flat in Surbiton and spent weekends at Elm Cottage.

Margaret was determined to earn her own income, and her success in this area was impressive both in its results and in the work her earnings represented. By dint of advances and royalties, as well as freelance work for periodicals and radio, her income rose steadily: from £368 in 1962–3, to £2176 in 1963–4, to £3823 in 1964–5. Her big year was 1966–7 when she was paid $7000 for the movie option and an additional $23,000 for film rights to *A Jest of God*. This windfall allowed Laurence to purchase Elm Cottage from the Maclean family. Although she may have felt vulnerable, she had the determination and capacity to meet her practical needs head-on. In fact, feelings of vulnerability spurred her into action.

The letters from 1962, when Laurence left Canada and Wiseman had just returned, to 1973, when Laurence returned from England, encompass years of personal and professional anxiety, achievement, and consolidation for both writers. In Margaret's case, they begin with revisions to the manuscript of *The Stone Angel*, after it arrives safely in England and when she realizes that her writer's instincts about its form and voice have been right. They end with the successful completion of revisions to the final draft of *The Diviners*, two weeks before her departure from England when she learns that she has been acclaimed as interim chair of the embryonic Writers' Union of Canada. For Adele, this period opens when she is becalmed in Winnipeg following her return home from four years in New York, an abortive trip to China, rejection of her play by her literary agent, and serious illness in England. This period also encompasses important personal events, first among them her marriage to Dmitry Stone, a marine biologist, and the birth of their daughter, Tamara. The period ends with McClelland and

Stewart's offer to publish *Crackpot*, Wiseman's second novel, which she had begun after her move to Montreal in the fall of 1963.

The family situations of the two women were very different from each other. The major personal developments in Laurence's life – marriage, the birth of her children, the breakdown of her marriage – had taken place prior to her departure for England. For Wiseman, similar events – love, marriage, stepchildren, the birth of her daughter – awaited her in Montreal. In both Winnipeg and Montreal, Wiseman was close to family – her parents in the West, her sister in Montreal – and to old friends. She had the personal and emotional security that such proximity provided. For Laurence, no such network existed in England. Although she treasured the friendships of people like Lovat Dickson, Alan Maclean, the English novelist Alex Baron and his wife, Delores, and her old friends from Somaliland days, Gus and Sheila Andrzejewski, she was essentially on her own as far as her domestic and emotional life was concerned. Canadian friends were either physically removed, like Nadine Asante, whom she had known in Vancouver and who was living in Glasgow, or recently met, like Alice Frick, who had worked with the drama section of the CBC in Toronto and was living in London and trying to make a living from freelance work. For Laurence, these circumstances intensified the psychological and creative importance that her correspondence with Wiseman had always had. Of Laurence's 306 extant letters to Wiseman, approximately one-third were written during her years in England, the most intense period being from 1962 to late summer 1969, when Laurence left England to begin her year as writer-in-residence at Massey College, University of Toronto.

The descriptive amplitude of Laurence's early letters to Wiseman disappeared, along with the rituals of another life and the decorous language of another time. A new voice had emerged – colloquial, resolute, often profane, anecdotal, and sometimes very funny. The intensity remained, but it was complemented by hard-won inner strength. In spite of waves of fear and what to her were bouts of lethargy during her first months on her own with her children, Laurence was able to do what she had been incapable of doing in previous years – laugh at herself. She was also able to accomplish a tremendous amount of work. While the letters reflect a sense of a situation in which she feels herself very much at sea, the record attests to action, decision, and accomplishment. Her letters to Wiseman, and later her letters to Al Purdy – and theirs to her – became her lifeline. She commented to Adele that 'in some peculiar way I exist only as an extension of my typewriter. I know that isn't true, but I sometimes feel as though it were true. In fact, often. The letters to friends are the same, really – the typewriter is my radio set, from which I send out messages – this is in some way my main contact with life' (27 November 1968). Her situation in London deepened what George Woodcock has noted, her 'obvious and at times overbearing need.'[5]

For Margaret Laurence, the Elmcot years were her most productive period. They were initiated by an act that was necessary and reckless – the shipping by sea mail of the only copy of her draft of *The Stone Angel* – an act that she viewed in retrospect as a half-hearted attempt to get rid of the manuscript, closely followed by almost unbearable worry about its safe passage. It was almost as if, in her newly found sense of purpose and in the face of her and Jack's families' disapproval at what she was doing, Margaret was prepared to let fate confirm or deny the rightness of her action. Amidst the confusion of moving and getting settled in London, the fate of the manuscript fuelled an inner turmoil and pent-up energy that Laurence directed at its revision when it arrived safely weeks after it had been mailed. Then, as always, she revised with decision and dispatch.

In her letters to Wiseman, Laurence talked volubly about the general challenges and particular details of her novels. Her pattern of incubation, false start, lamentation, and eventual revelation of the true project was consistent throughout her writing career. She would write without revising; only when the draft was complete would she return to it for revision. She described herself to Adele as writing 'in a way similar to the Stanislawski (sp?) Method' (24 January 1965), that is, from inside her characters. Adele's method was more methodical, in part by habit and in part in response to her teaching schedule: she wrote and revised chapter by chapter.

Their letters reflect this difference in approach. Laurence's have one overarching preoccupation – writing, the writer, and her world. All that she did took place in the context of her work and her children. In Wiseman's letters, writing is a topic of discussion that takes its place alongside other subjects; her letters do not articulate her writer's preoccupations. Wiseman alludes to her imaginative challenges and pleasures – 'The "how to do" is tough, isn't it? But it's the key, & worth sweating over. It's so lovely when you finally know, & it begins to shape. If the "how to do" ever stopped bugging one it would be a sure sign that something had gone wrong, – a numbness of sensitivity had set in at the nerve ends, – the beginning of artistic death' (5 May 1967). For her part, Laurence's letters are vivid and dramatic narratives whose tone, language, and voice vividly dramatize her vocation. In some cases, and to Laurence's great surprise, Wiseman was silent about her work. When Laurence received a complimentary copy of *Old Markets, New World* (1964), she wrote, 'Heavens, girl, you are a dark horse! I never even knew it was coming out!' (23 December 1964).

When Margaret Laurence returned to Canada in 1973 and settled in Lakefield the following year, she and Adele saw each other fairly often, though not as often as they would have liked because Adele, her husband Dmitry, and their daughter were living outside Toronto in Kleinburg and then in Maple, and Margaret did not drive. They did, however, telephone each other frequently, often several times a week. Even when she was visiting in Toronto with friends like Clara and Morley Thomas, Margaret would often speak by phone with Adele. When Adele and Dmitry moved to Toronto in February 1977, personal visits became much more frequent because Laurence could travel easily by bus between Lakefield and Toronto. In spite of occasional bouts of panic at the size of her telephone bill, Laurence maintained that the telephone to her was like the car to others – an indispensable means of communication.

The letters of this period were often prompted by issues and events – censorship, the Writers' Union of Canada, the sale of personal papers – but there were also letters about a host of other topics: children, Wiseman's 'doll show,' which was a presentation based on the dolls her mother had made over the years, house renovations, writer Hubert Evans's honorary degree, typewriters, critics, shared holidays, and highly amused speculations about future literary scholars poring over the Laurence–Wiseman correspondence. Because she was better known, Laurence in particular felt the responsibilities of being a public figure and accepted that role, including the chancellorship of Trent University in the early 1980s. For Wiseman, the 1970s and 1980s were also busy decades. She had been ecstatic – and Margaret with her – when, at the age of forty-one, she had given birth to her daughter, Tamara, in June 1969. The 1970s and 1980s were primarily her child-raising years, and much of her energy was taken up by Tamara and the care of her stepsons.

There were, however, other achievements for Wiseman. She was writer-in-residence at Massey College in 1975–6 and in 1978 she published *Old Woman at Play*, a book about her mother, her mother's dolls, and the creative process. In 1981 she was finally able to go to China with a group of six other Canadian writers who had been invited by the Chinese Writers' Association. Margaret and Adele were also able to look after each other during periods of surgical recuperation. Since the mid-1970s, they had become respected elders of the literary 'tribe,' as Laurence loved to characterize the company of Canadian writers. Both were honoured and bemused by their status and delighted at the successes of other women writers such as Margaret Atwood, Marian Engel, and Alice Munro.

Throughout their careers, the two women had encouraged each other unstintingly and, in the process of going through what Margaret Laurence called 'this vale of tears,' they had shared moments of doubt and fear, of triumph and achievement. It was a richly rounded friendship that allowed them to cry and laugh together. In one instance, when *Crackpot* was rejected by Viking Press in New York, Laurence had sent Wiseman what was to have been a comforting telegram, but which was, in the event, hilariously mistranslated by the telegraph office as 'VIKING IS IN SPAIN TRANOPF LETTER FOLLOWS LOVE MARGARET' [Viking is insane. Try Knopf]. Several years later, while writing *The Diviners*, Laurence ruefully noted in a letter that Wiseman had begun to appear as a character in the novel. Wiseman's reply was gleeful: 'So you're going to put me in a book! Ha ha! I guess I'm just one of those people; sculptors itch to sculpt me; painters to paint me; musicians to orches-trate me' (31 December 1972). They treasured these moments as the leaven that sometimes helped to put pressure and expectation into humorous perspective. In one aspect of their later lives they were radically different. Margaret Laurence found public appearances an ordeal, and she would shake from nervousness, although her voice never failed her. Her consent to be chancellor of Trent was all the more a mark of her esteem for the position and the institution. For her part, Adele Wiseman was a natural performer and speaker who took great delight in presenting her doll show to many different audiences. It was inevitable, however, that both learned how to fill their roles in ways that did justice to expectations of them.

Sadly, both women died much too soon, Margaret Laurence on 5 January 1987 at the age of sixty, and Adele Wiseman on 1 June 1992 just after her sixty-fourth birthday. As a legacy, their letters attest to mutual friendship, love, and respect, which are freshened upon every reading of their correspondence. We, like them, have every reason to be grateful.

Notes

1 Margaret Laurence, *Dance on the Earth: A Memoir* (Toronto: McClelland and Stewart, 1989), 7
2 W.L. Morton, *Manitoba: A History* (Toronto: University of Toronto Press, 1957), 274
3 Clara Thomas, *All My Sisters: Essays on the Work of Canadian Women Writers* (Ottawa: Tecumseh, 1994), 297
4 Laurence, *Dance on the Earth,* 157
5 George Woodcock, 'Personal Interest,' *Canadian Literature* 140 (Spring 1994): 104

A Note on the Text

Margaret Laurence's and Adele Wiseman's papers are held in Archives and Special Collections, Scott Library, York University, and contain the exchange of letters between the two women. From the first undated letter written by Laurence sometime in the fall of 1947 to the last – also Laurence's – dated 12 November 1986, the exchange traces a close personal friendship that spanned forty years. In the entire correspondence, 306 letters are from Laurence, while only 83 are written by Wiseman. There are no extant Wiseman letters to Laurence in either collection prior to 1962; the first letter from Wiseman to Laurence is dated 20 August 1962.

The reasons for this disparity stem from a combination of circumstance, personality, and choice. Both women travelled great distances and changed residences on numerous occasions. Wiseman was by nature a saver who kept everything, while Laurence hated clutter and was inclined to houseclean furiously when she was moving or gearing up for writing. At different times, each destroyed letters at the request of the other. Certainly both sorted through their and each other's papers immediately prior to their official sale. In addition, from the earliest stages of her career, Wiseman possessed a sense of the professional side of her vocation and began deliberately accumulating a personal archive. Laurence came to this stage much later. The effect of this history, especially as it applies to the first twenty years of their correspondence, is effectively to mute Wiseman's presence and voice.

From 1947 to 1973, letters were Laurence's and Wiseman's primary means of communication. They lived at great physical distances from each other, and the rhythms of the mail ensured a fairly regular exchange of letters, if we can extrapolate from Laurence's portion of the correspondence. After Laurence's return to Canada in 1973, the regularity of their letters was broken and, with it, the narrative rhythm encouraged by the delivery schedules of the postal system. There was a falling away of habit and continuity as the telephone and personal visits replaced letters as their primary means of communicating. Letters tended (though not always) to become extraordinary rather than ordinary and were more often than not prompted by occasions, events, and causes; they were no longer the regular record of patterns and events of daily living. There were intervals where, usually in the wake of large telephone bills, Wiseman and Laurence would resolve to resume letter writing. This initiative, however, would last only until the telephone reasserted itself.

For this volume we have drawn from among the original letters included in the writers' papers. Despite the relative lack of letters by Wiseman, this volume is designed to provide as representative a sense as possible of both women, the continuity and constancy of their friendship, and their ongoing preoccupations: their writing, their personal lives, and the public causes they took up.

In preparing this volume we have kept editorial intervention to a minimum. Idiosyncratic spellings have been retained, obvious typographical errors have been corrected, and supplementary information, when required for clarity, has been inserted in square brackets. Quotation marks and the placement of punctuation in relation to quotation marks have been made consistent with University of Toronto Press style. The format for addresses and dates has been standardized. The first time it is used, an address is reproduced with all the information that appears in the original, and thereafter an abbreviated form is given. To prevent any confusion in the reading of the letters in this volume, all postscripts appear at the end of the letter rather than at the beginning where lack of space sometimes occasioned the writers to put them. Margins have been standardized for addresses, salutations, and signatures.

The letters in the collection were either handwritten or typewritten. In keeping with typographical convention, titles, words, or phrases underlined in the originals are set in italics. Multiple underlining in the originals is indicated here by single underlining in addition to the italic setting. Notes have been prepared for a broad readership. The information they provide is current to the date of the letter, except where the context requires additional information.

We have omitted letters of incidental interest and letters that reiterate what our selection already covers. Wherever possible in the period following 1962, when there are extant Wiseman letters, our selection is designed to provide a sense of a dialogue of two voices. Letters are reproduced in their entirety except in rare cases where material is no longer pertinent or has been omitted at the request of Margaret Laurence's or Adele Wiseman's children. Such deletions have been indicated by ellipses in square brackets, while material lost as a result of damaged originals has been noted by dashes in square brackets.

THE LETTERS

Dear Adele, Mary, Abe, Mo, et. al –²

Stranded.

Neepawa, as usual, is so very much like itself.

Nausea (*real*, not mental), as usual, has set in, the uncomfortable accompaniment of great mental stress & strain. However, your voyageur is making valiant attempts to control the digestive system, & so far I haven't thrown up on anyone's oriental rugs.

I am writing to you because if I don't I shall explode (mentally that is.) Jack is at St. Norbert, & I forgot to tell him to go to the postoffice there for mail, so I'm sure he wouldn't think of it, so I don't think there's any point writing to him. If you see him, however, tell him from me that he's the most wonderful guy in the world & when I see him on Saturday I'll fall on his neck & weep.

I know it's ridiculous to be writing to you all so soon, especially as I'll be seeing you in a week, & I'm sorry if this epistle appears a trifle disjointed, but my need is great, believe me.

We are all going to the lake tomorrow, about 20 people. Gay fun. Who should we ask? Well, 'A' isn't speaking to 'B' now, you know. Oh yes, they are, I saw them say hello on the street. Well 'A' has never *liked* 'B,' but they get along *very* well together.(?!) Ok, Settled. Both 'A' & 'B' will come. But what about 'C,' who is really such a bore?

Oh, we have to ask *her*, well, you know – we just *can't* leave her out. And by the way, I heard the most *dreadful* thing, girls, about 'C's' daughter – it seems she was in a cafe one night & she – No! She didn't! Oh, my dear, she certainly did! I wouldn't *dream* of telling her mother, of course. ⁓⁓⁓ tra la la – the flowers that bloom in the spring.

♪ ♪ ♫ 0 0 0 ♪ ♫

And of course, there is the story of the poor little Polish DP³ girl that the minister's wife met on a bus – she wanted to take Medicine here & had 2 yrs medical training in Poland, but of course is working now as a nurse's aide. Moral of the story? Why, simply that she's *so* cheerful about it all, such a wonderful girl, perhaps someday she'll go through with her medical training. What's that? No money? Ah, but my dear, such wonderful *spirit*! So determined. Poor child, her family, she said, was taken to Russia. (Dreadful people, the Russians – no sense of *freedom*.) [I told them about Yvette, but they were unimpressed.] I'm

probably being very unkind. But perhaps you will forgive me. I miss
you all very much. We'll see you on Monday nite, eh?

Regards to you all, & to
Mr & Mrs Wiseman

Peggy (alias 'Prairie Flower')

1 As Margaret Laurence indicates in *Dance on the Earth*, this letter was written shortly
after her marriage to Jack Laurence on 13 September 1947.
2 The members of Adele Wiseman's family: her sister Miriam (Mary), her brother
Morris (Mo), and a family friend, Abe. Wiseman's other brother was Harry.
3 The postwar abbreviation for displaced person, that is, refugee

1, Fairfax Mansions,[1]
Finchley Rd.,
London N.W. 3,
England
28 January 1950

Dear Adele:

You will be wondering what has happened to us ... I'm afraid my
correspondence, carried on so nobly before Xmas, has been let slip of
late. Hope you got my airletter of thanks for the parcel ... we have really
enjoyed the things you and the family sent, and have just finished the
tobacco a few days ago ... it's amazing how long we spun it out! Also
hope you got our long letter sent to all of you before Christmas. Adele,
I do hope you and Mary have got jobs now ... we are very concerned
about you ... please write and let us know how things are. We had a
letter yesterday from Jim Freedman,[2] saying he was having a terrible
time finding work ... things must be getting pretty awful in Canada.
Have you done anything about shorthand or something like that?

The long-awaited day has arrived at last ... the Canadian Tribune has
published one of my poems.[3] I suppose I should be properly casual
about the whole thing, but actually I was, and am, tremendously
pleased and encouraged. They also wrote a very nice letter, enclosing
a tear sheet of the page, which I thought was extremely thoughtful of
them. I don't know whether you get the Trib, but it was in the
January 9 issue, not, of course, under my name. Very nice layout,
complete with 2 photographs appropriate to the subject of the poem. It

isn't a terribly good poem, but neither is it (by my standards) a propaganda piece. That is, I feel that a strictly propaganda poem is one where the propaganda matters more than the poem. A real poem, no matter how many flaws it may have, is one in which the idea and the form are inextricably united, the one impossible without the other. Whether it comes off, of course, is quite another matter. At any rate, I was very encouraged at their printing this particular one. In their letter they said they had just received another poem which I had sent them, but didn't say whether or not they would print it ... I rather hope they do, as it is a better poem, on the whole, and is about the revolt of the Italian peasants which began in earnest last fall.[4]

Another stroke of luck ... we have recently won £64 in the Football Pools! By the old rate of exchange, that is about $250!!! Honestly, we could hardly believe it, as it is the first time that either of us has ever won anything. The Pools, in case you don't know, are a form of gambling on the results of the football matches held throughout England during the winter. We have been putting exactly 1 shilling (20 cents) a week, on the Pools, no more, no less. Everyone in this country plays the Pools, but since there are only about 40 prizes every week, needless to say many people put their shilling on, every week for years and years and never win. We were absurdly happy about this 'found money,' and have decided to spend it recklessly. Half of it will go towards our holidays, which we fervently hope to spend in France and Italy. The rest is being spent on concerts, theatres, ballet, clothes and books. We have already seen a play called 'The Heiress' on the strength of the Pools money ... the play is actually a very fine adaptation of Henry James' novel 'Washington Square.' We are also going to another one called 'Black Chiffon,' and have also been to several concerts lately at the Albert Hall, one of them being a Beethoven concert in which Sir Malcolm Sargent conducted the London Philharmonic Orchestra in Beethoven's 9th Symphony, with a choir of nearly 200 voices! It is really an experience to hear (and see) it ... we have heard it once before, and expected it to be not quite so terrific this time, but it was. The choir was all dressed in white (the women, i.e., who composed most of the choir ... the men were in evening dress and were at the back, so that you got the view of the huge group of women in white gowns completely unbroken by any other color.) The most tremendous moment in the whole thing comes, I think, in the last movement, where the choir stands up and begins to sing Schiller's Ode to Joy. The brotherhood of man theme is repeated, of course, throughout the whole last movement ...

'By thy magic is united
What stern custom parted wide,
All mankind are brothers plighted ...' etc.

Beethoven was really a revolutionary, respectable as his music may be today. My advice to a progressive rally would be to invest in a really good orchestra, conductor and massed choir; perform Beethoven's Ninth, with the Ode to Joy being sung in English; then take up the collection immediately afterwards! The result would be stupendous!

With our Pool money, also, we are in the process of buying a few more clothes to combat the English weather. I am trying to persuade Jack to get a really good English wool pullover, plus another pair of grey flannel trousers. He is very difficult when it comes to clothes, as he insists on buying all kinds of things for me, out of our Pool money, but keeps saying he doesn't need anything, which of course is sheer nonsense. Many couples have the difficulty of each wanting to buy new things for himself or herself, but we have just the opposite trouble ... I have to persuade Jack to buy things for himself, and vice versa. We went downtown last weekend to buy a few things for me, and Jack went slightly mad, going from store to store saying 'I think you need a new dress' or 'How about a new coat?' etc.etc. We finally ended up with a lovely wool dress, in blue and white check; a brown tweed coat, long enough for me to wear a fairly long dress with it without having the dress show much underneath the coat; a black silk skirt; and a really lovely rust and blue silk scarf from Libertys (one of the poshest stores in London!). Honestly, it was quite fantastic, but, I must say, wonderful.

We saw the Italian film 'The Bicycle Thieves' not long ago ... when it comes to Wpg for heaven's sake don't miss it, as it is one of the best films ever produced. It is the story of an Italian worker, who has been unemployed for a long time. He gets a job putting up posters, and then - finds out that he needs a bicycle for the job, so the family (himself, his wife, and their 8 or 10 year-old son) pawn the bed-linen and get back his old bicycle, which he had previously pawned. His first day out on the job, the bicycle is stolen, and the rest of the picture is the story of how the worker and his little son tried to trace the stolen bike. Through the streets of Rome; the markets; the churches (and the film really slams the churches, who are holding services to honor the poor, while the workers of the city starve); the cafes; etc. etc. the father and son hunt for the bicycle. When they finally find it, they discover that it has been taken, not by a professional thief, but by a workingclass lad who is in just as desperate straits as they are. It is a really wonderful, human, fully conscious, film. And all the parts except one bit-part are taken by people who had never acted before!! The child is really remarkable, as is Lamberto Maggiorani, who takes the role of the father. I saw an item in the Daily Worker not long ago, which said that Maggiorani had worked in a factory until he got the part for the film, and afterwards, had gone back to the factory, but had been laid off, along with most of the other workers at the plant, shortly after. He has been without work for months now, and when interviewed he waved a bunch of press-clippings, all very keen, and said 'You can't eat press-clippings ... How they would laugh if they could see me now.' His own son has just had his 11th birthday, but there were no gifts. (Sideline to this story ... my boss[5] had occasion to go down to the Italian Embassy in London last week, and said she has never seen such luxurious surroundings, everything new and up-to-date and lovely. Need I say more?)

Well, Adele, I think I must close now and get lunch. It is Saturday morning, and the room feels like the Arctic. Do write soon and let us know how everyone is getting along. If you see Roland and Addie,[6] tell them I shall write to them early next week.

Our best wishes to you and Mary, and to the whole family, and to anyone you happen to see who knows us.

Peg

1 In the summer of 1949 the Laurences had moved to England where Jack Laurence worked for Sir William Halcrow and Partners.
2 A friend from Winnipeg
3 'Let My Voice Live' by 'Meg – (A Canadian in England)' was published in *Canadian Tribune*, 9 January 1950, 15. The text is as follows:

> I am a childless woman, old,
> And like my frail world, bled to grey.
> A dry husk, my seasons' fruitfulness
> Dead as those lads whose bones now melt
> Like lifeless leaves into that hillside
> Hideously mellow with their fallen flesh,
>
> Joachim was like his father, grey-dusk eyes,
> And laughter warming as tea after the chills of hunger.
> Ben, sixteen that last year, had a stooping walk
> From too much living in sunless basement rooms.
> These memories threaten.

To settle again an empty heart is hard,
And I am tired, having seen death glisten
Like a dank wedding-ring on both my hands.

Children, they say, are born again to women now.
Oh, you women with fruitful wombs,
Know that the young can make your hearts contract
With anguish sharp as stones of many an endless road,
Fearing that their quick-flexing bodies, too,
Will be seared and shamed. War, the glorious,
The exalted? Think of my kind, and judge.
You women, looking now at your children
(So small, so hardly-stirring in sleep,
Their slight hair soft to touch as moth's antenna) ...
Only this plea from my gathering silence ...
    Let my voice live in your angry voices
    Crying stronger than any malevolent rising storm,
    'Life for our sons, and for man's sake, peace!'

4 This poem was apparently never published.
5 Margaret Laurence was working in a London employment agency for a Mrs Berman.
6 Roland and Addie Penner. He had been Wiseman's classmate at the University of Manitoba and had graduated in 1949.

1, Fairfax Mansions
12 June 1950

Dear Adele:

We got your letter this morning and felt terrible to think that you thought we hadn't answered your last request ... it was our fault for not explaining ... but as soon as I got your former letter I wrote to you, and Jack wrote also, a week later ... BUT we sent these letters by sea-mail, as I will explain later. I should have written before to say they were on their way. The reason, I am sorry to say, that I had to send the letter sea-mail was that they wanted 10 shillings to send it airmail, and I couldn't afford it! However, I hope it reaches you fairly soon. In it I included all the correspondence, plus copies of my own correspondence, re: jobs for you. I also sent a book 'Jewish Social Work in Great Britain,' which a Jewish social work organization kindly sent me. As I said to you in my letter, Adele, I do feel that the Jewish organizations are your best bet. They were the people whom I thought were the most helpful when I made enquiries. They have a lot of young people's organizations, like YWCA clubs, and with your playground experience I think you'd stand a good chance to get taken on there as group leader or junior program worker, etc. Which would be very much in your line. I went into all this in my letter, which pray to god you get shortly. The Min. of Education never answered my letter, but the London County Council did, and enclosed a form to be sent to the Min of Ed to see if you would be eligible as a teacher in the state primary schools. I sent this on with the letter, and think perhaps you should send it to the Min of Ed airmail. But as I said before, I think the Jewish social work organizations are your best bet. Now, re: your recent questions ...

1) *the British state school term*: (fall season) begins, as near as I can find out, about September 15.

2) *Passage on ship*: Jack and I both think that, if you have quite decided to come to England, and if financially possible, you should take the passage on the Samaria, because otherwise you may have trouble in getting passage over this fall. If you get here before the school term opens, you can always get a temporary job. Or, if you work for a social organization, it won't matter anyway. The Jewish Social Work place sent an address (which I forwarded, along with the other things) of an organization that supplies clerical staff for Jewish welfare agencies, and the man said in his letter it might be possible to fix you up there if necessary. Please let us know as soon as you know definitely when you're coming, and we'll try to fix up a place for you to live.

3) *Food etc.*: You are allowed to bring a certain amount (I forget how much ... they'll tell you at the place where you book passage) of tobacco or cigarettes, and would advise you to bring all you are allowed, as it is horribly expensive here. Food is pretty good here now, with tinned meats, biscuits, jellies, rice, syrup, fruit juices, etc., now off the ration and quite easy to get. Tinned meat is fairly expensive, so you might like to bring some. Also, tinned fruit is hard to get. Package Jello puddings are not available either, and would be nice for you to have, as you could prepare them in your room. Don't bring butter or fats, as they are quite available now, and altho rationed, the ration is quite sufficient. Tea is also available, and coffee (but the coffee isn't very good, so you might like to bring a pound). I wouldn't advise you to bring much food, as the situation is better than you might think. Also, don't under any circumstances bring a lot of soap and cosmetics, as these are easy to get here. Soap is rationed, but the ration is so large we've never used all ours. I don't think there's really anything we need, Adele, so just bring things for your own needs. Kleenex, etc., is easy to get here also.

4) Clothes: Just about the same as at home, really. It would be advisable to bring 2 or 3 cotton dresses, as the summer here is quite warm. For winter wear: a medium heavy coat; stout oxfords or other shoes; several sweaters (if possible, a few cardigans to wear with skirts and blouses for work); any suits you may have; a raincoat, if possible; an umbrella, if possible; and do for heavens sake bring at least one good wool dress, as houses are poorly heated in winter, and you'll need a wool to keep from freezing when you go out in the evenings to someone's house! You will want to bring, also, some nylons for yourself. Don't bring any for me, Adele, as I still have quite a few pairs, and my mother will send me more when I want them ... save your money and your luggage space for yourself!!

5) Customs: You're allowed to bring almost anything, except liquor and excess tobacco (you can find out the customs regulations from the CPR or CNR there).

I'll write again soon and tell you more about our plans, as they stand at present. In the meantime, I do hope everything works out all right for you, Adele. If there's anything else we can do, let us know. Best of luck!.

Love,

Peg

P.S. Jack has applied for a job in Somaliland, Africa, so we may be seeing some more of the world. Will let you know about it as soon as we hear ourselves.

P.S. find out if you can bring some sugar – the ration is very small (½ lb per person per wk)

1, Fairfax Mansions
19 July 1950

Dear Adele:

It is so nice to be able to write unadulterated good news to someone for a change! Well, kid, your troubles are over ... for awhile, anyway! I went to see Miss Gerson at the Stepney Jewish Girls Club,[1] and had a long talk with her about you. She could not, of course, commit herself to employing you on a permanent basis, but she said that she would be glad to have you come to the Club as soon as you arrive in London. The setup is this (if it's ok. with you): Jack and I will meet you at the docks

(I think you dock at Tilbury, London), and take you home with us for a meal. Then, afterwards, we will take you and your luggage to the Stepney Girls Club, where you can move right in. If Miss Gerson is away (she may still be at camp with some of the girls' clubs) you will be met by Miss Woolf,[2] at the Club, who will show you around. Then, when you've settled in, you can begin work on a part-time basis, in exchange for your room and board and some pocket-money. Your duties will be mainly concerned with group activities at the Club ... helping the group leaders with the junior club activities, and all that sort of thing, much the same sort of work as you're now doing in your playground. Miss Gerson is very charming, and altho' she said she would have to talk to you first before she could officially take you on on that board-and-room basis, she did say she felt sure that it would be quite all right ... that your qualifications seemed good, and that you looked like 'a charming girl' from your photo. Also, the reason why I feel so confident about it is that she wouldn't have said you could move into a room there as soon as you arrive if she hadn't been pretty sure she'd like you enough to have you working there! The job, Adele, you must understand, is not on a full-pay basis, but is definitely room-and-board in exchange for part-time services. Also, there is some pocket-money allowance, which we didn't discuss. As far as a more permanent job is concerned, Miss Gerson said that when she saw you and saw how you got along with the clubs etc., she might discuss a full-time paid job with you, and if there isn't an opening at the Stepney Club, she could put you in contact with any of the other Jewish organizations who need similar staff. I do hope this is ok. with you, Adele, and that you think the arrangement is all right. In my opinion it has these advantages: 1) room and board provided from the moment you land, so you won't have to spend your savings; 2) part-time work for awhile, so you will be able to see a lot of London in the interim; 3) an 'in' with the Jewish social work agencies, so that, if they like you, they'll do their darndest to get you some full-time full-pay type of job; 4) interesting work with East End London youngsters ... a really fine way of getting to know that side of London (the East End, as you know, is the workingclass area). Honestly, Adele, at the distance which you are still from England, you couldn't do any better about a job. You'll be certain of food and a room, and you'll make valuable contacts. I hope you'll be as pleased as I am with the situation ... I think it sounds swell. Your room is a nice large one, plainly furnished, but quite adequate. Bath-room is right next door. You may have to share it, but I said you wouldn't mind that. Miss

Gerson asked what was your object in coming to England, and what sort of job you ultimately wanted. I hope you approve of my answer ... I told her you wanted to write, but realized a) you couldn't earn a living at it; and b) you couldn't write in a vacuum, but needed some creative work to do as well, and that therefore you thought you'd like some sort of social service type work. I hope I didn't say the wrong thing, but that seemed nearest to the truth, and also expedient. She said the Stepney Jewish Girls' Club is a recognized training centre for social workers, and if you are interested in receiving training (they give classes as well as practical work), you and she could discuss it when you arrive. My advice to you is to think quite seriously of this, as I think it might be a damn good thing. She said the Club is fairly Orthodox, but not 100% ... she said she was glad you weren't completely Orthodox, as their food there isn't always absolutely so, altho' of course they keep a kosher kitchen. Adele, I do hope you don't think I've committed you too far ... but I thought that, since she said you could go there directly, it would be best to jump at the chance. You could always refuse later if something better turned up. But as I say, I think it's a good way of making contact with that type of social group-work. Miss Gerson and her staff seem very nice, and I'm sure you'll like them. There was also a marvellous collection of tiny kids there when I was there ... playing in the nursery. I do hope you'll approve of everything. Please let me know. Love from Jack and myself to you and the family.

Peg

1 Phyllis Gerson (1903–90) was an English social worker and warden of the Stepney Jewish Girls (B'nai B'rith) Club and Settlement in London.
2 Miss Woolf was an employee at the Stepney Jewish Girls Club.

27 December 1950

Dear Adele –

Well, here are your two stormy petrels, at the moment off the coast of Portugal.[1] We expect to pass Cape St. Vincent about midnight, and proceed to Gibraltar.

But to begin at the beginning – . We had a smooth channel crossing, thanks to fairly good weather plus your pills! When we got to Rotter-dam, however, we discovered to our horror that the 'Tigre' had been held up in Antwerp owing to fog, & might not call at Rotterdam for a few days. That was putting it mildly – we were stranded in Rotterdam for 5 days! We got to know that ugly little port town a whole lot better than we wanted to! Prices were high, & we had the devil of a time finding a restaurant where we could eat a meal at less than 9/-(each!). Finally we found a nice place, 'De Drie Steden,' in a workingclass area, & ate our noon meals there. For our evening meal we would buy rolls & cheese & fruit, which we smuggled guiltily into our unfortunately high-class hotel, planning always to say loudly, 'nice pottery we bought today,' or some such thing, à la tourisme, if one of the hotel staff glanced too suspiciously at our round little brownpaper parcel! Late at night we would creep out & deposit the fruit peelings etc in a nearby 'singel,' or canal. Apart from that, we managed quite well in the matter of meals, and were surprised to find that a great many Dutch people speak passable English. Not all, however ... we did have some trouble in that respect. One day, in our 'cheap' restaurant, we decided that we would like some apple pie for dessert. The waitress spoke only a little English. We tried everything we could think of ... 'apple,' 'apfel,' 'pomme,' 'strudel,' etc. No good. Finally Jack drew gay little sketches of apples and pies on the paper tablecloth. His art, however, must not be of a very high order, for we still drew a complete blank. Finally we marched in a determined little procession to the front of the restaurant, where we pointed out what we thought looked good from among a lot of pastries on the counter. Mine turned out to be a 'slagroomwafel,' or waffle with whipped cream in between the 2 portions. It was lovely, so after that we ordered only that one pastry for dessert, developing quite a good Dutch accent in respect to that one word!

We saw quite a lot of interesting things in Rotterdam, for it is really quite an interesting town, despite our first feeling of antagonism towards it because of the delay. Much of Rotterdam was destroyed during the war, and they've done a wonderful job of rebuilding. There are a lot of ultra-modern buildings. One of these is the Museum Boymans, where an amazing amount of fine things are to be found. These include several Rembrandts, some Rubens, a lot of very good gothic things, some early Van-Gogh landscapes, and some very fine modern things ... an Epstein bronze, a Henry Moore bronze, an early Picasso, and a lot of Zadkine sculptures. We saw some of the latter's work in Paris, and were very impressed. His 'Orpheus,' in the Boymans, is done in bronze, very angular and tree-like, with his lyre growing out of his ribs like a branch. – Rotterdam hasn't done badly in re: a museum – the town is only about twice the size of Winnipeg! The building itself is one of the finest for its purpose that we've seen, being all done in grey marble and white stone, and divided up into innumerable small galleries, instead of only a few large rooms, thus giving 2 additional walls to each section and avoiding crowding of exhibits. The whole place is full of wonderfully large windows, which give a feeling of light and air throughout. Incidentally, this is the museum that housed one of the most famous of the 'phoney Vermeers' ... painted, if you remember, by one Van Meegeren during the war, and accepted for years by all the experts as being genuine Vermeers. This one was, I think, called 'Christ at the Home of Mary and Martha,' altho' I'm not sure.[2] The museum was so proud of it that they had a print of it put on the cover of their official catalogue, and now, since to reprint said catalogue would be too expensive, there it remains, altho' the picture has long since disappeared. We recognized the print, and asked about it, and the staff seemed genuinely embarrassed ... no one knew, or would say, what had become of the picture, which, to my mind, is a fine one, forgery or not.

One day we went to Delft, the little town famous for a) Vermeer and b) Delft blue pottery. It is a small town with rambling cobbled streets and high square houses. The 'singel' runs through the center of town, and in the market place is the town cathedral, the same church that Vermeer painted. This naturally gives it a sentimental and artistic value, but in actuality, it is a hideous church ... Gothic (14th century), but with none of the mounting lines or impression of having grown out of the earth and striving towards heaven that one does (quite genuinely, I believe, despite all Ruskin's sentimental nonsense on this point)[3] find in French and English gothic. It is red brick, which in itself cuts the vertical lines and breaks the upward thrust of the building.

Delft pottery, blue and white, is in all shops, until one gets a bit sick of it. It is quite nice, but awfully traditional in design. We liked much better the modern ceramics display of the Handicrafts Centre, which has its chief branch in Delft, thus carrying on in a modern way the traditional local industry. This stuff, however, was all individually made, and we liked it so much that we spent far too much money and bought several pieces of it. Some of the ones we got have simple, almost primitive designs ... grotesque birds and fishes in heavy brown lines on a light brown background, and touched in with blue. Some were incredibly delicate in grey-green, with dark blue spindly-line patterns of leaves and flowers. It must be very satisfying to be able to make things like that yourself.

Well, finally, after what seemed an eternity in Rotterdam, the 'Tigre' arrived, and we got on board. Our suite is extremely nice, a sittingroom, bedroom, and bathroom. We are the only passengers on board, altho' we may pick up some others in Genoa. We eat with the Captain and his wife, and are the only 4 people in the dining room! The Captain, fortunately for us, speaks quite good English, and his wife a little bit.

(*Dec. 28*) – Several of the ship's officers also speak English, so we manage. Altho' ordinarily, the officers have their own dining room, they all gathered together in the Captain's dining room for Xmas dinner, which, according to Norwegian custom, is served on Christmas eve, and most of the celebrations take place then. They call it 'Jule' (pronounced 'Yule'). The Christmas dinner and celebrations were very interesting indeed. There was a terrific dinner ... turkey and all the trimmings, and the drinks (all free!) ranged through beer, aqua vite (a national drink with them ... a sort of strong liquor made from potatoes ... quite nice, but very potent!), curacuo (sp?), and scotch whiskey ... 5 or 6 26 oz bottles of the latter being consumed between 7 p.m. and 1 a.m. The Captain, who is a dear soul, very fat and jolly, got very drunk and became more and more like Raimu[4] as the evening went on, going into elaborate pantomime about a huge parcel of presents that had been left, he said, by Jura Nissen (I'm not sure of the spelling ... but it's like our Santa Klaus, and as we abbreviate and say 'Santa,' so they call him 'Nissen' ... he looks more like a troll than our idea of Father Christmas, being short and stocky and elf-like). Anyway, the Captain was afraid the bundle of parcels might also contain an atom bomb, so he stalked it carefully for a full half-hour before opening. Presently the parcels were given out, and Jack and I discovered much to our surprise that there were some for us, too! I got a little marzipan pig, plus a box of genuine marischino chocolates with real liqueur inside! Jack was given (believe it or not) a 26 of real scotch whiskey! We nearly passed out with shock! The best thing, however, was the verse which was attached to my box of chocolates. We thought it was quite an admirable effort, being in English rhyming verse. It was signed 'officers on board,' and went:

'To our little sporty guest,
A happy sailors' "Julefest." '

!!!What do you think of that? Despite the questionable adjective, I thought it was very nice indeed. Also, they explained carefully, if unnecessarily, that 'Julefest' was a Norwegian word. After the presents,

we sang Xmas carols, these being, naturally, in Norwegian, and mostly
with unfamiliar tunes. The tunes were good, we thought, mostly being
in a minor key, and you should have seen Jack and me singing the
Norwegian words lustily, with the help of a little songbook! When in
Rome, they say ... We decided that we'd soon be fluent in the language,
if only we could ascertain what the words meant! The only words we
understood were 'Jesus' and 'Halleluja,' which we sang with particular
emphasis, to show they had significance for us, unlike the rest of the
words. We had a long talk with the Wireless Operator, who speaks
excellent Eng., about the relative merits of Ibsen and Shakespeare, and
upon his remarking that 'our country once ruled your country,' we
drank to the Vikings. Oh yes ... one word we did know was 'Skol.'
Despite the language difficulty, everyone was awfully friendly, and I
think it was without doubt the most interesting Christmas we've had.

There hasn't been much sea-sickness so far. J has been perfectly all
right, and I was sick once, in the Bay of Biscay, as I had suspected that
I would be. Since then, we're ok. We made a faux pas the other day,
tho' ... the Captain's wife wasn't down for lunch, and we, assuming that
it was sea-sickness, made kindly enquiries after her health, remarking
on how terrible mal de mer could be, only to discover that it was not so
much sea-sickness as change of life! I should hate to be sick again, as
the food is so good on board. However, I think I've found my sea-legs
now.

We pass Gibraltar tonight, and hope to be at Marseilles for New
Years, and as the crew naturally wants a holiday to celebrate New
Year's eve, they are working like mad to keep the ship on time.

I've been going ahead with my story not too badly, having finished
Chapter III (rough draft!) yesterday.[5] I've done 25 shorthand pages since
leaving London, and now must transcribe them ... if only they would
turn out to be as good as one feels they are in the first flush of finishing
a chapter! Still, it is good to be able to devote more time to it. How is
your story coming along? And how is the New Regime For Accomplish-
ing Much? Still in effect, I hope. Be discouraged, if you must, at times,
Adele, but for heaven's sake don't give up! Not that you would be
likely to. But it will get done, and it *will* be good, if only you can keep
working at it like mad! It doesn't matter if you can't get much done at
one time, just so it goes ahead steadily.

I'm reading 'The Brothers Karamazov' now. It is a joy to read ... I've
never read a book that impressed me so much with its sharpness of
perception, vividness of dialogue, and way of catching the full

complexity of its characters. It really is tremendous. They say that Dostoevsky wrote much of his work without even going back and reading it over again ... that, in fact, much of it is just the way it first came from his pen. My God! To think of what that means ...

Well, the stewardess has just arrived with tea, so I must close. One always seems to be eating aboard ship ... I shall probably be grotesque by the time I arrive in Africa ... with so much food and so little exercise, I'll put on pounds if I'm not careful.

I'll write again when we arrive, Adele ... did we give you our address? It's HARGEISA, Brit. Somaliland, East Africa. We won't be there, however, until about the middle of January.

Hope everything is all right with you, and, especially, that you're finding some time for your own work. Give our regards to your family, when you write, will you?

Best regards from both of us,

Peg

1 The Laurences were en route by sea for Somaliland via Aden.
2 In 1945 the Dutch painter Hans van Meegeren was called upon to defend himself against charges that he had sold paintings by Jan Vermeer (1632–75) to Hermann Goering during the Second World War. Van Meegeren demonstrated that he had forged works attributed to the Dutch master. Among these was *Christ in the House of Martha and Mary*.
3 Laurence is alluding to John Ruskin (1819–1900) and his essay on 'The Nature of Gothic' in *The Stones of Venice* (1851–3), vol. 2, chap. 6.
4 Stage name of French actor Jules Auguste César Muraire (1883–1946), whose films include *Fanny* (1932) and *Un carnet de bal* (1937)
5 Laurence was working on a novel, set in a small prairie town, about a love affair between a Canadian girl and a Ukrainian boy.

Sheikh,
Somaliland Protectorate
12 February 1951

Dear Adele:

No doubt you have the impression now that we died en route. I'm terribly sorry we haven't written sooner. Ever since we arrived, so much has happened that we've hardly had time to draw our breath.

To begin with, then, we had five really good days in Genoa on our way out here, which was very fortunate for us as we hadn't expected that long a time there. From there we proceeded to Port Said, where we had a day, and then on through the Suez Canal and the Red Sea to Aden. At Aden, we disembarked, and got on a very dirty little tramp steamer to come across to Berbera, and from Berbera we travelled by truck to Hargeisa along the worst roads in the world. It is a barren, semi-desert land in most places, with miles and miles of sand stretching away into the distance, and in front the line of hills, showing red-brown in the brilliant sunlight. A few prickly bushes, the odd flat-topped tree, and many varieties of cactus are the only growing things, and since this is the dry season, they are brown and dry now. Occasionally one sees a water-hole, or a river-bed (called 'tug') that is still a bit moist, and then the scene changes at once ... bright green grass, bullrushes, a tangle of palms and pepper trees, marvellously green and alive. But for the most part, the land is empty; the sky is open from one side of the horizon to the other; the yellow sand glistens with mica, and slides down into long ribbed dunes; and the prickly little bushes dig their tenacious roots down, finding in that unrewarding soil the means of a scant existence. Then, in all that expanse of sand and sky, a figure appears, a man standing calm and straight, and looking at you with a sort of dignified detachment. It is a Somali herdsman, a tall brown-skinned man dressed in his traditional brownish-orange robe, and carrying his long wooden stave. The small herd of black-headed sheep cluster around him. The camp is nearby ... a few angry looking camels, very thin now since the lack of water is terrible; the nomad's tents (akhals) made of woven grass and twigs; old men and children sitting in front of the camp; and women in their long robes helping with the camels and flocks. The Somali people are really quite amazing. A mixture of Arab and Negro, they tend to be very handsome people, the men tall and sharp-featured, and the women very tiny and having beautiful soft features and enormous dark brown eyes. The women wear voluminous robes of red and yellow and black, with a head scarf. They are very shy, and will not speak much to you at first, and walk with downcast eyes. A contrast to the assertive men. The remarkable thing about the Somalis, tho', is their terrific pride and dignity ... they are, I imagine, about the poorest people in the world, and their country is about the poorest, also, but they walk erect and proud, and look you squarely in the eye, and what is more, they love their barren little land. One would have thought that their harsh life would have broken them long ago, but not so. Most of them are nomadic herdsmen, and live by travelling from water-hole to grazing grounds. The water holes are only pools of brackish evil-smelling water, and the grazing is mostly dry grazing, but somehow they and their flocks keep alive, altho' each year many do die from either thirst or starvation. Jack's job will be to try and put in some small dams (ballehs) in the tugs, to hold some of the water after the rainy season, as it usually sinks into the sand within 24 hours. The tug in spate is a roaring river, which lasts only a day! His job will be terribly difficult, and he's already working awfully hard, doing research and compiling rainfall figures, etc. He will be on safari most of the time, and I hope to go with him in a month or so when he'll be setting up camp for a week or so at a time. He's been given good equipment ... a new Landrover (a sort of modified jeep), a truck, etc. We also have two 'boys' now! It was hard at first to get used to the servant idea, but we figured that at least we could try to be as fair as possible with them, which is a lot more than a lot of people here are. Our boys are Ismail (who will go with J on trek) and Mohammed (who will stay here at Sheikh with me, and whom I'm attempting to train as a cook!) They're both nice kids, in their late teens, and so far we've managed to get on very well with them, by trusting them and treating them like human beings, despite the fact that so many people here told us never to trust our boys; that all Somalis are thieves; etc etc etc.

The really great thing I've been saving till last ... we've got a house, and it's a nice house, too! We won't be at Hargeisa after all, but here at Sheikh, which is the best place in Somaliland. It is a mountain station, right in the heart of the hills, very high up, where the wind is never still. It is one of the few places that is reasonably green all year around, and the climate is absolutely perfect. I'll continue this on airletter # 2.

To continue about Sheikh ... the mountains are speckled with trees growing along the gorges, and our house is situated at [the] end of the settlement where we can look out and see the whole valley and the hills. Across the valley is the big white tomb of the important sheik (Mohammedan priest) after whom the place is named. Our front door is like a picture-frame, and the picture contains the soft line of hills; the red sand of the valley and the blue-green rocks; the green flat-topped trees; a flock of tiny white sheep, grazing a few feet from the house, and tended by a brown-robed Somali woman with a scarlet headscarf. The yerki (little boy) is there too, with his little switch of dried grass, rounding up the stragglers in the flock. I think it is the quiet one notices most about Sheikh. During the whole sunny day, only the odd scrap of birdsong; the strange minor-key chanting of the boys as they work; the early morning clank of water-tins as the Somali woman brings up our three donkey-loads of water each morning; the frantic chirp of the yerki, a little boy so tiny that one can hardly see how he copes with the relatively large cows he drives through the valley; and the occasional tic-tic-tic of a lizard in the walls of the house. There is a strange air of peace here, almost a Shangri-la atmosphere. I suppose the best thing about Sheikh, from the Somali point of view, is that it has permanent water in the valley, and the camels here are fatter than almost anywhere else in the country. That doesn't mean the flocks and camels are *fat* ... merely that every rib does not show, as it does with the animals in most parts of Somaliland at this season.

Our house is really very nice. From the outside it doesn't look so hot ... it's a timber house, painted green, and is a bit shabby. But inside it's ideal. We have a good-sized livingroom with a big stone fireplace (quite necessary some evenings!); a big bedroom; a bathroom with a sink and concrete bathtub; a small kitchen; plenty of cupboard space; and a cookhouse outside. The floors are all concrete, and we haven't enough carpets yet, but otherwise the place now looks very nice (we think). I've made the curtains for the livingroom and bedroom (10 in all ... thank heaven the windows are small), in unbleached cotton, printed with potato block-prints. The livingroom ones are done with a pattern of 3 autumn leaves ... green, rust and brown. I've also done two cushions for two of our wicker-seated chairs ... these cushions are also in unbleached cotton, and I've embroidered a large snail (one of the few things I can draw!) on each, in green and yellow. Also I've done a cushion for our couch, with a block-print of green butterflies that looks quite good. Our bedroom curtains are done in block-prints of sunflowers ... some turquoise with yellow centres and some dark blue with yellow. Please forgive my rattling on about domestic details ... but the last week I've really been surprisingly housewifely! I hope, at this point, never to see another curtain hem!

I haven't got down to writing yet here, but I did chap. III on the boat, and hope to settle down again this week, as Jack will be away again and I've now got the house pretty well organized. The only other Europeans here are connected with the school, as the chief govt school for Somalis is situated here. The principal and his wife are extremely nice people, very interested in literature, and the others are passable. Also, no one here (as contrasted with Hargeisa, where we really were hardly ever sober!) is a heavy drinker, which is a great blessing! As soon as Jack gets things organized on trek, I hope to go with him a good deal, as I think I could write just as well (or nearly so) there as here, and also I want to learn more about the country. We've made a small beginning with the language, but it is awfully difficult, as it contains many sounds not made in English at all.

Must go now. I do hope everything is ok with you, Adele, and that your writing is going forward, and that the job's all right, and that you aren't discouraged. Please write soon (our address is just: Sheikh, Somaliland Protectorate, E. Africa). We're very anxious to hear from you. I do wish you could visit us here, Adele, you'd be awfully interested in the country. Please give our love to your mom and dad and Mary and Mo, when you write, and tell them I *will* write when the smoke clears a little ... we've hardly had time for anything lately. Also, our regards to Winnie[1] and Miss Gerson.

1 Winnifred Taylor (b. 1907) was an employee at the Stepney Club.

Sheikh
2 May 1951

Dear Adele:

How about a crafty line from you? We are beginning to think that all our friends have deserted us ... we've had so little mail for about a month, and all of it has been from our respective mothers. Please buck up our morale and write to us! By the way, a horrible thought has just struck me ... we don't owe you a letter by any chance, do we? Anyway, how are your plans for Miriam's visit? Are you still going to hitchhike? And have you heard anything about anyone at home? We never hear anything about people in Winnipeg, except from you, Adele ... honestly, if it weren't for the news you tell us, we wouldn't know if Wpg was still there! Anyway, how are you, Adele, and how is your writing? That is the question. I have been slipping badly this month, having only got one chapter nearly done, as I've been mainly collecting information about Somaliland. I've also been trying to learn Somali ... a hideous task, since it must be the hardest language in existence. So far, Hersi, our interpreter, who is teaching me, and Abdi, our driver, and Mohamed, can understand what I say in Somali ... but all the other Somalis think I am speaking English. It is most disheartening! Of course, I can only say silly things so far, such as 'the country is looking well this morning; there are plenty of clouds in the sky ... do you think it will rain?' and so on. What I really want to do is to be able to understand the Somali stories and poems, of which there are a huge number, all unwritten, of course, but a vast body of folk-literature passed on from generation to generation. Some of these poems are highly complex, and also very symbolic, and the more ignorant Somalis can't understand them half the time. The Sheikhs, and other wadaads (holy men) and notables, are always arguing about the interpretation of a poem ... it's just like a college at home in that way! I don't know any of the poems yet, but have had a few odd lines translated for me ... one is 'In the green Haud[1] there is a tree for poverty to sit under.' It sounds just like Eliot,[2] doesn't it? I don't really think I shall ever be able to speak enough Somali to understand the poems, however, as they are in very literary Somali, and not at all easy. The Somalis are great orators and talkers, and always act out a story while they are telling it. It seems strange that a people without a written language should be so much more talented along literary lines than in any other branch of art. Most of the poems are not really recited ... they are chanted, and some of the tunes in themselves are lovely. Most are in the minor-key, like Arabic or Indian music, and very haunting and melancholy. I have also been discovering a lot of interesting Somali words ... there is a Polish chap here, Goosh Andrzejewski,[3] who is studying the Somali language, and Jack and I have become quite good friends with Goosh and Sheila (his wife). He has let me go through his files, and I've copied out a lot of interesting words. Most of these relate to Somali customs, or magic, or religion, and I've been also asking Hassan Adan and Ahmed Mahmoud, two of the Somali teachers at the Sheikh school, about these customs, so have been finding out quite a lot. Some of the words, however, are very lyrical or witty in themselves. 'Waharwaallis,' for example, is a type of low bush with pale mauve flowers, and the name means 'that which makes the little goats jump' ... Another good one is 'marooro' ... a kind of herb which has an acid taste in the morning, but is fairly sweet in the evening ... and the name is also used as a nic-name for a woman!

There has been a lot of excitement in Sheikh lately, as a few nights ago a man was taken by a lion in the Sheikh Pass, not far from here. Last night, a lion took a boy in the same hills. At this time of year, the people in the Guban, or coastal plain, are moving up through the mountains, on their way to the Haud, or inland grazing grounds, and they take their flocks and camels through the Pass at night. Since there were flocks around, then, it is believed that this lion is a man-eater. A man here at Sheikh claims to have seen a lion two nights ago on the road, but this is more doubtful, although about fifty people claim to have seen clear lion-tracks. But Jack went over the next morning and couldn't find a track at all. Jack hopefully cleaned the rifle, but I don't suppose we shall get close enough to a lion to take a potshot at it. At least, I hope to God we don't. Jack is away at Hargeisa for a few days now, and in the meantime, I don't intend to go out much at night!

Please write soon. Love from both of us,

Peg

1 The Haud is a plateau area of Somaliland and a major wet-season grazing area for Somali camel herds. It is also subject to long periods of severe drought. It was here that Jack Laurence constructed a series of 'ballehs' or earthen dams to hold rain-water during the fierce drought season.
2 Thomas Stearns Eliot (1888–1965), Anglo-American modernist poet
3 B.W. (Bogumil) Andrzejewski (b. 1917), a Polish poet, had been given a Colonial Office research grant to study Somali language and literature. He was to become an expert in the field and later taught at the London School of African and Oriental Studies from 1952 to 1982.

Sheikh
15 June 1951

Dear Adele:

Thanks for your last letter, which we received last week [—] both over-come with admiration for you in re: your walking [—] think it was absolutely terrific of you to get all that [—] You know, you should write an article for a Canadian mag [—] they'd probably print it like anything. I'm so glad about Mary going to England, you'll have a wonderful time together. Did I tell you that I hope my mom will be able to come to London when we're on our leave and meet us there? We can't afford to go back to Canada, and anyway, we don't want to, as we want to see Italy and France before it's too late, and we'll spend a month in England, I think. I hope my mom can make the trip ... we would pay her fare, if only she can leave my old devil of a grandfather for the time. She hasn't had much enjoyment in her life, and I think this would mean quite a lot to her.

I'm sorry to hear about Alvin[1] in Paris (sounds like the title of a children's book ... Alvin in Paris ...). I think you are 100% right about Paris, Adele, and we were so pleased to hear your ideas on the subject, because they agreed so perfectly with our own! We felt when we were there that it was like some magic potion, incredibly sweet to the taste, but rotting the brains of all but the very strong. I know I couldn't work there for five minutes ... I'd be out in the sidewalk cafes the whole time, watching the world go by, talking with fascinating people, and never doing anything. I think you're wise not to go there to work ... it's a wonderful place for a holiday, and maybe the Parisians (sp?) themselves can take it more casually, but it's a bit much for us!

I'm glad Esther[2] is so well on the way ... pray God it's ok this time. So Tema's got a boy? Have you ever seen them, Adele? ... I don't suppose so.

If you know any news about people from home, do let us know ... our only source of news is you!

How is your book?[3] From the sound of your letter, and thoughts on Paris etc., I thought you had been working on it ... I hope so. How is it coming along? Let me know the details some time. Where have you got to with it? Etc.

I'm finished chapter 8 in mine, and have only three more chapters to do, but I'm beginning to feel the thing is much too long, and I don't know if I can cut it down properly. It's kind of top-heavy, particularly since half-way through I introduced an entirely new theme (it really did seem to arise quite naturally, so I let it take its course, so to speak). The girl falls in love with a young Ukrainian boy she's known at college, and fluctuates between a) unconscious prejudice against his background, expressed at first in a sort of fear of his making love to her, even while she's very attracted to him, and later in a desire for him to leave the small-town (and his family) forever, so that he can be disassociated from them in her own mind; b) a later realization of the prejudice of those who think they have no prejudices, and the consequent violent reaction ... against her family, to whom Ukrainians are beyond the pale ... and a desire to marry him at once, just because he *is* Ukrainian. Does that sound crazy? I don't think it is, really, but it's so hard to explain in a few words. And even harder to get across in the story, without actually saying any of these things, but merely showing it in the actions of the people, and so on. It's certainly not a very original theme, but in this case, it seems to fit in with all the rest of the story. However, there is still too much attempted, in one way ... too many people, too many themes ... the thing doesn't hold together properly. Maybe I've learned something from it, though. The next book I try will be infinitely shorter and more compact. The trouble with a first novel is that one tries to put everything into it, all the things you know. Which is probably silly. I'm very fortunate, though, because this is a good place to work. We've been out on trek for nearly a month now, right away into the desert, with no one to bother us. I still never seem to have enough time, though ... I'm studying Somali, which is a hellish language, and I'm teaching Mohamed and Arabetto (our young truck-driver, named thus because he's half Arab and half Somali) to write and read English, and I have to think up lessons for them and try to draw pictures to illustrate words ... and you know how artistic I am ... my pictures look like nothing on earth! I'm also keeping extensive diaries, with, probably, the ulterior motive of writing a book about this country when we leave ... this diary business is more complicated than it sounds, as I write about 40 notebook pages every couple of days, and how I'll ever weed it all out when the time comes, I just don't know. There are so many things to describe, especially the Somalis, who are a fascinating people, tremendously complex. From time to time I try to describe one of our chaps in words, and I wonder what makes me think I could ever write a novel.

I'll continue on airletter #2 ... I didn't tell you any of the things I meant to do in this letter.

AIRLETTER #2

We've had quite an exciting month ... we always do, [—] is always happening. A few weeks ago, we saw and killed [—] poison snake we've come across. It was a huge thing [—] feet long and very fat, a dark brown with black and [—] its back, and a cream-colored belly. Its fangs [—] wasn't as alarmed as I thought I'd be, as by this time [—] aren't very numerous. Also, we are living in the back [—] truck, so it's like a modern prairie schooner! We also [—] a big dog-like creature, pale brown with dark spots, [—] and bastardly in appearance. Incidentally, it was a hermaphrodite [—]. The chaps tell us that many hyenas are this way.

Day before yesterday we had a fantastic experience. In the night, I awoke and thought I saw a black shape trying to creep into the caravan underneath the mosquito net. I was very sleepy, though, so I merely shone my torch on it, and of course there was nothing there. But in the morning we found that thieves had reached in and taken our radio, all Jack's expensive engineering equipment ... theodolite, sliderules, etc, his briefcase, with all the records of the work done to date on the balleh scheme, our typewriter, and various other things!! We felt absolutely sick, as we thought they'd dash across the border into Abyssinia and get rid of the stuff before we could catch them. Not so, however. We found that they'd left a spear and a stick here, evidently getting scared when I woke up and yelled, and these weapons were the means of identifying them at a local mud-and-wattle coffee-shop. We found, after a great deal of clever talking and expert tactics on the part of our driver and interpreter, that one thief was still at the coffee-shop, and that the coffee-shop owner was presumably in league with the thieves (and later we found he is the 'brains' of quite a large outfit). With Hersi and Abdi threatening death and destruction, the tribesmen finally persuaded the thief to give himself up, and he actually led Jack to the spot where all the stuff was hidden. He seemed quite non-plussed, and casually asked Jack for a cigarette! We seem, however, to have stumbled into a sort of minor crime-ring, so we shall have to take the matter up with the police. There aren't many thieves in S'land ... not professional ones, anyway ... and those who are here are notorious, and known to all Somalis. Our chaps knew this man at once as a recognized thief.

I wish you could see some of the people here, Adele. The degree of physical beauty among the young Somalis is absolutely incredible, when one considers their uncertain diet and the fact that sometimes they are reduced to starvation. If you search Mayfair and the Champs Elysees and Fifth Avenue, you won't see women any more beautiful than some of the Somali girls I've seen. I never noticed beauty in women much before, having always concentrated my attention on the male sex, but it is impossible not to admire these girls, just as it is impossible not to admire a perfectly constructed flower. They mature young, and theirs is an extremely rich and voluptuous beauty. Straight shoulders, high firm breasts, small but not pinched waists, round plump hips, and love-ly arms. Skin a light brown ... the most highly esteemed color being 'assan' ... a coppery brown. Their facial bones are strong and well-defined under a very soft-appearing flesh and skin, and the shape of the face is rounded delicately, and tapers into a small neat chin. There is a softness and mellowness about them, and their eyes are large and dark with long lashes. Their carriage is superb ... they walk erect, with a perfection of balance gained, perhaps, from carrying jars and baskets on their heads, and they seem to step in a gliding fashion, like a ballet dancer. The men are a complete contrast, as they should be. Handsome-ness is the keynote with a good-looking Somali man (and there are very many). Straight sharp features and keen eyes; a tall, usually thin build, and long fine hands. Their faces are a harmonious blend of Arabic and negroid, with the sharpness of the one tempered, and the squatness of the other drawn in, clarified and defined. They, too, have good carriage, and it is a fine sight to see a young herdsman in his brownish orange robe, striding across the desert with his spear slung casually across his shoulders. One of the best looking men I've ever seen is Ahmed Abdillahi, a young tribal chieftain. We've known him for some time, and he came to our camp the other day, looking magnificent in a new blue and white shirt and a white lungi (robe) and an embroidered turban. He carried a wonderfully carved brass-bound spear. I don't describe him facetiously (sp?) ... he *did* look magnificent ... that's the only word for him. Actually, in his presence, I can never think of a single Somali word to say ... somehow you don't want to say anything that might sound stupid to him. He's got a broad but thin face, with heavy well-defined bones; wide nostrils; deep-set eyes that are keen and serious. He's a very tall man, with well-muscled arms and legs and a long straight torso. He has a strange unshakeable kind of poise ... the look of a man who knows his own worth and is not afraid of it. He walks with the grace of a leopard. I don't know how some of the pukka sahibs[4] feel about him, but I don't see how they could help feeling rather small and a bit petty. Well, enough. Must go. Do write soon.

Love from both of us,

Peg

1 Alvin Goldman, a friend from Winnipeg
2 Esther Wiseman, wife of Adele's brother Harry
3 Wiseman had begun writing the novel that was to be published as *The Sacrifice* (1956).
4 Anglo-Indian colonial term for European

Hargeisa,[1]
British Somaliland Protectorate,
E. Africa
4 September 1951

Dear Adele:

I haven't written for so long that I feel terribly guilty. I hope you'll forgive me. The past two months have been the most hectic yet, and we're both hoping we won't have such a frantic time again. But more of that later. First, thanks ever so much for your 2 letters. Jack and I are really filled with admiration for you and Miriam, doing that terrific walking trip through England, and then continuing on the continent. The Wisemans really are a remarkable family! I think it's absolutely wonderful to have seen so much in such a short time, and with limited finances. I'm glad you're staying in Italy, Adele. Good luck to you ... I hope you find a job.[2] We will be going to Italy for part of our leave, so if you're still there, who knows? ... we may meet again in Rome or somewhere![3]

As far as we're concerned, the past months have been both interesting and nerve-wracking. We had to go up to Djibouti, in French Somaliland, so that Jack could collect the Caterpillar tractors that were coming to that port, for his job. We expected to be away only a few weeks, but as it happened, we spent nearly 2 months, all told, on the trip! First, we came to Hargeisa, and discovered the boat was delayed, so we went out into the Haud to do some more surveying in the meantime. We stayed there about a week, and then proceeded to Hargeisa again, and thence to Borama, a station high up in the mountains, close to Ethiopia. When we got there, we got a telegram saying the boat was again delayed, 10 days, and so we stayed in Borama for the time. It was extremely pleasant, because the country there is lovely ... big jagged mountains, ragged thorn-laden acacia trees, candalabra trees that look like ordinary trees as far as their trunks are concerned, but have cactuslike branches that point towards the sky like enormous stiff green fingers. The candalabra were in bloom then, and on the end of each branch there was a huge scarlet or yellow flower. We also went to visit Amoud, which is the ruins of an old Arab trading city, thought to be over a thousand years old. This is a fascinating spot. The walls of many buildings are still standing, and one can get a terrific idea of what the place looked like when it was still alive. But now the candalabra trees and the wild vines have overgrown the town, and one feels a strange sense of desolation looking at it, as though the trees and thorn bushes were the real rulers of the country, and might have to wait a few hundred years, but would ultimately overcome any settlements, including our own.

From Borama we went to Zeilah, which is right on the coast. It was, in a sense, a terrible time to be at Zeilah, because the coastal plain is hot as hades during the kharif (the summer monsoon) which is blowing now. Zeilah was also extremely interesting. It used to be one of the chief ports in this part of the world. The Greeks and Romans traded there, and called it Aulites (and the Somalis still call the Zeilah people the

'Audal,' from the ancient name). Somaliland was known then as the 'Regio Cinnamomifera,' because they thought that cinnamon came from here. Actually, it didn't, as it was brought from Ceylon and India and traded to the Greeks and Romans at Aulites. After the ancient world ceased to use Aulites, the port was in the hands of the Arabs for hundreds of years. It was a chief center for trade in ostrich feathers, myrrh and frankincense, and slaves. It remained a slave-port until the early 1800's, believe it or not. To Zeilah, in the 1400's, came Sheikh Ibrahim Abu Zarbay, who was one of the Hadrami saints from Arabia who brought the Muslem religion to S'land. His tomb can still be seen at Zeilah. In the 1500's, the King of Zeilah was an Arab, Mohamed Ga'anyer (Small Hand), who set out to conquer Ethiopia, for the Muslem faith. His great armies swept out from Zeilah into Ethiopia, and would probably have succeeded in conquering the Christian kingdom, had it not been for the Portuguese who thought that the Ethiopian king was an embodiment of the medieval legend of Prester John, and therefore sent armies in to help their co-religionist.

But now Zeilah is dying. It is only a collection of little brushwood huts, bleached and greyed by the sun and the sea-wind, and a few crumbling stone or mud-brick buildings with doors warped and askew. Even the pearl-divers, who used to get small pink-coloured pearls from the sea there, no longer ply their trade, and the dhows are rotting at the wharf. But still, one cannot help feeling that there is still some echo of the city's past glory clinging around the dusty salt-smelling town and the fading, ruined buildings.

Djibouti is quite another matter. We were forced to stay there for 10 days, as the boat took a devil of a long time to get unloaded. Fortunately, we stayed with the British Consul there, so it wasn't so bad. But I've never been in such an unbearably hot place. Djibouti ... the shabby little Paris of the East. And does it stink! This country is Paradise compared to French S'land. The magala or native quarter there is about 100 times worse than here ... the Somalis live in dirty little shacks made out of rusted old flattened kerosene tins, and I've never seen such poverty in my life. The natural consequence of this is that the place is full of thieves and general sharpers, and most of the Somalis there appear to have been corrupted beyond all redemption ... and no wonder. Who wouldn't, living in a place like that? The French, on the other hand, have got houses and apartment blocks that look like a city in Europe or America ... lovely modern bungalows; modern apartment blocks with acres of windows; great creamy yellow office buildings. It is quite a contrast. Then the French attitude is very strange ... you find that, officially, they believe in liberty, fraternity and equality, and yet ... no one believes in it or acts by it. In Brit. S'land, where practically no one believes in fraternity with Somalis, the Somali people are treated with 100% more respect and friendliness than they are in Djibouti. The French officials appeared to us to be pompous and brutal, on the whole, towards the Somalis. It is very strange. Anyway, it was an extremely interesting 10 days, as Djibouti must have all possible types in it ... wizened little Arab dockers from the Yemen, who look weak as a child, but who, they tell me, are tremendously tough; Somalis and Danikil[4] and Ethiopians and Galla[5] and various assorted African peoples; sleek Indian businessmen in snowy white suits; young Frenchmen with morose handsome faces, wearing white uniforms and white topees; French middleclass matrons, who looked pale and exhausted and fat; French priests in long white robes, riding bicycles; Senegal policemen ... big strapping muscular chaps in khaki and wearing a red fez, and with a super-military air that has apparently been dinned into them by the French (or else they were always warlike ... probably both) who like their colonial police to come from another colony and not to be fussy about beating up on people of the country in which they work; Indian women in lovely silks and wearing the veils of purdah; little yellowed Arabs driving donkey-carts of charcoal into the city; paunchy Greek storekeepers and their women; prostitutes of nearly every race and hue; and so on. It is a most fascinating place.

Jack nearly collapsed after our Djibouti trip, since he had to work all day, every day, on the docks, in the burning sun, trying to get the Cats unloaded and onto the diesel truck that was to take them back to Zeilah and thence to Hargeisa. He had an Italian foreman who spoke no English, and the chap who operated the one inadequate crane that Djibouti port possesses spoke nothing but French. Jack was therefore having to direct the operations; show people what to do; ward off the hordes of interested spectators waiting for a chance to pinch tools; and at the same time cope with 4 languages ... French, English, Somali and Italian. Everything had to be conveyed through about 3 or 4 people, and information got garbled en-route. It really was the most fantastic strain for him. One day he came home and couldn't see ... he quite literally was temporarily blind ... the Consul told us it was sheer heat-exhaustion. I nearly went crazy worrying about him.

But our troubles, alas, were not at an end. We finally got back to Zeilah with all 3 Cats and the 2 big scrapers, and then we had to load up the first Cat on the diesel and get back to Hargeisa, through sand that we knew might bog the heavy diesel down. And it did. We set out from Zeilah at 3 p.m. By 12 midnight we'd gone 25 miles, and we'd sweated like anything all the way! What didn't happen! The diesel got stuck in the loose sand. Then Jack got a PWD tractor to haul it out. Then the tractor pulled too fast at the wrong moment, and the diesel's steering broke. Jack and Brandolini fixed the whole steering apparatus with bits of wire, sitting out in the middle of the desert, with night coming on and a sandstorm blowing up, and cursing in several languages. It really was the most fantastic thing. Then night came with a bang, as it does here, and the sand began to blow. We had to get the diesel out, as if we didn't, by morning it would be up to the axles in sand, and no one for hundreds of miles to help us get it out. Jack was absolutely magnificent, as usual, being in about 40 places at once, with everyone, including Brandolini, depending on him for every detail ... I honestly think if he hadn't been there, they'd all just have sat down quietly and let the bloody truck stay in the sand. But finally he got everyone going, and once they got started, the spirit of the occasion affected everyone and they began to work like crazy. Which was just as well, since it took us hours and hours even then. We got to Hargeisa 2 days later (the trip normally is 1 day ... it took us 3), and by that time Jack was worn out. For 2 months we'd been moving constantly, and he'd had so much organizing and general messing about to do that it wasn't funny. So when we got here, we took stock and decided we'd have to change things or they'd be taking him back to England in a stretcher. So we began a campaign to get a house in Hargeisa, and finally succeeded in moving into a stone bungalow ... a guest house, almost in the back yard of Government House, and next door to the Governor's private secretary. Not an ideal place to be, but better than moving around so much. We did like Sheikh, but it was far too long a distance from Hargeisa and from most of J's work. So we went up to Sheikh last week and moved all our stuff down here. We've got a very nice and comfortable house, and feel quite lucky, all in all. Our address will be Hargeisa, from now on.

I've been terribly busy all these past months. First of all, I've been keeping a diary, or rather a series of descriptions and interesting bits of information, with an eye to a possible series of articles or something in a year or so. Secondly, I've begun a new phase in writing. I must admit I haven't worked on my novel for a hell of a time, and now feel that the whole thing will have to be completely re-written. What set this off was the beginning of some writing about this country ... about 2 months ago I wrote a short story, and a few weeks ago, I wrote another 2 stories, about Somaliland, or rather, set in an East African colony, without mentioning any names. Listen, Adele, they're good! Pardon this unpardonable attitude of pride, but really, I honestly think they are. I think, as a matter of fact, they're the only good things I've ever written in prose, except for odd passages here and there. But I mean as a whole. Jack thinks so, too. Adele, it really is the first time I've ever written anything that he thought was good, as a whole. There have been odd bits in the novel that he liked, and his criticism was always very helpful, but this time it was a bit different. I think this is for 2 reasons: a) for the first time in my life I really tried to write as I thought my characters would think, and not as I thought myself ... i.e. both stories are without propaganda entirely; b) they are both written mainly in conversation. I am beginning to feel that this may be the start of a new way of doing things. I'm unsure of the method, of course, but I do feel it's the most hopeful thing that's happened. Because, on reading over the novel, I find that a good deal of the conversation seems quite good, but the descriptive passages, especially those describing people's reactions and feelings, are really pretty bloody. It seems that when I go much beyond conversation, I get pompous and rather unsubtle. I seem to do better sticking to what people actually say, and letting the reactions and feelings and any deeper significance show up between the lines, rather than actually stating it. I don't know if this will lead to anything, but I feel quite hopeful at the moment. The only thing is ... were they merely freaks, or can I repeat the same method and pull it off? Time will tell. But I've come to the conclusion that propaganda in any form is not for me. In many ways I regret it. But there it is.

The other thing I've been doing is translating Somali poetry and stories. Not by myself, of course, because I still speak only a little Somali, and couldn't possibly understand most of the poetry. But I had the good fortune to get to know Goosh Andrzejewski, a Polish chap who was out here with his English wife, studying the Somali language. He is something of an expert in the Somali tongue, being about the only European who can talk to them on a wide variety of topics, including the basic ones of love and war etc. His assistant, Musa Ismail, a Somali, is terribly keen on the Somali literature. And so, between the 3 of us, we've been working. Goosh and Sheila have gone back to England now, unfortunately, but I did manage, before they left, to get the literal translation of a good many poems and stories. I am now in the process of turning these into what I fondly hope is literary English. I have tried all along to be as true as possible to the original, and yet not to be too hidebound and thereby lose the implied meaning in the original. In some of the poems I've added a line, in order to explain something that was implied in the Somali, or perhaps phrased something in 6 words instead of one, because often a Somali word is very compressed and there is no single counterpart for it in English. It is very difficult to resist putting one's own bits and pieces of thought into the poems, but I think I've avoided that, in the main, by not adding one single word that was not either there in Somali or directly implied. When possible, I've translated exactly, but of course the process of putting it into more or less literary English lies in the choice of words ... there are, I discover, an awful lot of synonyms in English. But the difficulties will be obvious from a few examples: in one love poem, the word 'place' occurs, but in the Somali, a special word is used, which means 'place' and also means 'the grace of God,' implying that the place referred to was highly blessed or particularily fortunate in some way. I've translated that by including the second meaning ... 'a place of Allah's kindly grace' ... which is really what it means, altho' only one word is used in Somali. I don't know how successful these translations have been so far ... it's always very difficult to translate poetry properly. There are 2 main kinds of poetry in Somali, altho' actually 8 or 9 kinds do exist. Apart from the 2 main kinds, however, the others are difficult to tell apart, except to a Somali, because the only difference is in rhythm and in the point in the line where the break occurs. All Somali literature is unwritten, and yet there is a huge body of it, and it all has its set literary conventions and rules. It is uneven, of course, and some of it is mighty poor stuff, but much of it is fresh and imaginative and original. The two main kinds are a) belwo ... literally 'a trifle' ... the short lyric lovesongs, which are set to music and sung, mainly by the young men. When sung, they have a rhythmic syncopated beat, very similar to American jazz. The old men affect to scorn the belwo, in much the same way as older chaps at home will scorn jazz. These belwo are usually not more than 3 or 4 lines long, altho' they are often sung in ballad form, with 10 or 15 put together, and a chorus; b) the gabay are the long, semi-epic poems, dealing with every subject from love to war, altho' the emphasis is generally on war or politics or philosophy. These poems are written in literary Somali (or rather, composed, since none are written), a language which has its own vocabulary, much of which is unknown to the average young Somali, unlearned as yet in gabay composing.

They are not sung, but are chanted, in a sort of monotonous but rhythmical way ... very boring if you can't understand Somali, but highly interesting when translated. I have only 2 or 3 gabay, because most are much too difficult to be easily explained. The short stories are legion ... the Somalis excel in story-telling, but as there is not much room in these airletter forms, perhaps you'd rather have a few examples of the belwo. Here they are:[6]

1)

    Since, when you die, delight
    By earth's silence will be stilled,
    Then let not now the priest
    Drive you from your song.

....

2)

    A man enchanted by the waking dream
    That enters like a djinn, his heart to own,
    Can never sleep, Amiina – I have been
    Away, these nights, walking the clouds of heaven.

....

3)

    Woman, lovely as lightning at dawn,
    Speak to me even once.

....

4)

    So perfect are her teeth, one might mistake
    Their whiteness for the palest inner bark
    Cut from a place of Allah's kindly grace
    Where new rains fell and the galol tree flourished,
    And fashioned into a vessel, bound around
    with pearls, pink-glowing, garnered from Zeilah's sea.
        (# this poem refers to the light brown or pink line across
        the teeth, common here, and considered a mark of great beauty.)

....

5)

    All your young beauty is to me
    Like a place where the new grass sways
    After the blessing of the rain,
    When the sun unveils its light.

....

6)

    Turn not away in scorn.
    One day a grave will prove,
    The frailty of that face,
    And worms its grace enjoy.
    Let me enjoy you now ...
    Turn not away in scorn.

....

7)

    The curving of your breasts
    Like apples sweet and small,
    Tolmoom, I will know again
    When night turns dusk to dark.

....

These are a few of the ones that I think are the best. Perhaps not a typical bunch, because, whatever their flaws, many are slighter. Still, I do think they show a good deal of emotion and sensitivity ... at least; I hope the translations get that across to some extent, because it is really there in the original. It is difficult now to get translations of belwo, because Goosh and Musa aren't here any longer, and no one else knows enough English to translate exactly. Also, Hersi, our interpreter, is much too delicate to translate most of them anyway! Must go now. Do write soon. I hope you find work in Italy, Adele ... we'll keep our fingers crossed for you. Love from us both,

Peg

1 The Laurences had left Sheikh and established a permanent base in the town of Hargeisa.
2 Wiseman was to stay in Rome until the following autumn when she returned to Winnipeg. While in Rome, she taught at the Overseas School.
3 The Laurences did visit Wiseman in Rome in June 1952.
4 People of the Galla region of southern Ethiopia
5 The Oromo people, who are the largest ethnic group in Ethiopia
6 These were all included in *A Tree for Poverty: Somali Poetry and Prose* (1954).

Hargeisa
9 November 1951

Dear Adele:

We were so pleased to hear from you, and to learn that you [are in] Italy now. I do hope you've got a job now, and that everything's all right for you. Also, that you're learning Italian ... you probably speak it fluently by now! Jack is learning Italian, also, and so, theo[retically] am I, altho' I haven't got around to doing anything with it as [yet]. We've got an Italian foreman on Jack's job, so he has to learn a [little] Italian in order to be able to speak with Gino, who speaks no En[glish.]

I'm very glad that you're working on your book now ... how is it coming along? How much have you got done? Where are you at with [it?] And so on.

I've abandoned my novel for the time being. The reason is simple ... it stinks. It really wasn't what I wanted at all, and I couldn't seem to get it written down properly. Then I started writing stories set in East Africa, and, possibly due more to fluke than anything, the first two really were quite good. So I've kept on, and have now written four and sent them to various publications. I am not being too hopeful about it, however. But I do feel that I've hit on a style that's at least more successful than the way I wrote before. Also, here, somehow, there's so much to write about. That is, nothing is at all the way it seems on the surface ... the myth of the poor downtrodden and exploited African is just as wrong as the myth of the ferocious and ungrateful African. Both the Somalis and the Europeans here seem to be very much a collection of individuals ... perhaps as one sees more of the world, one tends to think less in terms of generalizations and more in terms of individuals. You can't say, 'the typical Somali' or 'the typical British colonial officer' ... there's no such thing. But in the relationships between Europeans and Europeans, far away from their homes, and between individual Europeans and individual Somalis, there is a wealth of possibility for short stories. If one was only a Steinbeck or a Hemingway or even ... now that I come to think of it ... a Kipling! But still, I do feel more encouraged about my writing than I ever have before ... not wildly enthusiastic, you understand, but just a bit hopeful. Sometimes I feel guilty about my good fortune in having so much time to write ... but on the other hand, it's only for a year ... it won't last forever! I spend most of each day at my typewriter, either writing notes on what's been happening, or the things I've seen of Somali life, or the things I've found out about Somali beliefs and culture; or else I am working at the Somali poems and stories ... I've collected quite a few, but of course can only get them slowly and painstakingly, through English-speaking Somalis, and thus miss a good deal ... also, I may never even hear some of the best stories, as they naturally don't know what I want to hear, and just tell me any stories that happen to arise naturally out of what has been happening or what we've been talking about. The rest of the time I spend writing stories. I've only done four so far ... it takes a lot of time ... so much more than one thinks it's going to.

Enough of this. We've been out in camp in the Haud now for three weeks, and are really enjoying it. I don't think we'll feel very happy about going back to live permanently in some city, now that we've spent so much time in camp. It is a very good life. Jack's got the first balleh nearly finished, despite tremendous difficulties with the machinery, and in getting supplies of grease and oil etc. We've got a huge camp now ... nearly 30 people in all, and we even have a mobile workshop with an electric generator, so we have electric light! It is not like camping at home. We live in the back of the big truck, and in the daytime we have a little brushwood hut, called a 'Wob,' made by weaving branches together and filling in the spaces with bunches of greyish silver weeds, like dried herbs, which have a pleasant hay-like smell. These clumps of weed hang down from the ceiling of the Wob, and when the sun shines through them, they look like silver tinsel that one puts on Christmas trees. Aside from writing, I spend a lot of time talking to people ... partly in English and partly in my very terrible Somali. The other day, two very shy country women came to see me ... and after a lot of polite talk about flocks and children, they finally asked me if I had anything which would relieve their menstrual pain! Coming from these so-called 'Children of Nature,' I was naturally a little startled. I had to explain that I had nothing, and that it was just like childbirth ... a natural pain that only God could relieve, in His own good time. It is surprising how much one relies on God here ... the Somalis only understand some things in those terms. Ultimately, one finds oneself saying, also, like they do, 'We'll be going to Hargeisa tomorrow ... if God wills,' and so on. Living in this harsh impoverished country, they'd go nuts without their faith in God.

Incidentally, we were very interested in your description of Italy ... what terrible contrasts there must be there. We talked to the R.C. padre here, not long ago, who visited Rome in Holy Year, and he hadn't noticed the poverty at all. He talked a lot about the buildings and Italian food. It made us kind of sick. Must go. Please write soon.

Love from both of us,

Peg

P.S. we'll be in Italy probably around the middle of June to the middle of July ... will you still be there, or where?
P.S.2. what about your boyfriend? or is there anyone else now? Please give details!
P.S.3 – Did you [—] those airletters [—] you c/o the S[—]

AIRLETTER #2

Hargesia
9 November 1951
Dear Adele:

I tried to cram everything onto the other airletter, [—] short of airletter forms, but now I found this one, so [—] the letter.

The country around here is quite pretty at the moment [—] it ever is ... the grass is tall and green, and the thorn [—] still got green leaves. All the Habr Awal tribe is on [—] this country now. We heard that their camels have a sick [—] and they're moving away from their usual grazing grounds, [—] change of grass will help their stock. We watch them move [—] early mornings. The burden camels plod along, 12 in a [—] of one camel tied to the rope that goes around the neck of [—] camel. They are led by the Somali women and girls ... the [—] (who are gorgeous) in their best and brightest clothes ... red [—] blue and gold and green robes, gold earrings and necklaces. [—] like Queens of Sheba, every last one of them. The girls grow old quickly here, but in their youth they are really beautiful. They save all their old clothes for herding the flocks when they're at their semi-permanent camps, and wear all their finery when they're moving, for after all, they're only strolling along, leading the camels. They don't get much opportunity of dressing up, these country women, for their lives are 99% hard work ... they work far harder than the men, and grow old and embittered and shrewish by the time they're thirty. It is really sad to see. The burden camels have a sort of saddle-blanket of brown moss, and on top of this, the bundles of grass mats that cover the akhals or huts are tied. Then, on top of everything, the semi-circular poles that form the framework of the akhal. The other burden camels carry the cooking vessels, and the big clay water vessels, in wicker baskets. The children and the old men always look after the flocks of sheep and goats. In this country, the young always herd the youngest animals, and one sees a flock of miniature goats, racing madly along, followed by a tiny Somali boy with his little switch of grass or twig, both child and animals scurrying to keep pace with their parent creatures. The men herd the camels, that is, the camels that are not used to carry burdens. They take a path well away from the road, and crossing the big plain near our camp, one can see the camel herds in the distance, dozens and dozens of great fawn-colored beasts moving leisurely along, eating the grass as they go, and followed by the herders, singing their high-pitched shrill songs to keep the herd together.

At night, as we sit in our 'Wob,' we can hear the songs that the wind carries in from the camps of nearby Somalis, faint mournful tunes, accompanied by the distant sound of clapping hands.

I discovered a few interesting beliefs of the 'miiyii' or country people here, the other day, from a passing tribesman, who stopped to chat. Apparently the Somalis believe that crows 'tookei,' live to be 300 or 400 years old, and that it is very bad luck to kill a crow. If you kill one, you could boil the meat for as long as you like ... for *years* ... and the flesh would not get soft, but would still remain hard and solid! Another thing ... the little greyish blue pigeons ... 'qolii,' are supposed to have a strange gift. When they are old and weak, they retire to the nest where they were hatched, and sit there for a few months, during which time they completely renew themselves. Their feathers are completely changed for a new set, and their bodies become strong and firm again, and when they emerge, they are young birds again! Interesting comparison with the phoenix.

But although the Somalis have some weird beliefs about things like that, they also have a lot of genuine knowledge about the animals and birds, etc. Like most cultures, theirs is a mixture of odd beliefs and true knowledge. A case in point ... in a book on Somaliland, published in the 1850's, which I read a short time ago, the author, an Englishman, says that malaria is prevalent in Somaliland, and that the Somalis have a quaint belief that it is caused by the bites of mosquitoes![1] It looks odd to see it printed there like that ... apparently the Somalis knew all about it, long before we did. The Englishman says, with his superior western knowledge, that of course any fool knows that malaria is caused by impure water-supply and not by any insect!

I must go now, as it's getting dark. Jack has just switched on the electric light plant, and Mohamedyero (Little Mohamed) has come in with the knives and forks for dinner. He tells me, with an enormous and appealing smile, that the 'aul' (gazelle) that Abdi shot today is 'sidii wan-ki' ... like a ram ... meaning it is very fat and has a lot of meat! We will have a venison dinner ... I wish you could be with us! Mohamed is bringing the soup, so I must close.

Please write soon, and give us all the news about yourself, and whether you've met any new men, and about the book, and your job, etc. Give our love to your family when you write, won't you?

Love from us,

Peg

P.S. It was terrible about Max Haskell[2] – we were very shocked to hear it. What actually happened, or does anyone know?

1 *First Footsteps in East Africa* (1856) by Sir Richard Burton (1821–90). This detail is mentioned in the first chapter, 'Departure from Aden.'
2 Not traced

Hargeisa
30 January 1952

Dear Adele:

This will probably come like a voice from the grave, it is so long since we have heard from each other. I hope you receive this letter – I'll send it to Rome, and if I don't hear from you in a month or so I'll write to Miriam ... I'm a bit alarmed at not having heard, and also I feel very guilty at not having written to you. I hope you are all right, and that you have a job etc.

How is your writing? Is the novel still coming along well? Please write and let us know how everything is with you. Have you learned Italian yet? I expect you've already gained an impressive fluency. Have you seen the Michaelangelo at the Cistine (sp?) Chapel? What is it like? Etc, etc.

Also, have you heard any news about anyone we know at home? We heard from Bob Hallstead[1] some months ago, but I think I told you about that. We don't hear from anyone in Wpg, I suppose because we don't write any letters to anyone there! How are your mom and dad and Miriam and everybody? How I'd like to see you all again! How is Abe? I wish you hadn't known him so long, Adele – it would be marvellous if you married him someday! Match-making as usual ... please forgive me. Perhaps you've already met an Italian Count or someone. Gosh, I would like to see you again ... letters are so unsatisfactory, aren't they?

Now for us. Much has happened. To begin with, I took a job here at the Secretariat, in the Confidential Office, for awhile, and it was terribly interesting. But unfortunately I had to give it up, as (surprisingly enough after all this time) I became pregnant! I thought I would be quite all right, being healthy as an ox, but you can never tell. It appears there are certain complications, and the doctor said I must quit work and rest a lot or I'd probably lose the baby. The same trouble as Esther ... I tend to miscarry, it seems. However, since I began taking it very easy I've felt a lot better, so perhaps it will be all right. I'm trying not to count on it too much yet, though. I'm about 2½ months now. If I'm ok for another 2 months I'll probably be all right.

The only thing is that it could have happened at a more convenient time. It will, I'm afraid, completely mess up our leave. I think Italy may be out of the question. Both Jack and I feel very sad at this, naturally, but it's just one of those things. I don't know quite what we'll do, but I think we shall go to England about the middle of June, and try to see a bit of the country first, and then park ourselves in some pre-arranged place, not London, someplace like Devon where we want to go anyway, and await the arrival. We will have to stay in England for a few months afterwards, if all goes well, but then we want to come back East again. We shan't be returning to Somaliland, as the work here is so well organized now that a good foreman can carry it on, and it would be a waste of Jack's time to stay on a job where there is so little experience to be gained. It was good experience this year, but another year would be simply repetition. We'd like to come back to Africa, someplace, though. Where will you be in the summer? Still Italy? We *may* be able to get to Paris for a few days ... perhaps we could meet there. I do hope we can see you, Adele ... it would be such a shame to be so close and not to see you again. Let us know what your plans are, won't you?

On the whole I've been pretty well, except that I feel deathly sick every evening. Also, I appear to have grown a bit feeble-minded, which is rather trying. That is, I find it terribly difficult to concentrate on my writing. I've been trying for 2 weeks to settle a plot of a short story. It is a good story, about an eastern Jew in Africa, and is based to some extent on fact ... i.e. the character of the man, not the plot itself. I know exactly what I want, but when I try to plan it out it gets absurdly tangled up, and I find myself in a confusion of the Jewish and Muslem religions, ineffectually leafing through the Old Testament and the Qoran! From time to time I wonder if I shall become a permanent vege-table, but perhaps this isn't likely. All my stories so far have come back like homing pigeons, blast them. However, the one I sent to the Atlantic Monthly had a personal letter instead of the printed rejection slip ... how one squeezes bread from a stone, or blood from a turnip or whatever it is! I have sent them all out again. It takes so long to hear. Also, I have discovered that most magazines send the scripts back all covered with coffee stains etc., which is most annoying as you have to type the offending pages all over again and then they don't look the same as the rest. I'm blowed if I'm going to type a whole script over again, though. The trouble is, too, that there are only about 6 places, in England and America, that one can send stories to anyway.

I've finished translating a whole lot of Somali poems and stories. Some of the stories are not proper translations, but are paraphrases of stories told to me partly in Somali but mainly in English. I don't know what I'll do with them all now, as I don't think they would be very appealing to a publisher. Still, it was interesting work and I'm not sorry I did it.[2]

I'm in Hargeisa all the time now, naturally, and Jack is still out in camp. He gets in every weekend, from Friday night to Sunday morning, so it could be worse. It's rather lonely for both of us, though, especially for him. I go and see some other European women here, and some of them are really quite nice, but not what you would call soul-mates. Most of them I'm not at all fond of, but I suppose it is very fortunate that there are a few pleasant ones. A few Somali girls come to call on me quite frequently, and they are charming, altho' it is a little difficult for us to converse very freely, since my Somali is so limited, and Mohamed has to translate most of what we say to one another. Then, sometimes, Ali Farah the Midgan (an outcast tribe), who makes sandals and bows and arrows and spears and who can get anything for you if you'll pay enough, drops around to see me and tries to sell me all manner of peculiar things. He is a grand old chap, and I enjoy talking with him – his people used to be the country's hunters, and he is still very handy with a bow and arrow, and sometimes demonstrates his skill. They are small people, rather squat and more dark than the Somali, and the older type of Midgan shows in his features that he comes from an older race than the Somali and a more negroid race. Apart from these people, I'm afraid my social contacts are nil. Still, life is never dull. I have an unfortunate tendency to sleep all the time now, which alarms me because I cannot resist it. But I suppose I must bow to the inevitable.

Jack is working very hard, but is not worrying as much as before. He is really very well despite the hard work, and is much more relaxed than he was some months ago. It is good to have the job on a working basis now ... there were so many irritating delays at one time. He is nearly finished the third balleh now.

I must go now, as Mohamed has my supper (about 3 lettuce leaves and a tomato) ready. He keeps telling me I'm not eating anything, but I can't in the evenings. Mohamed is very pleased about the child, and keeps telling me I mustn't walk fast 'like a man' now, but must be very careful. I get a pint of milk (horrible stuff) a day, and he practically forces it down my throat, coming in from time to time and saying sternly 'You *haven't* had your milk yet!' until I feel so guilty that I drink it. He is an awfully nice kid, really, and we shall miss him when we leave. After a whole year of tribal conferences etc he still hasn't got his wife to come and live with him ... it is sad that a boy of 19 should have such an unhappy marriage.

Do write soon, Adele, and let us know all about everything. When you're writing home, please give our love to your family.

Love from both Jack and myself,

Peg

LATER:

We received your letter today, so I'm adding a note before sending this. We were so glad to hear from you, Adele, but very sorry to hear about your crisis ... I hope you're feeling better now. I may be opinionated, but I think if he didn't fall for you straight away he must be nuts. I'm terribly sorry it turned out badly ... there is so little one can say, as all this Tennysonian bunk about 'better to have loved and lost'[3] is pretty cold comfort, as I know from past experience.

I wish you could get to Israel ... I think it would be a wonderful experience, no matter how hard it might be. I would so much like to go there some time for a visit ... perhaps if you got there we could come and see you at some point ... or do they let outsiders in at the present time (with food difficulties and so on)? If we were Jewish, I think we'd go and work there like a shot ... it must be about the most interesting country in the world at the moment, and it would be very good to participate in it.

Our own plans look a bit different from what I said before in this letter. It now appears that we will probably be able to fly back to England after all (we thought they wouldn't let a woman go by plane if she was more than 6 months pregnant), so *if* they let us stop off for a week or so at Rome, we will do so. We will leave about the middle of June from here. I do hope we can get to Rome, partly to see Rome and partly to see you. I'd hate not to see you again, Adele, since God knows where we shall all be in another year. If we can't get to Rome, will you be stopping off in England before going back to Canada? If so, we might be able to see you then. If we have a flat anywhere, you could come and stay with us. As soon as we know more definitely about things, we'll let you know. We should be able to arrange something.

It was good to hear some news of people at home. I'm so glad Clarice is doing well. Also Abe ... we should write to him some time ... perhaps you could send us his address. I was surprised to hear about Max Cohen[4] ... it's good that he seems to have pulled himself together at last. I'm glad your family is all right ... give them our love, won't you?

Must go now. Please write again soon ... we do like getting letters from you so much. And take care of yourself ... don't try starving or anything, will you? As an economy, I mean. I hope the book will progress again now.

Love from Jack and myself,

Peg

1 Robert Nathaniel Hallstead (1907–67) had joined the English department at United College in 1946–7 during Laurence's last undergraduate year.
2 They would eventually appear in *A Tree for Poverty*.
3 Alfred Lord Tennyson (1809–92), *In Memoriam A.H.H.* (1850), Canto 27
4 M. (Max) Charles Cohen (b. 1926), freelance writer for radio and television.

c/o Sir Wm. Halcrow & Partners,
Box 1621, Accra,
Gold Coast, West Africa
1 December 1952

Dear Adele:

I can hardly apologize enough for not writing sooner, but honestly, we have seemed to be moving at top speed ever since we saw you last.[1] Also, since we've been out here, it is only in the last week that our sea-kit has arrived, and with it the typewriter, and I just couldn't write a decent letter longhand. Anyway, I hope you'll forgive us.

I hope you're getting on ok. at home now. What are the job prospects, and what are the prospects for getting back to Europe????? How is everyone at home? Who is there now? TELL US ALL! Also, please give our regards to everyone there, and our fondest love to your mom.

I'm enclosing a few pictures of Jocelyn, taken when she was 2 months old. It is hard to believe that she is now over 3 months old. She has changed so much since you saw her!

To begin at the beginning ... our last few weeks before leaving England were really awful. Not only did we have all the preparations to get through, but also we had a calamity with the baby. She caught an awful chill in that blasted icebox of a flat, and had convulsions and really was ill. We rushed her into hospital, and for the first week they didn't know what the trouble was. Actually, they never did find out ... they figured it must have been caused by the chill, though, as there was nothing else they could find wrong. After the first week, when her temperature still wasn't down, the doctor said they'd have to take off some spinal fluid to do the tests for meningitis. At this, you can imagine how I felt. I've never been so worried in my life. However, the next day her temperature went down, and stayed down, and she made a speedy recovery after that. The doctor said it must have been a virus infection due to her cold. She has been perfectly well since ... no trouble at all. But you can imagine how worried we were. Also, we didn't know if I was going to be able to come out here with Jack, and indeed, we didn't know for sure until three days before we took off! Jocelyn got out of hospital on a Monday, and we left on the Thursday. Also ... an additional trouble was that her vaccination didn't take the first time, and we couldn't have her done while she was sick, so she had to be done the day she got out of hospital, and I was terrified for a time that that might have a bad effect on her. However, it didn't. We had a grand trip out here, and the baby was perfect ... never cried at all. But our last weeks in England were far from cheerful. It was bitterly cold, and of course I had to trek over to the hospital every four hours to feed her. I thought we would all die of chill before we got away.

This country, in comparison, seems like paradise. We have all been very well ever since arriving here, and the baby in particular is really thriving. She is getting a nice tan, and looks tremendously fit and healthy. She weighs 14 lbs. now. She can hold up her head, and is very interested in everything around her. She has a number of weird gurgles and chortles that she makes now, to express approval, and she seems more like a person every day, rather than just an infant.

The climate here is wonderful. It is quite hot, but we love it. The hot season is beginning now, and although it is quite humid, we don't find it too hot as yet at all. We haven't seen much of the country yet, owing to the lack of transport, but now we have bought a small second-hand Standard, so we will get out more. The firm has built a row of bungalows about 5 miles from the city proper, and we have one of these. It is very modern in design, and is much more posh than we had expected ... hardwood floors in halls and bedrooms; polished tile floors in diningroom and livingroom; huge plateglass windows in the livingroom; walls in the diningroom that open up completely, allowing a through current of air; tiled bathroom and kitchen; etc. There is a large livingroom; diningroom; 2 bedrooms; bathroom; lavatory; kitchen; store; and cookhouse outside. It is really lovely. We may have to move to a small place called Tema where the new port is to be built, probably in about 6 months time. We shall be sorry to leave this house, but quite glad to be at Tema, which is a lovely spot right on the sea, with palms all around, and quite uninhabited except for a small African village. It is the sort of place that really suits us better than a city.

Accra is very large, by African standards. The market place in particular is interesting, for the variety of people one sees there. The West African people do not seem to us as good-looking as the Somalis, especially the women. Where the Somali women walked like queens, these women tend rather to slouch along. The men, however, although their features aren't as fine as the Somalis, are marvellously built, probably owing to a diet of fish, fresh fruit, and groundnuts ... cheap and nourishing. You would enjoy seeing some of the men, Adele ... what muscles! There is a peculiar kind of cotton material printed in Holland, woven in Manchester, made especially for the African market, and both men and women are to be seen in the market wearing robes made from it. It is called locally 'mammy cloth' and is done in bright bold colours and patterns. It is most attractive to see the people in these robes. Many men, of course, wear European-style work-shirts and shorts, and educated men and women dress entirely in the European mode.

Christianity is the predominant monotheism here, altho' there are quite a few Muslims as well. It seems to be a blend of European Christianity, plus something of the old African paganism and super-stition. The old gods die slowly, and Christianity, in particular, does not seem to transplant here in Africa as well as Islam does.

There are about 13 newspapers published daily in English, as well as some vernacular ones. These are extremely interesting, as they give one a line on the country's general feeling about the political situation here. The country is well on its way to self-government, having a Prime Minister (Kwame Nkrumah, who seems a very intelligent and sincere young man ... the country has a good leader in him, I think),[2] mainly African government Ministers, and an elected parliament. The Governor is an Englishman,[3] of course, as are most of the District and Provincial Commissioners. Most of the High Court Judges are Africans. The country is therefore midway between being under the Colonial Office and ruling itself. Nationalism is very strong, and in particular among the young educated men one sees a real enthusiasm for the future of the country as an independent nation. We have not as yet met any of the educated Africans, but hope to do so soon through the university here at Achimota, not far from Accra. But the newspapers are always printing articles dealing with various aspects of the country's future and its problems. There seems to be an admirable tendency among many educated people here now to emphasize the importance of keeping many features of the old African culture ... literature, music, dancing, the arts in general, as well as certain features of the tribal system, and adapting these to the modern world rather than imitating slavishly the European modes of culture. It is a fascinating place to be, really, as one feels it is typical of both the old and the new Africa. In the interior, the tribal system still holds good; the chief religions are still the old idol ones; witch-doctors and magic are still prevalent. And yet here in Accra you find people at the other extreme ... African doctors, lawyers, writers, judges, etc. From the little we have seen of the country, I think we are going to enjoy being here.

Jack is working at present on a new road that is to be built between here and Tema, the place where the new port is to be. He finds the work interesting and worthwhile, although he is terribly busy and finds each day too short. Still, it is better that way.

We have been lucky with neighbors. The people on one side of us are extremely nice ... she was in the Army for a long time, and is a highly intelligent and practical girl ... just my age, which is nice. On the other side, the people have a three-year old girl, so we are working a mutual baby-sitting arrangement, which is nice for all of us. However, I'm afraid Lois (the mother of the little girl), while pleasant and friendly, will never be much of a bosom pal. She was brought up in a wealthy family in England; never worked, didn't want her child when it came along and therefore left it to the care of her mother largely; and can't seem to cope out here at all. She said to me the other day that she hated roughing it. I stared at her in amazement as I thought of these luxurious bungalows, complete with electricity, running water, and servants! Jack and I couldn't help wondering what she would have thought of our home in the back of a Bedford three ton truck in S'land. However, I know the tropics don't suit all people, so I suppose I ought to be more sympathetic. I hope to god she doesn't go home ... there will be our baby-sitting arrangement finished. I sound like a selfish brute, don't I? Well, I am. So there.

Did those pictures you took ever turn out, Adele? I do hope so. Incidentally, I'm going to write to the Kramers this week ... I feel so badly that I haven't written to anyone up to now. I do hope Sylvia is ok[4] ... have you heard from them?

Gosh, I wish you could get back to Europe some time when we are there, Adele ... I somehow feel it won't be so very long until we meet again. How is your book? Progressing well, I hope. Don't let anything or anyone put you off from continuing it, will you? How is Esther? Was she ok this time? I do hope so.

Please write soon and let us know how you are and all about people in Winnipeg. Do you ever see the Marshalls?[5] Their son must be pretty big by now. If you see them, give them our love. Also anyone else we know.

Love from us both,

Peg

---

1 Wiseman had visited the Laurences in the fall of 1952 while she was en route from Rome to Winnipeg. The Laurences had gone to London on leave to await the birth of their daughter, Jocelyn, who arrived on 28 August 1952.

2 Kwame Nkrumah (1909–72) was leader of the massively popular Convention People's Party and was prime minister of Gold Coast (1952–7). He remained as prime minister of post-independence Ghana (1957–60) and then in 1960 became president of the Republic of Ghana until his ouster in 1966.

3 Sir Charles Arden-Clarke (1898–1962)

4 Winnipeg friends of the Laurences

5 John and Christine Marshall. John Marshall had been best man at the Laurences' wedding.

c/o Sir Wm. Halcrow & Partners
16 February 1953

Dear Adele:

We were so glad to get your letter today, and to learn that you have a job.[1] It sounds like a good thing. Of course, it will mean that the book doesn't get done as quickly, but as you say, you're far enough with it now that you know you will finish it, and the job will give you the opportunity to save something.

It was good to get news of people at home. The girl you mention is Sylvia Kushner ... she was a good friend of ours. Jack knew her a long time before I did. She is a very nice person ... if Miriam sees her again, please give her our regards. I'm glad Abe is getting married, and I hope the girl is really nice. Could you give him our best wishes if you're writing to him? I was surprised to hear that Sid Warhaft is married,[2] and also Max Cohen. Did Sid marry anyone we know? I'm glad the Kramers are ok, and also that they got our letter ... we weren't quite sure of the address. What is Vic doing now? I hope they write to us.

The C.B.C. seems awfully slow, Adele. I suppose all such places are. I've written six scripts, about 6 pages each, double-spaced, which to me seemed close to 15 minutes ... maybe I read slowly, I don't know. I'm going to send them off as soon as I can get them typed up properly. I suppose we'll have left this country before I hear ... that is the worst of moving around.[3]

I had some good news the other day ... one of the stories I wrote (set in Somaliland) has been accepted by 'Story' Magazine in the States. It is the mag. edited by Whit Burnett, and they wanted the story of mine for 'Story' in book-form, which I gather is a collection of short stories published quarterly.[4] The letter was dated July 14. I got it about three weeks ago. It had been sent to Somaliland, and they had kept it in the

P.O. there from July until December ... can you imagine it! Naturally, I wrote at once, trying not to sound too eager. I was afraid they might not want it after such a long lapse of time. I got a letter back the other day, however, and they still want it, thank the lord. It'll go in a later volume, as it is too late now for the Spring 1953 issue. In the first letter, Mr. Burnett asked if I had a novel they might consider. Of course, I haven't. So I wrote and said I had quite a few short stories (omitting to mention that only about 5 are completed) and would they be interested in a collection of them. In the last letter, he said volumes of stories by a single writer don't sell very well, and they would rather see me work on a novel. After my first abortive effort, I don't feel at all sure I could write a novel, but perhaps I will have a crack at it. It would be set in S'land. The other one (unfinished) was top-heavy and had about 10 times too many sub-plots etc, and every character was a major one, which was silly. Perhaps if I keep the main plot simple, and limit the major characters to a few, it might turn out better. There is plenty of local colour in Somaliland for the setting. I had a lot of ideas for things, but they were all for short stories. Lately I have been considering the situation from the novel angle, but haven't reached any conclusions as yet. The trouble is that life there has so many varying aspects, it would be difficult to make a unified novel. Maybe it would be possible, though. There doesn't seem much point in writing only stories if they're not going to stand a chance of getting published. The story was 'The Uncertain Flowering,' about the adolescent girl who went out for the holidays to visit her parents in the colony ... do you by any chance remember it? After a decent interval, I'm going to send them some of the other stories ... they said I could. It is hard not to seem too eager, isn't it, when in fact one is?

You'd think I'd have lots of time to write, wouldn't you? But I haven't. Jocelyn takes up a lot of time, and I also have to supervise a lot in the house, as cleanliness is the only way of avoiding diseases here. I can't work at all in the evenings, as a) I am too tired here ... we normally go to bed about 9 p.m.; and b) the typewriter would wake the baby anyway. I get in about 2 to 3 hours work a day, that's all. Still, it's quite a lot really.

Jocelyn is fine. At 5½ months, she now weighs 18 lbs, which is quite a lot. She can sit up by herself now, although a bit unsteadily, and she is getting her first tooth. She is still awfully good. I have had to wean her, unfortunately, so she now takes a powdered milk mixture from a spoon and cup ... no bottles. She is getting very entertaining now, and Jack is very fond of her, thank goodness.

I heard recently that the collection of Somali poems and stories I translated cannot be published by the E. African Lit. Bureau, so the Som. govt is having it published by the govt press in Aden.[5] It won't be as nice a job, but I don't care about that so long as it gets printed somehow.

Please write soon, Adele ... we love to hear from you. How is Esther's baby?[6] Please give our regards to all the family.

Love,

Peg

P.S. The Story Press is a good bet for your novel. Address:
Whit Burnett, Editor,
The Story Press,
Main Street, Setauket.
Long Island, New York, U.S.A.

1 Wiseman had two jobs – as tutor and essay marker in the Department of English, University of Manitoba, and as a technical assistant in an entomological laboratory.
2 Sid Warhaft (d. 1976) was working on his PhD for Northwestern University. He later joined the Department of English, University of Manitoba.
3 Laurence had submitted the scripts about Somaliland for broadcast. Elizabeth Long of the CBC initially declined them and in September 1953 offered $50 to have Laurence rewrite them. Laurence refused and asked that the material be returned to her. At the CBC's request, she added a short article on the technical aspects of Jack Laurence's work in Somaliland and sent the lot back to the CBC in November.
4 'Uncertain Flowering' was published in Story: The Magazine of the Short Story in Book Form, no. 4 (1953): 9–34. Whit Burnett (1899–1973) had founded the bimonthly magazine with Martha Foley in 1931.
5 The publication information on the title page of A Tree for Poverty states: 'Published for the Somaliland Protectorate by the Eagle Press. Kampala. Nairobi. Dar Es Salaalm.' The book was printed by W. Boyd & Co. (Printers) Ltd., Nairobi.
6 Harry and Esther Wiseman's son Arnold had recently been born.

c/o Sir Wm. Halcrow & Partners
8 June 1953

Dear Adele:

I don't remember who owes who a letter, but it seems quite awhile since I've written to you. I hope everything's ok with you and that your book is progressing well. How is the family? And how is Harry and Esther's baby?

I've begun to think I might do a radio series on this country after all, and will begin to jot down things as soon as I can find a minute. There seems to be so much to do, and despite having servants, so darned little time. It appears that many records of African music exist and can be bought here, so perhaps one could get permission to use them in a talk. We are hearing some tonight, and will buy the ones we like, and hope to find someone who can explain them to us ... it shouldn't be too difficult. Any talk on this country would of necessity emphasize the new Africa rather than the old tribal culture, for the former is the dominant thing here. There is, evidently, a very good calypso-type song called 'Nkrumah, Nkrumah,' which I hope to get. Nkrumah as you know is the P.M. here.

I've been working quite hard on the novel set in S'land, although it goes ahead slowly.[1] I've done about 3 chapters, which is nearly 100 pages, and that depresses me, when I consider that, for example, Graham Greene's really terrific novel 'The Power and the Glory' is only about 250 pages. I don't know how people manage to compress like that ... perhaps it comes only with years of experience. I try very hard to be brief, but find I am always spreading myself to dozens of pages where a couple should suffice. I keep getting chummy letters from Whit Burnett saying he hopes a good deal of it will be done by August, when he and his wife return from France. Well, of course, it *won't*, which is a sad thought. I know that sort of letter is absolutely standard, but it cannot help but spur me on. However, there is a limit, especially with the baby to look after. Also, I don't especially like this idea of sending someone a rough or semi-final draft, do you? Particularly of the first few chapters ... they are so important, yet how can they be put into final form until the whole thing is done at least in draft? I have heard that the Somali script ... poems and stories, maybe you remember it? ... is being published now by a Nairobi firm, at the expense of the S'land govt, which is really quite handsome of them, as it will cost them quite a bit no doubt. Gus Andrzejewski, at the School of Oriental Studies, is now sending me further literal translation of poems, which I'm working on. We are now getting into the more complex Somali poems, the long 'gabei,' and these are very fine in Somali but terrible to translate with anything the same effect. I am glad to be going on with them, however, partly for their own sake and partly because it keeps the Somali mode of thought and expression fresh in my mind.

Enough of this. We are very well, except that our house was robbed last week. The thieves got in through the windows in Jocelyn's room. Fortunately we woke up when they had just gone into the livingroom, and they fled. They only got about £17 worth of stuff, nothing of any great value and all replaceable, thank goodness. The thing that worried me was the baby ... thieves don't usually harm anyone, but one can't help wondering what would have happened had she suddenly started to yell. We found an enormous crowbar outside her window. She was wide awake throughout, but quite quiet and didn't seem in the least alarmed. Thieves are one distinct disadvantage of this country. The watchman was, as always, fast asleep on the front doorstep.

We are seriously considering returning to Canada after this tour. We like it here, but not well enough to come back, especially since the job doesn't seem to be leading anywhere in particular. In many ways I'd like to return, especially to see people, but I certainly hope we don't have to stay for the rest of our lives.

Jocelyn is well, and getting very sturdy and active. She can nearly stand up by herself now, and says 'mum mum' and 'da da.' She waves goodbye, but usually at the wrong time, such as when people are arriving. She is a problem now, though, as she's so active and wants to do so many things that she can't manage yet, such as standing and walking. She is always tumbling over when sitting in her cot or on the floor, and her forehead is constantly scarlet from bashing it on something when she falls. Still, she doesn't seem to mind. She is getting to look more like Jack, and her hair is almost blonde now.

I haven't heard from the CBC. I suppose it is too soon.

Please write soon and let us know all about everything.

Love to all from all of us,

Peg

P.S. June 10 – Haven't managed to get this posted yet. We got your letter today – many thanks. I'm so glad the Stobies like your book – that is *really good*.[2] Keep on with the good work, whatever you do. Someday, Adele, that is going to be a really fine novel.

I'm glad you saw Miss Gerson again – doesn't it seem a long time since you first thought of going to England?

My story is in the publication that will come out Oct or Nov 53.

P.S. 2. Give our regards to Abe when you see him, & also to Sylvia Kushner & anyone else who still remembers us. Have you ever met Bob Hallstead yet, Adele? Eng. Dept, United College. He's a grand person & so is his wife. Address – 538 Jefferson Ave. Sometimes I think how much I'd like to see everyone again. Do you think we shall ever meet again in Italy, Adele, or was that just the Happy Time? I grow nostalgic – perhaps I am getting old.

P.S. 3. We've had 2 spitting cobras out by our chicken pen lately. They are said to aim at the eyes, & to have perfect accuracy in throwing venom, up to 9 feet. A cheerful thought.

1 The novel was never completed or published.
2 Margaret and John Stobie were members of the Department of English, University of Manitoba.

c/o Sir Wm. Halcrow & Partners
14 December 1953

Dear Adele:

Thanks very much for your Christmas card, which arrived by the last mail and also thanks for enclosing the book review[1] – very encouraging, and sometimes I feel I could do with a little encouragement! Thanks a lot.

Also, thanks very much for sending my address to Malcolm Ross. I got a letter from him the other day, saying he is now editor of Queen's Quarterly[2] and asking if I could send any Somali poems or my own short stories, for him to consider. Unfortunately the poems are pretty much tied up now until they're published by the Som. govt, but I told him when I replied that I'm still working on further translations and explained my collaboration with Gus Andrzejewski on the poems, and I said I'd write to Gus and see if he would agree to sending extracts from some 'gabei' to Queen's Quarterly ... I think that would be better than reprinting some of the first collection. I also sent a story to him – it may not be the type he wants, I don't know, but I thought I'd send it anyway. It's 'Amiina,' the story about the Somali girl and the European bloke who shot himself – I re-wrote it considerably before sending it, as I realized on re-reading it after a year that it needed a lot of touching up. Funny how one doesn't realize at the time. It was the first of the Somali stories I wrote, and isn't as good as it might be, but I think it's quite a lot better since I re-wrote it. In any case, no harm trying. I'm grateful to you, Adele, for putting him in touch with me.

I haven't heard from the CBC yet and can only hope they got the scripts. The more I think about it, the more foolish I feel about it – never mind, it was partly their fault – her letter was very ambiguous.

I've got about 25 pages done on the novel now – it seems like a very small bit after all the time I've spent on it. A year now. I've decided not to divide it into chapters ... it doesn't fall that way naturally. It's got two parts, really, and within those parts it's made up of related but separate episodes – I don't know whether that's a bad thing or not, but I don't think it can be helped, because it takes place in two worlds, so to speak, the Somali and the European. I had hoped to have the first draft done by the time we go home on leave, but I won't even have part one done. Still, I think now it is better to get it done more or less as I want it, especially the first fifty pages – if I can establish the right tone, I feel it may carry on under its own steam – at least, I like to think so.

We still haven't heard whether we're coming back here or not, and Jack is getting very fed up with not knowing – I don't blame him, it's very awkward not knowing whether to start looking for another job or not. The firm will almost definitely ask him to come back, as the Chief Engineer wants him, but the only question is salary – will they offer him what he thinks he ought to get?? I hope now that we do come back – I have become unexpectedly fond of this place.

Jocelyn is chattering like a magpie now. I've shown her the wrapped parcels for Christmas, and told her 'Christmas is coming.' She hasn't a clue what it means, but knows it is something exciting, and now says excitedly, 'Chrisum coming – coming see you!' I don't know why 'coming see you' – perhaps she thinks it is a person. We're going to have a tree for her this year. She puts quite a few words together now, and when we take her out it is a constant running commentary – 'hallo, lizard!' 'Look – cows!' etc. etc.

Must go now. Do write soon. I hope your novel's progressing rapidly. It must be wonderful to have it so nearly done. You know, I really admire the way you've stuck with it, Adele, and I honestly believe it won't be too long before I'm receiving my autographed copy of it! I'm really looking forward to reading it – by the way, what are you going to call it?

Love to all,

Peg

1 Not traced

2 Malcolm Ross (b. 1911) had been a professor of English at the University of
Manitoba from 1945 to 1950. Laurence had been a student in his course on Milton
and seventeenth-century thought. While in the Department of English at Queen's
University, in Kingston, Ontario (1950–62), Ross was editor of *Queen's Quarterly*, a
scholarly journal of articles, reviews, and creative writing.

c/o Sir Wm. Halcrow & Partners
16 January [1954]

Dear Adele –

I know I do not actually owe you a letter, having written only about a
week ago, but tonight you are the only person I feel like writing to,
since Jack is at the moment going through Episode #4 of my story, & I
am sitting here trying not to chew my nails. Jack is a very good critic,
you know. If he says it stinks, then it does in fact stink. The first two
times he read this episode, he tore it to bits (it had then been re-written
about five times already), so I hope he thinks it stands up better this
time. I am fed up with it. I wish I could disagree with J's criticisms –
but they are so damned logical & sound – I always wonder why I didn't
see it myself. If I ever write anything with any merit, it will be largely
due to him – he's always getting me to rework things until they're at
least the best I can do – I sometimes think that I myself would never
operate at full strength otherwise. I have, including this episode, the
discouragingly small amount of 26 pages done to date on the story. But
I am damned if I'll press on like I did before & then have to chuck it all
again. I am doing the story mainly from the European woman's point
of view. In the (necessary) places where the Somali world is the setting,
it is mainly seen through the Somali girl's eyes – this combination is
risky, obviously, but better, I think, than my original idea of writing it
from the man's (D.C's)¹ point of view. I have not got the necessary
scope of talent to write from a man's point of view. I feel more relaxed
about it now that I am not struggling against my own nature. - Sorry to
pour out all this, Adele - it is only because I know how well you know
the anxiety that the whole thing may not turn out right.

We are all well. Jocelyn is chattering like anything. She is getting to
the exhibitionist age – tonight she paraded out into the compound with
no clothes on, & her pot stuck on her head saying gleefully, 'Shira see
hatta (hat) on!' The other day she nestled up to Jack & cooed softly, 'I
love you, daddy,' which we thought was very sweet – then the next

minute grinned wickedly & announced 'I love *Doss*-alyn!' (Jocelyn –
That is the way she says her name.)

Before I forget – we've had to put our leave forward & now won't be
going until the end of April – we will probably be in Wpg the third
week of May. I *hope* you'll still be there – you must be!

Sorry to write such an unsatisfactory letter! Hope your story's going
well. Love from us all.

Peg

P.S. Jack says Episode #4 is ok now – Thank god.

1 District Commissioner

c/o Sir Wm. Halcrow & Partners
7 April 1954

Dear Adele;

It was good to get your letter – thanks very much about the party – as
far as arrangements are concerned, we can settle it when we get there,
but whatever you want will be ok with us. It is very good of you and
your mom and dad to be putting us up and everything – honestly, it is
wonderful of you, and we really appreciate it. We leave three weeks
today – I can hardly believe it!

I got a letter from Elizabeth Long at the CBC, saying they got my
scripts, for the second time, and are sending a cheque ($50) (That seems
like quite a lot to me. The scripts aren't very good.) – so that is settled,
thank goodness. She said the cheque would go out sometime within 6
weeks – I wonder if that means the material is to be used about that
time – if it isn't used before then, which I don't imagine it will, we'll be
in Canada – I'd kind of like to hear the scripts, even though she said
she was sending copies of them (the re-written ones, you know). She
said she had rewritten them herself, as the script writer she had picked
out to do the job had a baby. Really, Elizabeth and I are getting so
chatty in letters, after having nearly had a stand-up fight via the mails!
It's funny, in a way. I got a letter (2 in fact) from Malcolm Ross – in the
first, he returned the story 'Amiina,' as it didn't strike him as typical of
what is happening in Africa.[1] He said he didn't like the story of the
'pathetic' Englishman and the 'vicious' native girl. I wrote him, perhaps

foolishly, a long long letter, in which I said: a) he had missed the point of the story entirely; b) but if he had missed it, it was obviously my fault as the story couldn't have got it across – for one thing, there wasn't enough background material; c) the Englishman wasn't pathetic, and the native girl was certainly not vicious, in fact, if anything, quite the contrary was true of both; d) the English boy was not destroyed, as M.R. said, by the native girl – he in fact destroyed himself, symbolically as well as literally, by the naivete of his love – having before hated the Africans, he found his 'pet' African, the one who justified all the others, and so began to accept the whole race, but his love, like his hatred, was lacking in true understanding of their motives, attitudes, reactions, etc. In the end, because he accepts Amiina as 'good,' good by his English standards, he is of course disillusioned, and turns once more – from love to hatred. The naivete of Europeans who must think the Africans are either entirely bad or entirely good – always, of course, judging by European standards – that is more or less the theme. Anyway, I suppose it was silly to explain it all, since obviously the story failed, but I did so because I hated to think Ross had the idea that I'd got to the point where I'd write simple little tales about pathetic Englishmen and vicious native girls. By the way, when you write to him, *don't* mention my saying all this, will you? I don't want him to think I feel churlish about his rejecting the story – I think he was quite right, it didn't get across what it was meant to. Perhaps I ought to have left well enough alone, but I didn't – I decided to send him another story, which I've done.[2] No harm trying, anyway. In his second letter he said the Somali 'gabei' had arrived, and he wasn't sure yet whether it could be used – it is pretty long, although I only sent him half of it. It's not really very good poetry by our standards – but I think it's quite interesting in its setting. I hope he uses it.

Now I've done nothing except talk about writing. You know, except for Jack – who is always a very helpful critic – I never talk to anyone about writing – in fact, most people here don't know how I spend all my time, and probably think I'm lazy as hell. It's such a relief to be able to write to you about it – I expect you sometimes feel, too, that it's odd that such an important area of one's life is shared with so few people, in fact, hardly any. I'm sorry you won't get the Stobies' criticism of your novel sooner – it will be hard to wait. I hope it's not too long.* What are you going to do – I mean, to whom are you going to send it? Can I see it when we get there? I'm so anxious to read it.

We're all well. Jocelyn has taken to 'writing pussy cats' on the walls and also to smearing herself and the house with blue chalk – today she looked like an 'ancient Briton blue with woad.'[3] Must go. We'll be seeing you soon.

Love to you all,

Peg

* I mean the waiting, not the novel!

1 The story has not been traced.
2 Laurence had sent another story set in Somaliland which Ross had initially accepted. However, he returned it, apparently at Laurence's request, when she sent him a copy of 'Drummer of All the World,' which Laurence considered a far superior story.
3 Laurence's paraphrase of textbook descriptions of Picts, the original inhabitants of the British Isles.

c/o Chief Engineer, Port of Tema,
P.O. Box 1, Tema,
Gold Coast, W. Africa
20 June 1955

Dear Adele:

We were so glad to get your letter the other day. I'm really glad to learn that the novel is shaping up ok. I felt sure that it would. I think it is quite right what you say – you did compress too much at the end, and I can certainly see why, as I am having to fight the same temptation myself right now. However, I feel certain your book will be ok now that you've got down to it once more. I'm really delighted to hear that part of the novel is to be read on the CBC – I wish I could hear it done. That's really good, Adele, and apart from being good in itself, it may prove useful when you are sending the novel to a publisher. I'm sure all these things add up. No kidding, I really am pleased!

Re: plans – we were glad to hear that you'll probably be going to England in Sept or Oct., as I shall be going back to London the middle of October with the kids.[1] Jack isn't due for leave until the beginning of December, but my mother and aunt will be going to England in September, so I'll take the children and join them in London in October.

Do you anticipate being in London for some time? I certainly hope so. It would be wonderful to see you again, and it seems quite likely at the moment that we'll be in England at the same time. Keep us posted about your plans and address, and we'll do the same. Incidentally, if by any chance you should go before expected or in some way not have our address in England, you can always get in touch with us in London through our friends the Colliers – F.C. Collier, 63 Shaftesbury Ave., Kenton, Harrow, Middlesex. They're in the phone book, also. We don't know yet where we'll be staying, of course, but hope to get a flat in London somewhere.

I did hear from Malcolm Ross, and they're going to print my story, which is nice.[2] It will go in several issues from now, apparently, I think in the winter issue. I'm glad he decided to take it. Re: the novel – I've got 19 out of 25 chapters done, but won't get the others finished before the baby arrives. I hope to get, at most, one or two more done. I'm approaching the climax, where nearly everyone either dies of abortion, gets shot, goes off their rocker or something. Just like Hamlet (there the resemblance begins and ends.) The end is so much the most difficult. I thought the beginning would be harder than the ending, but it isn't so. I remember what you said a long time ago when you were working on the ending of yours – the last chapters when everything either jells or doesn't jell. I feel just like that about it. It is so hard to see it in perspective. I have terrible spells of feeling the characters are weak and unconvincing. Sometimes I think about the 'hero' – if he was my husband, I'd give him a good swift kick, and about the 'heroine' – who cares what happens to such a nitwit anyway; and about the Somali girl – is she (horrible thought) a conventional portrayal of the 'native girl'?? Also, the recurring fear is – is the thing going to be interesting? It's interesting to me, but will it be to anyone else? However, I suppose everyone feels these things. I feel now I've got to finish it whatever it's like. There have been so many novels set in Africa lately, that probably no one will be publishing them by the time this is done. Also, it is non-political, and most of the novels nowadays about Africa seem only concerned with axe-grinding against the 'white man's burden.' One difference with my story, anyway – it's not primarily concerned with the type of European who hates Africa, but with the type who is completely bound up with it. And not, I hope, in the manner of so many Africa-lovers in novels – 'God! the Masai are wonderful people! Nature's gentlemen!' – that sort of thing makes me sick.

Jocelyn is well, except for minor scars of battle. She bashed her head on the concrete floor tonight, and went to bed sporting a huge bandage all over her forehead – whatever is wrong, she has to have a bandage on it. She has taken once more to saying her prayers at night, and she intones them in a voice that could be heard miles away. The religious effect is slightly offset by the fact that she insists on following them with a loud rendition of 'I'm a Little Teapot.' She was out in the car with Jack the other day, and apparently as soon as they got going she said triumphantly, 'Well mummy's not here, so I guess we can go really fast now, eh?' She thinks her parents are pretty dumb, I guess – she is always correcting us now. – Jack was talking about a rug some of our neighbors have just got, and he said 'It's a better quality than ours.' She said, 'I don't know why you call it a quality, Daddy. It's not a quality – it's a rug.' Today I accidentally bumped into her, and she said haughtily, 'You mustn't bump into people like that, when they're just standing here drinking their orange juice.' Sometimes Jack and I feel we're just two weatherbeaten old souls on the verge of senility! I suppose this goes on until she's about 25!

Jack and I are both well. I look like a mountain. Only 1 month, thank goodness. The doc says the infant is small, however, and may be late (cheering thought). Write soon.

Love to all,

Peg

1 Laurence was pregnant at the time of writing. David Laurence was born on 9 August 1955.
2 'Drummer of All the World' appeared in *Queen's Quarterly* 63 (Winter 1956): 487–504.

c/o Chief Engineer, Port of Tema
10 July 1956

Dear Adele;

How are you? Do you owe me a letter or do I owe you one? I'm getting a bit confused mentally these days. It is now approaching 6 months since I began working until 2 or 3 a.m. four nights a week, and I think the strain is beginning to show! I feel at the moment rather discouraged,

as I'm afraid I'm just about at the end of my tether, and I haven't
finished the story yet. Can't get rid of headaches, and feel generally
beat-up. However, I have a very strong constitution, thank god, and so
if I can only make a last burst and finish the damn thing off (rough
draft, you understand) I shall then take about three weeks off and do
nothing but sleep. I hope the effort proves worth it. Did you feel
discouraged when you were nearing the end? I feel awful. I think the
story is terrible. It is probably the worst piece of prose in history. Also,
who am I to write about Africa? I don't know a damn thing about it,
relatively speaking. I've had the nerve to write half the thing from an
African's point of view. Also, it's too long (344 pages now and with an
estimated 50 to go). (Time out while I remove David from under the
table where I am working!) The Europeans will hate the European parts
and the Africans will hate the African parts. Never mind – it has a good
title. 'This Side Jordan.'[1] From the Book of Joshua, as a matter of fact,
but it's suitable. I'm sorry to bore you with all this, but you're the only
person I know who will understand. I was looking over my ¾ finished
Somaliland novel and maybe it's not as bad as I thought – maybe I'll
finish it after this one. But this one is different, somehow – I feel
strangely fanatical about it. (Excuse me a moment – David is standing
on his head and appears about ready to collapse.)

Jack's mom said in her last letter that your talk was going to be on
the CBC soon.[2] I certainly wish I could have heard it. What was the gist
of it? How soon is the book coming out? I'm so anxious to see it. It sure
is wonderful that Gollancz is taking it in Eng.[3]

I read Mordecai Richler's book 'Son of a Lesser Hero' (terrible title).[4]
Gosh, Adele, you've been keeping something from us all these
years – why didn't you tell us Jews were such stinkers? Seriously, I
thought the picture he gave of the Jewish community was appalling.
Everyone in the book was a first-class heel. It made me feel like
vomiting. Also, there were no real problems, if you know what I mean.
One felt they were all contrived and one didn't care how it all worked
out anyway. I kept thinking of your book and of the penetrating and yet
deeply sympathetic analysis of the Jewish community you've done. You
have something that, more than anything, Richler seems to lack, and
without which no writer can ever be great and maybe not even good,
and that quality is love and compassion. Beside it, R's novel seems like
a pack of cheap tricks.

The kids are wonderful, which is to say they are so full of energy
they'd be unbearable if they had any more. Jocelyn is entertaining as

usual. The other day she came in with a picture she had cut from a magazine – it was a sylph-like glamour girl. 'I've got something Mummy would like to be!' she cried, 'Wouldn't you like to be SLIM like this girl? You'd better keep it as your diet picture!' Yesterday we were playing a pretend game, and she said 'Let's pretend David is my baby brother.' Then she stopped, and considered, and said, 'He *is* my baby brother, too.' Then she said, 'I'm pretending *and* realing.' That solved the whole problem.

David goes like a bomb all day long. He crawls very fast, too fast, and is on the verge of walking. He is a terror, and has a terrible temper and an equally large amount of charm. At the moment he is sitting beside the record cabinet, saying thoughtfully, 'No. No.' He knows he's not meant to open it, but in a minute he will do so anyway. He says 'No!' to himself but keeps on doing exactly as he wants anyway. If one says 'No' to him he either pretends not to hear or else roars in an insulted way.

Must go now. Please ignore my disjointed rambling at the beginning of this letter. Actually, things are going quite well, and I don't honestly think the story is working out too badly, if I can only finish it quickly while the spirit moves me.

Please write soon.

Love,

Peg

P.S. Did Metro and Kay's baby arrive ok?
P.S.2. I will be 30 in 4 days time. Life is passing.

1 The novel was published in 1960 by McClelland and Stewart in Canada, Macmillan in London, and St Martin's Press in New York.
2 While in London, Wiseman had recorded for CBC Winnipeg a talk for the series *Writers' Problems.*
3 Victor Gollancz published *The Sacrifice* on 22 October 1956.
4 *Son of a Smaller Hero* (1955)

c/o Chief Engineer, Port of Tema
23 July 1956

Dear Adele:

It strikes me I wrote you a pretty stupid letter before, all full of my own
doubts and depressions. Very sorry. Actually, things are going quite
well, I think. I've got one more episode to do in the first draft, then a
heck of a lot of fixing up (parts I've decided to change since they were
first written, etc) to do before I start turning my attention to re-writing
proper. In other words, the story has to be hammered into shape before
I start worrying overmuch about the style. Maybe that's wrong – I don't
know. I think perhaps in the past I may have fussed over writing too
much, bleeding it to death in the process. I'm going to try not to spend
too terribly long on the re-writing. I want to bash it off to a publisher,
and if it's no good, I think I'll start another. Don't get me wrong – it
isn't that I believe in writing too quickly. I don't. But I feel my great
flaw in the past has been mulling over something much too long, and
kind of losing the thread in the process. This, I may say, will be the
third novel I have written (the other 2 never got quite finished as they
were no good, especially the first – the second, the one set in Somaliland, I still have some feeble hopes for). I am thirty years old. This is
not good enough. I'm sorry I keep chattering on about all this to you.
The thing is, I can't talk about it to anyone except Jack, and altho' he is
wonderful about it, and has an excellent critical mind, he hasn't actually
done this kind of work himself. I often feel I am leading a double life
– do you? It seems a kind of irony to me that the thing in life which is
most important to me, next to my husband and kids, is something I can
never talk about, never let anyone know about, even. Too much talking
about one's work can be a bad thing – and I don't ever want to become
a member of a mutual back-slapping or soul-searching group. But it
seems sometimes strange to me that this past tour something important
has happened to me, and Jack is the only one who knows anything
about it. One feels sometimes it must show, but it doesn't. I am a
mother and housewife. Full stop. Thank god, at least Jack has followed
it every step of the way – it would be unbearable if there wasn't
anyone. Anyway, things work towards their conclusion – the general
election here is over, and thank god it went the right way, otherwise I'd
have had to change the whole novel! I was chewing my nails lest the
nationalists should get in, and everyone thought I was balmy! The story
isn't a political one, politics are only dealt with indirectly – it isn't in

any sense partisan in the political-party sense. But it is in the broad sense. The nationalists here represent a return to the past, the C.P.P. (Nkrumah's party)[1] despite their widespread corruption, represents a forward move. I spent a day not long ago with the principal of an African school here – Mr. O'Reilly-Wright. A showboy. Very charming, very intelligent, but a bit of a twister under the surface. He was very good to me – I visited every classroom and saw the work, etc. Met all the teachers. Most interesting. A third-rate African school is featured in my story – that is why I wanted to see if my impressions had been correct. They were. But Mr. O'R-W's school is a relatively high-class one – government accepted, and all that. And altho' the scholastic standards are higher than I had imagined, the physical conditions are about three hundred percent worse. You should only see the lavatories! I was delighted to find that I hadn't been wrong – only in my school I hadn't been nearly sordid enough. That can be fixed. And yet the strange thing is that O'Reilly-Wright is a good man in many ways. He was going to the U.S.A. on a trip (has since gone) and he spent a long time asking me about it. He was scared, Adele – he is a respected citizen here, and he was scared of what he would find there. I didn't pull any punches – no use in giving him a false impression. But I did tell him that since his trip is being arranged by U.S. Information Service, he could expect personally only courtesy and friendliness – he wouldn't be allowed to see the other places. I referred him to 'Black Boy' (R. Wright) which he had never read.[2]

Have you read Kingsley Amis' book 'That Uncertain Feeling?'[3] If not, please do so at once. It is TERRIFIC. It is everything I love in a novel – realistic in the right sense, mocking at all the phoney values, etc. Somerset Maugham has said Kingsley Amis is vulgar etc., and that is quite right. Our generation probably is. We don't have the money to live in villas in France. We worry about who's going to pay the gas bill. S. Maugham doesn't like that much. Too bad for him. At one point, the hero (?) in K.A.'s book meets some types on the street who say to him 'Where is pain and bitter laughter?' He is about to strike his breast and say 'In here, friend,' when he realizes they have actually said 'Where is piano and bit of life?' He is dreaming, Tristran like, about his illicit love,[4] and swallows a mouthful of tea-leaves.

Love,

Peg

P.S. Kingsley Amis is Welsh, & *very* good. makes Mordecai Richler look pale.

P.S.2. *NB!!* My mom heard your talk – she said – 'Adele's voice records very well – she had a down-to-earth approach to her subject that I liked very much. I thought it was the best one I've heard of that series.' Congratulations! My mom is quite a sharp person, you know & she wouldn't say it unless she really meant it.

1 Convention People's Party founded by Nkrumah in 1949
2 Richard Wright's (1908–60) novel was published in 1945.
3 Kingsley Amis's (1922–95) work appeared in 1955.
4 An allusion to the tragic medieval romance of adulterous love between the knight Tristan and the Irish princess Isolde

P.O. Box 1, Tema
31 July 1956

Dear Adele:

I was so glad to get your letters yesterday. Listen, as soon as Gollancz publishes your book in October, will you please buy me a copy and I'll send you the money. No quibbling, now – I always think it is a mistake for an author to give away free copies – let your friends help the sales! I'm so glad the book is coming out so soon, and also with Viking even sooner. I was thrilled to hear about the reviews – they sound really wonderful. Which is what the book deserves. I don't know how you feel about it, but I think I would be inclined to take more notice of a favourable but also critical review by D. Daiches than the more ecstatic ones of some of the others.[1] That man is terrific. He has obviously given thought to the review, not done it just as an emotional impression. And if it is critical in some places, well – that just makes the fact that it is generally favourable mean more. I can see what you mean by the finished product of a novel being something of an anti-climax, but right now I would be prepared to take that chance! Anyway, after Oct 20, I shall be watching The Sunday Times and The Observer and the N.S. & N. for reviews of your book.[2]

At the moment, I'm laid low with a terrible cold. At least, not laid low, as I have to get up and look after the kids, but I feel pretty terrible. I have a slightly fevered feeling – so anything I say in this letter about my story should not be taken too seriously.

Re: my story. It has two themes, really. It is told partly from the point
of view of Nathaniel, an African schoolteacher who has the equivalent
of about a grade 9 education, and partly from the point of view of
Miranda, the young wife of a European accountant in a British firm
here. It is really the story of her attempt to make friends with a few
sample Africans (i.e. Nathaniel and his wife Aya); her serious but
blundering attempts to understand them; and her final realization that
intellectual 'racial tolerance' is not enough – it is, in fact, only the
beginning. She fails, of course, as we all do who try the same thing and
with the same naivete, but she begins to realize why she has failed. At
one point, near the end, she realizes that she has never even asked
herself whether or not she *liked* Nathaniel and his wife. They were
always in the nature of 'exhibit A' to her. And to them, inevitably, her
attempts at friendliness have been embarrassing and she has seemed
both clumsy and patronizing to them. Miranda's husband, Johnnie
Kestoe, is a young Liverpool Irishman who has made his own way in
the world. Charming and tender towards his wife, he is also impatient
at her insistence on making friends with Africans. He has no use for
Africans at all. Like most self-made men, he has a front of great self-
reliance and energy, but in fact he needs Miranda more than she needs
him, and he despises in Africans what he fears in himself – the newness
of their educated position and their inability to cope with it; their
frequent weakness and hesitancy when faced with the modern competi-
tive business world; etc. Miranda is the daughter of a Church of
England bishop, and thinks she has broken away from her class, but is
influenced by her background much more than she realizes. Miranda,
anxious both to make friendly overtures towards Nathaniel and to
convince her husband that Africans are ok, persuades Nathaniel to see
Johnnie and ask him if there are any job possibilities for some of his
(N's students). Nathaniel is worried about his students, as the Progress
Grammar School is a very second-rate one and he thinks they are
turning out boys who believe themselves to be educated but actually
have few qualifications. Also, he sees himself succeeding brilliantly with
some of his students and being praised by high govt Africans for
helping to build the new Ghana. So he agrees to go. He does go.
Johnnie is doubtful, but agrees to see the boys. Johnnie sees the boys.
Only one is any good at all, and Johnnie hires him – as a messenger.
The boy has had ideas about the brave new Ghana, and now, still
believing himself to be well educated and a leader-type, he is con-
demned to sit in the dust in front of Alkirk Moore & Bright's offices,

waiting for someone to give him errands to run. Miranda is disappointed at this failure but she does not see the terrible significance it has
for Nathaniel. Both Miranda and Aya are expecting babies about the
same time, and they are actually in hospital at the same time (straining
credulity, this? But I was in hospital with 2 women I knew very well,
when I had David – if it is too much of a coincidence, I can't help it).
Aya is in the throes of labour, and is also very frightened at being in a
'European' hospital (it is the govt one). Miranda insists on coming in to
her cubicle, asking her constantly how she feels, is there anything
anyone can do etc etc. Inevitably, Aya turns on her and for the first time
tells her the truth that Nathaniel has been too embarrassed to tell –
Miranda is not wanted. Why doesn't she go away?

Miranda is shocked and hurt by this. But a short time later, having
her own child, she begins to understand that it is difficult for anyone to
enter into another's pain. If she could not understand Aya's simple
physical pain, how much less Nathaniel's – a torment of resentments
against Europeans, hatred of his own primitive past, fears of his own
inability to cope with the civilized world. That, more or less, is a very
shortened summary of Miranda's story, altho' of course much more
happens than that – for one thing, her gradual understanding of the
undercurrents of fear and anxiety in her own (the Eur) community –
they are all waiting, knowing soon they must be replaced by Africans,
hating the Africans whom they consider to be incompetent to take over,
fearing their own future – they have all got too used to the easy life
here and none of them know how they'll ever be able to cope at home
in England again.

As for Nathaniel's story, only part of it is his relationship with
Miranda. The main thing about him is that he stands, as he tells his
uncle at one point, 'Between today and tomorrow.' His uncle says that
is nowhere. He dreams of the past glories of Ghana, and the glory that
will be in the future, but he doesn't know how to achieve it. He is only
semi-educated, and knows it. He is not very far removed from his forest
past, and he fears that. The old Africa both disgusts and fascinates him.
He is repelled by its superstitions and its cruelty and fear. But he also
longs for its safety, the security of the tribe and the little village where
a man did not have to stand alone or make his own decisions. His
family keeps wanting him to go back. His uncle offers to find a job for
him as clerk to a chief. But to Nathaniel that represents a defeat – a
return to the past. His wife and his mother-in-law both try to persuade
him to go back, and often he finds it hard to withstand them. But the

new Ghana to him means education, and he feels he would be betraying himself to go back to his village. At the same time, he knows that Progress Grammar is a crooked outfit, and Jacob Abraham Mensah, its principal, is only out for what he can get. Nathaniel is pulled between a past that is unquestionably more honest (but is going nowhere, with its paraphernalia of fetish, fear and cruelty) – and a present that is corrupt but is definitely on its way towards independence and the new Ghana. In the end, of course, he decides to stay. There are some symbols running through Nathaniel's story – they came quite of themselves and weren't planned, but seemed to fit. Principally, the River is to him the old gods (Tano, God of the River and Lord of the Forest, is one reason why) and the safety of the old life. The River is, in a sense, the womb with all its dark safety. But in a gradual understanding that is climaxed in a religious meeting, Nathaniel sees the River is also Jordan. It is for him to cross. But in the end he knows he will never see the full flowering of the promised land, the new Ghana. Nathaniel is of the generation of Moses & Aaron – he has been too [–]. He names his son Joshua. And at the end he says to his son 'You'll know what to do with it all, won't you? You'll know how to make it all work.'* Of course there is more to the story than that, but that is roughly an outline of the two themes. Nathaniel's story is told in very emotional terms, and Miranda's is on a much more subdued level, as I think would be the case.

It is a very plain story in the sense that nothing much happens, I suppose. No one is raped or seduced, there are no riots or anything like that. Maybe not enough happens. I don't know. It is called 'This Side Jordan.' I don't know – when I summarize it like that, it doesn't seem spectacular enough. But I'm so sick of books about Africa full of wildly dancing tribesmen, human sacrifices, and Europeans who are always drunk and always leaping in and out of bed with each other. That isn't the Africa I know. Maybe the Africa I know hasn't got enough sensation to make it book material. We shall see. I can see there's a lot of work still to do.

Must go. Hope this hasn't been too dull. Please write soon.

Love,

Peg

* I should have said that Nathaniel sees finally that there is more to crossing Jordan than just Independence Day – when independence is gained, that will only be the beginning. I suppose in a sense the gaining

of Independence & the breaking away both from the old Africa & from European domination in this country is mirrored in the story of this individual man, but I have not pressed the analogy or indeed pointed it out at all. I guess it is there if anyone cares to see it.

P.S. the story is *not* autobiographical.

P.S.2. this didn't get mailed & it is now the middle of Aug. Sorry. We just got today an announcement of Mac Price's marriage to a girl named Margaret Tupper, in Wpg.

1 David Daiches (b. 1912), critic and author, was University Lecturer in English at Cambridge. In a letter to Marshall Best of Viking Press, dated 4 July 1956, Daiches gave a balanced review of *The Sacrifice*.

2 *The Sacrifice* was reviewed in the *Sunday Times*, 21 October 1956, 7. It was not, however, reviewed in either the *Observer* or the *New Statesman and Nation*.

2226 Windsor Rd.,[1]
Victoria, B.C.
17 March 1957

Dear Adele:

I hope you did not find my last letter incoherent. I have been working like the devil ever since arriving, typing out that damn manuscript, and now it is finished. I have sent it to the Atlantic Monthly Novel Contest – I haven't a hope of winning, of course, but they are taking several scripts besides the winning one, so I might as well have a bash.[2] In any event, they virtually promise to return the scripts pretty promptly if they are not being considered, so I don't think the time waste will be too much. I shall then, I think, send it to MacMillans of Canada – and what the dickens is that man's name, Adele?[3] I cannot remember. I think he might think it was a bit odd, though, don't you, getting a script addressed to him personally? Or do you? I don't want it to appear that I am trying to use influence or anything – not that I would have any scruples, you understand, only if I were in the publishing business, I would tend to be put off by any such tactics. I sort of feel I should chuck it in an old shoe box or something and send it rather quietly. Of course I know all this is quite stupid.

Well, now that it is done I don't know what to do with myself, and feel very lost without it, as though a lot of people I knew suddenly went away. Also, I wonder how long I will go before I start anything else. Quite awhile, I hope, as I feel I must get settled down somewhere first, and I have an overpowering urge to make up to my family (ie. husband and kids) for all the neglect they have endured over the past year. Not really neglect, you know, but half my mind was elsewhere. I wonder what I shall want to write about next? You know that previous half-finished novel on Somaliland? I think maybe I can do something with it, but I would have to begin all over again. Its trouble, I can see now, was a basic lack of simplicity – a theme should be as simple as birth or death – something that can be summed up in a single sentence and yet whose ramifications are so wide that it can never be entirely said at all. The theme of that one wasn't simple – it was superficially very complicated because I didn't really know what I was trying to say and therefore camouflaged it with intricacies of plot. I think I loved Somaliland too much to write about it so soon after being there. Perhaps at this distance I can see what it was a little more clearly. I don't know. And someday I would like to write a novel about an old woman. Old age is something which interests me more and more – the myriad ways people meet it, some pretending it doesn't exist, some terrified by every physical deterioration because that final appointment is something they cannot face, some trying to balance the demands and routine of this life with an increasing need to gather together the threads of the spirit so that when the thing comes they will be ready – whether it turns out to be a death or only another birth. I think birth is the greatest experience of life, right until the end, and then death is the greatest experience. There are times when I can believe that the revelation of death will be something so vast we are incapable of imagining it. I read a joke the other day – a little boy says to another, 'Why does your Grandad read the Bible so much?' and the first boy replies 'I think he's cramming for his finals.' I thought that was very funny, and also very touching, in an odd way. I picture a very old woman who knows she is dying, and who despises her family's sympathy and solicitude and also pities it, because she knows they think her mind has partly gone – and they will never realize that she is moving with tremendous excitement – part fear and part eagerness – towards a great and inevitable happening, just as years before she experienced birth. I probably sound off my rocker. It is only because you are the only person, apart from Jack, to whom I can spout these vague and half-formed ideas.

Jack is coming back a little earlier than expected, and will reach Montreal April 20. I'm not sure when he will land in England. I'm ticking off the days, needless to say.

I've heard a lot of good comments on your book, and mom saved me some reviews, which were wonderful. How is the research coming for the new project? Please write and tell all about everything.

Kids fine. Please write soon.

Love,

Peg

P.S. I have lost 10 lbs! Am living on celery & cottage cheese.

1 Margaret Laurence and her children had returned to Canada in January 1957 and were staying with Laurence's mother who had recently undergone an operation for cancer. Jack Laurence followed in April.
2 No award was given for 1957.
3 Possibly John Morgan Gray (1907–78), president of the Macmillan Company of Canada, or Kildare Dobbs (b. 1923), one of Macmillan's editors

1540 St. Georges Ave,
N. Vancouver, B.C.
1 December 1957

Dear Adele –

I'm sorry not to have written before, but we have had a rather chaotic time for the past few months.

In the first place, we looked for a house & finally found one – then, when we thought everything was settled, it turned out that the contractor-owner was trying to pull a fast one & to involve us in a third mortgage which would have ruined us financially. We were lucky to get out of the whole mess with only a $20 legal fee – and next time, we'll be *very* careful! We've decided not to look for a house until Spring, as our situation is so uncertain – Jack doesn't know if his firm will succeed in establishing itself or will go broke![1] However, we are hanging on for the moment, as engineers are finding it hard to get jobs here now.

Secondly, after a long and painful illness, my mother died in September.[2] I spent the 3 weeks before her death, in Victoria. I knew it would only be a matter of days, & I wanted to be there. I think that was the most ghastly period I've ever lived through. I had the children there – & was trying not to upset them. My 2 aunts[3] were there, & we took turns going to see mother in the hospital. For the first week, she was rational, & so I was able to talk with her. My brother[4] spent his holidays there, & so the two of us used to visit her together. She knew she was dying, but she never said so – I think she was trying to make it easier for us. She got weaker & weaker, & the pain made it necessary for her to have morphine all the time. One evening when Robert & I went to see her, she had slipped into irrationality. I hope I never have to do anything as difficult again, Adele, as to talk to her about people who had been dead for 20 years, as though they were alive & might enter the room at any moment. Only one thing she was really clear about – my brother & myself. She said 'God bless you' to us when we left – I don't remember her ever saying that before in my life. I think I knew then that I'd never see her again – not her real self. The next day she was unconscious, & she never regained consciousness. But she lived another week. I never thought I would pray for someone to die, but I did then. It didn't seem fair that a person who had had such a hard life should have such a hard death. If I ever have to suffer like that, I hope I'll be able to take it with such strength of spirit as she did, all through that year of illness.

Anyway, I guess I was pretty close to breaking-point after my mom's death. But shortly afterwards we had another blow – Jack became very ill & had to have an operation for kidney stones. My aunt came over to be with me & help with the kids so I could go to see Jack in hospital. Then my aunt & both kids came down with Asian 'flu! Honestly, Adele, for a few weeks I thought I would go out of my mind. I guess I hit the bottle pretty hard, & I swear that's the only way I got through those weeks. However, things ultimately straightened out. Jack is still at home, but after 2 sets of complications (an infection & an abscess) he now seems almost well.

Re: my book – a blow there, too. The Atlantic sent it back. However, it is not too gloomy a prospect – their criticisms were absolutely right, Adele – 100% right. They said the African parts were fine, etc, *but* the European characters were not 'fully realized.' And I can see now how shallowly portrayed the Eur. characters are. The director of At. Monthly wrote a long personal letter, in which he suggested re-writing the Eur. parts, & said they wanted to re-consider the script if I re-wrote the Eur. parts. So that is what I am doing. I have just begun – I ought never to have tried to write it so quickly. I am re-doing it, taking Johnnie Kestoe as the central white character, & his character parallels that of Nathaniel in such a natural & inevitable way I don't know why I didn't see it before. I guess it'll take 2 or 3 years. I'm also marking Eng essays for

UBC to make money, as we have been hard hit by J's illness. PLEASE
WRITE!

Much love,

Peg

1 Jack Laurence had been hired by H.H. Minshall and Associates Limited the previous spring. The firm had been established in June 1956.
2 Margaret Simpson Weymss died in Victoria on 25 September 1957.
3 Her mother's sisters, Ruby Simpson and Velma Simpson Feltham
4 Robert Weymss (1933–86)

(WHEN WRITING, PLEASE USE
VANCOUVER ADDRESS:
3556 W. 21st.,
Vancouver 8, B.C.)

Fort St. John, B.C.
14 August [1958]

Dear Adele:

Well, here we are in the Far North! Jack has been, for some months,
Resident Engineer on the dismantling of the old Peace River Bridge that
fell down. He has been up here since the beginning of May, and in July
I came up with the children for the summer. We (the kids and I) go
back the end of August, as Jocelyn begins school in September. Jack
hopes to be back home by the end of September, and will have to come
up here again for the final dismantling of the bridge towers next winter.
We have had a really idyllic summer – beautiful countryside, mountains,
northern rivers, etc; picnics, swimming, berry-picking; Stampede and the
full Wild-West atmosphere for the kids. This is a wonderful country, and
Jack and I often feel we would like to settle down somewhere like this –
in the Cariboo country, perhaps. But how to earn a living? Maybe
someday we'll have a brilliant idea on the subject. At the moment it's
impossible. But both of us are country people at heart, you know. We
don't really care too much about cities. Farming, however, is out. We
know nothing about it, and I would drop dead if I had to approach a
chicken at close quarters. But we keep talking about it – we have some
wild and wonderful schemes for 'our own business,' but no capital!

I was so glad to get your letter, some time ago now, and to learn that
you are working on a play.[1] So what if it takes years? Quality is the thing,
not quantity, as long as you can manage to get three square meals a day

in the interim. I know it'll be good when it's finished, however long it may take.

I think the last time I wrote to you I was still more or less in the woods, but I think maybe I've pulled out now. We had a long depressing time for awhile there, but we seem to be ok now. Working outdoors has done Jack a lot of good – he hasn't looked as well in a long time as he does now. It was lucky, his getting assigned this job at this particular time. I, too, have settled down and stopped feeling sorry for myself, largely anyway. The only reason I felt depressed for such a long time was that I felt I'd never be able to finish this damn novel. Finally, however, I got back to it, and now have the first draft finished. I have to re-write certain sections, but the back of it is broken, anyway. I threw out 25 chapters of the 50, and started all over again. I cannot understand now how I could have written it the way I did the first time. I only had half a novel. But the other half was there – waiting to be picked up, as it were – only I hadn't seen it before. I don't know how much better it is this time, but a good deal, I think. I did the European chapters from the man's point of view, this time, which I ought to have done the first time. Actually, it's a hell of a lot better this time. I know. But is it good enough? Well, this time I like reading it aloud to myself, after everyone else is in bed, and that's a good sign! This is not as egotistic as it sounds – quite the contrary, actually. There is no job in the world in which one puts greater effort with less assurance of success and less knowledge of the true quality of one's work. You know all this, of course. Gosh, I'd like to see you, Adele, and talk about all these things. Incidentally, if ever you should be able to get to Vancouver, we have lots of room in our house – did I mention it before? Our house is yours, for as long as you care to stay. Sometimes I think of ten years ago in Winnipeg, and it seems about a century. We had all the answers then, didn't we? Only we never knew how many questions there would be.

Please visit us sometime. Anyway, write. How ARE you, anyway? Are you happy in your work (do I hear you say 'drop dead!')? We haven't so many friends, either, you know. One gets to value them more and more, perhaps because they really are so few and far between.

Good luck with the play – and with everything.

Love from us all,

Peg

P.S. I saw in the paper that Malcolm Ross is teaching this summer at UBC. I'm hoping he may still be there when I get back, but I don't know. I'd so much like to see him.

I'm going to mark essays next winter, if UBC still wants me to. It is quite interesting work, especially since the chap for whom I mark essays is a real prince.[2] We work very well together, and see many things the same way. It's quite a well-paid job, actually, but I don't want to spend as much time at it as I did last winter. Much of my time then, however, was spent in poring over the grammar text.

P.S.2. Please don't think I'm enamoured of the Catholic theology. I'm not. It interests me in exactly the same way as the West African Akan peoples' worship of Nyankopon, the sun-god, interests me. And there are many parallels, too. All religions seem to have a good many primitive aspects, but I don't think that is an entirely bad thing, either.

The European character, Johnnie, goes back to the R.C. Church at the end of the book. I didn't know whether he was going to or not, but he did. For him, it was necessary. But there is a subtle point which I don't really emphasize – the European is the one who returns to the past, in this fashion. The African, for all his weakness, does not.

1 *The Lovebound: A Tragi-Comedy* was printed privately in 1960.
2 Gordon Elliott (b. 1920) was a member of the English department.

                                        3556 West 21st Ave.
                                        13 May 1959
Dear Adele –

The irony of human relationships is always, it seems, that one's friends are never there when one needs them, & if they should ever need you, you are of course two thousand miles away. There are only two people in this world that I'd like to talk to tonight. One is yourself, in New York.[1] The other is Michael,[2] & he is in England. So.

I was glad to get your letter. I subsequently learned from UBC sources that they are having the Drama course, not the Fiction, this summer. So I guess you will not be here. I took the opportunity to give you as good a build-up as I could, with Jan de Bruyn,[3] who is an associate of Jake Zilber's,[4] & who also teaches Creative Writing here. I was seeing him in connection with 'Prism,' a literary (horrible word) magazine he & a few others are starting here. He asked me if I knew any other writers, & I gave him your address. I hope you don't mind. He has read your novel & was very impressed with it. The only aspect of 'Prism' which distinguishes it from a dozen such is the fact that they intend to publish mainly original stuff, *not* literary criticism. This will be a pleasant change.

I met Jan de Bruyn because I submitted a story to 'Prism' – (one edition is probably all they will be able to finance unless the Canada Council loosens up). De Bruyn liked the story but thought there were certain weaknesses, so I re-wrote it, & it is much better, but quite long, so I don't think they will take it anyway.[5] His committee of three has to pass judgement & they undoubtedly won't like it, the bleeders. How I hate publishers, editors, etc. Of course if they liked my work I would probably love them like anything. I got a short story back from the Atlantic Monthly today – why I keep trying there, only god knows. They sent a lovely letter, saying amid other things, that although the story 'didn't fit their requirements' etc, they felt I 'have a facility which held our attention.' The only snag is that the letter was mimeographed. What hypocrisy! If they don't like it, fair enough – why try to gild the pill? I mind that far more than the rejection slip. It seems so condescending, somehow. Of course, the thing I have to get used to is the question of standards. As soon as a publication, even the At. Monthly, rejects a story, I begin thinking maybe it is no good for anything at all. And maybe it isn't. How can one tell? Without periodic encouragement, how can one possibly know if one's own standards are any good or not? This is not, as you will have perceived, the central problem. The main point is – if one is writing, & more or less gambling one's whole existence on it, & cheating family & etc of one's time & care, & putting into it very nearly the whole of identity, & it turns out to be no good – what will you say then? 'God, I bought the wrong stock? I invested in a mine that wasn't capable of production?' Sometimes I think the Beat Generation have the answer – a complete rejection of this known world & its values. But of course that is impossible for me. Because I don't entirely reject the standards of this world, or I could not care about them at all. Fragmented & un-absolute as all our values are, at this atomic point, I can't place myself in the Beat's position of saying it doesn't matter. Because basically, I care. I care terribly – not to be a 'success' (neon-type, cocktail, autographing type – that leaves me cold), but to know that *somebody* (even one) whose standards are more or less mine, doesn't think everything I've done is a total loss. That's all. Also, despite the (in a way) enviable mystic position of the Beats (who are this half-century's literary figures, whether we like them or not), it cannot be a solution to me to produce solely for the work itself, because what I try to write about is rooted in this world. It is not a purely private vision. I can't be that much alone. The work itself is *most* of it – one does it, presumably, to create a private world in which somehow one can breathe better than in this one, but in the final analysis, in my view, the private world has to become public. If it remains private, it is shrivelled as a stillborn child. One wants to get rid of it, finally, to bear it, to cease to be obsessed with it – & this can only be done if it is published, & hence forgotten. So there we are. What all this waffling amounts to is that I am bloody discouraged with myself & my own ability to create living creatures on the printed page. I read Joyce Cary's 'Mr. Johnson'[6] not long ago, & I could have wept in rage & frustration – and admiration – because he had done it. How?

I have done only 3 short stories since I finished that godforsaken novel which no one in their right mind would consider publishing. Maybe the stories are better. Maybe not. I don't know. There are a dozen, at least, more which I want to do, & will, & there is the only answer & the enigma as well – I'll do the bloody things even if no one will publish them, because it is the only pleasure in life, apart from sex & one's children. I wish to heaven I could drop the whole sorry business & become a Good Housekeeping Mom, complete with home-baked bread & glamour, but I can't, so why talk.

And now I have taken all this long letter talking about myself, Adele, when I didn't mean to in the slightest. You will understand.

If you get the chance to come here to teach, you will of course stay at our place, I hope, if you'd like to. I do wish I could see you & talk with you. Don't let 'them' (the undefinable 'them' – the enemy) beat you into writing anything sooner than you want to. I wish you were here. God bless you. I feel perfectly bloody but will no doubt recover as usual. Kids are well. Jocelyn just recovered from measles. David as individualistic as ever – life will be very hard on him, I fear and know.

Love from all,

Peg

P.S. Write soon.
P.S. Dorothy Parker sounds awful & pathetic.[7]

1 Wiseman was awarded a Guggenheim fellowship in October 1957. She moved to New York where she lived until her departure for Japan in June 1961.
2 Probably Michael Wilson, whom Laurence and her husband had known when Wilson was a district commissioner in Somaliland.

3 Jan De Bruyn, member of the English department at the University of British Columbia and editor of *Prism International*.

4 Jake Zilber was a member of the Creative Writing Committee of the UBC Department of English.

5 'The Merchant of Heaven' was published in the first number of *Prism International* (September 1959): 52–74. Laurence published three others in this periodical: 'Godman's Master,' 1, 3 (Spring 1960): 46–64; an excerpt from *This Side Jordan* 2, 1 (Fall 1960): 4–12; and 'The Tomorrow-Tamer,' 3, 1 (Fall 1961): 36–54.

6 Joyce Cary's (1888–1957) *Mr. Johnson* (1939) was the last of his four novels set in West Africa – the other three were *Aissa Saved* (1932), *An American Visitor* (1933), and *The African Witch* (1936) – that dramatized the clash between Africans and their British overseers.

7 Dorothy Parker (1893–1967), New York poet, short-story writer, and critic, was famous for her sardonic wit.

3556 West 21st Ave.
14 May 1959

Dear Adele –

Please ignore the puerile outpourings contained in my last letter. I apologise for inflicting my self-pity on you. I didn't even give you any news. However, I am going to turn over a new leaf. This always happens in the Spring – both the discouragement & the new resolutions. I'm going to: a) be cheerful; b) be sensible; c) lose ten pounds; d) stop being obsessed with writing ('Another short story? I can take it or leave it – '). Talking of weight, I have been losing this same 10 lbs every spring. Why wasn't I born the slim sylph-type?[1]

We are all well. Jack is still with the same firm, although for how long we don't know. The firm is doing better now, but Jack doesn't really feel the work is quite his cup of tea. It may be, of course, that they will get a job in which he could be Resident Engineer, & he would be happier on a job like that – he's not very keen about work which is all office work & no site work. We are hoping there will be an outdoor job this summer, in a place where I could go with him, with the kids, as we did last summer.

I was very interested in your description of the others at the writers' retreat or whatever it was.[2] I have read one of Kubly's books & liked it very much.[3] Also recently read Malcolm Cowley's book on Modern Writers & thought it was excellent.[4] The others mostly sounded very odd and sort of discouraging.

Re: my novel (?) – have sent it to McClelland & Stewart because Gordon (the chap whose essays I mark – he teaches English to engineers) wrote to Jack McClelland about it,[5] & J. McC wrote to me. I haven't heard. I don't think they'll take it, though, so perhaps I should try MacMillans afterwards. I'll wait & see. I don't really think enough happens in the novel. It is not, as they say, 'action-packed.' Anyway, I'm not certain I like the ending now. Maybe it is naive – I don't know. It ends on a definite note of hope. When I get the script back, I am going to let it sit for awhile, & see what I think in 6 months or so. I'm glad you're still doing the play. The play 'A Raisin In The Sun'[6] showed that the work of a new & young playwright *can* be accepted. I hope finances improve for you. Please write.

Love,

Peg

1 At this part in the letter, Laurence had written and crossed out the following paragraph: 'I enclose $2 – would you mind sending me some American 5¢ stamps? I need them for return postage or scripts. Many thanks.' Then she had added in the margin: 'May 19 – We drove to Bellingham last weekend, so I got the U.S. stamps there! (Very simple – we had forgotten we lived near the border.)'
2 Wiseman had been at the MacDowell Colony, an artists' retreat in Peterborough, New Hampshire, that had been the home of Edward A. MacDowell (1861–1908), composer, pianist, and teacher.
3 Herbert Kubly (b. 1915), author of fiction and non-fiction, was a MacDowell fellow from 1956 to 1962.
4 Malcolm Cowley (1898–1989), American critic, poet, and editor. Laurence is probably referring to *Exile's Return: A Narrative of Ideas* (1934), his study of American literary modernism.
5 John Gordon McClelland (b. 1922), president, McClelland and Stewart Publishers
6 Lorraine Hansberry's (1930–65) play was published in 1959.

3556 West 21st Ave.
10 September 1959

Dear Adele:

Many thanks for your letter, which arrived this morning. I will tell you why you haven't heard from us for so long. About a month ago I had a long letter all written to you, but I burned it because it was so gloomy. I thought I would wait until I could write a little more cheerfully.

We just heard the other day about your grant from the Canada Council – congratulations![1] It is wonderful that you got it. I can, however, appreciate your problem – are you honour bound to do with the money what they've announced you'll do with it? What I really mean is – are you *bound*, honour or no? Maybe you could work part of the time in Israel. I envy you setting off for far places. I wish we were. Perhaps we will one day. We are both going to take Spanish classes at UBC this winter. So if there was ever a chance to get a job in South America ... Anyway, that is in the distant future. When will you be going, or do you know yet? I wish we could see you before you depart. However, I'm afraid there isn't much chance of that, unless you could by any chance get to Vancouver.

Is your short story going to be read on the CBC?[2] If so, please let me know when, if you know. It's odd how long one can work on something, and finish it innumerable times, only to discover it isn't yet right and needs more work. I think I am too impatient. I expect to finish things too quickly. And on the other hand, I am never quite happy about anything I've written – I find it hard to say 'This is now finished.' I agree with you – this is a fool's game, and nobody would begin it if they knew how hard it was going to be. But by the time you find out, you're hooked, addicted. You can't leave it.

Re: my novel (?) – McClelland & Stewart have said that they will publish it, *if* they can find an American publisher to bring it out simultaneously. Or a British publisher. Macmillan in England heard about it, through Michael Wilson, and wrote asking to see the script. I forwarded the information to McC & S, figuring this was the ethical thing to do, and they have sent the script to Macmillan. Haven't heard yet. They haven't had any success yet with American publishers. They told me they had sent it to the Atlantic (not realizing it had already been there twice, although in different form each time ... the Atlantic must be getting pretty bored with that story!). Apparently the Atlantic sent it back to McC & S, saying it had been a near thing and was rejected mainly because they already have a number of African novels on their list. This 'near thing' business no longer encourages me – it is like saying that someone is almost alive. However, one good thing – McClelland & Stewart seemed very pleased about it, so if it confirms their opinion of the book, I suppose it has had some good effect. An awful thing – they (McC & S) wrote saying they needed very badly another 2 copies of the novel, and would I please send them. So I had to type it all out – I nearly blinded myself in the process, as I did the whole thing in 2 weeks, 300 pages, and was so bored by it, having seen it so many thousands of times before. If McC & S don't find an American or British publisher, I am right back where I started, so god knows what I will do then. If Macmillan in England doesn't take it, I suppose it wouldn't be much use sending it to Macmillan in Toronto. Or would it? Anyway, I can but wait and see. Claire Pratt, who is McC & S's chief editor or reader or something, likes it, so that is perhaps encouraging. She is E.J.'s daughter.[3]

I have been bashing away at short stories. The long one I was working on is being published in the first issue of 'Prism.' Not much, but something. I sent a story to Queen's Quarterly, and the editor[4] (not Malcolm Ross any more) sent it back saying he would have liked to print it, but they have a lot of fiction on hand and the story is a long one, and would I send it to Tamarack Review. I had already sent a story (another one) to T.R., and Robert Weaver[5] sent it back saying he would have liked to publish it, but they already had a lot of fiction on hand, and the story was really rather long. A vicious circle, obviously. I have these 3 short stories (all long) now, and want to send them to Macmillan's in England, who publish each year a collection of long short stories called 'Winter's Tales.'[6] But alas, I have sent 2 of them to other publications, where they certainly won't be accepted, and haven't received them back. Why do editors keep scripts for months and months and months? Anyway, I am going to try to do a few shorter stories. I want to do about a dozen, set in Africa, and have ideas for more than that, but some of them will have to be long, I'm afraid. Perhaps the only chance is to get enough and send them to a publisher in the hope that they will be published as a collection. I don't know. This, at any rate, is my long-term project. I want to get as many published in periodicals as possible. I'll have two published when this one comes out in Prism, and if I can get 4 or 5 taken somewhere, anywhere, they might stand a better chance of being taken by a publisher as a collection. It will take years. Very difficult. By the way, do you happen to know for sure what the ethical and legal position is, regarding sending scripts to more than one place at a time? I know it wouldn't be done, to submit a script to more than one periodical. But I'm wondering if I could submit to 'Winter's Tales' the scripts that are out already but which will almost certainly *not* be taken by the publications concerned.

Enough of this. The house this morning seems terribly quiet. Jocelyn is back at school, in Grade Two, and this morning David began playschool. There is a co-operative playschool at our United Church, so he is going there. It will, I hope, be very good for him. I used to get very fed-up listening to his voice yakking at me all morning, but now that he's not here, I miss him. It was ever thus. Jocelyn is making good progress, too good in a few subjects such as reading – she gets books from the public library which are marked 10 to 14 years, and reads them with comprehension, so god knows what she thinks of the Grade 2 readers which are really excessively simple. She is not so good in arithmetic and printing. David is an odd little character. For his birthday he wanted only 2 things – a real hand-drill and a real pipe-wrench. He got both. Seemed rather peculiar presents for a four year old, but he explained that he really needed them badly to do his work with his tools. The back yard is full of his bridges, dams, irrigation systems, parking lots, etc. He is a complete dunce when it comes to colouring, painting, drawing, remembering rhymes, etc etc. And he isn't interested in songs, although he rather enjoys stories. But on machinery and tools he is really quite remarkable. He uses all the basic carpenter's tools, including saw, vice, hammer, wrench, screwdriver, drill, spanner, etc. And his understanding of the way machinery works is astounding to me. He is very aggressive and at the same time very shy, a not uncommon combination.

Jack is still working for the same firm. In some ways he is not very happy with his job, but doesn't quite know what to do about it at this point. He feels it is not quite his line of country, but it is hard to know what would be better. However, the firm is doing better now, and getting more jobs, and there is a chance that soon there will be some jobs within his firm which might interest him much more. I hope so.

Must go. Do write and let us know when you expect to go abroad. Also, how is the play coming along? Very hard to say, I know. But if it is progressing, that is the main thing.

Love from us all,

Peg

1 Wiseman had just been awarded a six-month Canada Council Arts Fellowship.
2 Possibly 'On Winnipeg' (Wiseman Papers 1991 – 012/16)
3 Claire Pratt (1921–95), daughter of poet E.J. Pratt (1882–1964), and at this time associate editor at McClelland and Stewart
4 John Edwin Hodgetts (b. 1917), a member of the Department of Political Science at Queen's University
5 Robert Weaver (b. 1921). Editor, anthologist, and radio producer, he founded the

Tamarack Review (1956–82). He had also launched and produced the CBC radio program *Anthology* (1953–85), which featured new and established Canadian writers.

6 Four of Laurence's short stories appeared in the annual anthology: 'The Perfume Sea,' 6 (1960): 83–120; 'The Rain Child,' 8 (1962): 105–42; 'The Sound of the Singing,' 9 (1963): 62–104; and 'The Mask of the Bear,' 11 (1965): 37–61.

[3556 West 21st Ave.]
1 December 1959

Dear Adele –

Macmillan in England has accepted it!¹
  Hurrah!
    Hurrah!
      HURRAH!
[They want 10,000 words deleted. A mere bagatelle! And it *is* too long – they're right.]
  Love from your erstwhile pessimistic but now fantastically optimistic friend –

JML

1 *This Side Jordan* (1960) was published in Toronto by McClelland and Stewart, in London by Macmillan, and in New York by St Martin's Press.

3556 West 21st Ave.
6 May 1960

Dear Adele:

Very glad to get your letter. The MacDowell Colony sounds like paradise. I especially like the sound of the bungalows – a room of one's own. Sometimes I think of that sort of place with fervent longing. I can't really complain, however, as the den is really a room of my own, in a sense, although everybody and his dog tramples through it from morning to night, bringing with them bubble gum, hurt knees, and complaints about the nefarious behaviour of others. Seriously, I'm very glad you are there – it sounds like a good place in which to work. I'm glad, also, that you're progressing with the play. Too bad about the Canada Council. If you have to take a job, why not try again (if not this year, next) to get on here at UBC teaching Creative Writing (whatever that means)? I saw Jake Zilber a short while ago, and gave him the most terrific pep-talk about you. I'm sure, actually, you could get much better jobs – my point of view is purely selfish – I'd just like you to come to Vancouver, that's all. Although it would be a nice place to work, UBC, as the campus is very beautiful etc. The English department seems to have a number of factions, each stabbing the other in the back, but I do not think it would be any different a situation at any other university. And I think you would really like a number of people in the department.

I think I told you that my novel's been taken by St. Martin's Press in New York. They have accepted the revised version, thank the lord, and they say that any suggestions they have now are of a minor nature and can be done when the proofs are done. I still don't know when it's coming out – just vaguely in the fall. I hate the thought of the proofs – to tell you the truth, I'm bored with the damn thing and will be very happy when I never have to look at it again. I had another story in 'Prism,' entitled 'Godman's Master,'[1] a story about a dwarf who was being used as an oracle by a fetish priest and who was freed by a young pharmacist, who then found he could not get rid of the grateful and also helpless dwarf. Etc. etc. I've been working on some more short stories. I've got two done, but I am going to let them sit for awhile. I want to write as many as possible (ie about 4 or 5) this summer, and then spend the winter re-writing them and finishing them. I know now that I cannot trust my own judgement for quite awhile after I have finished the first draft of a story, so I am beginning what a friend calls the 'quick-frozen pie method.' It seems to work better, for me to put something away for some considerable time, before I send it off anywhere. I want to do about 12 short stories set in W. Africa. I've got 7 done (4 of these published or accepted for publication – not very many).[2] The last one, just completed, is a light and rather satirical one, although with undertones (I hope). I really want to start another novel, but I want to do the short stories first, because I've had the ideas for them for so long, and they got put away because of the first novel, so I feel if I don't do them now, they'll never get done. The ideas for them are not very fully worked out, of course, and I do not write very quickly. This doesn't matter, except that I have some of the ideas for a novel worked out and I am anxious to start on it – it began as a short story, and I realized finally that it couldn't be done as a story. My main trouble is, as always, impatience – I want to do everything all at once, in five minutes before dinner. But alas, impossible.

I'm finished with essay marking for the summer, thank goodness. At the end of the term I had to do 250 essays in less than 2 weeks, and it almost killed me. However, the cheque made me revive somewhat. The book-review man on the Vancouver Sun[3] (who fortunately appeared to like my stories in Prism) phoned me today and asked me if I'd review books. I said I would be delighted, but began to consider afterwards whether or not I'd be able to do reviews, as I haven't done anything like that for years.[4] However, the paper certainly will not want anything of an academic nature, so maybe it will be all right. I do not feel like slaving very much over a review for a daily paper, as it seems to me wasted effort, but on the other hand, as they pay $10 to $15 per review, one is almost honour-bound to try, at least to give value for the money. I don't suppose there will be too many, anyway, as he has lots of people reviewing for that page. I will give away the review copies for Christmas presents.

Jack is away at Revelstoke for a couple of months. He is working on a new bridge. He's not very happy about his present job, as the firm doesn't seem to be expanding and Jack finds he has to do a lot of work in which he isn't interested. So – we are again at the crossroads. There is a possibility that he will be offered a very good job with a firm here (very complex situation re: the man who is in the post now, etc. I won't go into details), and if he is, he will take it, as it is the sort of thing he has always hoped for, but the kind of job one doesn't apply for – it has to be offered, if you know what I mean. A kind of administrative job, for which a firm does not advertise. If it doesn't work out, I think he is going to apply for a job in Nigeria. I don't really mind which way it works out, except that I hope for his sake that he gets the job here, as he really wants it. I would love to go to Africa again, but of course there is the problem of the children. In some parts of Nigeria, English schools exist. Do not get the idea that I would not send our children to school with Africans – I would be delighted to do so, but in African primary schools the education is in the local dialect for the first 3 years, so that's not much use to us. I would not mind sending them to boarding school when they are 10, but would not be keen on doing so before then. A great problem, really. However, if it seems the best thing for Jack's work, we will go, and with no regrets. We'll work out the school angle somehow. I hope only that I don't have to teach them myself – I would be a rotten teacher. But we shall see. I wish I didn't feel so split about it, though – I worry about the kids, and yet when I think of Nigeria, I want so much to go and see what it is like. It is quite like Ghana, of course, in many ways.

The kids are fine. Jocelyn is just finishing Grade Two, and has done very well. She is particularly good in reading, and reads about 4 large books from the public library every week, so Grade 2 reading seems rather simple stuff to her. Arithmetic comes less easily, and she has been practising with Jack several times a week, but now that he is not here, she is stuck, for my arithmetic is about Grade One level. I am trying not to let her know that I still add on my fingers. When she gets into fractions, she leaves me behind. She is a very social child, and appears to be out-going, but only to people who do not know her. Underneath, she worries quite a lot about school, although we do our best to calm her, and I am always having to reassure her, etc. We have never urged her to do better work, and she has always been conscientious, so why she worries I don't know. She is such an easy person to get along with, though, and has such a wonderful sense of humour. She even laughs at my feeble jokes, and that is really kind-hearted, believe me. David has had a good year at playschool, and has been transformed from a solitary savage into a reasonably social, semi-civilized human being, who can now play with another child for as much as an hour without poking the other kid in the eye. Progress. He is a dear, actually, although still rather barbaric, and is fantastically imaginative. He builds hundreds of boats, from boards and nails and spools and wire, and he paints them and puts sails on them, and we all trip over them in every corner of the house. I cannot clean his room, because he nearly has a fit if I touch his precious collection of what he calls 'good junk' – wire, old batteries, string, elastics, pieces of wood, stones, nails, old bottles, boxes, etc. etc. I can't remember if I told you this remark before – if so, please forgive me. But not long ago, I heard David talking to Jocelyn in the following gentle manner: 'Boys just go rushing through the world, beating down everything that's in their way. Boys are made out of steel, so they can blast the sugar-and-spice girls!' I know the thought isn't too commendable, but the drama of the expression! We all looked at Princess Margaret's wedding on TV tonight, and of course I bawled like the Missouri all through the ceremony. David said curiously, 'Why on earth are you dripping?,' and I had to explain apologetically that I always cry at all weddings, so he asked me if I'd cried at my own. He seemed very amused when I said I hadn't, as I was too busy answering the questions. He thought the ceremony was riotously funny, especially as the Archbishop kept talking about the 'Father, Son and Holy Ghost,' and as David said 'we know ghosts aren't real. How come he doesn't know?' This was reminiscent of the night when he said 'If God is in outer space, and the Americans can't get a rocket down yet with a man in it, I certainly don't believe God can hear what I'm saying.' Prayers were therefore stopped for quite some time, as I couldn't help seeing his point of view – outer space, after all, is a long way off. The concept of any other sort of deity of an indwelling nature is, I'm afraid, too abstract for a five-year-old, and would be alarming rather than otherwise, I think. But David is a scientist at heart, it seems to me. He wants to be an electrical engineer, and is always tinkering with the little light Jack fixed for him with a flashlight bulb and a bunch of old batteries. I think of David's despairing cry one day – 'When am I going to be old enough to know all about electricity?' He wants to know, but he also realizes dimly that he cannot know about electricity until he is very much wiser in a lot of other things. He knows about alternating currents, although he doesn't understand it, and can fix the wires on his signal light in the proper way. Jack finds his questions hard to deal with, because David constantly wants to know things which cannot be simply explained. In other ways, however, in art and colouring and cutting-out with scissors, etc etc, he is really ham-fisted. I refuse to believe that a child who can handle perfectly well a hand-drill and saw and all kinds of tools, is incapable of handling a pair of scissors, but there it is. I don't care, and would be quite happy to let him develop along the lines of his own interests, but unfortunately a school program demands that a child develop along all lines, not just a few. All I hope is that he is lucky enough to have teachers with patience, because the kind of child he is can easily be discouraged altogether by teachers who like best the children who are averagely good in everything.

Well, here I am, talking like Dr. Spock.[5] Sorry. I forgot to tell you – if Jack does get this new job, he would be spending the summer, probably, in the north, and we would go with him. It would be fun, as we would live in a trailer. Fun for a short while – I don't think trailer life would suit me for long, but it would be interesting. Also, I want someday to do 2 things: 1) live in a trailer settlement, on a work site – this is the way of life of thousands of construction workers; and 2) to get to know some iron-workers, the high steel men, for Jack's descriptions of them, their superstitions, their fantastic pride in their work, their resentment of all engineers, etc., seem fascinating to me. Perhaps the next time I write I will know what's going to happen. I hope so.

In the meantime, please write – you're the only person to whom I can really blow off steam about my work. Strangely enough, I now know quite a number of writers, but only one person here can I talk to very much about writing. The others seem on such a high level of abstraction that they leave me behind – the atmosphere is too rarified for me – I have to keep my feet on the ground or I don't know what I'm talking about. Sometimes I don't think they do, either, but that may be only a sense of inferiority on my part. I was at a party at Earle Birney's not long ago[6] (Birney wasn't there – he is a fine man, in my opinion, very unassuming and rather gentle) and I really felt a sense of utter hopelessness. The purpose of art; the consciousness or otherwise of symbolism; the direct communication of experience – these are all subjects which one naturally thinks quite a lot about, in private, but when they are discussed in such a theoretical way, without being tied to concrete examples, one feels as though the whole thing is simply a lot of phoney baloney. Or at least, I do. I guess one must realize one's own limitations, and at this point in my life, I am beginning to know mine – I really and honestly do not even want to attempt anything fancy. I can only do one thing – I can tell stories, tales, or what-have-you. And that, quite simply, is all I can do. This is not, and never will be, first-rate stuff, but for what it is, it is honest, and my talking pretentiously about art is not going to make it first-rate stuff. So – after that evening (at which I was so quiet I almost scared myself, this not being my normal behaviour) I swore to myself never to discuss the subject again, but only to talk about things which I can tie to some sort of reality (no doubt limited) that I can partially comprehend. Nuts to the nature of art.

I digress. I had meant to wind up this letter and say goodbye. Please write.

Love from us all,

Peg

P.S. Did I tell you what finally happened re: the photograph of me? I had one taken by a Hungarian ex-nobleman name of Esterhazy, and it turned out very well – I can actually look at it without wanting to throw up.

1 *Prism International* 1, 3 (Spring 1960): 46–64
2 Including 'Godman's Master,' Laurence had, in fact, published or had accepted for publication five stories. The other three that had appeared were: 'Drummer of All the World,' *Queen's Quarterly* 63 (Winter 1956): 487–504; 'The Merchant of Heaven,' *Prism International* 1, 1 (September 1959): 52–74; and 'The Perfume Sea,' *Winter's Tales* 6 (1960): 83–120. Laurence was about to publish 'A Gourdful of Glory' in *Tamarack Review* 17 (Autumn 1960): 5–20.

3 Donald Stainsby

4 Laurence's review of William Conton's *The African* appeared in the *Vancouver Sun*, 14 May 1960, 5.

5 Dr Benjamin Spock (b. 1903), renowned American pediatrician, most famous for the millions of copies and numerous editions of his perennial best-seller, *Baby and Child Care* (1946)

6 Earle Birney (1904–95), poet and teacher, was a member of the Department of English and the Creative Writing Program of the University of British Columbia from 1946 to 1965.

3556 West 21st Ave.
21 July [1960]

Dear Adele:

I was so glad to hear from you. It's bad luck about the Canada Council, but I was delighted at the tone of your letter – you sounded more cheerful than you have in a long time, due no doubt to the fact that the play is coming along well. I'm *really pleased* to hear it, & to see you thumbing your nose at the Can. Council & just going on and *producing* – that is the old Wiseman spirit! Gosh, I'd like to see you, kid, & talk over everything. So much to say. Your play will be terrific when it's done, I know. You have a wisdom that I've never achieved – you are patient about your writing, & wait for the light to dawn, whereas I am too impatient always.

I'd like to send you the story that's coming out in *Winter's Tales* – I think they'll send me 3 free copies, so I'll send you one. In October. Tamarack Review has taken a story of mine[1] – did I tell you? I'll send you that one if they send me more than 1 free copy – I'm not really all that mean about the price, but I don't know where to buy one. But now, Adele, I have come to the end of the supply, & have no more stories to submit anywhere. I've got two that aren't finished yet, & I have germ ideas for about 8 more, but *I will not hurry them*. I am going to start the incubation method – putting a story away for a few months, as that seems the only way of gaining enough perspective on it. If I submit too soon, I write to the publication & ask for the script back, as I want to revise it. I've done that too many times. My great trouble with these African stories is to be *simple* enough. To relax and let the characters speak for themselves – not to *mean* but to *be*. I think I am getting more professional re: the general movement of a story. Let's face it – I believe in *plot*. But the people are the main thing – to set them free so they live their own lives. I want to begin a novel, but won't hurry that, either. I have the beginning of the concept for a novel, & if it turned out right it would (I hope) be better than the first one. However, that is a very long-term project.

At the moment I am confined to bed. I've spent 3 weeks in the hospital, undergoing all kinds of x-rays etc, & they finally discovered that the source of my trouble was my gall-bladder, which had stones & was coated with cholesterol. So they opened me up & removed the gall-bladder. I'm home now, but still rather shaky. I've made very good progress, however. I was stunned to discover I had a twelve-inch incision, & was glad I had not known beforehand that they were going to slit me from top to bottom like a gutted mackerel. I've healed pretty quickly & really feel better than I have in a year, except rather weak still, of course. My aunt is here, & a teenage girl from next door comes in to do the housework.

Jack got the job he wanted – the firm is Wright's Canadian Ropes – They make steel cables for bridges, etc. He is their Plant Engineer, & finds the work interesting and stimulating. He has a chance to use his own ideas, which is what he needs. I hope it will work out for him. So far it seems promising.

I've been reviewing books for the Vancouver Sun, & like doing it very much. I don't do very high-class reviews, but I guess they're ok for a daily paper.[2] I get to keep the review copies. I'm going to give up the essay marking this year – I feel I've been spreading myself too thin & it isn't right, not for myself or the family. I'm going to have to stop burning the midnight oil quite so much. I'm sorry about the essays, as I enjoyed doing them & also learned a great deal. But what with essays & those awful revisions on the novel, I got myself really at the end of my tether, & I'm not going to do that again. When I was in hospital, I reviewed my life like a drowning man is said to do, & could see how stupid I'd been to get myself in the position of having no reserves of energy or calm.

A very strange thing has happened to me. A short time ago I received a parcel & a letter from Jack McClelland, of McC & Stewart. It was the manuscript of Pat Blondal's second novel, *A Candle To Light The Sun*.[3] Jack McC (obviously totally unaware that I had known Pat) asked me to read it & said he would like my opinion of it. They will publish it in October, & why they should want my opinion I simply do not know. I have written to him & asked him why. But it seems very odd, a trick of fate. My ancient Presbyterian conscience tells me straightaway that this is a judgement on me for the sins of malice & envy, & then I have to smile at this reaction, as it is so much like some of the small-town prairie characters in Pat's novel! It will be hard for me to write an impartial comment, I fear. Actually, it is a most remarkable novel, Adele, *quite unlike* her first (which seemed very Ladies' Home Journal to me). This one is enormous – some 500 pages, & I do not think she had time to revise it much. It would have been better to have been cut in places, but even as it stands it is quite an achievement. She attempts such a lot – an over-all picture of a small prairie town & all its people; an historical picture of the late 30's & the war & the post-war years & our generation, a wonderfully complex analysis & picture of a man's search for his own identity & meaning. All this in one book. I saw it described, you will remember, as 'a Canadian *Peyton Place*'[4] & no doubt this comment will help sales, but as a comment on the novel it is a terrible lie. This is no Peyton Place – it is a serious novel, done with subtlety & great compassion. Am I being influenced too much by her death? I don't think so, really. You know how it is, Adele – when you begin to read, another set of faculties takes over, & you become almost compulsively honest because you couldn't bear it if someone else approached your own work in anything other than an honestly critical way. I think her novel is really one of the best things on a prairie town that I've ever read, & it is much more as well. Her style is oddly jerky in the beginning, & this bothers me a little, but later it grows smoother & less noticeable, & this is an improvement, I think. It is a good book – if she had lived to work more on it, it would have been truly excellent, but even as it stands it is a remarkable job. I wish I could have told her so. It is all rather strange, isn't it?

Must go. Please write. I do hope your way becomes clear & that your finances won't be too difficult – could you get a part-time job? Life is very complicated, trying to live and work at the same time, two ways of life which so often seem at odds with one another. I have that, too, but in a different way. I always feel that my writing is stolen time, in a way. Perhaps if we did not have these constant tensions we wouldn't write at all. I don't know. I have no answers for anything any more, do you? Just to work somehow, & combine this with reality in some fashion, never quite achieving the hoped-for balance. But I wish you didn't need to worry about money – it seems so damned unfair, Adele, in this fat society, that a person like yourself, doing the work you are doing, should have to consider money at all. Anyway, I wish you luck & I hope something will turn up. But you're working well, anyway, & that is the main thing.

The kids are fine – they grow very tall and handsome, & astonish me all the time to think that they are mine. They are becoming independent, & that is good. Jocelyn goes into Grade 3, & David has one more year of playschool. They are very tanned this summer, & their hair is bleached golden by the sun. Being away from them for 3 weeks makes me see them more clearly now. They seem so beautiful that it frightens me – like the Chinese pretending their beloved sons were girls, lest the gods see and strike. Nonsense. I am growing ridiculous in my old age.

Anyway, Adele, I hope still that one of these days you'll get up here & stay with us for awhile.

Love from us all,

Peg

1 'A Gourdful of Glory' (see p. 119, n. 2)
2 Between 6 May and 21 July, Laurence had reviewed William Conton's *The African* (14 May), Giuseppe de Lampedusa's *The Leopard* (28 May), Dan Jacobson's *Evidence of Love* (18 June), and Conrad Richter's *The Waters of Kronos* (2 July).
3 Patricia Jenkins Blondal (1926–59) had been Laurence's classmate at United College. Her first-written novel, *From Heaven with a Shout*, was published in 1963, three years after *A Candle to Light the Sun*.
4 The novel *Peyton Place* (1956), by Grace Metalious, became a sensational North American best-seller on the basis of its depiction of the sexual mores of middle-class, small-town America.

3556 West 21st Ave.
3 December 1960

Dear Adele:

Thanks for your card and letter, and for your encouraging remarks re: the book. I've had quite a number of reviews now, mostly from England, and on the whole they are kind. The London Times pans the book,[1] saying that the relationships of white and black are of limited psychological interest, but they do certainly pick out the novel's weakest points very neatly, which none of the other reviews have done – it is the only review to point out the flaws of construction which seem so glaring to me that I thought every review would mention them. I remember your saying how you wished that someone would read your book as carefully as you wrote it – few do, it seems. The Statesman gave it a very good review (hallelujah!) but said the ending was 'suspiciously sunny.'[2] Richard Church, in the Bookman, on the other hand, also gave it a very good review but said the ending was despairing and showed the impossibility of understanding between blacks and whites. This disparity of opinion can only be regarded as encouraging, and at least so far no one has called the book 'dull' – the only really damning word in my vocabulary. I thought I would be a nervous wreck when the reviews came out, but I do not find that I am really much affected one way or another. When you look at a whole sheaf of reviews, and each presents a different interpretation (quite naturally), you can't really take any of them very seriously. Especially the good ones, which unfortunately (or perhaps fortunately) one tends to believe less than the bad ones. As a matter of fact, I appear to be able to take criticism much better than praise – are you that way, too? Criticism merely stiffens one's spine, but there is something about praise that is oddly depressing. I don't mean from people who are close friends or whose judgement you trust. For example, I am very glad you liked the book, and that does not depress me – it heartens me tremendously. But – I'm not expressing myself clearly here, I know – after I read quite a number of favourable reviews, I felt as though I didn't want to see any more – I only wanted to go away quietly somewhere and forget about the whole thing. Perhaps basically it is a fear reaction – one is frightened at good reviews, because one may start to believe them? I don't think that it is likely, really, because I know that novel's flaws better than anyone. It is amateurish in many ways, because it is the work of an amateur – I don't apologize for that. But I hope so much that the next one will be better. The European characters in this one do not emerge clearly, I feel, and I would like to think I would do a better job next time. But here is the other fear – the first time, a novel is written with tremendous intensity and hardly any know-how. One can never be that innocent again, and I think that what I am feeling at the moment could be summarized thus: I may have got one or two characters across with reasonable conviction and warmth the first time, almost by accident, but what of beginning another novel when one knows so much more about the pitfalls and snares that can happen? This actually is a very old and stale dilemma – am I a one-shot novelist? I always felt that if I could ever get this novel published, that would be all I would expect out of life, but of course it is not the end but the beginning and at this point the next step looks more difficult than the first. I see now that I began by telling you how cool I was about the matter of reviews, and have ended up in a very un-cool way. The thing is that I know I have a good story (or I believe so, anyway) for the next novel, and some people who are contradictory and interesting – and I find I'm afraid to start it, because I don't want to foul it up. I think the thing to do will be not to begin for quite awhile yet, and to indulge in what you used to call 'creative laziness.' It'll come by itself, quite likely, when it's ready. I hope so. But it is a far more difficult proposition than the first one.

I was so glad to hear that Macleans took your story[3] and that the reimbursement will be reasonably good. We look forward to seeing it. It's so important right now that you don't have to break off working on the play, as you seem to be forging ahead with it. I'd so much like to see it – all in good time. I still hope that one of these years, when we have our retreat built at Point Roberts (did I tell you we now own part of the U.S.A?) you'll be able to come up for a holiday, and we will talk far into the night over bottles of California wine.

Speaking of wine, ours is ready now and I wish I could send you a few bottles. It is really good. We have 3 different kinds of grape wine, 3 of peach wine and one of orange wine. We named them all after B.C. place names – Lillooet, Uclulet, Walhachin, Nicola, Keremeos, etc. For six months our basement has been like a brewery. We are now authorities on the art of winemaking, and go around casually letting fall such phrases as 'we'll soon have to rack the lees,' etc.

'Winter's Tales' is now out, but I can't send you a copy as I only have 2 and am absurdly reluctant to part with them. However, St. Martin's Press very cleverly sold the story which appears in 'Winter's Tales 6' to the Sat.Eve.Post, much to my astonishment.[4] They have cut it quite a bit, but have done a masterful job of cutting, and anyway I don't care, because it is printed in W.T. in its entirety. It'll come out in Jan. or Feb., I think. I had a story in Tamarack Review last issue, but now that I see it in print I don't think it really comes off very well, so I'm not sending it to you either. Apparently the Saturday Review is going to run quite a long review of my novel, and St. Martin's just sent me a copy of it – it has been done by Mary Renault,[5] which is a piece of very good luck, especially as she liked the book.

Jack has been in the Yukon for about three weeks, but I expect him back this weekend. We want to go to Seattle for the weekend, if we can, just to get away from home and young ones, but goodness knows whether we'll make it or not. It depends upon when he gets back. He loves his job now, though, and finds it full of variety, which is wonderful. He's terribly busy, but he prefers it that way. He phoned the other day from a place called Toad River, which sounds pretty dreary, and said the work was really interesting but the evenings were awful – he was getting bushed after only a few weeks, he said.

After your novel came out, did you get any letters from eccentrics?

I got a letter the other day from a gentleman who said he thought it would be a fine idea if I were to finance and promote his 2 books, as yet unwritten. His subject: flying saucers, which he has been fortunate enough to observe at close enough range to identify their pilots.

Jack McClelland of McC & Stewart was out here not long ago, and had a cocktail party for my book and others, but as I happened to be the only local author, I had to be perfectly charming to all newspapermen and booksellers etc. I guess I was, but I wouldn't like to depend upon it. It reminded me of the first time I met the governor of Somaliland, and got plastered. Gordon Elliott, who was there that evening at the publisher's party, assures me I simply became more and more ladylike as the hours passed, but that may be pure kindness on his part. I detest making a fool of myself. I wonder why I do, then, so frequently? I hate that kind of party, anyway, everyone shouting in everyone else's ear and not really able to say anything. Jack McClelland is very nice – very charming, and has the faculty for making whoever he is talking to at the moment feel that they are the most important person in the world to him right then – a real talent, if you ask me. I liked him very much.

The kids are flourishing, but the cat has fleas. I am nearly going insane, spraying the house and dusting the cat with flea powder. But apart from that, we are well and reasonably in our right minds. Two of Jack's sisters will be in Victoria for Christmas, with their families, so there will be ten children and I can hardly bear to think about it. Noel, Noel.

Love from us all. Please write. By the way, Jocelyn, who hasn't seen you since England, says she remembers you perfectly and is going to send you a Christmas card. She says modestly that she may enclose a few examples of long and short division and the times-tables.

Peg

P.S. I went the other day to what is, I believe, known as an 'autographing party,' at a local bookshop. It seemed daft to me, because I wouldn't walk across the street to get even Ernest Hemingway's signature, but it seems that some people do not feel that way about it. The owner of the bookshop, a rather jaded Englishman who seems like a younger edition of Noel Coward, very thoughtfully regaled me with stories of all the writers who had either committed suicide after their first novels or else taken to drugs or drink. I felt like saying, 'well, don't get your hopes up as far as I'm concerned.'

1 'Muddling into Maturity,' *Times Literary Supplement*, 4 November 1960, 705
2 Gerda Charles, 'New Novels,' *New Statesman and Nation* 19 November 1960, 800, 802
3 'Duel in the Kitchen,' *Maclean's*, 7 January 1961, 22–3
4 'The Exiles' (an abridgement of 'The Perfume Sea') appeared in *Saturday Evening Post*, 3 June 1961, 28–9.
5 'On Understanding Africa,' *Saturday Review*, 10 December 1960, 23–4

3556 West 21st Ave.
22 January 1961

Dear Adele:

First, and most important, I've sent your ad to the Vancouver Sun, and I trust it will appear next week-end – it will be the 28th, not the 29th, as the Sun comes out on Saturday, not Sunday, but I guess that won't matter.[1] I've asked them to send the bill to me, and to forward any replies here. Anything received will be sent to you at once, airmail. I certainly wish you luck. The trip to China sounds like a marvellous idea, if the wherewithal can be found. Of course, the best way to go to China is via Vancouver!! Please. A book on China would be, one would think, a goldmine, as so little has been done on it.[2] If you and Amy go, I will be green-eyed with envy. However, I can't complain, and I don't, actually. Re; your suggestion that I apply to the Canada Council – I considered it, and then thought that the only thing I could legitimately say is that I would like a cleaning-woman for the mornings, but I don't think that would go down too well with them – sounds kind of mundane, don't you think? No attic in Paris stuff. I am getting to be a worse housekeeper all the time, as I write in the mornings now, and do my housework (supposedly) in the afternoons. I haven't got much to show for it, either, in the way of writing. But as always I am far too impatient, and this is a great fault.

Secondly, we read with great pleasure your story in *Maclean's*. I noticed at once that they had changed the title,[3] and wondered why, and was a bit annoyed to find out why. Your title was miles better – had imagination and would have aroused a reader's curiosity. Theirs was dull and ordinary, which is too bad. The thing I liked best about the story was that I could almost hear your voice telling it, which is quite an achievement – your voice as a child, I mean, but it had your touch, which I liked enormously. The detail I liked best was the bit about the aunt's mended sox...she was a perfectionist. Do you know what it reminded me of? The cousin of Abraham's (which he told as his wife's cousin) who went insane and became a Christian. I don't know why I should think of that – the same slightly zany slightly bittersweet humour. It's a good story, Adele. Wish there were more of them. But you've accomplished a hell of a lot, if the play is nearly done. I heard your interview on CBC the other evening, and thought you were struggling hard against great odds, as the interviewer didn't seem to know what to ask, and didn't help you at all. It was not a great success, but that is not your fault. In these interviews (as I now know, to my cost) a great deal depends on the interviewer – does he ask leading questions, but questions that are possible to answer? If not, you can't help floundering somewhat. I had the same thing happen. I did an interview with a local radio chap here, and it was broadcast nationally, and it was simply disastrous. Horrible. I sounded like a new United Church minister in his first sermon, who has to cope not only with nervousness but with a speech defect. The chap who did it had not read my book, didn't know what to ask, and I was terribly nervous, so between us we really goofed. I did a later interview with Eileen Laurie of CBC, and it was ok. She is an old pro.

Re: John Gray, and Macmillan. I feel badly that he should feel badly about it, and I blame myself to some extent.[4] The thing was this, Adele – when I finished the novel, a friend here wrote to McClelland and told him I had this script, and he wrote and asked to see it. So of course (at that point, feeling no one would ever take it) I sent it along, and that was that. I had intended to send it to John Gray, and would have done so if McClelland hadn't written. As you will see, it was sheer accident. In a way it might have been better if it had been done by Macmillan in Canada, as it was Macmillan in both the States and England. I must say, however, that Jack McClelland has been wonderful to me, and I have no complaints on that score. They've done their best for the book, and I couldn't have asked for more. But if you ever have a chance to explain to John Gray that it wasn't done out of any feeling against him, I would be grateful.

Thanks for the clipping. You know, I am really in a quandry (sp?) at the moment. I've abandoned work on the novel I told you about. I am carrying on with short stories, as I have a number of stories I still want to write about Africa, shreds of ideas which I've been carting around for years, and I find I can work on them. But the novel – I don't know – I feel at the moment (a) sick of Africa, except as far as short stories (which aren't as probing as a novel – not mine, anyway) are concerned;

and (b) I don't feel I know enough to write this novel. Maybe after a few years something in some quite different form will emerge. Right now I think I'd like to come back home. This, of course, coincides with my own state of mind. I feel I'm here to stay, for better or worse, and that I don't need to go away any more, in fact can't go away. It's here, and in me, and I can't run forever to countries (real or imaginary) which I like because they didn't know me when I was young. If that makes any sense to you. I hated being here, for several years, you know. But now, for the first time, I feel the urge to write about the only people I can possibly know about from the inside. I feel that novel on Africa is very superficial, and I can't help that. The next will probably not be publishable, because it will not have the admitted advantage of timeliness or the exotic flavour of foreign lands, which (let's face it) helped considerably with the first. I don't want to write a 'Canadian novel.' It's just that I feel I might at last be able to look at people here without blinking. Having hated my own country most of my life, I am now beginning to see why. It's the mirror in which one's own face appears, and like Queen Elizabeth the First, you smash the mirrors but that doesn't change yourself after all. Very strange. I am glad I did not write anything set in this country, before, because it would have been done untruthfully, with bitterness, but perhaps not any more. I don't know. I really only want to finish these short stories, perhaps do something with all the huge diaries I still have from our time in Somaliland, and then put paid to that phase of my life. It's over, and I have a strange sense of release and relief.

I'll let you know the moment any reply to the ad appears, and I'll send the ad as well. I hope something will transpire. Please write.

Love from us all,

Peg

P.S.1. did I tell you – I've changed my name to Margaret? Not because of the novel, but because it did give me an opportunity to take the plunge, which I've wanted to do for years. I've always detested my name, and only you and Jack and one other very close friend now call me 'Peg,' which I don't mind so much – it was Peggy I hated, so I have killed her off (I hope).

P.S.2. – I sent a copy of Pat's book to you[5] – did you get it? I didn't pay for it – I got 2 copies, naturally, free. I got one from McC & Stewart, as they had used one of my comments on the dust-jacket (strangely, not on the jacket which you've got, which was a review copy). The other I got from the *Sun*, to review, which was certainly odd, as they didn't know I'd known Pat. I knew (superstitiously) that they would send it to me to review. I gave it a very good review, which I think was pretty honest, although I have no means of knowing.

P.S.3. The story of mine will come out in the Sat.Eve.Post in March, I think. I have now an agent[6] (which seems very fancy, and I have my doubts about it) and he has recently sold another story to the Post,[7] which is very surprising, but very good news as far as I'm concerned. I know one is supposed to be snobbish about these things, but the story wasn't written with the Post in mind, and if they want to buy it, that's their business and I'm glad to have the money.

P.S.4. Had tea with Ethel Wilson[8] the other day. She is terrific. A lady, in the best, wisest, most gracious sense. I was very impressed by her, and felt one would not dare say anything one didn't mean, for she would spot it at once.

1 Wiseman had asked Laurence to place an ad appealing for funds to help finance Wiseman's projected trip to China with her British photographer friend Amy Zahl. The advertisement, which appeared, among other places, in the Business Personals of the classified section of the *Toronto Telegram*, was the following: 'Noted Canadian writer with publication outlet, journeying to the Orient to create a travel book for your delight. She will dedicate the book individually to those adventurous spirits who help to make it possible by contributing $500 and over. Box 85 Tely' (28 January 1961, 46). The ad also appeared in the *Montreal Star*, but was refused by the *Vancouver Sun* and the *Winnipeg Tribune*. There is no evidence that the initiative was successful.

2 Wiseman and Zahl got as far as Hong Kong but were refused admission to China, and so the projected book was not written. 'How to Go to China,' an account of Wiseman's successful trip in the summer of 1981, appeared in *Chinada: Memoirs of the Gang of Seven* (1982), 98–128, and in Wiseman's *Memoirs of a Book-Molesting Childhood* (1987), 91–116.

3 'A Duel in the Kitchen,' (see p. 127, n. 3) had as its original title 'On Wings of Tongue.'

4 John Gray had apparently expected Laurence to submit *This Side Jordan* to Macmillan Canada for possible publication.

5 Blondal's *A Candle to Light the Sun*, which Laurence reviewed in the *Vancouver Sun*, 21 January 1961

6 Willis Kingsley Wing of New York, whom Laurence had retained through Jack McClelland. He was also Wiseman's agent in 1961–2.

7 Probably 'The Spell of the Distant Drum,' an abridgement of 'The Voices of Adamo,' which was published sixteen months later in the *Saturday Evening Post*, 5 May 1962, 24–5.

8 Ethel Wilson (1888–1980) was a Canadian novelist and Vancouver resident.

3556 West 21st Ave.
29 March 1961

Dear Adele:

This is the third letter I have begun in answer to your last one. The others I tore up, as they were so permeated with pessimism of a personal nature that it did not seem well-omened to send them, especially as your letter was so much more cheerful than you've been in a long time. I was really pleased to hear the note of optimism in your letter, and I feel you really will get to China. In fact, I predict it confidently. (I'm thinking of starting a gypsy fortune-telling business as a sideline). Seriously, things seem to be looking up for you, and I'm delighted. I'm also very glad you saw Willis Wing, and hope he may be able to help you. In the meantime, I will keep my fingers crossed and light a candle for you, mentally at least.

The pessimism on my part was owing to my persistent feelings of doubt about the novel which I had begun. At every point I felt very unhappy about it, and tried approaching it from all sorts of different viewpoints, but nothing seemed right. I had originally done it as a short story, and then had felt it should be developed further. For a long time I thought my lack of confidence in beginning it was simply due to the common doubts about a second novel, but I am sure now that is not the case. One really ought to listen to the inner voices, and I suppose in the long run one does, but sometimes it takes quite awhile for them to penetrate into the conscious mind. I think I knew, really, deep down, all along, that a) I did not have the necessary background or knowledge to bring this story off as a novel, and b) I do not honestly want to write another novel set in Africa – at least, I do not have any real need to write one, and therefore I can't. I think one is often influenced by other people even when one doesn't want to be, and when they don't have any intention of influencing, one way or another. I think I began this novel because McClelland assured me there wouldn't be any use in attempting a collection of short stories until I had written another novel. It sounds pretty awful, put that way, doesn't it – as though I were feeble-minded or something. But I think that is what happened. I had been previously going along nicely with short stories. I certainly don't blame McClelland, or anyone except myself, for this abortive attempt at a novel. But what I really want to do is what I was doing before – to continue writing these short stories until I've done the ones I want to do, and then no doubt something will turn up. I know one thing now

– when I do try another novel, it will certainly not be set in Africa. I had an odd experience when I was attempting this now-abandoned novel – I kept thinking of an entirely different set of characters – they kept creeping in, as it were, to disturb my thoughts, and they were (and are) all people here, in this country. God knows I have no desire to write a 'Canadian' novel in that horrible nationalistic, stilted sense, but if they happen to live here, that's another thing. One of these days something may take shape in that direction. But for now I've gone back to the short stories, with a kind of relief, as though I have shed a great weight from my mind. The idea for the novel can be told as a short story, and I'm reasonably confident about being able to do that. It should never have been considered as a novel, that's all. There are a few other short stories I want to do, with African settings, and then I will not want to write about Africa again. You will see, of course, why I have had all these mental difficulties – strangely enough, I really want to write about my own people, for the first time in my life, and yet, because everything I have ever sold has been about Africa, I cannot help feeling that a large part of any recent good fortune in this regard has been due to the timeliness of the subject rather than the quality of the writing and that when I write *not* about Africa, that will be the end of anything being published. However, it can't be helped – a person can only write about the things that really interest them, and as far as I'm concerned, I'm extremely interested in doing perhaps 3 or 4 more stories set in Africa (for which I've had the germ of an idea for a long time), and after that, I'm not interested any more. The most difficult thing seems to be the maintaining of at least a reasonable degree of honesty with oneself, and the ability to go your own way. One other thing I want to do some time, although it's not likely to amount to much, and that is to see what I can do with the voluminous diaries I kept while we were in Somaliland.[1] Perhaps they wouldn't be of interest to anyone except ourselves – I don't know. They are swollen with tons of verbiage, but if I can go through and weed out all the theorizing and the boring bits, it is just possible that something might remain. I'm going to try, anyway, although I think it isn't likely that anyone's experiences in a remote corner of the globe, ten years ago, would be of general interest. No one could read them in their present form, so I intend to copy out the interesting parts, if only so that my grandchildren can read them (they will probably not be interested, either, but after awhile the script may have some historical value!) I'm glad I didn't try to do this years ago, as the thing would then have been filled with pompous theories about colonial administration etc, and now I only want to include the things that actually happened. This will be a kind of labour of love. Then, as the sun sinks slowly in the west, we say goodbye to ... etc. But without regrets, now, at last, and about time, too.

A maddening thing happened the other day. As you know, I'd been reviewing books for the Vancouver Sun, and suddenly the publisher[2] decided to discontinue the book page, for no reason that anyone can discover, other than, as he says, the fact that the Sun's book page is not as good as the N.Y. Times or the Observer, which seems a very odd point of view, rather like telling a creative writer he might as well quit if he can't write as well as Graham Greene. Not that I'm all that certain of the quality of the N.Y. Times, but the Observer is certainly tops. But so what? Anyway, the annoying thing is that when a number of people wrote in, complaining about the book page being removed, they received letters back from the publisher, in which he said, among other noxious comments, that the book page is only interesting to those who are reviewing books and who enjoy seeing their names in print. Considering that the whole deal was (I thought) a business arrangement, in which the reviewer got paid and also got to keep the book, I thought his comment was a little uncalled-for. Damn it, my pride felt hurt! I don't mind his thinking that way, if he wants to, but I didn't feel it was necessary to reply in that vein to anyone who wrote in about the matter. Anyway, the main thing is that it seems a pity that a city the size of Vancouver shouldn't have any book reviews in a newspaper. At least, that is my point of view. The guy who was the book editor is so worked up about it that he is considering going elsewhere, which is also a pity, as he is one of the very few who believe a Canadian book has to be judged like any other book – in other words, it doesn't automatically stink because it is Canadian, nor is it automatically marvellous. Many people here are still very much one way or the other, it seems to me. What amuses me is how many people in Vancouver now claim to have been bosom buddies with Malcolm Lowry[3] – you can bet your bottom dollar they didn't feel that way when he was a drunk at Dollarton, but now he's been discovered by the literary reviews in Paris, and so the picture has changed, and also he is safely dead, which is such a comfort, as he can now be translated into whatever legend is most pleasing. Earle Birney is an exception – he is absolutely straight, and a wonderful guy, in my estimation.

Let me know what happens. Did I tell you Willis Wing sold another story of mine to SatEvePost? I was very surprised, to say the least.

Some friends of ours from Ireland, who had lived here and then gone back to Ireland and hated it, have recently returned and have been searching for a house. In the meantime, we have had 2 of their 5 kids staying with us, so at the moment our place is a veritable circus, and I am due to enter the provincial mental hospital at any time. Actually, they're good kids, and don't mind that I yell at them as though they were my own.

We heard Mort Sahl[4] here last night, and thought he was brilliant.

I have to go out and buy Easter eggs. One damn thing after another – you just get over Christmas, when it's Valentine's Day, and by the time you've recovered from that, it's Easter. On top of that, David's kindergarten teacher has quit and so he'll be home for the summer a month earlier than expected. However, I don't mind quite so much now, as I am not any longer trying to do the impossible in the form of that horrible novel which for a while was haunting me and giving me nightmares and indigestion.

Good luck. Good luck. Good luck.

Love,

Peg

P.S. We've just put down 20 gal. new grape wine. The peach is no good – a complete flop.

1 *The Prophet's Camel Bell*, an account of the Laurences' year in Somaliland, was published in 1963 by McClelland and Stewart and by Macmillan.
2 Donald Cameron Cromie (b. 1915), president and publisher of the *Vancouver Sun*
3 Malcolm Lowry (1909-57), expatriate English writer, lived in a cottage at Dollarton beach, near Vancouver, between 1937 and 1954.
4 Mort Sahl (b. 1927), American entertainer and political satirist

3556 West 21st Ave.
5 September 1961

Dear old downhearted pal:

What is this calamity Jane business? You will indeed ride again, and when you do, Wing and everyone else will flock around you and tell you they knew all the time that your play was terrific – different, of course, but terrific. I have come to the conclusion that most people in this world are wise after the event. I'm damn sorry he didn't have a more favourable reaction, but I am not astonished. He is, after all, an agent who has an eye to what will SELL (magic word). Naturally. Your play, although I don't know a thing about it, is, I imagine, just as 'off-beat' as your novel. Which is something in its favour, probably, but it does make it more difficult to get it accepted. What can we do about this sort of thing? I feel intensely sympathetic about this situation, as I feel I will be involved in the same sort of thing in a year or two, when I finish the novel I am working on now. Wing won't like it. Probably the publishers won't like it. And even worse, if it ever gets published, a great many old ladies of whom I am extremely fond will never speak. to me again. It is not a sensational novel. No seductions. No rapes. No murders. It's not 'timely' – i.e. it is not about Africa or any other 'newsworthy' place. It is not the novel I intended to write. It is the work of a lunatic, I think. It has hardly anything to recommend it to the general public. But I can't help it. I made two false starts on 2 separate novels that I'd had in mind for some time and found I could not write either one. Very nicely plotted, they were, but dead as doornails. Then this daft old lady came along, and I will say about her that she is one hell of an old lady, a real tartar. She's crabby, snobbish, difficult, proud as lucifer for no reason, a trial to her family, etc. She's also – I forgot to mention – dying. The outcome is known from the first page. The whole thing is nuts – I should have my head examined. Who wants to read about an old lady who is *not* the common public concept of what an old lady should be? Obviously no one. Sometimes I feel so depressed about this, I think I will take up ceramics or something soothing. But I can't help it, Adele. I have to go on and write it. It's necessary, and I cannot do it in any other way than the way it comes. It, too, is a tragi-comedy – isn't life, generally? I can't get away from this sense of the ludicrous – how many people at the moment of death speak immortal words? Most of us will be gasping for a kidney basin to throw up in. If I were old, I would not be philosophical – I would be furious at being pushed around. This is not a popular thought. So what do I do? Write about a lavender-and-lace character, full of wisdom and religion? A grand old pioneer, beloved by all? In my experience, pioneers are pig-headed old egotists who can't relinquish the reins. If there's one thing that gives me a pain in the neck, it is certainly pioneers. This is not an acceptable point of view. And yet every last one of them is more to be pitied than blamed, but not pitied in a condescending way. This whole novel is something that goes so far back, with me, and is such a wrenching up of my background, that it is difficult for me to be honest enough. The main problem is that if it ever gets published, which is unlikely, considering its nature (which will be called morbid although it is also so full of the ludicrous), IF it ever gets published, a lot of people will be mortally wounded and offended, and I feel really sorry about that, but I don't know what to do about it. However, so many people can never realize that one creates characters – or they are, rather, given to you – and that they are not copied from individual persons etc.

I don't mean to imply that writers always know best – only that no one else always knows best, either. In the long run, what can you do except write what interests you, and hope that someone somewhere will find it interesting also? Why don't you send the play to another agent and at least get another opinion? Or why not try the Manitoba Theatre? What can you lose? Why don't you write to J. Hirsch about it, and see what he says?[1] Please, please don't consider re-writing anything until you have someone else's opinion. I wonder if it might stand a better chance in England.

I enclose Kildare Dobbs' review of my novel.[2] At first I wondered why it was so vitriolic, and also so relatively loaded with smart cracks, but I learned that he spent a year or so in East Africa, so I guess he knows all about the soul of Africa. He had a poem in Tamarack Review a short time ago, called African Poem,[3] which was quite good poetry, I think, but its general outlook was that of the European who dislikes much of his own civilization and who finds in so-called primitive cultures the bloody splendour lacking in ours – almost the 'noble savage' outlook. However, sad as it may be to these seekers after some lost Garden of Eden, the noble savages these days are tending to feel they could do with a little less splendour and a little more sanitation. Perhaps I am bitter. Actually, I met Dobbs here not so long ago, and thought he was quite a nice guy. He was certainly very enthusiastic about your writing, Adele, and I don't think you need to worry about Macmillan in your present situation – Dobbs said that he and John Grey both felt they'd stake their lives on your turning up finally with something very good from that trip. So relax.

You asked me to tell you something funny. This isn't so very funny, but it's the best I can do at the moment. We saw in Izak Dinesen's 'Shadows On The Grass'[4] a mention of a Danish chap who had done some research into Somali literature and customs, and had written a book on it, so we went to great lengths to obtain the book, which is 'The Horn of Africa,' by John Bucholzer.[5] He has taken a trip through British Somaliland, and his chapters on his experiences are quite interesting, although superficial. But when we came to the chapters on Somali literature, I got the shock of my life. He had lifted the whole thing from that book of mine, the Somali translations. I didn't so much mind that he had taken my translations of poems and stories, because folk literature belongs to everyone, although I rather resented the fact that he implied he had simply gone out into the desert and sat around campfires and then taken down all these glorious songs and stories directly from the Somali. (Actually, it was rather odd – he must have taken my English translations and put them into Danish, and then his English translator put them back into English, and the results are quite astonishingly close to my English translations, so at least they were translated accurately). I thought he should not have pretended that direct translations are so easy, but this was not what really bothered me. The thing was that he had taken paragraphs and sections directly out of my introduction, and all my conclusions and ideas about Somali literature were presented as his own – and in my words! He had, once again, put these sentences into Danish, but when they were translated back into English, they are still astonishingly close to my sentences – in many cases, nearly identical. This was completely direct copying on his part, with no acknowledgement of source or anything. Even if he had acknowledged the sources, he should not steal whole paragraphs etc. I am very annoyed about this, and I'll write to his English publishers, although it won't do me any good, as I have no intention of taking legal action, although what he has done is in fact an infringement of the law of copyright. Maddening, isn't it? If I ever write about our Somaliland days, I'll tell the whole story – the bastard, it would serve him right.

I'm glad to hear about Amy. Please give her my sincere good wishes. I certainly hope your China visa comes through, Adele, and that the picture looks a little brighter by now as far as that aspect of the trip is concerned. What about articles on Hong Kong? There are so many Chinese people in Canada from there, you might find the articles would be of great interest in this country. Anyway, good luck, and please keep us posted. I wish there were something more constructive I could say, but you know we are thinking about you and hoping everything will work out, especially re: the play, which I do hope you will send to someone else. Could your English publisher advise you?

All the best, kid.

Love from us all,

Peg

P.S.   Kids are well. David started school this morning, and when he came home he said, 'It was great. It's funny – I feel bigger now.' I told him he even looked bigger. Jocelyn is in Grade 4 this year. I just remembered something genuinely funny – a friend of ours, also a writer, called around this morning and in the course of conversation it came out that she, too, is writing a book about an old lady! We are thinking of forming a society ... S.P.O.O.L. ... Society for the Prevention of Obscurity to Old Ladies.

We went to our cottage for our holidays,[6] and Jack worked all the time, putting cedar shakes on the outside of the bungalow. Busman's holiday. But he said he enjoyed it! Our place is really nice now, I wish you could see it.

1 In 1958 John Hirsch (1930–89), theatre director and administrator, combined Theatre 77 and the Winnipeg Little Theatre Centre into the Manitoba Theatre Centre with Hirsch as its first artistic director.
2 'Outside Africa,' *Canadian Literature* 8 (Spring 1961): 62–3. Dobbs, a writer and a co-editor of the *Tamarack Review*, was at this time an editor with Macmillan Canada. He had been with the British Colonial Service in Tanganyika from 1948 until immigrating to Canada in 1952.
3 *Tamarack Review* 19 (Spring 1961): 61–6
4 Isak Dinesen was the pseudonym of the Danish writer Karen Dinesen Blixen (1885–1962). *Shadows on the Grass* (1960) is a collection of African sketches set in Kenya.
5 Buchholzer's study was published in London in 1959 by Angus and Robertson.
6 The Laurences had bought a cottage at Port Roberts, Washington, just across the border.

3556 West 21st Ave.
8 October 1961

Dear Adele –

I hope this letter reaches you, as you may be in China by now.[1] I worry about you – are you really ok, etc? Not that we could do anything, from this distance, but anyway we worry & hope you are at least eating regularly & drinking boiled water & looking after yourself & so on. What about the articles? I wish I'd written sooner in reply to your last letter. I have written no letters for awhile, having been absorbed to a total degree by this damn novel.

DON'T GIVE UP ON THE PLAY! ! ! ! ! ! !

This is very important. If you do give up trying to get it accepted, what will happen? A hundred years from now, if the western world is still intact (which is admittedly unlikely) someone will produce your play & everyone will say what a terrific piece of work, but you will unfortunately not be around to gather either the plaudits or the shekels. So keep on with trying to get it produced. Standards, I have come to see, are so variable & individual that the writer _must_ write to please himself first, & then he can only hope that someone will share his viewpoint enough to want to enter his territory. _You_ are the only one who knows how the play should go. If you really know in yourself that it's done the way you want it, for heaven's sake leave it alone – don't mess around with it. I think that it will find someone who will produce it, ultimately.

It's so difficult, I find, to maintain any sort of faith in oneself. I haven't got an ounce of it myself, for all the way in which I write to you. Maybe I'm hoping to convince myself as well as you. I fluctuate between extremes, re: this novel, & may yet become a manic-depressive. I've finished (almost) the first draft, & although it needs a lot more work, I can see now the shape of it. I wrote it in a kind of single-minded burst of activity, letting the thing go where it seemed to want to go, & at the time I was (& still am, basically) completely convinced by the main character. But I'm beginning to anticipate the pitfalls – for one thing, it is written very simply and directly, for the simple reason that I am not clever enough to write it any other way, & in any event I still have a strong feeling for direct & simple writing, even though this style is perhaps almost archaic now. For another thing, it is by no means a new theme – but what is? I feel, in a rather protective way, that it could easily be called unsophisticated, because in fact it is, but what I'm trying to imply in it isn't really simple at all, of course. Maybe it's too obvious? Maybe it's not obvious enough? Well, this way lies madness, as you know. So what can you do except go ahead & do it as you see it yourself, even if everyone else who ever sees it thinks it is perfectly horrible or, even worse, boringly naive or just plain boring. I have brooded over this so much lately that it has got to stop. Kind friends & acquaintances still say from time to time very peculiar things such as 'how does it feel to be a successful writer?' and I look at them oddly as though they were speaking to me in Hindustani. I feel I haven't really learned a thing about writing except that no one really knows what is good & what is bad. So you might as well write to please yourself & not worry about anything else. I have now decided that I'm finished with worrying (about things like 'is it any good?' 'is it no good?' etc). It's just too great a drain on the energy, & I haven't enough to spare. I think that this process (i.e. of getting to trust your own judgement, & to attempt *honestly* to write what you feel & not what you're supposed to feel) – I think you have gone through this in the past 2 years & have come to much the same conclusions, haven't you? I've thought a lot lately about some of your comments re: the play, & how you've felt you had to go on & do it your way, whatever anyone said. You might like to know that I have been considerably heartened by remembering what you said of your own experience in this regard. This book (?) of mine, you see, has been written almost entirely without conscious thought, & although the conscious thought will enter into the re-writing, on the first time through I simply put down the story as the old lady told it to me (so to speak) & let it go where it wanted, & only when I was halfway through did I realize how it all tied together & what the theme was. I didn't know it had a theme before, nor did I know the purpose or meaning of some of the events & objects in the story, until gradually it became clear. Now I wonder if one can really trust the subconscious in this way, or if it is all an illusion, which has meaning for me but perhaps to another person will seem only an excessively simple & far-fetched tale? I can't know, but I'm trying very hard to follow your example in this way, & take the thing on faith, for the moment, anyway. I am terrified at the thought of submitting the manuscript, ultimately, somewhere. I never felt so hesitant about the first novel. Strange, isn't it?

I never seem to talk of the external world in my letters to you, possibly because I know very few people to whom I can talk about the interior battles, so you get it all. Sorry. Anyway, we are all quite well. The kids are fine – David is in Grade 1 & very pleased that he is learning to read, at last. Jocelyn is involved with Grade 4, Brownies, piano lessons, & dancing – but doesn't seem to be much bothered by what seems a rather full schedule. Jack & I are having a lot of fun lately in making wine from real grapes, with the help of an Italian friend. I'm still marking essays, doing about 4 book reviews a month, & this year (don't faint) I'm teaching Sunday school in the Unitarian Church. Sometimes I feel I have too much to do, but I guess I don't, really. Jack finds his job very interesting still, & always has too much to do, but in general we both feel quite happy here now, if it weren't for the ever-present threat of fallout, bombs, etc.

Please write. We certainly hope you are okay. And please – don't give up on the play!

Love from us all,

Peg

1 In fact, Wiseman was in London, where she had flown from Hong Kong at the beginning of October to attend the wedding of her friend Amy Zahl to David Gottlieb.
Wiseman would remain in London until her return to Canada the following April.

3556 West 21st Ave.
5 August [1962]

Dear Adele:

I'm sorry I've been so long in replying. For the past month, I've been at
sixes and sevens, or something, owing to a variety of causes. We've had
various relatives visiting for most of July, and although I was glad to
see them, there was a certain amount of confusion etc, with lots of
children tearing around madly in all directions. Last week I decided I
must get away from everything, so I packed up myself and the kids and
went out to the cottage at Point Roberts. I thoroughly enjoyed it, but the
kids were bored stiff, as they had no friends there. They put on a rather
touching act of enjoying every minute, as they knew it meant a lot to
me, but when finally David came down with some kind of 'flu, I
decided I wouldn't fight the inevitable any longer, so returned to town.
We'll probably only go out for weekends, and perhaps that will be just
as well. My inclination is to say 'When I was a kid, *I* was never bored!'
etc, but then I recall that at Clear Lake, there were always a lot of my
friends staying at nearby cottages, so that made quite a difference. The
real reason why I needed some peace and quiet was all connected with
writing, as usual.

My book on Somaliland (did I tell you the title – 'The Prophet's
Camel Bell') has been accepted by Macmillan in England. I'm very glad
about this, with some reservations. I hope that the English acceptance
may encourage McClelland & Stewart to take it in Canada, but we will
see. St. Martin's has turned it down, as they don't think it would sell in
the U.S. Willis Wing is trying to place it with another Amer publisher,
but so far without success.[1] St. Martin's wrote me a strangely apologetic
letter, in which they said they thought it was a charming and informa-
tive book (damning with faint praise?) but wouldn't take it as they felt
the American sales would be disappointing, etc, and then they pointed
out the exact amount (sixteen hundred and eighty four dollars) that they
had spent on ads and publicity for 'This Side Jordan,' despite which the
sales were disappointing – what do they think I should do, cry into my
gin-and-lime over the $1684? Why didn't they make it $1685, anyway?
Well, maybe Wing will find another Amer publisher, but I doubt it.

Anyway, it is good (I guess) that it is being published in England, at least. My reservations are concerned with the book itself, which (a) doesn't seem to me to count, really, as it is non-fiction, and (b) does not seem at this point to be what I wanted to write at all, anyway by which I mean that I think the material was there but I did not do justice to it – I wish I didn't realize this.

(Brief pause for station identification – I have just been out to the kitchen, to discover that the birthday cake which I made for Jack's birthday tomorrow and just finished icing, has sagged – one layer has slipped off the other layer – how the devil could that happen? I am beset by mysterious djinn!)

Anyway, I feel dissatisfied with this book, and yet I do not think I can do it any better. I am finished with it. I feel like writing to Macmillan and telling them to forget the whole thing, and perhaps at some point I will wish I had done so, but I won't – that's the irony of it. The script isn't terrible – just mediocre. I think it is too nice – I feel it will offend no one, although I didn't intend it to be that way. Not that I would go out of my way to offend anyone unnecessarily, but I think the whole thing is too bland. But I do not feel I can re-write it. I am not sufficiently interested in it, at this point. I wrote it as honestly as I could, and worked on it obsessively for 8 months, but I've had it, now, even though I now feel it is too superficial.

I wish I could persuade the publishers to do a book of short stories, but there is not much chance of this, at least not for a good long time.[2] I've got 10 W. African short stories, of which all but one have been or will be published somewhere. Tamarack Review accepted one not long ago, for their winter issue (I think),[3] and another will be in the next issue of Macmillan's *Winter Tales*.[4] But apparently you have to have 2 or 3 novels to your credit (or whatever) before anyone will risk short stories, as a book.

I have abandoned the old lady novel. I may return to it one day, if I can see how to do it properly, but right now I can see only that it is boring. This is the one thing that is not permitted. The whole thing really is very poor, and right now I feel I can only cut my losses and put it away. I feel intensely depressed about it, needless to say, especially as I wonder if I can write anything about this country. I can see now why I found it easier to write stories etc set in Africa – it is a kind of screen, an evasion, so that one need never make oneself vulnerable. Also, when I write about people here, my old inhibitions come up all over again. Maybe I could do something with stories set here if I weren't living here. I don't know. Also, I am troubled by what I take to be North American sophisticated cynicism – a great many writers, some of whom I admire very much, protect themselves from attack by attacking first – i.e. everything, basically, is rotten, and what the hell? This is okay, but I feel that I am incapable of sustained despair – I don't think there is much doubt that we are going to blow ourselves to pieces one of these days, but I cannot accept the view that there is absolutely no health in us or that life is completely meaningless, and because I feel this way, I often feel that anything I write about people here will be naive or perhaps merely corny, and for this reason I have gone to any lengths to avoid writing about the situations which really concerned and moved me. I have the feeling that the novel about the old lady represented such an evasion. Perhaps in the long run there is no way other than to look inwardly and personally, and take the risk. I think the important thing is to go on doing something, and not to be paralysed by one's doubts and uncertainties, but of course this is easier said than done. Anyway, that is the state of things at the moment. My family and friends, not unnaturally, feel I ought to be happy because of the S'land book being accepted in England, and I guess I am, in many ways, but one cannot help feeling – what next? I wish I knew a lot more, or else a lot less.

Re: Jack's job – at the moment, he has several irons in the fire, so to speak, and we are anxiously awaiting news of several jobs for which he has applied, in various distant spots. I hope one or another will work out, as he is getting progressively more fed up with his job here, and we would both like to go elsewhere, if possible, despite the fact that when I begin to think of it in practical terms, I worry about the kids' education etc. But no doubt all that would work out, too, when the time came. I'll let you know as soon as we hear anything.

How is the China book?[5] I was glad to hear you were making such good progress with it. I can certainly appreciate your problems in writing about yourself, directly. I agree that to avoid coyness is not as simple as one feels it ought to be – when is an anecdote amusing, and when merely simpering? I sweated over that one for months. However, I do not have any doubt that you will achieve the tone you want. If you can write it the way you would talk it, you're set. I'm glad that John Gray will publish the play if an Amer publisher can be found – goddamn Amer publishers, I say! They are the persistent fly in the ointment. If one could feel that this is because their standards are so high, well and good, but of course it is not this at all. What about England?

I know that your play will be produced one day, but I just hope it will not be very far in the future, that's all. Still, it is completed, and you have done it the way you wanted it, and that is something not to be under-estimated.

How did the party at the Yeos go? Yes, we know the people. Marion Metcalfe was married previously to Ross Woodman, and now to Gren Yeo. Jack went around with Marion at college for a time, and I, briefly, went out with Gren, which is kind of odd, in a way, maybe. We'd be interested to hear how they are, etc, and also news of anyone else we know. Glad you ran into Hallstead – I'm very fond of him and his wife.

(Brief pause for cake checking – thank God, the blasted thing is still all in one piece! Jack's birthday is Aug 6, and David's is Aug 9, so this week we are always inundated with tons of uneaten cake. Jack doesn't even like cake very much, but I, sentimentally, always make him a birthday cake – my reason, ridiculously, is that he never had one as a kid – it's a little late, now, I know, but I somehow cannot help making this futile gesture each year, and he takes it in the spirit it is offered, I guess, not really as a cake.)

I met the other day George Lamming, the W. Indian writer (one of his novels was 'In The Castle Of My Skin') who is here at the moment on a Canada Council something-or-other.[6] He was unfortunately very drunk that night, so was lucid only in spells, but I thought he was terrific. Not only a very talented writer, but the kind of personality that hits you like the spirit of god between the eyes. Very revolutionary in outlook, and with the strength of his convictions, but not in any sense liable to write merely propaganda. If he stops off in Winnipeg and you have the chance to talk with him, try to do so.

Well, having poured out all my troubles, as usual, I now close in the hope that you'll write soon and pour out all yours. I don't know what I would do if I could not write from time to time and tell you about all these things that plague me. One cannot usually talk about them to anyone, and although Jack, God knows, is sympathetic and would always listen, I feel he is quite patient enough about my writing and the withdrawn times which it involves, without listening to a constant spate of my uncertainties. Anyway, he knows them without my saying. But sometimes it is a relief to get them off one's chest. Another thing – before you ever had anything published, you could talk about your worries re: writing, but somehow this becomes much more difficult now, because one's non-writing friends tend to feel that once you have anything published, you are set forevermore, and if you feel you aren't, you must be some kind of a nut. Have you had this experience? 'Well you don't need to worry,' they say, 'because you know the publisher will at least give serious consideration to what you've written now.' This is not what is worrying, of course. My real concern is if I can write anything worth publishing, and also how to get down at least some slight suggestion of the complexities which did not bother me at one time because I did not see they were there. Please write and tell me I am not really going off my rocker, and that this kind of split personality (the public self and the other) is quite normal, really.

And most of all, good luck with the China book. I'm anxious to hear how it's going.

Love from us all,

Peg

1 *The Prophet's Camel Bell* was published in the United States by Knopf as *New Wind in a Dry Land* on the same day, 15 June 1964, as Knopf also published *The Tomorrow-Tamer* and *The Stone Angel*.
2 McClelland and Stewart and Macmillan published Canadian and British editions of *The Tomorrow-Tamer* in 1963.
3 'The Pure Diamond Man,' *Tamarack Review* 26 (Winter 1963): 3–21
4 'The Sound of the Singing,' *Winter's Tales* 9 (1963): 62–104
5 The project never saw print.
6 George Lamming (b. 1927) was in Vancouver on a Canada Council fellowship.

490 Burrows Ave.,
Wpg. 4, Man.
20 August 1962

Dear Peggy,

I was on the point of replying to your other letter, when yours arrived this morning, so I'm sitting right down to reply lest you should worry about it. Don't worry, I shall do as you ask as soon as I'm finished this. I've very often had the same feeling about a letter I've written when in an emotional state, the fear of being disloyal, the fear of giving oneself away, the fear of exposing what's private.[1] Usually the fact is that one is so filled with these fears even when one is writing that one says a lot less than one thought one was saying and leaves the recipient slightly puzzled by one's stern injunction to destroy this letter. But I will and I certainly won't mention it to anyone. I have far too much respect and fondness for both you and Jack to mistake this for anything but the kind of readjustment that takes place periodically between intelligent, loving people who need to be honest with each other. I guess you've let this pile up for a long time Peg, so that now that it's come into the open it's done so with the force of a lot of repression released behind it, – what I'm trying to say is that you're still probably awash with various waves of emotion, guilt, relief, love, etc., etc., which haven't relaxed to their proper proportions yet. I wish you could talk to someone about it, simply to talk away the jagged edges, and am sorry that you're so far away. Not that there's anything anyone can do to help in such a personal thing, but I know what a relief a willing ear can bring. I know how much you've always dreaded Jack's disapproval, or what you thought would be Jack's disapproval, and what this rebellion must have cost you, – at least I imagine it must seem like a rebellion in terms of what you've conceived your relationship to Jack to be. And yet, who knows, maybe complete submission isn't what Jack's wanted from you all along? Perhaps asking him to pass judgment on your 'private area,' – in this case your writing, is a kind of imposition on him too? It shifts your own responsibility for your private self onto him too, something which, ultimately, you've found to be impossible to bear because it reduces yourself to less than a whole person in your own mind, and something which I'm sure Jack doesn't need. Jack is far too big a guy and too capable in his own right to need the reassurance that you're not competing with him. So what has happened is a kind of habit pattern's been set up in which you've both been trapped. You rebel against what you've invited, Jack's views on work which you haven't allowed yourself to develop completely in what should be airtight, – the crucible of your own imagination, – and Jack, since he does have a marked literary turn of mind allowing himself to do what you seem to demand. What you really want is reassurance from him. What he gives you is what you say you want, – critical appraisal, at a time when you're too unsure of the thread to be able really to bear it. I suspect that Jack would be just as content to say proudly, – and of the pride I'm sure, – 'This is my wife, I don't know much about what she's busy hatching till it's nearly done, and some of it I don't know that I necessarily approve of entirely, but it's hers, and I'm proud of her as a person.' Corny sounding, ain't it? And presumptuous. Perhaps I ought to tear this up and not send it, because how can I presume to know what life is like for you both? What I am sure of is that you'll work this thing out all right. Of course you need to have faith in your own judgment. Of course you need to make your own mistakes about your work. Perhaps you do need to be by yourself for awhile, if only to help you realize what really constitutes your marriage, aside from all these accretions which dependence and habit have allowed to grow up. I know you'll see what you and Jack have really got is something aside from all that, and the realignment will probably be a relief to both of you.

Has Jack got a good prospect? It would necessitate that you figure out what to do with the kids, schooling, etc., anyway. So it would be a fairly natural thing for you to stay with them in London for awhile anyway, if London is where you want them to be educated, during the transition period. You don't say anything about times, so I don't know how imminent these moves of yours are. I am delighted that you've decided that you want to apply for a Canada Council Grant. I've been annoyed frankly that you haven't before. If you don't deserve one who the hell does? Where the hell is all that money going to anyway? What continues to fascinate me is the number of civil servants who have permanent, pensionable positions in which all they have to do is to simply turn people like us down when we apply for measly one year grants. Phooey.

Write to THE CANADA COUNCIL,
    P.O. BOX 97, STATION D,
    OTTAWA, ONT.

Tell them that you are a Canadian novelist and would like to apply for a fellowship, and ask them to send you the necessary application forms and grant prospectus. They will then send the stuff. Write right away because the first time I applied I missed, apparently, because I missed the final entry date, which that year was in November I think. But it may shift, so get going on it right away. Now, when you get the entry forms and they ask all kinds of questions re what you've written and accomplished before, don't be shy. List in detail where you've had stories published, books, fellowships, prizes, – all of them. And right from the start, – don't forget the Somali book of poems etc. Oh yes, apply for the senior fellowship for writers, – I think it's $4,000. Don't downgrade yourself. You're no bloody undergraduate. They'll also ask for a plan of what you intend to do, or work on when you've got the fellowship. Let them know it's a story that takes place in Canada. That's another thing they like to hear. And good luck. As I recall the year I tried the list of successful applicants came out in February.

By the way your analysis of your attitude to Africa and its relation to your work and yourself is very interesting. Of course, doesn't all our work have something to do with our very most intrinsic selves? And it doesn't hurt to discover what it was, afterwards, either ourselves or our work. It just prepares us for the next struggle, as people and as writers.

The pictures of the kids were wonderful. God they're sweet looking kids. – I've just torn your letter up and flushed it down the john, – I'm compulsive about these things, – instructions are instructions. If you're moving soon will you be coming through Winnipeg? If so couldn't you stop over? I'm bound to be here, – I am beginning to wonder for how much longer. I've sent off the three trial chapters[2] to Willis Wing and am now awaiting his reply re whether Harpers wants them or not. If not I have to look for a job, – what? I'm not exactly fitted for anything. But we'll see when the time comes. Meanwhile, I'm here, and you're welcome. And if I've said anything too presumptuous in the above please forgive. And write soon and tell me how you're doing.

love,

Adele

1 After a long period of tension and frustration, Margaret Laurence had clashed with her husband over their personal differences and his criticism of her old lady novel. She had told him that she would not accompany him to his next job in Pakistan and that, instead, she and their children would go to England where she would try to make her living as a full-time writer.
2 An apparent reference to Wiseman's projected book on China

3556 West 21st Ave.
29 August 1962

Dear Adele:

Many thanks for replying so promptly to my letter, and for understanding so well (on the basis of my having given you so few facts) the essence of my difficulties. I have simmered down to some extent now, and think that things will work out quite well. I have written to the Can Council, but have not yet heard or received forms. It is still not quite certain about Jack's job, but it appears there will be little doubt that he will get it and will be going to Pakistan. However, we do not want to count any chickens yet. But we have discussed the whole thing, and we now feel that this will be the opportunity I have long needed, to stand on my own feet for a while and learn to trust my own judgement. If he goes to Pakistan, he may have to go fairly quickly. I will remain here for the moment, and will go to England later this fall, probably November, or as soon as I am able to rent our house here and make the necessary arrangements. I will go whether the Can Council kicks through or not, but it would certainly help if I could be in that way self-supporting.[1] However, we shall see. The main thing now is that I believe I can do it all right, although it will certainly not be without many qualms when the time comes. All this is very complicated, but perhaps when we go to England, I will be able to stop off for a day in Winnipeg – I would very much like to see you, needless to say, and to have the opportunity for both of us to catch up on what has really been happening, which one doesn't and can't deal with in letters. All the things which I have recently realised about myself, etc, now seem so obvious that I really wonder how I could have not seen them for so long. It takes me so painfully long to learn anything at all. But I feel free, or reasonably so, from the sense of despair that has been with me for some years now, so I don't really mind the slowness of growth. As far as I am concerned, this will be the opportunity to terminate a kind of delayed adolescence, at the advanced age of 36, and it is really now or never. I feel now that it will work out both to my advantage and Jack's, if things go as we hope and trust.

I think McClelland & Stewart are going to turn down my Somaliland book, but I wish they would let me know one way or another. Jack McC expressed such confidence before he ever saw the script that I think he is embarrassed to write me now. However, that is his dilemma, not mine. At least it will come out in England, and perhaps that is a good thing, although I still wish I would have done a better job with the script. It was my last painful breaking of ties with Africa, and as such it is too restrained in parts, out of the fear of being too unrestrained. But it is finished and I am not going to waste any more time thinking about it. I have managed to get some wonderful photographs for it, from an old friend,[2] so that is a help. Dead silence from American publishers. But what the hell? Corragio – Avanti![3]

Please write. Your letter did more to encourage me than you can possibly know.

Love from us all,

Peg

1 Laurence was unsuccessful.

2 C.J. (Bob) Martin had been employed by the British Colonial Office and remained with them, serving in Africa until March 1961 when he joined the British Broadcasting Corporation as program organizer for its Somali Section.

3 A reference to Wiseman's year in Rome in 1951–2. The phrase *Coraggio – avanti* means 'take heart and go forward.'

35 Heath Hurst Rd.,
London, N.W. 3,
England
25 November 1962[1]

Dear Adele:

Did you get my letter? Did I write to you before or after I moved into this flat? Unfortunately, I can't remember. I will assume that I wrote before I moved in here, so if I repeat myself, forgive me. I was terribly lucky to find a flat in the area I know best – I really love this part of London. Our flat is in one of those red brick houses, and although the ceilings are high and the rooms are therefore impossible to heat, I really like it. We're close to Hampstead Heath – I walked up there with the kids today, and got lost! No kidding, we were totally without any sense of direction, and I had visions of camping under a tree for the night, like Colin Wilson, only he no doubt was not accompanied by 2 little kids, which makes a difference – what would 'The Outsider' have been like if Wilson had had a family up there on the Heath with him?[2] The mind boggles at the thought. I took the kids to the Science Museum yesterday, and David was fascinated by the models of old trains and boats. We're really covering London in a very unsystematic but enjoyable way. The week before we went to the Zoo – the kids liked the elephants best. I said to David, 'You've never seen a real live elephant before, have you?' And he said, with complete logic, considering my wording, 'No, and I've never seen a dead one, either.'

Did I tell you that Alan Maclean[3] suggested to me that Macmillan might like to do a book of my short stories?[4] I nearly dropped dead with surprise, as this is what I have been hoping for, lo these many years. I don't know what his reaction to them will be, of course, as he has only read the 2 that have been in 'Winter's Tales,'[5] but I have spent the last 2 weeks typing them all out – 250 pp manuscript. I have finished them now, thank God – a boring job, as I had typed them all out many times before. I only hope they do decide to do a book. By the way, the parcel from Wpg arrived, with my novel manuscript.[6] I don't think it reads too badly. It's kind of an offbeat story, in a way – which really means that I personally find it very interesting but I have grave doubts that many people would share my point of view. But basically, Adele, it is written as I wanted to do it – I had begun on re-writing, following J's criticism, and find now that what I re-wrote is pure unadulterated crap. It was better the first time. I am not trying to write an historical novel, after all. What the hell do I care when they were using steam tractors on the prairies? This kind of thing. I had begun to try to make it into something that it was not intended to be – in order to widen its appeal. I only succeeded in turning it into something bloody awful. I threw away, the other day, all the re-written parts and will stick to the first draft, come hell or high water. The old lady knew what she was doing when she told me her life story – at least, that is what I feel now, anyway. We will see.

How are you? How are you feeling, physically and mentally? Please write. I am kind of anxious at not hearing from you. Are you okay? PLEASE WRITE!! I don't worry about many people in this world, but those I worry about, I worry like anything.

Personally, life goes on, in a manner of speaking. After the initial elation at being here, and settled in a flat, etc etc, came the inevitable letdown. Not exactly letdown, but for quite a few weeks I had been so totally absorbed by the immediate problems of getting organized for the trip and getting organized here – flat, school, etc – that I didn't have time to think of anything else, not much, anyway. Now I have time. A mixed blessing.

I have not seen much of old friends here, as I find that I do not want to see much of them. The burden of explanations, polite enquiries on their part, etc, seems almost intolerable. Also, I have not got a phone yet, and I find that phoning from a pay-phone is very hard on my nerves – I can't hear, for one thing. But this is just an excuse. I feel lonely as hell, but I don't phone people – I will, in time, of course. Right now I enjoy walking down the street and not knowing one single person, no one at all. This is probably not healthy, but I don't care. I'm not at a loss for things to do – keeping the kids to their schedule, and working at writing fills all my time. About half the time I feel pretty good, and can work hopefully. The other half I feel depressed, lonely, empty, bereft, and just plain lousy. I do not feel homesick – this is one emotion I have never felt in my life. But there are a few (very few) people I would like to see and talk with – maybe this is a type of homesickness, after all – the only kind of home I seem to value anyway, those half dozen people who are members of my tribe. In other respects, I feel I would like to remain here forever – right here, where I am now. I hope to Christ I feel differently in a year or so. Did I tell you – the Can. Council wrote to say their decision won't be until February? Well, I will put that possibility firmly from mind – they undoubtedly won't give me a cent, anyway. I got back the money the agent had taken for income tax – he had taken it off mistakenly, thank goodness. Of course, I have to pay the tax in April, so let us hope I have something with which to pay it. Cost of living is HIGH. Especially for smokers. As my friend in Glasgow says, 'You will find some things cheaper than in Canada – like bird cages, for instance.' By the way, I have just become a terrific admirer of orthodox Judaism – the reason is that my landlady and her daughter tell me they are always home on a Friday, so they don't mind if I go out then (they don't need to keep an eye on the kids, but I wouldn't go out unless some adult were in the house.) So far I have only been out once. I have this terrific feeling that I should force myself to go alone into a pub, but I don't know if I will ever overcome my Canadian inhibitions sufficiently. Must go. No more space. PLEASE WRITE.

Love,

Peg

P.S. I have joined CND,[7] but haven't yet gone to a meeting. I haven't gone to the Unitarian church here yet, as I keep feeling reluctant about it – they are somehow too cheery and positive-thinking for my present frame of mind.

1 Laurence and her children had arrived in London on 22 October and she had taken a flat in Hampstead.
2 Colin Wilson (b. 1931) had been catapulted to prominence by the ecstatic reception of his first book, *The Outsider* (1956), a study of existentialist writing, thought, and personality. Publicity around the publication of the book described how, in the early 1950s, he had spent his days writing in the British Museum and had slept in a tent pitched on the public grounds of Hampstead Heath.
3 Alan Duart Maclean (b. 1924) was a director of Macmillan in England and editor of many numbers of *Winter's Tales*, Macmillan's annual anthology.
4 *The Tomorrow-Tamer* (1961)
5 'The Perfume Sea,' 6 (1960): 83–120 and 'The Rain-Child,' 8 (1962): 105–42
6 Exceeding her baggage weight limit for air travel, Laurence had shipped the only copy of the draft of *The Stone Angel* by sea to London.

7 Campaign for Nuclear Disarmament, a British organization established in 1958 to fight against nuclear arms. In the 1950s and 1960s it organized large demonstrations including protest marches to Aldermaston, Berkshire, the location of the Atomic Energy Research Establishment factory.

35 Heath Hurst Road,
2 January 1963

Dear Adele:

I can always judge whether or not I really want to write to a person by where I start on an airletter form. With the Christmas thank-you letters which I have just been slogging over, I start about 6 inches down the page, and even type double-space on some of them! I got your letter this morning, and I was so damn glad to hear you in such a cheerful mood. I'm glad you went early and stayed late at those Xmas parties, and the hell with the dyspepsia. I'm sorry about the vigils with the friend's mother – reality, as you say, comes in pretty forcibly at such times. I don't know, though – I think that if flesh-and-blood life did not hit one forcibly from time to time, either painfully or joyfully, everything would become shadowy and insubstantial, work, oneself, everything. The only trouble, for me anyway, is that when life hits me it usually hits me with such a wallop. Anyway, I am so glad to hear you talking excitedly about Riel.[1] I couldn't agree more. I have always felt so drawn to that strange man and have always wondered why his story had not been done, in dramatic terms I mean, over and over again, instead of mainly being done in history books, etc. A play on Riel was done on CBC-TV about a year ago,[2] I think, but unfortunately I did not see it. Anyway, with that kind of story (or myth or whatever one sees in it), the possibilities are endless. By the way, should you ever require the historical data, I guess Winnipeg is about the best place for that, isn't it? Two things come to mind. First, Mary Mindess[3] did a lot of work in the provincial archives at one time, when she was writing a booklet called 'City Of The Rivers,' which was published by the Tourist Bureau or some such thing – it was a very good piece of work, too. Anyway, she would know exactly where to look, and she is also a friend of Hart Bowsfield[4] (whom I used to know quite well, too) who works in the prov. archives. The second thing that comes to mind is that another person who knows a hell of a lot about Riel is Gordon Elliott, my very dear friend from U.B.C., who teaches English now but is actually an historian. Gord was going to write a book on Riel but changed his mind as he was too bound up with other things at the time – it was to have been a history book type of thing, of course. He is teaching at Prince George, on a university extension course this year, but can always be reached c/o English Dept, University of British Columbia, Vancouver 8, B.C. Maybe this wouldn't be of any help, but I suppose the fact-finding has to come first, before one could know what to make of it – maybe enough facts exist in 'Strange Empire' (which I don't know).[5] In any event, more power to you. By the way, I didn't take your comments on the novel as a harangue – I felt, rather, that they confirmed what is essentially my own point of view, that things have to be done in their own way, and that one must trust the characters enough to put the whole thing down as they tell it, and not try to muck about with it too much. One must, as it were, listen. You know what I mean. If one is misled (I speak in this vague way as it is less painful – I mean *me*, *I*, not one) into following advice, however well-meant, which conflicts with the true basic concept of the thing itself, then that is a kind of betrayal of oneself. However, to appreciate what it was like, as far as I was concerned, ask yourself what you would have felt like if Peg Stobie[6] had been a man and your husband? I guess, Adele, the whole absurd thing was that for a whole year I was making some kind of lunatic attempt to convince myself that I must be wrong about that novel, because if I weren't wrong, it indicated a lack of communication, on the personal level, which I had long known to be the case but which I simply could not face except in my solitary late-night sessions with the wine jug. This novel means such a hell of a lot to me, simply because it is me. One wants it to be read with comprehension. I don't mean the characters are me, naturally, although some of them are, in some ways, as must surely always be the case. My own dilemma, I see now, is closest to Hagar's son John – in fact, he is the person whom I feel the most for – all this is meaningless, as you haven't read the script, but I say it in case the thing is ever published (I am an optimist at heart). Anyway, I am pretty certain now that the things which I thought were there, actually are there, and must be said in this way. I finished the revisions on New Year's Eve, which I took to be a good omen.

I am now in that agony of apprehension about it – is it too obvious, or is it not clearly enough stated, etc. But there comes a time when you have to let it go, so I'm going to type it out when the kids have gone back to school (holidays last until Jan. 7) and see what Macmillan's have to say about it. You know, Adele, it is written so much in Hagar's voice that sometimes I think it needs to be read aloud. That was another insane thing I considered doing, months ago when I was in the depths – re-writing it in the 3rd person. Impossible, however – she is speaking; that is simply a fact. Re: short stories – at the moment, I have no interest in writing them. If I ever do feel like it, then of course I will, but right now that is not what interests me. Anyway, the way I feel about *Hagar* at the moment is that if Macmillan's thinks it is unpublishable, I will feel disappointed, but I will still disagree with them. 'Here stand I; God help me, I can do no other.' I have always been very drawn to those words of Martin Luther's.[7] Imagine what it must have taken, to say that in the face of the whole Establishment of the western world, when it is so difficult to say it even of issues on an infinitely smaller scale (however, not smaller to me). So – we will see.

I got a letter from Alex Baron,[8] and phoned him when he and his wife were in London over Christmas. They said they would try to get over and see me, but I got another letter a few days later, saying their car had broken down in the cold weather and snow which we have had, so they went back to Hove. However, I hope to see them soon. I have made very little effort to see people, Adele – I have been kind of preoccupied, I guess. I want to see people, and yet I don't seem to get around to it. I will, in time. Maybe when I get a phone, if I ever do. But I'm not concerned. I am trying, for the first time in years, to live a less scheduled life, and to do things when I feel like it – for me, at this point, this is very difficult. My God, my instinct in coming here was absolutely right. If I hadn't, I'd have been done for, as I now see very clearly. You ask what I hear from Jack.[9] He is well, and working very hard. He misses us. I can't write to anyone, not even you, about him, really, Adele. Many complexities, concealed too long – I am not certain about anything in this area only about my work at present.

Love,

Peg

P.S. I hope you find work. Have you got any irons in the fire, as it were? It is bloody awful that a writer can't earn a living from writing.

1 Louis David Riel (1844-85), Manitoba Métis leader executed for treason for his part in the Northwest Rebellion. Wiseman was later to write *Testimonial Dinner*, a play incorporating Riel as a character. It was privately printed in 1978.

2 John Coulter's (1888–1930) *Riel*, first performed in 1950, was shown on 23 and 30 April 1961 on *GM Presents* with Bruno Gerussi as Riel.

3 Mary Turnbull Mindess had been at United College with Laurence. Her husband, Bill, was employed by the CBC.

4 Hartwell Bowsfield (b. 1922), Canadian historian

5 *Strange Empire: A Narrative of the Northwest* (1952), by the American historian Joseph Kinsey Howard (1906–51), was the first account of the Métis uprising that was directed to American readers.

6 Margaret Stobie was a member of the English department at the University of Manitoba.

7 As the inaugurator of the Protestant Reformation, Martin Luther (1483–1546) was accused of heresy. In 1521, he was ordered to renounce his 'errors' before a formal assembly that had been convened at Worms to condemn Luther as a heretic. His famous reply was given on this occasion.

8 Joseph Alexander Baron (b. 1917), novelist, and his wife Delores. His last novel had been *Seeing Life* (1958) and he was about to publish *The Low Life* (1963).

9 Jack Laurence had been working in Pakistan since the previous October.

35 Heath Hurst Road,
14 February [1963] –
VALENTINE'S DAY.

Dear Adele:

ALAN MACLEAN (MACMILLAN'S) LIKES *HAGAR*! HE LIKES IT! CAN IT BE TRUE? He has just phoned, and I am in something like a state of shock. He thinks it needs to be cut, somewhat, as it moves rather slowly in the beginning, and I feel that this is a justified criticism, as I had thought myself that it took rather a long time to get really moving. So I'll do some cutting in the first chapters. He also wonders about the title, thinking it makes it sound like an Old Testament tale, so I will give thought to that, also. I had felt many times that the title ought perhaps to contain something more of the book's theme, but couldn't think of a suitable title. Maybe one will come to me. Basically, however, he thinks it comes off. He says he knows this kind of old lady very well, and that he finds her entire predicament and her death very moving. Adele, I feel as though my faith in life, in myself, in everything, has been miraculously restored to me. Of course, this novel meant a lot more than it should have done, to me, as in a way it was (or became) a whole test of my own judgement – and luckily, I had got to the point where I knew that although it might not say anything to anyone else, it did say a lot to me, so perhaps really that was the true restoration of faith – I think so. Nevertheless, in terms of novels, it meant the transition from writing about Africa to writing about my own people, the only ones I know from the inside, so on that level also it had almost too much significance for me. Oh God.

I can still hardly believe it. Now we will have to see where we go from here. I have been trying to write 5 minute talks to submit to the BBC for the Women's Hour, and have given it up as impossible. They seem so corny that I am ashamed to submit them. Let's face it – I can't write unless my heart's in it, and so from the £ and $ point of view, that is just too bad for me. I received a polite refusal from the British Council today, for a job I'd applied for. I am so unqualified for a job, that is the snag. Also, who wants to hire a woman who has 2 kids, when obviously if the kids get sick or something, my mind will be pre-occupied and I will probably stay home from work? Well, all these things will work out, no doubt. I have been so damn worried about things lately, but thank God now this has happened about the novel, anyway. The main thing is – if it actually does say something to someone else, then I wasn't off my rocker. The real crux of the matter is that one must not be dependent upon anyone else's point of view, and therefore I ought not to be moved too much either by acceptance or rejection of my work. But my uncertainties about myself were so marked and of such long standing that I cannot help feeling an enormous relief to hear that Alan likes the book – this is unavoidable, at this point. The next hurdle is to restore myself to a sufficiently calm state to begin work again.

   Please write.

                              Love,

                              Peg

                              35 Heath Hurst Road
                              12 June 1963

Dear Adele:

Was I ever glad to get your letter the other day. Its somewhat fantastic tone (Polish majors; sad burglars) was just what I needed to improve my morale, which at that point was pretty low. This introductory piece for the major's book sounds like a good thing.[1] Are they going to pay fairly well? I hope so. It is, as you say, a damned odd world. No, you hadn't written about your burglary, but the encounter with the young burglar sounds both funny and sad. You could do a good job on an article on it.[2] Someone told me (I can't remember who it was – that's odd) that they'd seen your article on Hong Kong in Weekend.[3] Could you send me a copy? I'd like to see it.

I don't quite know what I've told you and what I haven't, in my battle with the BBC. They accepted my series of folk tales for the Hausa Service,[4] and the department that handles payments wrote and said they trusted 4 guineas for each script would be acceptable to me. I wrote back and told them that as I had done a lot of research, I had hoped to get slightly more than 4 gns (I had hoped to get 10 gns, the bastards), and they wrote back and said in view of what I said, they were prepared to pay me – what do you think? – half a guinea more per script! I really had to laugh, but I didn't refuse, naturally, as what good would that do, so I wrote and thanked them for agreeing to offer me slightly more than 4 gns ... slightly being the operative word. I have sent the same series of scripts to the CBC and to Radio Uganda (where I know a guy), but am not too hopeful. Bob Weaver has taken a short story of mine for CBC Wed. Night,[5] so that is $350, which is better than the BBC pays for anything. Otherwise, the money situation is poor and prospects do not look good. I'm getting £100 more on 'Hagar' than on the others, but so far no word of what Jack McClelland is going to fork over, and as far as American publishers on all 3 books, either Willis Wing has goofed or else I am just unlucky, because St. Martin's has decided not to take the S'land book after all – Sherman Baker[6] has quit, and St. M's is going to change policy and do mainly textbooks, and so far W.W. has not found another Amer publisher. So that means all 3 will come out in England and Canada, but not the U.S., which is a tragedy, financially speaking.[7] I don't know what in hell to do, Adele, about this money question. The thing is – I am okay at the moment, but on the money Jack sends me, which is really quite a reasonable sum, I can live and pay rent but still the kids' clothes and my own etc come out of my money, which leads me to feel it is costing me too damn much entirely to live, and I don't know how to cut down – I could stop smoking, I know, and never buy even beer, but I WON'T! GODDAMN IT, I JUST WILL NOT! Main problem: I know now that I want to stay here, and I am pretty sure I want to stay here by myself. I know this is a hurtful decision, and that if I carry it through, there will be hell to pay on all sides. But what can I do, Adele? I cannot face anything else, now. I love it here. I love living here, and working here, and I guess I just like living on my own, as well. I am no longer a nervous wreck, as once (this previous state, I should say, I do not blame on anybody – there is no blame on either side, as far as I am concerned ... it is not so simple as that). However, apart from questions of responsibility and of children, the thing remains that I can't stay unless I can support myself,

and how can I? I really do not know. Not by writing, that is for damn
sure. So what I have done at the moment is a complete evasion of the
problem. I am simply pretending it does not exist, at least until next
Xmas, when J comes on leave. I have suddenly begun writing this
novel, and it is coming along. What it will turn out to be, I have no
idea. Maybe lousy. Maybe okay. Who knows? Who can know, at this
point? This is the terrible thing. You spend time at someone else's
expense, on work that you have no idea whether it will work out or not.
But I must do it this way, as the alternative is not to write it, and if I do
not do it now, I may never get up my nerve again. I have the feeling
(very protective) that no one else will like it, but I don't seem to care
much about that. I like writing it, and that is all that matters. It is a
lunatic project in all ways, but it is the only thing to be done. It is not
the thing itself that worries me – it's there, all right, I'm convinced of
that, just as I'm convinced the people are there (I *know* them – I mean
they exist for me), but can I get it out? I'm not even thinking about can
I or can't I, because if I do, I won't be able to. I've been working every
morning, slow and steady, for exactly one week, and trying not to think
about it too much in between. I would go out of my mind if I dwelt too
much on the thought that I produce so damn slowly, and why can't I
churn out thousands of stories and make some real money and so on.
I know what you mean, Adele – this is the way you work, and how can
you help it? But when I think of what I earn (laughable) and when I
think of the dough that is paid out for stories by various publications,
this induces a kind of semi-hysteria in me, so I simply must not think
about it. I got a letter from W. Wing the other day, enclosing some
comments on a story of mine which he had been peddling around un-
successfully. The comments from such magazines as Good Housekeeping were hilarious ... 'this story has some moments, but we do not think
our ladies would care for the basically hostile relationship of the
husband and wife' ... it was not any hell of a story, just about an old
man who resented his wife's conformist notions of redecorating their
house, and retaliated by carving his own fantastic tombstone.[8] But what
hope with G. Housekeeping et al? Ladies Home Journal said 'this story
is too far out for us' ... God, Adele, me far out? ME? It is to laugh. But
still, some part of me (the non-financial) was more pleased about this
than about the stories sold to Sat. Eve. Post. However, I was compen-
sated for all this by receiving from Macmillan's the block-pull of the
cover for 'The Tomorrow-Tamer' (the Afr. short stories), and it is really
a stunner – black and white and scarlet, and really terrific.

I agree so much with you that you can't work by anyone else's standards of what you ought to be doing. The one thing we must admit to ourselves is that we are not lazy. It may appear to be so, but honestly it is not. I seem to waste so much time. But I don't know how to do it any other way.

Many strange things have been happening. I agreed a long time ago to be one of the speakers at the Canadian Universities Society Literary Supper (!!), mainly because Rache Lovat Dickson,[9] who is a wonderful man, asked me. The awful day rolled around, and the topic was 'The Writer – Man of Letters or Voice of a Generation?' Who could make any sense of that one? Rache told me I should not write it all out, script-like, but ought to use brief headings and so make it more spontaneous-appearing. I followed his advice, and sweated blood, but it seemed to go off okay. I only did a brief sketch of some things happening in Canadian and W. Afr writing, taking the view that both were really Voice of a Land, and that the strained nationalism of our early writing ultimately gives way to true writing which is concerned only with the creation of individual and unique life on the printed page, etc etc. I gave an enthusiastic account of A. Wiseman's 'The Sacrifice,' in this regard, naturally. Blair Fraser[10] was one of the other speakers – he is a very nice guy – and Rumer Godden[11] was another – she was not nearly as formidable as I had imagined she would be. Lovat Dickson is a man in a million. However, I did a terrible thing not long ago – he invited me over to his place for dinner, and it happened his wife was away in Yugoslavia, and I got stoned and wept on his shoulder – how could I? I don't think he minded, in fact I think he was quite pleased in some odd way, so I don't feel too badly (is this an improvement? Yes, I really think it must be, as a few short months ago I would have spent days and days in guilty remorse over this kind of thing).

I went to the wedding of Robert Yeatman, one of the men at Macmillan's, and it was a very posh wedding in the country, at the bride's home, and she seems to come of an ancient and blue-blooded county family. Robert is a very nice guy, and I like him a great deal. It was really interesting to see the people who milled around on the lawn with champagne glasses afterwards – a look at the other side of the fence, you might say. Alan Maclean had been unable to drive me down, as he was arriving late, but asked me beforehand to go back with him, which I did. Muriel Spark[12] was with him, and she turned out to be unexpectedly appealing – rather vixenish, as you might expect, but not having in personal life (at least, to a casual view) the biting wit of her writing. I liked her, anyway. When we left, the bride's father was at the door, bidding guests farewell, and as we tripped lightly out and thanked him etc, he said vaguely (very confused by this time, obviously), 'Oh yes – you were the singers?' Alan, who is the soul of politeness on the surface but underneath has a very non-conformist view and a terrific sense of humour, said no, actually, we weren't the singers, we were – ah – from Macmillan's, as it were. Later, Alan said what a fool he'd been – he ought to have said, 'Yes, we're the singers, and what's more, we haven't been paid yet.' It was a lovely ending to the day, and we sang evangelical hymns and Victorian musical-hall ballads ('She's only a bird in a gilded cage ...' etc) all the way home. Alan is always sober, having once been an alcoholic, and he is the only person I know here, apart from Gus Andrezejewski, who is really a good influence on me. I always remain sober and yet happy when I am with either of them.

Bob Weaver wrote to say he was going on a trip out west, so I expect you've seen him. I like him so much, and wish I hadn't met him at a time when I was slightly demented.

Frances Bolton, the 21 year old daughter of some old friends of Jack's (and, in a sense, mine) has come over to spend the summer with me. The arrangement is that she will take the kids on outings on weekends while they are at school, and on daily outings when they are on holidays, in exchange for room and board, thus providing herself with the opportunity for seeing London and me with the opportunity of (a) writing every day, without my beloved but distracting sprouts around, and (b) getting away to Glasgow for a week, to see a good friend of mine there who is married to a Ghanaian medical student.[13] Also, maybe other weekends elsewhere, if any invitations appear. I'm going to phone Alex Baron and his wife. I liked them so much, but would prefer to talk with them without the kids being there all the time.

The kids are doing well in school, and I am hoping and praying that Jocelyn will get into the Grammar School which we have applied for. We have had the interview with the headmistress, but as 50 more girls are interviewed than there are places for, it is very uncertain. We'll hear in about 2 weeks time. The primary and secondary schools seem better to me than in Canada – a more stimulating and challenging program entirely – not so much Dick and Jane garbage, and they are at least a year ahead in arithmetic. David greatly enjoys his weekly classes in Science, where they do simple experiments and also learn about the planets etc. He has a very scientific mind, and has progressed here in an unbelievable way. I told the kids that since I sold the story to CBC, we would each take £1 and spend it on books, which we did, and Jocelyn got 6 paperbacks, very good ones, an assortment of fiction, but David got all science books ... 'What Is A Solar System,' etc. He spends hours reading them, and then gives forth with all kinds of strange facts about the relative sizes of the earth and the sun, etc.

I have thousands of letters to write, but I have spent almost the whole evening writing to you, because I seemed to have so much to tell you. Please write soon. These communications from members of my tribe mean more to me than anything else, I think. At times, life seems utterly bloody to me, but I have to admit as well that I am getting better at enjoying what is here and now, without asking 'do I have the right to enjoy it?' etc. The Presbyterians will be the death of me, probably, but we struggle on, and so on. Please write. I hope the CBC pays well for the Hong Kong articles.[14]

Love,

Peg

1 Wiseman wrote the foreword to Severyn R. Kulesza, *Modern Riding* (1966), 7–12
2 'My Burglar' was broadcast on CBC Winnipeg's *Prairie Talks* on 29 May 1963.
3 'Where Learning Means Hope: Hong Kong's Canadian Club Does What It Can to Aid Worthy Pupils,' *Weekend Magazine*, 18 May 1963, 18, 20, 45
4 Gus Andrzejewski had introduced Margaret Laurence to the producer of the Hausa Section, BBC African Service, and she had agreed to write ten scripts on worldwide folk tales on some common themes. She was paid a total of £47.
5 'The Crying of the Loons'
6 F. Sherman Baker had been vice-president and editor-in-chief at St Martin's Press.
7 Willis Wing withdrew the manuscript from St Martin's and later succeeded in placing it, *The Tomorrow-Tamer*, and *The Stone Angel* for publication with Knopf.
8 Not traced
9 Horatio Lovat Dickson (1902–87), expatriate Canadian, author, editor, and director of Macmillan in London. He was the first to accept *This Side Jordan* for publication.
10 Blair Fraser (1909–68), Canadian journalist and Ottawa editor of *Maclean's*
11 Pseudonym of British novelist, playwright, and poet Margaret Rumer Godden Haynes-Dixon (b. 1907) whose work was published by Macmillan
12 Scottish novelist (b. 1918) whose best-known work is *The Prime of Miss Jean Brodie* (1961)
13 Nadine Asante, whom Laurence had met in Vancouver
14 In late June, Wiseman recorded five talks for CBC Winnipeg on her China trip, two of which were 'Junk Hunting at Home and Abroad' and 'On Food and Eating.' She was paid $55 for each.

35 Heath Hurst Road
17 August 1963

Dear Adele:

Thanks for your letter – I especially appreciated your comments on my war with the cockroaches. I am happy to report that I won, at least I think so. I have not seen any of the little buggers around for over a week now, so let us hope for the best. Kay[1] departed, none the wiser, and Frances, her daughter, left a week ago, still under the impression that we had beetles. I am relieved to hear that you don't think of lavender as being quite 'me.' It makes me wonder what scent is 'me': could it be the coarse reek of cheap red wine? That, plus the odour of frying meatballs (my domestic side), plus Chanel #5 (my eternally optimistic nature).

Yes, I understand what you mean about not being able to park yourself on me. As a matter of fact, if you did come to London, I would much rather you paid rent for the room, so don't thank me for nothing, kiddo! I don't think it would work out well any other way, and maybe it wouldn't work out well under any circumstances, as we might tend to spend too much time in talking, and also both of us need to be alone a great deal of the time. Anyway, the door is always open, Adele, with or without rent, etc, as I think you know quite well, and I feel the same about whatever place you might be living in. I'm very glad to hear about your teaching job in Montreal.[2] I know quite well what you mean by not wanting to mark all your own papers. I, also, was an anxious marker, and could not put in for more than 15 minutes each essay, considering the length of essay, but in fact used to spend about half an hour on most of them, writing lengthy comments etc. and worrying about the mark I'd assigned. That way, you would not have any time for your own work at all. Maybe you can get some reviewing work to do – a review of a novel for a newspaper doesn't take all that long to do, and although they don't pay much, it is something. Anyway, good luck and blessings, etc.

I think your only trouble with sending the play to Alice Frick[3] is that, while she is undoubtedly a very good judge of what is likely to produce well on radio or TV, the deeper levels would not likely find much of a response with her. I may be doing her an injustice – I'm only going by her comments on books we had both read. Not that I am very goddamn deep, mind you, but – well, hell, you know what I mean. I thought about this after I'd written you, and thought maybe I had been too hasty. But I still have the feeling it might get a better reading here, somewhere.

I'll be getting another novel to read for Macmillan this week, so things may be looking up that way.[4] Also, Robt Yeatmen, of Macmillan's, has arranged for me to have lunch with the woman who is in charge of BBC 'World of Books,' with an eye to possible review jobs. All this is crazy, though, in a way, for this reason – I have come to the conclusion that it would be harmful to too many people to break the whole pattern of my life at this point, and therefore what will probably happen is some kind of compromise, with me living here (I hope – I feel I can't even count on that) part of the time, and part of the time wherever J is working. The only justification I would have for doing otherwise is that I would like to stay here and the hell with everyone else, but I can't really act that way. Ironically, I now think it might be possible, within about a year, for me to earn enough, one way and another, to get by. However, I am trying not to think about all this kind of thing, as it is futile at the moment. The main thing is to get back to work. Since Fran left, I have been keeping regular working hours again. Have done the draft of a story in a week, but it needs a lot of further work. Anyway, it is good to get back to work. Can't contemplate the novel I want to do. I've goofed the beginning of it so many times that all I can do now is put it aside and let it take its own course, if it wants to, sometime. These stories, which I feel are no hell but I am intensely interested in them nevertheless as they are based on childhood persons, are the best thing to do right now. When I say no hell, I only mean they are simple and unfancy, but I care about them. Willis has just sold one of these to Sat Eve Post,[5] and I am elated about the dough. I still have that sneaking feeling that if the Post takes a story, it can't be much good, but I didn't write it for the Post, so what can you do? I mean, what can you do except put down what is there? Anyway, I'm very glad of the cash, needless to say.

The really tremendous news which I got yesterday is that Knopf has taken all 3 of my books! I can hardly believe that it is true, as I had just about given up hope of any of them being taken by an American publisher, especially a publisher of repute, as it were. So this is really good. Everything has now been settled with Jack McClelland, and we are on friendly terms, but I still don't know how he feels about 'Hagar' – he has only recently received the script, so I haven't heard yet. However, I am certain he will take it, now that Knopf has. I am willing to bet that both Knopf and McClelland will say it needs vast alterations, etc, and I am not prepared to do very much in this line, at this point. Am I getting unreasonable, or cynical, or just tired? They don't know any more about it than I do – this is my feeling now. It's written the way I want it written, for better or worse.

Dolores Baron phoned the other day, and I am going to their place for a weekend early in September. I thought it was very nice of her. I'm taking the kids as well, so it was probably brave as well as nice of her.

Please write. And good luck with the job in Montreal. And with everything.

Love,

Margaret

(Can you bear to refer to me as Margaret? This is becoming compulsive with me.) It has nothing much to do with my writing – it's something further back, at least I think so.

p.s. 'The Prophet's Camel Bell' came out here about a week ago. So far no reviews. Let us hope it gets one or two. I am not very impressed with it, as a book, but the photographs are nice. I am kind of disenchanted, as it were, where it is concerned, as I think it is not honest enough. I'll send you a copy when I get the Canadian ones. It had a lovely review on the BBC Somali Service[6] – written by the guy who took the pictures, some slight bias may have crept in!

1 Kaye Bolton, a Vancouver friend
2 Wiseman had been hired on contract by Sir George Williams University to teach first-year composition for the 1963–4 academic year. In September 1963, she was also hired by McGill to teach in the English department at Macdonald College. She taught at Macdonald College until the end of August 1969. She was awarded a leave of absence without pay in 1966–7, financed by the Quebec Ministry of Cultural Affairs.
3 Laurence had met Alice Frick the previous month. Frick had worked for the CBC radio drama department in Toronto from 1942 to 1954. At this time, she was living in London and working on a freelance basis for the BBC in the television drama section.
4 Laurence had begun assessing novel manuscripts for Macmillan and was paid five guineas for each reader's report.
5 She was mistaken. Ladies' Home Journal had bought and was to publish an abridged version of 'To Set Our House in Order,' March 1964, 80–2
6 Not traced

35 Heath Hurst Road
20 September 1963

Dear Adele:

I have been thinking about you a lot, and wondering if you are in
Montreal by now, and teaching, and how you are liking it, etc. I'm very
anxious to hear. I sure hope everything is going okay. Please write. I
know you'll be tremendously busy, beginning the job, but please
scribble a line and let me know how things are.

I seem to have gone into some kind of decline or something. When
I am really honest about it, I have to admit that I have not actually
written anything except one short story in months. Honestly, Adele, at
this point I feel that there are quite a few short stories which I want to
do, and this same damned old novel which I have begun about a
hundred times, and yet I do not do any of it. I don't know why, except
that I feel absolutely beat, for no particular reason. The less I do, the
more tired I feel. I know I will have to snap out of it. I've begun that
novel so bloody often, and each time it doesn't work – something just
isn't right about the approach, although I still feel that something is
there, and that there is a way to do it if I could only hit on it. I must
have written hundreds of pages and thrown them away. Recently, all I
really want to do is sleep. Marvellous escape mechanism, or something.
I sleep for hours, even in the daytime. I just lie in the sunshine, on my
bed (which is right beside the window) and sleep – I am so appalled by
this, as it seems a terrible waste of time. I don't know what the hell is
wrong with me. Whatever I do manage to write not only seems awful,
it *is* awful. I have the feeling that I have been through at least six major
battles and am now exhausted, but God knows I have not been doing
anything with myself all summer, except lazing around and reading and
brooding about things. No doubt this will pass, but inactivity is very
depressing, isn't it? It is not a lack of ideas, apparently, but some kind
of lack of sheer physical energy.

We went to Hove a few weeks ago, for the weekend, to stay with
Alex and Dolores Baron. I like them both so much, and thought it was
so nice of them to invite me down with the kids. They have a lovely
house, which Dolores has spent months in re-decorating, and it really
is beautiful, simple and elegant. I read Alex's last novel, 'The Low Life,'
and liked it very much. They are looking for a small flat in London, as
I think they feel a little isolated down at Brighton – Dolores comes up
to London about once a week, in connection with her work.

Mordecai Richler and his wife[1] came over last evening for dinner. Also Alice Frick, and Donald Bull (Esther Birney's brother). Florence had to go to Victoria station to meet their new Spanish au-pair girl, so she did not arrive until about 9.30, and we had dinner about 10 p.m., by which time I thought I was going to faint with hunger. I liked both of them quite well, although M seems pretty untalkative in the presence of people he doesn't know well. I think he was half sloshed by the time he got here, so maybe that was the trouble. After awhile he opened up and talked about his visit to a Canadian airbase in Germany, about which he's doing an article for Maclean's.[2]

I may be going out to Pakistan for November, if Jack can get the firm to pay my fare.[3] He wants me to go, and it would be a good opportunity to try to settle all these problems about what to do if he keeps on working abroad, re: kids schooling and so on. I don't know. I'm tired of thinking about the whole thing, to tell you the truth. He wants to work abroad, and this is obviously right for him, and I would like to stay here, but obviously can't, and the kids have got to get educated somehow. I suppose we will end up going back to Canada, to some place where none of us want to be, in order to be fair to everybody. British justice. I do not mean that as a crack at anyone, only fate. Nadine, my friend in Glasgow, is going to come down with her baby for the month and look after my kids, which is damn good of her. That is, if the firm will pay my fare.

Knopf does not like the title of 'The Prophet's Camel Bell.' They want to call it either 'The Camel Bell,' which stinks, in my opinion, or 'New Wind In A Dry Land,' which isn't bad, but isn't as good as the original title. However, I don't care very much. I am going to agree to the latter title. They don't like 'Hagar' either, and have suggested either 'Mrs. Shipley' or 'Old Lady Shipley,' both of which are so terrible, in my opinion, that they don't bear thinking about. Macmillan had felt some doubt about 'Hagar,' too, so when this letter arrived with Knopf's suggestions, I brooded violently over the whole thing, and was suddenly struck by the obviously right title, and I now prefer it to 'Hagar,' and am astonished that it did not occur to me six months ago, as it is an image which occurs in the first sentence of the novel and recurs throughout the book, and it is completely suitable, etc. 'The Stone Angel' – do you think it is okay? Macmillan have agreed, although it means a new jacket design, unfortunately. So I hope Knopf will agree, and not insist on either of their suggestions. I know I must not get to the point where I say, 'Go ahead, call it any damn thing you like,' or I will regret it later.

The Somaliland book, as I anticipated, has had very few reviews. A few good ones in The Telegraph, Guardian, etc.[4] But damn few. Some of the reviews in the provincial papers are good for the laughs, if nothing else. One said something like 'What she lacks in writing skill she makes up for in her determination to say nothing which will damage East-West relationships!!' Inscribe it on my tomb – she meant well.

PLEASE WRITE. Are you working at anything? Alice asked about the play again. I told her you had said it was with someone else, at the moment, that's all. My God, how I wish you were here, Adele – you are the only person right now that I would really like to talk to. Anyway, I hope the teaching job is interesting but not too demanding. Please write.

Love,

Margaret

1 Mordecai and Florence Richler lived in London from 1959 to 1972.
2 'The Social Side of the Cold War,' Maclean's, 16 November 1963, 28–9, 44–6
3 Laurence did go to Pakistan in November and wrote five short stories there.
4 David Holloway, 'Travels and Misadventures,' Daily Telegraph, 30 August 1963, and Christopher Wordsworth, 'The Seeing I,' Guardian, 20 September 1963, 9

35 Heath Hurst Road
27 December 1963

Dear Adele –

I am writing to you, not because I owe you a letter but out of pure bloody loneliness, which no doubt you will comprehend. I am due to move in 2 days' time,[1] & with my accustomed sense of panic, I have got everything packed NOW – what in hell am I going to do for the next 2 days?? This morning I went through the crisis period, in which I always feel that everything is impossible & I won't be able to pack all the things we own in the available number of boxes & suitcases. Now, however, I have actually stowed away everything except our pyjamas & toothbrushes & I am sitting here, drinking gin & water (mother's ruin) & wondering (a) how I can ever cope with the complex finances of a 5-bedroom house, & (b) how I can ever learn to light a coal fire, & (c) how one trains an 8-wks old puppy, which is the age ours will be when we get him on Jan. 2nd. If I manage to live through the first month in Elm Cottage, I may be okay. We had a quiet but pleasant Xmas, with 2 Canadian friends coming in for dinner, & on Boxing Day we went to Alice Frick's – she is really a nice person. Jack McClelland writes me that 'The Tomorrow Tamer' will be published in Canada in January – he is rather annoyed that the English edition has been on sale in Vancouver for some time.[2] I don't know how I can make any comment about this – I don't blame him for being mad, but I can't feel Macmillan's were wrong in publishing when they did. I hate being involved in this kind of bickering. I like Jack McC. such a lot, & can't bear to think he might be annoyed with me – but this is my affliction in regard to everybody I like, & one can't please everybody, after all, so you get to the point of feeling – the hell with it, take me or leave me, it's all the same to me – I can't change to suit everyone. The story I thought was coming out in SatEvePost is actually coming out in Ladies Home Journal – they have a joint editorial board. I must be biting the hand that feeds me, but I keep thinking – if it is coming out in LHJ, it must be a pretty rotten story. How can you win? I had to speak to Macmillan's salesmen last week about my writing – traumatic experience, or so I thought it would be. Actually it was okay, & I gassed on about *The Stone Angel*, & afterwards they presented me with a copy of *The Golden Bough*, which I thought was very handsome of them. I feel like saying 'You should sell my books because I need the money' – but I didn't.

Love,

M

P.S. PLEASE WRITE! (To Elm Cottage)

1 Laurence had rented the summer home of Alan Maclean's family in the village of Penn. It was to be her home for the next ten years and became affectionately known as 'Elmcot.'
2 *The Tomorrow-Tamer* had been published in England in the first week of October.

Elm Cottage, Beacon Hill,
Penn, Nr. High Wycombe,
Bucks., England
17 January 1964

Dear Adele –

It is precisely midnight, and I am sitting in the kitchen, trying to get the coal fire to go. It went out this afternoon because I neglected it, on account of the fact that David & I were putting down lino in the lavatory. Now the bloody goddamn stove has been refusing to burn all evening, & I am determined to get it back into some kind of life before I go to bed, or else it will be too horrible to be imagined, in the cold grey dawn. Everything about the cottage is fine except for 2 things – (1) the coal boiler in the kitchen, which heats the water for the bathroom & also heats both bathroom & kitchen, & which I find *impossibly* difficult to deal with; & (2) the fact that I keep feeling I am going to go broke in heating this house in winter. (I thought I would write longhand so I wouldn't waken the dog, but it's no use.) Honestly, to sum things up, what I appear to have taken on is this: an old and certainly uneconomical house, which I think is going to cost the earth to heat, and which has various drawbacks such as the coal boiler, but which feels really like home to me nevertheless and in which I do not seem to feel lonely even though I am by myself most of the time. It is a house which people have loved and cared about, and one feels that, somehow. It was rented to American service families for some time, and has been very much neglected, and now it really needs attention and work. The livingroom has lovely red tile floors, a bay window overlooking the garden, and a beautiful fireplace. There are 5 bedrooms, one of which I hope ultimately to be able to rent. It really is a marvellous house, and I love it, and I think we will be extremely happy here if I manage to survive the first few months. At the moment I am in the last stages of sheer physical exhaustion, having been working harder than I have ever done in my entire life, turfing out old junk, scrubbing floors and walls, painting woodwork and furniture, making curtains, re-finishing old oak tables etc etc, as well as getting the children outfitted for their new schools and attempting to maintain some kind of semblance of calm during their period of re-adjustment, and also looking after the dog, who is only 8 weeks old and requires almost as much attention as a human infant. In the long run, however, maybe you are right when you say that I will always think that these crises are the end of the world but won't entirely collapse, etc. I was so damn glad to get your letter. I had been feeling that I was doomed to spend the rest of my life doing nothing but domestic work, but your letter heartened me considerably. Actually, the domestic work is not done with any sense of grudge, as I find that I really love this place and would like to fix it up properly – it needs loving care, and will, I think, reward anyone who gives it that. I would like to stay here forever, but probably that will not be possible. Anyway, I am not thinking of the future, as I don't know at all what will happen. The kids love the house, and are very pleased to be here, as they each have their own quite large room, and also a playroom downstairs, with plenty of cupboards for toys etc, and a large garden which promises to be a good thing in the warmer weather. David loves his new school, as it is very small and therefore not difficult to get used to. Jocelyn will be okay, also, I think, although her school is very large (over 1000 girls) and therefore more difficult to enter as a new pupil. I would like not to have to change their schools again for awhile. But when Jack and also all my in-laws write to me, they all say 'how marvellous that you only had to sign a lease for a year' – the subtle pressures upon one are enormous. Also, if I go broke in the midst of this deal I won't really have any choice except to return to that goddamn house in Vancouver. He who pays the piper calls the tune. However, I am *not* worrying about money at the moment, really – something may turn up, and any money I've ever made has been made accidentally anyway, not by trying consciously to make it. I had a story in the last issue of Tamarack Review,[1] and Bob Weaver paid me more for it than I had expected, which was certainly very nice of him. I haven't done any writing since moving, needless to say, as I've been totally absorbed in getting the house into livable condition. Another two weeks should see most of the basic work done. I got an advance copy of 'The Stone Angel,' and it looks okay, although the cover is rather a drab shade of brown. It is coming out in March, I think. Don't know when in Canada.[2]

The dog has begun to wail – oh God. He has been very good the past few nights, but is really like a baby and does kick up a fuss sometimes at night. His name is Ringo – he is named after one of the Beatles, pop singers. Jocelyn is a Beatle fan. Their most popular record is 'Twist and Shout,' and believe me, our little Beatle has certainly done his share of twisting and shouting. However, he is also very appealing, and the kids adore him. I, too, am kind of fond of him, God knows why, as he is such a nuisance.

When you say your disorganized life, what do you mean? Your lectures etc sound as though they are very demanding, in terms of time, etc. What about work? I hope you are getting more done than I am these days. I haven't even typed out the stories I wrote in Pakistan. I tried to write some very short ones, for the CBC, but it didn't work out, so I have abandoned the idea of doing anything except writing whatever comes along. I know what I want to tackle for the next novel but the thought still scares the hell out of me. Maybe this will pass. I wish you were here to talk with. Please write.

Love,

Margaret

1 'Mask of Beaten Gold,' *Tamarack Review* 26 (Winter 1963): 3–21. She had been paid £32.
2 *The Stone Angel* was published in Canada on 23 May.

Elm Cottage
25 June 1964

Dear Adele:

I was so damn glad to get your letter, but appalled to think that I had not written to you for some considerable time.[1] I find this hard to believe, probably because I so often talk to you, and sometimes one forgets that you aren't hearing what I'm saying! I don't know how I could manage in life, if it weren't for these conversations with absent friends. Is a tape-recorder the answer, I ask myself? Probably not. Anyway, recently I have done absolutely nothing in the way of writing, but have been totally involved in what is known as domestic life, of one kind and another. Jack arrived back on leave the beginning of June, and I met him in Athens. We spent 12 days in Greece, I feeling as usual somewhat guilty about enjoying the marvellously beautiful country while knowing that about 99% of Greeks are earning less per day than I spend on cigarettes, etc. But in fact it is a lovely country, geographically. What I liked best was the sight of wheat fields, ripe already in June, that pale white-gold of ripe wheat, with scarlet poppies growing in among the grain. Also I liked the wine, which is by me the best in the world. Also the cheese is the best, and the bread, and the olives. If I lived in Greece, I would exist on a diet of bread, cheese, olives and retzina, and would never be sober. Lucky for me I live in a country where wine is not cheap. We decided we would have to compromise, as I prefer to go to one spot and stay there and look around rather slowly, and Jack likes to zoom around like lightning and see a million places in a week. So we spent half our time in going on a bus tour around various parts of Greece, and the other half in sun-bathing and swimming at a beach near Athens. It worked out very well, and we both enjoyed both halves of the trip, to our mutual surprise. I thought the bus trip would probably be hell, but actually I did enjoy it. It was called, splendidly, the 'Four Day Ultra-Classical Tour' – try and beat that for a title! I am not all that keen on ancient ruins, and found them all only moderately interesting until Mycenae,[2] which really hit me. The stone roadway underneath the Lion Gate is grooved with the wheels of those distant chariots, and it is not so very difficult to hear Agamemnon returning, in the bitter dust and heat of the day, expecting with a calm and giant egotism to find all well within his fortress and nothing altered from the day he left. It was the only time in the trip when I was compelled to break away from the group (I tried very hard to *not* break away at any point) – and I went off and climbed the hill, where the tour wasn't taken, to the wreck of the palace on top of the mountain. Nothing there, and yet it was all still there. I thought something idiotic such as – thank God, alone at last – when all of a sudden up popped an entire family from behind one of the massive rock walls, and a small boy said in my own speech and accent, 'Hi.' So I said 'Hi,' where Agamemnon fell, and didn't know, really, which had the most meaning for me personally, the kid who spoke in a way I could understand, or the King of Men,[3] heroic but blinder than Oedipus, and the compelled queen. All very weird. The beach near Athens was lovely, and we did not do very much except eat and swim, and that suited me just fine. Now, back at Elm cottage, we are very busy with trying to see old friends and also some new friends of mine, but things seem to have been settling into some kind of workable something. Jack seems to like the house, thank God, and has decided to sell our house in Vancouver and make this his base for the next few years. He'll be going back to B.C. for about 2 weeks early in July, and then will come back here. He doesn't know yet where he will be going next, but possibly Africa again. I will stay here with the children. No need to repeat all the reasons to you – you know them all. Whatever we do isn't going to be perfect, but the main thing is to hold everything together somehow, or at least that is the way it seems to both of us at this point. A lot of it is up to me, to be at least reasonably realistic and calm, and actually I am trying, although still with the feeling that my best is none too good, but I suppose intention must count for something, or so I hope.

Re: Canada Council – thanks for your encouraging tirade, friend, but honestly I cannot and won't apply to them again unless I am in really dire financial need (at which point it wouldn't be any use, I know). I guess it is my pride or something. But I do also feel that I don't at this stage need the money desperately, so have some reservations in that direction as well. Anyway, it is too late for this year's set of applications. Please do not think I am a nitwit about this, Adele. It is only a kind of cultural oddity, my reaction to the Can. Council. It's something I can't help. When the chips are down, alas, I have many of Hagar's characteristics – I cannot really bear to feel beholden to anyone. I do not think of this as a virtue, I may say – I think it is an affliction.

I loved your description of your furniture re-finishing. I sympathize from the depths of my heart. That paint-and-varnish-remover is pure poison. Also, isn't it odd how one can become involved so desperately in something like re-doing a piece of furniture? Or doing anything. I had the same wild energy when I fixed up the house here. David and I put down the linoleum as though we had been possessed by demons. Now I look at it, sometimes, from Jack's professionally careful viewpoint, and I see all the dozens of carpet tacks which we pounded in, and which wouldn't be there if we'd done the thing *properly*. But what the hell? If we hadn't done something, we'd still have been walking around on the bare floorboards upstairs. My definition of success – something that, however ghastly, is better than what was there before. All my definitions are getting simpler and simpler as the years go by – soon I will be speaking only in words of one syllable, probably.

Hope you saw Bob Weaver when he was in Montreal. I think he has done more good to Canadian writers than the Can. Council. I also like him very much, partly because I think he is a courageous man, who seldom complains. PLEASE WRITE. PLEASE WRITE IMMEDIATELY. IF NOT SOONER. What is this about which you speak with hope?

Love,

Margaret

p.s. give my love to Miriam, please.
p.s.2. I liked where you said you weren't much good at screwing tables. That line absolutely made my day.

1 Laurence had last written Wiseman on 10 April 1964.
2 Site of the advanced culture of mainland Greece whose civilization flourished between 1550 and 1100 BC. In Homer's *Iliad*, Agamemnon was the king of Mycenae and the Greek leader during the Trojan War. When he returned home, he was murdered by his wife Clytemnestra, and her lover. Laurence's experience is described in 'Sayonara, Agamemnon,' collected in *Heart of a Stranger* (1976).
3 This epithet is used in Book III of *The Iliad*.

Elm Cottage
12 September 1964

Dear Adele:

Where to begin? First, I hope you got my cable okay.[1] I thought that my first reaction to the play simply could not wait for 7 days or however long it takes an airletter. Which may be silly, but that is how I felt. Anyway, I think the play is terrific, Adele, and I also think it is one of those plays which communicate various things to various people – reactions can be, legitimately, as varied as readers, because one tends to take from it the things in it which are closest to oneself.[2] That is true of every work of art, probably. For me, the two things which emerged the most strongly were: the beautiful way in which each character comes across on both levels – ie. the symbolic and philosophical, plus the human individual flesh-and-blood level; and secondly, the way in which an absolutely straight appraisal of the human condition is possible, without any false idealism or sentimentality, and yet with a final affirmation of man's worth and value.

Previously, before I read the play, I had felt for a long time, as I told you, that it might be a good idea to have it published even if it could not be produced immediately. I now freely admit that I was wrong. I can see now why you have felt, yourself, all along, that the thing *had* to be produced. It does have to be produced. That is its natural medium – the theatre and the human voice, and it demands production. I think it comes across well in reading, and that it should also be published, but I feel very strongly now that it must be produced. Bob Weaver wrote to me recently and told me (among other things) that he and Esse Ljungh[3] were considering the play for radio and also that he hoped to show it to some theatrical groups in Toronto. I'm very glad, and hope that something may come of it. The only question I have about radio is that I think it would be better for TV, and best for stage, as it was intended. I think something would be lost in a radio production – maybe because I would like to *see* Hitzig and Yesh and Marina, etc. Especially Hitzig, who *must* be seen. He *is* seen, in fact, in the mind, but one feels that a visual production would present the thing as a total effect.

The humour is good, true, sharp, and points up in some way the pain of the whole. The play is painful to a really terrible degree, by the third act, but the final impression is one of affirmation of the individual's ability to earn his humanity, as well as a recognition of the evil (what else can you call it?) inherent not only in *them* but in *myself*, for what the play really says in the end is that it is never only a question of *them*. At least this is what it says to me.

I found the portrait of Cass a very frightening one, simply because he is capable of such deception and self-deception, and sometimes in dealing with this kind of thing, both in others and in oneself, one gets the feeling that it is very difficult to see him (it; these qualities) in any sort of honesty ... that one is in great danger, always, of being taken in.

The individual man came across as both dangerous and pathetic (the poetry he attempted; his latching onto 'his art,' etc). I also thought it was fantastically good the way you conveyed the insecure man's lust for power, combined with his basic fear of actually seizing power, combined with his violent fantasies, combined with the way in which he hid his *real* cruelties from himself; combined with his sado-maso-chism, which is always an attribute in some way or other of the authoritarian figure – this was brought out to just the right degree, in the scene in the cabin with Dora, where he begs her to punish him.

Nix I saw as Cass's more clearly dark self – the devil, in fact, cynical and un-human in an almost bewitched way, and this was one of the things in the play which for me had some echoes of Moby Dick. Other echoes of Melville – the references to Leviathan, I *know* the Biblical background of this, but in this setting it has for me connotations of the white whale as well, and the speech of sudden intense poetry of some of the passengers and crew. I think that these, plus Old Testament references, enrich the whole thing. When I say 'echo,' I do not mean you are purposely echoing anyone, not Melville or the O.T. – simply that these things, as one's roots, are *there*, and that they strike chords in the reader's mind, and reach deep into hidden places.

The character of Yesh comes across very movingly as himself, and very effectively as a kind of Jesus figure. This aspect is excellently done, because it is never overdrawn, never hammered at – it is suggested simply and with dignity, and left at that.

Abel, who is The Man, comes across with a kind of growing power. At first, he is only himself, a young seaman who is unsure of himself, who isn't the kind of man you would notice much, one way or another. He grows and develops in the reader's mind as he grows within himself and discovers that humanity has to be earned. Both sides of him (both as Abel and as The Man) are shown with honesty – no attempt is made to slur over the dark side or to evade the genuine love of the man through fear of being thought too emotional (this is a great fear of writers now, I think). The thing about Abel is that he actually *is* capable of destroying the child. In panic, in desperation, in a state of semi-hysteria, he could have thrown the child overboard. He could have done it. He didn't, but that isn't the point. He is shocked, himself, when Marina sees something about him that he doesn't see himself. On the other hand, he is also capable of going with Marina and dying with her because – is there ever any other reason? – he loves her. His dual nature has to be accepted, but he is portrayed as a being who possesses free will. He can choose. He cannot help containing within himself the component parts of good and evil (or whatever words one chooses to describe the creation and the destruction), but he can *help what he does.* He is a broken reed – he isn't a hero; he could capitulate at any moment. But he can choose love rather than hate. And once in his life, he does. He is tremendously moving as a character simply because his role as everyman is always and at every moment accompanied by the recognition of him, by the reader, as himself, as Abel Green.

Hertzl, to me, has some suggestions of Abraham in 'The Sacrifice,' and possibly this is because (although they are totally different men in so many ways), both contain the strong traditional faith. Herzl and Hitzig, as brothers, seem to me a fascinating presentation of two facets of the Jews ... the traditional religious aspect, strong, moving, sometimes oddly archaic and yet with a phenomenal ability to survive; and the contemporary aspect ... cynical, ironic, and yet in the end with a compassion hidden under wisecracks and a kind of bitter wisdom.

The character of Hitzig is the major character creation in the play, in my opinion. I think he is marvellously developed – his initial toughness and accompanying innocence, his gradual realization of the situation's reality, his temptation to get himself out and to leave the others, his final affirmation of his belonging with them, whatever happens, and most of all, the depth of the man's love combined with his constant seeing of himself in all his ludicrous aspects and his absolute lack of phoniness and his wry wisdom. His growing love for Dora is beautifully done – this love affair is the reverse of anything romantic, and because of this, it is (to me, anyway) enormously moving in all its odd ways – it is ludicrous, mad, humiliating, exultant, plain and earthbound, two middleaged people who are both very far from gods, goddesses, heroes, heroines (such as the tales Hitzig spins to Dora) – and yet in some way in the end it becomes Love itself, a mystery like creation. In the end, it is only love (the only direct contact with others, the only means of recognition that Others exist) which binds men to life. 'Love-bound,' finally, seems to me to convey the sense of the word 'bound' in two ways – 'bound' in the sense of *moving towards*; and 'bound' in the sense of *being anchored by* and even *being tied and confined by*.

The theme of redemption is dealt with in a way which was to me extremely thought-provoking, and I felt that the juxtaposition of Abel and Yesh, in the end, was very effectively done. Yesh, terribly touching and yet in some way curiously dated, remains (as himself and as Christ) alive among the gentiles. Abel dies among the Jews in order to earn *the*

man, the state of being a man. There is in the end no symbolic redemption and no Messiah ... only individual men earning their humanity, as
Abel earns it, and as Hitzig also earns it. Humanity, like freedom, like
salvation, isn't really transferable – either you discover it for yourself or
you don't. But the very act of one man's finding it, and earning it – this
is, in every way that matters, hope.

I expected the play to be too long, probably because you had been
rather downcast about it at one time and had said various people
questioned whether it was practical, in a produceable way. I really do
not have any qualifications to say even one word about theatre at all,
but in the reading of it, it did not strike me as too long. Very little could
be cut, it seemed to me, although perhaps something would change to
some extent in the production – details, I mean, not anything essential.
But nothing is superfluous; everything is there because it is needed and
because it has meaning. I do not know what the hell kind of theatre it
would make because that isn't my medium. I only know that in the
reading it has pace, that it moves in the sense of events and that it
moves also in the sense of inner things gradually becoming outer and
showing themselves. One criticism of it might possibly be that some
parts are too philosophical and even too obscure. I don't think this is so,
because it seems to me that contemporary theatre (and novels) must necessarily be trying to do a multitude of different things at the same time
and must therefore rely to some extent upon the viewer's or reader's
willingness to enter in and try to see and feel what is there – I think
that the significant change in English novels within our lifetime has
been the growing realization on the part of novelists of the truly
ambiguous and complex and uncertain nature of reality, and an attempt
to convey this in words while at the same time to convey individual
persons in that spontaneous and un-thought-out way – in other words,
to be saddled with the knowledge of what your writing means, and at
the same time to be able to forget that sufficiently in order to convey
flesh-and-blood in all its surprises. It seems to me that this is what you
have tried to grapple with in the play, and I think it has come off. In the
places where you have passengers and seamen [—].[4] In the deepest
sense, you appear to me [—] about the same things which concern me
and no doubt concern every writer, in some way or other – the ways in
which people continue to damage one another, and the ways in which
sometimes there can be healing; the basic importance of tradition as
one's place of belonging in a specific way, and the basic unimportance
of creeds and all these differences when one human is face to face in

any real way with another. My God, now I am stricken with self doubts and wonder if I have mis-interpreted all this? It doesn't matter, I guess, in one way. This is what I took from it, that's all. This is what it said to me. It will be less than what you intended, probably, and in some ways different – maybe that isn't important. Anyway, it spoke. In the end, what moves me the most is Hitzig seeing that there isn't any easy way out, and he and Dora trying to bargain for the other's life – this is utterly convincing; they don't do it because it is right or because they ought to – only because they cannot bear to see the other person cease to be; but in the end everyone can bear everything because what else is there to do? Only death ends it, but Herzl, going back to die, is greater than the Herzl who would have died if the boot had descended before. That is all that matters. It *has* to matter – this is the essence of our faith, without which 'life' ceases to be a different word from 'death.'

I have become rather emotional, I guess. It is because the play moved me very much. Anyway, write and let me know your reactions to my reactions, etc. Have I seen something of what you were trying to get across, or am I too subjective? I don't know, and in a way I don't care. All this is what it said to me. PLEASE WRITE.

Love,

Margaret

p.s. do you want the copy of the play back or not?

P.S.2. I'm not sure I understand the exact significance of Hitzig's voice at the end – 'No whalesblood on the hook?' but it has the evocative power of some poetry – it is eerie and moving, and it carries suggestions of the mystery at the heart of things. This is my first reaction – further thought will probably reveal other things as well in that part.

1 Laurence had cabled earlier in the day: 'FINISHED READING PLAY   IT IS TERRIFIC LETTER FOLLOWING   LOVE MARGARET.'
2 Wiseman's play *The Lovebound: A Tragi-Comedy* is set in late summer 1939 aboard an ancient freighter crowded with Jews who are fleeing Europe and are subsequently refused asylum in the Americas.
3 Esse Ljungh was a producer in the drama department at CBC Toronto.
4 The left-hand corner of the final page of the letter has been torn and lost.

> [1217 Drummond Street
> Apartment 21
> Montreal, Quebec]
> 23 September 1964

Dear Margaret,

Funny how when you most want to you find it hardest to express yourself. Yes, I got your wire & remarkable, – (because so acutely aware of & understanding of so much that I was trying to do) – letter, & found myself simply unable to reply because I can hardly believe it nowadays when somebody really gets it. I had just, when your wire came, heard from Mac Ross[1] in the nicest, sweetest, most apologetic way, that though it was in some ways a moving & impressive piece he was distressed by the cruel way I treated certain aspects, that I handled a subject worthy of compassion with lack of compassion, that I revealed an unbelievable depth of cynicism, that Hitzig is a Bob Hopeish[2] talking caricature. Cass is too much of a caricature to 'be convincing either as a person or as a symbol,' that he, – & someone he showed the play to, someone who knows people in the theatre, feel that the 'dialogue is over intellectualized and that the *people* are dwarfed by this,' that Abel's 'all for love substitution of himself for Yesh in the death-car' struck him as 'a rabbit-out of the hat piece of (plot) trickery at the end.' Poor man was terribly upset at the idea that he might be hurting my feelings. How could he know of the immense, frustrated bafflement his comments produced? Of course, it's pointless arguing. You're right; people either get it or they don't. One thing about this; people respond in extremes. I could feel that he was genuinely upset by the thing. Everybody who's seen it seems to have reacted with a degree of violence one way or the other. This is partly why I am more determined than ever that more people should have the opportunity to react. It belongs in the public domain. But I really am baffled about how to push it. I seem to have no talent for the peddling part of the business. By the way, Mac Ross wished me every good luck with it, & I believe him. I'm grateful for his honesty; he was not destructive, – really rather hurt, for some reason, & afraid of hurting me.

But can you understand how I felt when hard on his letters I received your wire & letter? You know how one tends to disbelieve positive reactions. When I got your wire, I thought, 'Well, she's my friend; maybe she's just being loyal.' (I was not casting aspersions on your literary judgment or honesty; just reacting with characteristic ebullient self-confidence). But your letter was too detailed for that; it was such a contrast, – accusing me of love instead of cruelty, of compassion instead of coldness & of various other qualities to offset my cynicism. Well kid, what can I say? Except thanks. When I see you I'll say much more. I can probably answer some of your queries more sensibly in person, just as I'm saving some of my queries for when I see you. At least I have the feeling that since you & a few others have actually read *my* play it does exist, and even if some of your interpretations are partly unexpected, they are still of *my* play, & logical to me, – not of some other thing, and are as valid as my interpretations. As long as the thing is accepted as itself in the public domain. What baffles me are all the readings of some other play. Well, okay, if only it is off my hands & where it belongs. If it's a true work it will fight its own battles.

I don't know yet what Bob Weaver has to say about it. A letter from the CBC was forwarded to me in Florida and must have arrived after I left. I've just written to ask Bob if it was from him, & if so, please to send me another copy.[3]

You can hang on to your copy of the play if you like, I have plenty more. The little note of ownership refers to the content, not the copy. I used it because so far I've only got it copyrighted in Canada, not the U.S. I'm going about that now, so on all copies I send I underline the obvious, & cause confusion.

Personal matters: things aren't going so well with my family at this point. Esther, my sister-in-law, Harry's wife, is very drastically ill. That's why I was in Florida. My parents are there now. At the moment there has been some remission, & we pray and hope. Hope seems to be strong enough to keep itself alive; perhaps it can be miraculously strong enough to keep someone you love alive too.

Term has begun again. This year, after paring away my extra teaching chores in the hope that I'll have more time to write, I find that I have a much tougher schedule on my regular job, must make the trek out 5 times a week, and am teaching in addition to two survey classes, (first year), a second year course in Modern Lit. Hey ho. I suppose I'll manage. And maybe I will get some writing done.

This has been a very egocentric letter. Please forgive. And reply, please, soon. I enjoyed your article in The Star.[4] It's good to read good sense well written.

love to the kids & Jack, & you!

Adele

1 Malcolm Ross
2 American entertainer (b. 1903)
3 Weaver did send a copy of his 4 September letter in which he told Wiseman that
   the two copies of her play had arrived safely, and that he and Esse Ljungh were
   going to be reading it as soon as possible.
4 'What's Novel about Canadian Novelists?' *Montreal Star*, 19 September 1964,
   Entertainment section, 2–3

Elm Cottage
2 October 1964

Dear Adele:

I'm terribly sorry to hear about Esther, as I had not realized before that
it was so serious, although you had mentioned that she was ill. Nothing
can be said – absolutely nothing, and we know this, but still I feel some
compulsion to say – I don't know what. I guess just that I'm thinking
of you, and all the family, and really hoping that she will get better, if
that is possible. There is so damn much pain that one hesitates to touch
anyone else's, in case you increase it, but with people you care about
you have to take that chance, I guess, just to let them know you wish
that everything was all right for them, even if it can't be.

I was, needless to say, intensely interested in your reactions to my
reactions re: the play. And in some way, greatly relieved that you did
feel I was talking about the play, not about something else. I don't know
what to think about Malcolm Ross's reactions, Adele – I find them very
puzzling, as 'cruelty' would be absolutely the last word which would
occur to me in connection with the play. How can he not have seen?
This is, of course, the question which I suppose has to occur at some
point, with someone you love and/or admire and who just has not at
all seen what you thought was there, in the writing. You've had this
before, I know, and I had it (traumatic experience, or something, in my
case) with Jack's reactions to The Stone Angel, which so shook me that
I had to put the script away for a year, and even tried (maybe) to half
get rid of it by packing it off with all the old tennis shoes in that parcel
we sent from your place and then worrying myself sick for 3 months
because I was sure it was lost in the post and there wasn't another copy.
All I know is that all this business damn near killed me (there were
other things as well, but this was one) and this wasn't because I
expected him to *like* it or even cared whether he did or not – what
bothered me was that he was apparently reading some other novel, not

the one I thought I'd written, and that what I was saying just did not communicate at all, not any part of what I saw in it. Anyway, I can now accept the fact that people's languages aren't the same, that's all. I have the feeling with Malcolm Ross that he is looking at your play from some quite different outlook, almost that he is thinking in some quite different idiom or something. My feeling was that his remarks seemed – is this an odd word to use? – dated. I thought – yes, that's the way people might have reacted at one time but not *now*. Not, I would have thought, now that (if nothing else) the whole mainstream of American (including Canadian) writing has been forced to express through bitter wisecracks some things which are too terrifying to be done justice to in any other way. We cannot risk, at this point, sentimentality – the situation is too serious for that. I'm thinking of Malcolm's comments on Hitzig and Cass, which strike me as having missed the point entirely. The thing I thought you achieved with Hitzig was that the quality of gentleness came through – that it wasn't wisecracks to the core, despite all his defenses, and this is something which many writers can't do at all – eg. Richler, where the wisecracks *aren't* made to reveal something else (except maybe in *Duddy Kravitz*). I like his work, but this is his limitation. Not yours.

I would so much like to see you and talk with you, about so god-damn many things. You have said in three letters recently, 'when I see you ...' etc., and so I am wondering if you have by any chance got some kind of plans for coming to England? I sincerely hope so. If you do think you may be able to get here in the near future, please remember that there is a room at Elm Cottage for you, for as long as you want to stay. If by any chance you could get here with a view to doing some work, if you wanted or were willing to live outside London, you could live here. I know there is this danger of you and I talking too much, and not working enough, but I don't really think that would happen.

I am still messing around with the beginning of something, but not with any great luck so far. However, I am not without hope. At the moment, working is a bit ludicrous, as I feel I'm no hell of a wife as it is, and can only try to concentrate on this aspect for the next month, as J will be leaving for Somaliland on Nov. 1st.

Please write. And try to clear enough time for yourself, to do your own work, or else if possible to move out for a time. If you should ever want to come here, kiddo, for any lengthy period of time, please do not think that this would in any financial way be a difficulty for me – I would charge you for your board, although no rent, okay? By the way, my new tenants are working out nicely – I've rented the flat to a very young couple, the guy in the Navy and home only weekends, and the girl a nicely easy-going kid with whom I get along fine. This is £5 p.w. but of course I have to pay income tax on it. Still, I hope it will pay for the heating and light, over the year.

Did I tell you about the woman's magazine article I did?[1] I thought it was terrible, but they accepted it and paid me quite a lot of money for it. I was pretty ashamed of it, though, and won't ever tackle that kind of thing again. (Unless I am really broke). My financial position is so peculiar that probably only another Scots Presbyterian could see my point of view, but never mind.

I'm glad I can keep the copy of the play. PLEASE WRITE.

Love,

Margaret

p.s.   the kids are fine – Jocelyn rapidly turning into a teen-ager, and David still absorbed with Hornby trains, Meccano, and tropical fish (alas).

1 'Mrs Stephens and Her Adopted Family' earned Laurence £157 and was apparently published in the *Woman's Mirror*, but it has not been traced.

Elm Cottage
19 November 1964

Dear Adele:

I've been composing bits of letters to you in my head for the past 2 weeks, but not alas on the typewriter – you know how it is. It was only when I got your letter this morning that I realized how long it had been since I got your previous letters. Anyway, I'm sorry I haven't replied sooner. The reason is that after Jack left,[1] on Nov. 2nd, I felt very depressed, thinking in many ways I should have gone to Africa with him, but I couldn't, etc etc, and all the complexities, and how much better one's intentions always are than one's performance, and all that kind of jazz, and I realized then quite abruptly that I had been in fact brooding about all this almost steadily for two years, and had more or less been doing fragments of work on the side, as it were, and I knew suddenly that I had to quit thinking and start working again or I would be a dead duck. So I started in on a short story the next day, and I haven't surfaced since, until today. It feels good to be working again, and also I feel suddenly quite cheerful about everything, and not so panic-stricken as previously. I don't know if the story is any good or not, but anyway, it is finished, although impossibly long and must be cut by about 10 pages, but God knows how. I've re-written it several times already, but it is still much too long. Maybe one of these days I will have the guts to tackle again the novel that I'm still *certain* is there. It's there, but will it emerge? I guess this relates to the quotation from Northrop Frye,[2] which I thought was intensely interesting. It seems to me that part of the difficulty in beginning anything is to relax enough to stop thinking and let the people go free and move by themselves, etc. All the thinking has been done beforehand, and will be done again in re-writing, which is a strictly analytical process, it seems to me – but in the first writing of anything, I often have this kind of mindless and disembodied feeling – do you? I feel as though, if I stop to think about it or wonder if I can do it, then I won't be able to. And in fact, I am trying not to read over anything while I'm writing it, not until it is finished in the first draft, because once I begin reading what I've written that day, it all seems like crap to me, and then I throw it out and start all over again and the same thing happens, and I don't get past paragraph one. But if I don't read it at all, until it's all out, then sometimes the story has been caught to some extent and put down, surrounded though it may be (and always is) by excess verbiage and sheer nonsense. This seems a very wasteful way of writing, but I don't seem able to do it any other way except just by putting down every damn thing that comes unbidden into my head and then sorting it all out afterwards. If I try to plan it out too neatly, and to avoid all this effort, then it comes out as stilted and false. My God, what a profession. I think it's like operating in two different gears or something – writing it for the first time, you're not working so much with your intelligence as with – hell, I don't know – intuition or something. But when you re-write it, you go into a different gear and become very critical and all that. Once I start writing something, I find it very hard to emerge and come out of it – don't you? It is as though the real world were fictional, and the inner world the real one. Everything seems very strange, and I have to take the dog for a walk and try to regain a footing here. I think I suffer from inertia – that is the only definition I can remember from High School Science ... 'Inertia is the tendency of a moving body to continue moving, or of a body at rest to remain at rest.' That is the story of my life!

I'm glad your classes are going okay, even though filled with so much routine work. Strange that you've got Tom Bolton in one of your classes. I hope he gets through.

Listen – PLEASE DON'T WRITE TOO MUCH OF YOUR NOVEL IN YOUR HEAD. Yes, I've written novels in my head – several (novels, i.e., not heads). Get it down, or nobody else will be able to see it. And there are quite a few of us who would like to, remember. You will, I know. I wish you had more time to work quietly at it without being bothered by finances, other jobs, personal troubles, etc, but this is true of us all, I guess, and maybe if we were living in some cosy cocoon, nothing would happen inside the head, either. God knows. Anyway, I hope you can save enough time for yourself, to get going on the novel. I was so damn glad to hear that you may be coming to England enroute to Israel next year. I am really lighting candles hopefully for that. I think the chances of my seeing you in Canada are pretty slender, to say the least. Anyway, if you do go to Israel, please try to work it so you can stay in England for a week or so on the way.

It must have been interesting to meet Irving Layton.[3] I like his poetry because I have the feeling, probably erroneous, that I can understand it. He must be a strange combination of genuine poet and terrific publicity-stuntman. At one time I think I would have found him intimidating, but not any more. I am getting tougher as I get older, I think.

I've been doing some book reviews for the BBC. They don't pay very well, but it is something, and also quite good experience. I hate recording them, as I get a very shut-in feeling in those little studios with no windows, and also I find it hard to read a script and make it sound reasonably spontaneous. I think the BBC likes my Canadian accent. Nice to cash in on one's nationality at some point. I've also been doing quite a bit of publisher's reading for Macmillan, and I rather like doing that, although I feel a weighty sense of responsibility when it comes to the really awful books, as I can hear someone else making similarly cutting remarks about a book of mine. I've just finished a report on what is probably the worst novel I've ever read.

Alex and Delores were down for Sunday lunch, the week before Jack left. It was nice to see them again. Alex always seems such a genuinely good person to me, and with a kind of hard-won wisdom, somehow. The kids and I are going to stay with them at Hove in a few weeks time, just for the weekend.

Had a letter from Jack, from Mogadiscio – he thinks he is going to like the job, and he is very happy to be back in the tropics. That is really the only place where he feels at all happy, you know. It is just too bad that I feel the reverse about it, as about so many things, at this point. Never mind. Things could have worked out much worse than they have, for both of us. This can't really be discussed in a letter.

The kids are fine. Jocelyn really looks like a young teenager now, and is getting much older in her concepts, quite suddenly, it seems. David still works on his many projects, and has just finished putting electric lights into our large dollhouse.

Please write soon. Also, let me know what's happened re: the play. I was talking to Alex about it, and told him what I thought of it, etc, and he said, very suddenly, that it had just struck him it might be very good for radio – the theatre of the mind, he said. Anyhow, good luck. In many ways it must be difficult for you to concentrate all your forces on any new work while you are still connected with the play. I wonder what about possibilities of its being done here in England?

Love from us all,

Margaret

ps. The editor of Woman's Mirror(!) which printed that ghastly article of mine, has just phoned to say would I like to do another article, this time on my own subject, and I have said I will. I must be mad. But honestly, Adele, there are 2 things involved – (a) money (naturally), and (b) I must keep some contacts, apart from the kids and personal friends, with the external world or I will become some kind of eccentric recluse. ps. what about your family situation? how is Esther?

1 Jack Laurence had gone to Somalia.
2 Northrop Frye (1912–91), Canadian literary critic and teacher. The quotation has not been traced.
3 Irving Layton (b. 1912) at this time was living and teaching in Montreal.

Elm Cottage
23 December 1964

Dear Adele:

A brief note, written in the midst of Xmas preparations – we are all going slightly mad these days, as we are having 2 couples to stay over Christmas, plus our neighbor's friends' kids (3 of them) who are great

pals of my kids. The Bryant kids arrived last night, and the five youngsters were up at 6 a.m. this morning, to go out to 'the Hidden Valley'
(a chalk pit nearby). Needless to say, mother did not rise at that hour.

Very very many thanks for OLD MARKETS, NEW WORLD.[1] Heavens, girl,
you are a dark horse! I never even knew it was coming out! The odd
thing was that I got my copy of Tamarack Review yesterday, and Macmillan's had an ad in it, which included the book, and I was immensely
curious, and then what should arrive this morning but the book itself.
I was so pleased, and I think it is a beautiful job. Your essay reminds
me of so many things in my own childhood – not markets, but when
you talk of the sleighs with the box-like huts built onto them, and the
way the kids used to hook rides. Anyway, it is a good piece of work,
Adele, and the pictures by Joe Rosenthal are terrific, aren't they? I also
was pleased to see what a lovely job of production they've done on the
book. I hope it sells well – it should mean a little money. I thought you
hit the right tone – evocative without ever being sentimental.

I have been in a state of blackest gloom for several weeks but am
pulling out of it now. I was going along okay for awhile, and proceeding with this novel, feeling that even if no one else ever sees anything
in it, at least I know it's what I have to do. Then I very foolishly broke
off to write a short story, thinking of next year's Winter's Tales and
wanting to submit one, and it turned out very very badly, and this
depressed me. I also had been quite unable to get going on the article
for Woman's Mirror, and then got a letter from another magazine,
asking if I'd do an article, and I began to feel horribly bogged down. It
is my old feeling of insecurity – I feel I must write an article instantly,
if anyone asks me to, as I can't afford to lose the opportunity. But I've
thought about this a lot, lately, and I know I must simply relax about
this, and not do any articles or short stories or any damn thing at all
until I've got more done on this novel, as I could keep delaying forever
in this way, and all the time when I'm *not* working on the novel, it is
bugging me like hell so that I cannot concentrate on anything else
anyway. So what with this, and feeling the necessity to concentrate on
Xmas, etc, I felt like giving up, but very stupidly so, of course. I tried
for such a long time to make some money that now I can hardly bear
to throw up any chances of doing so, but on the other hand, why did
I accumulate a certain amount if not to write the only thing that matters
to me? Anyway, please forgive all this brooding. When I feel I've got
more to do than I can possibly handle, it gives me an intensely frightened and paralysed feeling. I got like this in Vancouver, at one time,

when I was trying to write, doing essay-marking, book reviews, teaching Sunday School (yet!), and doing housework, plus trying to cope with kids. But it is easier now, because the decision to cut down on things is mine, now. I mean, it doesn't depend on anyone else. Anyway, when I think how much you have to cope with at the moment, I think I ought to be shot for complaining. I'm *not* actually complaining – just reflecting on the fact that it seems difficult to keep things going on some kind of even course. Please write soon. And congratulations on the Markets book – it is super.

Love from us all,

Margaret

1 Wiseman's illustrated essay about the old farmers' market on Winnipeg's North Main with Joe Rosenthal's drawings of Toronto's Kensington Market

Elm Cottage
31 December 1964

Dear Adele:

Got your letter this morning, and the main thing is – I'm terribly glad etc that you have got going on the novel, even if you have to do it in bits. As a matter of fact I felt what amounted to genuine envy – when you spoke about its being almost automatic writing, and the characters struggling to get out. This is what one always prays will happen, but doesn't happen just because you want it to. It's a kind of grace, given like all grace for reasons we don't know, but it can't be willed. If it happens, it is some kind of miracle. All that can be willed, I think, is that one sits down at the typewriter and does something. Anyway, once the thing has begun to come, nothing can stop it. Just try to unload as many essays on your marker as you possibly can – that's all.

I don't think my reasons for not applying to the Canada Council are all that different from yours. I do feel at the moment that I do not actually need the money, as I have enough to get by for 2 years if I am careful, but this wasn't really my only reason for not re-applying. I, also, felt as though I had asked for charity – and I really detested feeling like that. I detested having to write that letter, telling them why I thought I needed the dough – and although I did not by any means tell them the whole truth, I felt it wasn't any of their business to know anything at all about me. I don't know whether it was my egotism that suffered, or just my pride. Same thing, maybe. Anyway, I can certainly understand your feelings about not re-applying.

I can see to some extent your feeling about The Word. This is very similar, you know, to the old African superstition that you should never tell anyone *all* your name, as it gives them a power over you. In essence this is the same sort of thing, and I feel it in various different ways, such as the belief that it is fantastically dangerous to try to express verbally one's deepest inner reactions and convictions, because one is then somehow tied by one's own definitions, which are always inadequate. It is true that the expression is the end of innocence – the expressed thing then exists, not only because it is seen by other people but also because it takes on reality to oneself as well, whereas before it might have dwelt only in the limbo of fantasy. What bugs me about the word is that the more you know about it, the more mysterious it is perceived to be, so that sometimes one thinks of religious orders who have taken the vow of silence and you wonder if they aren't right after all. This is defeat, of course, at least in my terms, and you have to do the best you can with what you have – this cliché is quite literally true, like some clichés surprisingly are – but I am still left at this point with the knowledge that I do not know how to say what I have to say. This probably sounds as though I were discouraged, but in fact I'm not (like you weren't bitter, at the moment) – I have just found that I have to begin this novel again, as it isn't moving right, but I feel somewhat closer to the way than I did before, so I don't really mind. I know the character is there – I don't have any doubt at all about that – I've known her for too long to feel any doubt about her existence (she isn't me, by the way) – but the problem of method continues to bug me. The way of letting the thing find its own method is not working this time. Maybe the same thing never really works twice, and each time one has to hope that a new way will reveal itself – I don't mean *new* as such, only new to oneself. I was envious about your saying that this of yours is an odd one – my feeling about what I'm doing is that it isn't odd enough – I don't mean I value oddness for itself, and I know you do not either, but only that I feel the limitations of my own seeing ability – I just don't see far enough or deeply enough, and when I do see deeply enough, I seem to come back from down there on a visit empty-handed or at least without the means of expressing what I have discovered – without the elusive words, I suppose. God damn it. I cannot stop attempting this novel, because I know it is there, but I have not yet found the way to it. This gives me the feeling that I am somehow choking. I have recently come to the conclusion that this one will have to be written with my head, I mean with me directing operations, and this is a responsibility which I can hardly bear, as previously I felt that the character was in charge and all I had to do was put it down. But this time the person is very evasive, and this is part of her, and very understandable, but she is damn well making life impossible for me. I think that the grace for which one hopes will not come, perhaps, this time. Lacking it, I don't see any way except to put down as simply and directly as possible the things that happen, and to try not to tell lies. I don't believe this is enough, but it appears to be all I have to hand at the moment. Perhaps it will change. I've made so many bad beginnings on this one that anyone in their right mind would give it up and do something else. But I can't. It isn't that I'm not prepared to cut my losses – I am quite prepared to do this, and I tried. I tried to begin THREE other novels. But it isn't any use – this one has to be done, however inadequately. I don't remember when I first met her but I think it must have been about six years ago. Now I know so much about her that the whole thing seems impossible – I don't, after all, want to write a novel of 20,000 pages. In fact, my whole feeling about novels, these days, is that this is the tightest form possible, considering what one is trying to do within it. I actually remember myself thinking, years ago, that one had a certain amount of *space* in a novel – how could I have thought so? I suppose because I didn't know, then, how much there was to get in and how bloody complicated it all was. I don't have any doubts, at heart, that this one will get done – all I doubt is (a) whether it will be any good at all, and (b) whether I will salvage some fragments of sanity throughout. What breaks my heart, as they say, is that I KNOW what could be done with it – and I do not have enough resources to do it. Well, never mind. We are not dead yet. Have had a hellish couple of days – Jocelyn with tonsillitis (sp?), and the water pipes freezing. All is well now. HAPPY NEW YEAR (in 2 hours it will be 1965).

Love and good hope,

Margaret

p.s. I am very very glad that Esther is so much better.

Elm Cottage
24 January 1965

Dear Adele:

Sorry not to have answered sooner. I have been lower than a snake's belly this past fortnight, and have not wanted to see anyone, write to anyone or even phone anyone. You know the feeling. You could probably see from my last letter that things were going from worse to no-worse-there-is-none, mainly re: this novel. I had been trying to do it, off and on, for about 5 years. Have made innumerable starts on it during the past 2 years. This time, I thought I would just have to stick to it and do it, however terrible it might seem. But I can't, of course. I have just chucked the whole thing, because at last I know why I couldn't do it. I kept telling myself the character wasn't me, yet when the circumstances of my life changed, the plot changed, and she *would* persist in speaking in my voice. What one wants (I, anyway), prays for, needs most of all, perhaps, is to be released from the sound of one's own voice. But however often I tackled it, the same thing happened – always it was the one voice I did not want to hear. This might be viewed as an evasion on my part – fear, unwillingness to see oneself, etc – and at one time this was true, but not, I think, now. I would be prepared to go through with it, provided that what was being said was in some measure true, but I kept having this feeling that everything was somehow phoney and false. I had the same feeling (I still have) about 'The Prophet's Camel Bell,' as though I cannot ever speak the truth when I am speaking in my own voice. Does this sound absolutely mad? I don't know. All I know is that it is true. Only when the character is quite different from myself (at least in some essential ways, especially the ways of communicating to some extent with the outside) do I seem able to move with some certainty and to feel that the thing is real and authentic. I seem to have to write very close (maybe too close) to the character, but as far away as possible from myself (at least from my external self). Otherwise the whole thing becomes impossible – once it may have been impossible because of my deep puritanical inhibitions about self-revelation, but I think now this is not so much the case (although still true) – I think it is more the fact that what I say in my own voice hardly ever seems true to me – I suppose I have a very shaky sense of my own reality and can only be certain (or reasonably so) when I've taken on another cloak or temporarily become someone else. I said to someone a long time ago that The Stone Angel was written in a way similar to the Stanislawski (sp?) Method[1] – naturally, I was not speaking seriously, but now I wonder if maybe this wasn't true after all. I have this feeling which I've had for many years that I tell lies all the time except when I am speaking with the few members of my tribe whom I trust absolutely, and that in general I can't speak truthfully except through someone else's mouth. At one point in my life I tried to change all this. But it did not really change. I tell as many placating lies as I ever did ('everything is all right'; 'people are mostly nice'; 'I mean well and I know you do too' – etcetera). Only with a few people can I cut through this – only in places where I know I won't be despised or pitied, I suppose. Like the way I'm writing to you now. Doris Lessing can lie on the psychiatrist's couch and be making notes for a novel with one hand, but I can't.[2] (I couldn't even do the couch bit – I'm too bloody proud). So – for various reasons which I know to be true, I have chucked out that novel. The main objection to it, Adele, was that it was not good – it didn't come across; the people didn't live. That is, in the end, the only valid objection to anything. However, the process of throwing it out, and knowing why, is certainly not cheering to say the least. It seems to me that I learn with such painful slowness – all this I ought to have seen before, but I didn't. Also, another difficulty with me is that with this novel I seemed to get bogged down in complexities – I could see too many implications and couldn't be selective enough. The main trouble here must be that it is not good to know the entire meaning of the thing in advance. This is partly why one writes it – to discover what it means. If you know, already, everything (or nearly so) about it, why write it? If you know too much about its meaning, you (or I mean myself) do not communicate these complexities; you only become incoherent. Or trivial.

So what with one thing and another, I have been in a state of Celtic gloom. But this cannot last for so very long, thank God, with me. Some urge to survive, maybe. I've begun to work on something else, about which I can't say anything at all except that it is something to work at, and I don't know what it means and suspect it may mean nothing except that I have to work at something, but God knows. Hope is not a reasonable feeling; it is only a necessity of life, like breathing, maybe – it may not be preferable to dying but it seems to be. I think all I can do is to take the next 3 months to mess around with what may or may not be there (I feel I've deceived myself so often about this), and then in the spring turn to doing some articles which might make me some money. I said to you in my last letter that if some kind of grace didn't happen, one had to go on and do the thing anyway, and this is not possible, I find. If it just isn't working, if the bones don't live in the slightest, how can you go on? And why? That was how I felt about throwing that damn novel out. But the new thing which is always beginning – maybe that is an illusion, also? How can you tell? I suppose you can't, until later on.

Things on the surface are very peaceful, etc. By the way, you never mentioned 'Old Markets, New World' – how did you feel about it? I thought it was a beautiful job. I know it doesn't matter to you in the deepest ways or anything like that, but so what? I hope you got some money for it. Also, it was valid and genuine, in itself, for what it was, which was not broad in scope but this isn't important. The good thing, also, was that Macmillan's mentioned the play on the dust-jacket.

If you have some people (even one) in your novel, who are trying to get out and break through, etc, then you will be okay, however long it takes. I don't know why all this should be so difficult. On the surface, and to other people, it never is, is it? And I get the feeling that I am some kind of lunatic, making fantastic efforts to pretend to be sane, but also suspecting that it may be the other way around. The hell with it. Sometimes I feel the need to concentrate on something VERY SIMPLE, such as putting out bread for the birds, or taking the dog for a walk, or going to Wycombe with the kids to buy gym shoes and having hamburgers at the Wimpy Bar (known to David as 'our favourite restaurant' – which sounds good; it does not, I trust, occur to him that it is also the cheapest!) I am, however, luckily, not broke, at the moment.

Please write. (By the way, I wasn't surprised to hear about Tom B – he has been very very difficult, for many years, poor guy – the fact being that to have intelligent and determinedly well-adjusted parents unfortunately does not ensure being able to cope with life's horrors oneself).

Please write.

Love,

Margaret

p.s. Jack writes and asks me why I haven't sent him a copy of The Stone Angel. It was here in the house when he was on leave. He didn't read it, and I don't blame him. But why mention it now? I can't send him a copy. Pride? Hurt? Or what?

1 Professional name of Russian actor and producer Konstantin Sergeyevich Alekseyev (1863–1938), who developed a method of acting in which a realism based on the inner truth of a character is fundamental. His approach became widely influential in the United States after his visit there in 1923.

2 Doris Lessing (b. 1919), author of the novel *The Golden Notebook* (1962). Her most recent work was *African Stories* (1964). Laurence is commenting on how the experiences of psychotherapy are reflected in Lessing's fiction.

[1217 Drummond Street]
23 February 1965

Dear Margaret,

The other day I tore up one of these letters I'd written to you; scandalized my thrifty soul but spared you a tedious outpouring, which I'll now try to summarize. Leslie Fiedler,[1] whose children, you may recall, I used to baby sit with in Rome; – they, the ones who were at the time old enough to be sat with, (over several days when the parents were in Venice,) were lovely boys. There are also three girls, but two were babies and one not yet born. Anyway, Fiedler is one of the top critics and writers in what I guess is the current literary establishment in the U.S. You know, the ones who talk about each other in Esquire, and get chapters of their novels published there. These include Sol Bellow, William Styron, Norman Mailer, James Jones, etc. etc. Anyway, I went to hear him. He is a kind of system building critic; you may not agree with much of what he says, but it stimulates and can also illuminate. His wife was with him, and I talked to her about the kids; actually we got into an interesting argument but I'll save that to tell you about. Later, he asked me what I'd been doing. So I told him, in the way that I felt aggressive, self confident people like to be told, that I'd written a play which was the best thing that had been written about the Nazi holocaust yet. One thing I like about Fiedler is that he is frank, leaves himself open but says what he thinks. He said, 'You know what my first thought was when you said that? I thought, "*I wish you hadn't*."' Now he wasn't referring to the idea that I'd said it was the best; possibly he was thinking of the fact that I'd said I'd spent four years on it, but what he meant was that he wished I hadn't written about *that*. For the first time somebody really came out and told me what they feel about the whole thing. Of course I know it, but here at last someone came right out with it, without any reference to the work itself, which he of course had not even seen. If people feel that way before they even see the

work, the people who are supposedly most profoundly occupied with
the significant things of our age, am I out of step! Of course I know it;
I don't know why I take on so. I usually have this feeling when I've
come into contact with the most apparently 'activist' artists and thinkers.
And I notice they recoil from me too. He said, in his talk, one very
interesting thing which I felt was relevant for me anyway. He said that,
(speaking of the novel as an essentially minority form, and expression
of the passive minority being raped by the majority), that the relationship between minority and majority was unilateral; that is that the
majority imposed an image on the minority, (the gentiles on the Jews;
men on women; the whites on the blacks) but the minority are unable
to impose a return image of the majority on the latter. So that the terms
of 'reality,' or acceptable reality, within which whatever conflicts are to
be fought out are enacted, are the terms imposed by the majority. The
minority knows of the image of itself, and has numerous ways of reacting to it; fighting, partially accepting, etc. etc. And here am I, refusing
to play the game, determined to show the counter-image because I think
there are larger realities, and a greater majority, – all of humanity. The
implications of his reaction are that the counter-image is not even
acceptable to many of the minority, as long as it is possible to achieve
some comfort within the majority terms. So 'I wish you hadn't' it is to
be. The nuisance is that I, who have always had such highfalutin'
notions of the work of the artist as a social value have now realized that
I am writing to satisfy myself, whether I like it or not, because if these
terms hold this work anyway can't be acceptable to anyone else. Oh
well. At this point I just don't seem to have the energy to peddle the
play. It requires, or seems to, so much explanation and such a unique
set of circumstances for the possibility of a production to seem likely
and I simply want to get to work on this other thing, whatever it is; so
I'm stymied. By the way, I've finally copyrighted the play, as publication seems unlikely. So would you please put a notice like this © ADELE
WISEMAN, 1965 on your copy. Then it can be shown around; I don't
mean I want you to peddle it; I just mean that maybe what I will do
now is send copies around for scrutiny, where I would have hesitated
to before, not that there is essentially any difference.

About my coming to Europe, I've meant to mention this before; if I
want to get any work done it's most unlikely I'll take the Israel job.[2] It
will mean a heavier teaching load than I've got here, much less pay, and
the necessity to learn Hebrew. Knowing myself I can see this as pretty
full time. I have got to the point now where I realize that I will have to

make a radical change if I'm ever to get anything done. I'll see what happens this summer. Unfortunately I've not yet managed to save any money, though I'm going to put on a determined push. At the moment I'm daydreaming of burying myself somewhere in Trinidad or Tobago; I have myself a cushy but expensive nest here. Okay so I've had my bour*geois* sp? period. By the way I at last have a new marker who's a mature, intelligent woman, so that a third or so of the rest of my marking this year will be off my hands. Silly business, eh?

Enough of me. I'm glad you're agreeing that the lay-by of the novel is temporary. What's there will out. How I wish I could look forward to seeing you in the near future. Will write again shortly. Now I must to bed. I have to get up shortly after 6 a.m. By the way, you have often mentioned your attraction to wine. I think the only thing that saves me is a queasy gut. The temptation is increasingly there as one gets older and more, not less frustrated about all kinds of things.

love,

Adele

P.S. Love to the kids. Please write, to me and at your work. There are few other satisfactions.

1 At this time, Leslie Fiedler (b. 1917), American literary and cultural critic, was professor of English at the State University of New York at Buffalo. In 1951–3 he had been a Fulbright fellow and lecturer at the University of Rome and the University of Bologna.
2 Wiseman was hoping to teach at the Hebrew University of Jerusalem.

[Elm Cottage
5 April 1965]

Dear Adele –

Your letter arrived at a much-needed moment, when I was feeling relatively lousy, & believe me, it cheered me enormously. I'm okay now – as a matter of fact, the trouble seems to be these days that I can go along fairly happily, trying to get back to work, & even (a miracle!) enjoying working in the garden, etc, & then I receive a letter from Jack, & this at once plunges me right back into the whole situation. I want so desperately to *quit thinking* about it, but I am afraid that these epistles nearly knock me out each week, although he certainly doesn't intend them that way. I have to become a little more resistant to these upsets, I guess.

I really enjoyed your account of the wine-type playreading you gave – how in hell is your friend now? I dare not think! I'm glad to hear you've taken up wine drinking. I'm not a qualified judge when it comes to *good* wine, but I venture to say there are few people in the western world who know more about all the *cheap* varieties of wine, & how to get as much as possible for as little financial outlay as possible. I read in Maclean's the other day that a wine-drinker has a life-expectancy of TEN years more than a spirits drinker! How about that? The news made my day.

Your sea captain sounds super. Sea captain, yet! How do you *meet* such guys? All the men *I* know are either married, homosexual, or in another country. Well, we can't force the wheel of fate. I feel bloody awful sometimes when I think that my dancing (etc) days are more than likely over, but what the hell? I can't complain (not that I don't)! I've had more than my share of luck in this life, & also am not dead yet. What a good thing not to know what is going to happen – it gives one the feeling of living dangerously, in some (probably absurd) way. Got a sweet letter from Ethel Wilson – I'd written to tell her about myself & J. She is really a honey. Has had a bad time recently – arthritis much worse, & her husband quite ill.

Sometimes I have a strong hankering to return to Canada, you know. Maybe I will, when the kids have finished secondary school. I don't want to upset their schooling again. I love this house so much too, and can't bear to think of leaving, but in 7 or 8 years I think it will probably be in such poor shape that Alan will likely have to sell it. So I don't regard it as permanent. If it can be home for the kids for the next few years, that will be a good thing. It's odd, though – sometimes, now, I feel very lonely for my own countrymen – not *all* of them, mind you, but a few. I guess it is a question of a similar idiom, or maybe one always thinks the idiom will be more similar in some place where one isn't. Whereas in fact, it is really only a matter of one's tribal members, of whatever nationality. I've found a few here, thank God. I *do* see Gus & Sheila Andrzejewski quite often – in fact, was at their place last night.[1] Gus is one of the bravest & best. I'll never forget when I first came here, 2½ yrs ago, how he used to try, very very delicately, to hearten me by quoting me proverbs – 'Among the Borona Galla, there is a saying – .' I used his translations of Somali poetry for this article on the Mad Mullah,[2] but didn't need to collaborate on it, as all the available source material on the life of Mahammed 'Abdille Hasan is in one book written by an Englishman in 1923[3] – I'd read it years ago, but now re-read it, & based my article on that, plus Gus's own translations, plus my own inimitable interpretation – 'How far did the British view of Mahammed 'Ab. H. correspond to reality, & how much was it tinged with fantasy?' Etc. The article turned out so *long* and so detailed, it is nearly a thesis, & I am damn sure no one will ever publish it, but I've wanted for years to write it, so there it is. I've really done it now because I could do it with my conscious mind entirely, whereas the novel demands some kind of ability to tune into something which isn't conscious so much as intuitive, and for that you have to be a very attentive listener, which I couldn't be for awhile. However, I got the old script out today, & maybe it will be okay, at some point. I am longing to get back to it now, and I feel I will, now. Don't mistake me – it is no major opus – I'm not capable of that. It is just another novel, but the character seems for real. That is all I am capable of, & I don't underesti-mate it – this is *not* only false modesty. I can do a basically one-character novel with some truth. But not a wider-scale thing. You see, I am not capable of the sustained effort and the breadth of view that you are. No wonder you can't do articles or short stories, Adele. Your natural form is one which encompasses a great deal. Mine isn't. I have to put across my view a little at a time. I don't regret this in the slightest – I only recognize it as a fact, the way I am. I want (God willing) to do two novels, maybe three after this one, and all are more-or-less formed (the bones anyway) in my mind. But each is a particular character, not a large cast, & each depends utterly on tuning-in to that one person for the time it takes to write the novel. That is what I can (with luck, & maybe some grace) sometimes do, & all I pray is that I can keep on doing it until I've put down what is there, that's all. You, on the other hand, will never write many novels, or whatever, but each thing that you create has a very wide scope and has gathered around itself a kind of richness, perceptions on many levels. You won't ever write a handful of good or even very good novels – but you do have that one chance in ten million of writing a lasting one. This is what I think. However, for God's sake don't let this scare you! In the writing, it's a private thing, as we know, & what happens later to it is not your business, or mine. How much I want to talk with you! Maybe one day I'll feel financially secure enough to go on a visit. Write, please.

Love,

Margaret

1 Andrzejewski was at the time a faculty member at the School of African and Oriental Studies, University of London. He had recently published, with I.M. Lewis, *Somali Poetry: An Introduction* (1964).
2 The essay was eventually published as 'The Poem and the Spear' in *Heart of a Stranger* (1976). It describes the life of the early Somali nationalist leader Mohammed 'Abdille Hasan (1864–1920), who fought against the British and who became known to them as the 'Mad Mullah.'
3 Douglas J. Jardine, *The Mad Mullah of Somaliland* (1923)

Elm Cottage
17 August 1965

Dear Adele:

I can't believe I've been so long in answering your letter, but I have. The reason is that I have somehow been compelled to type out this novel from the handwritten scribble[1] and could not seem to stop myself, which was ludicrous, because the external circumstances were so unsuitable – the visitors have been continuing, and although I have been very glad to see them, or most of them, I feel at this point as though I'm operating some kind of hotel. I am damn fed up with changing bed linen in time for the next outfit, and making enormous meals. Bitch, bitch, etc, but at this juncture I feel like moaning, so I know you will understand and forgive. Two weeks ago Jack's aunt (ex-missionary – terribly intelligent and nice, and I do love her, but of course J has always been the white-haired boy, so rather awkward for me under the present circumstances) arrived for a few days, and the day she left, a Canadian friend who lives in London phoned to take me up on a long-standing invitation to visit, so she arrived and stayed a week, which was lovely but my God etc etc, and the day she left, my kids' three pals from Sussex arrived for a week, so we had the Fort X Gang again, and they were really marvellous, as a matter of fact, the 5 kids being a hell of a lot less bother than any number of adults. They all slept out in the tents for 2 nights, then got tired and decided to sleep in, but all the work was done by them – they put up the tents and took them down; I didn't lift a finger. They're getting very much more self-reliant, which is marvellous for one and all, me especially. I took the whole crew to Wycombe one day for a meal in a good restaurant and then a film, and they were wonderful – everyone on best behavior in restaurant, and I really enjoyed it, much to my surprise. Apart from that one expedition, they went everywhere alone – and wanted to, for my kids had told me in advance that what they really wanted was for me not to get in their way too much. A suggestion to which I readily agreed, I may say.

Anyway, somehow or other, I got the bloody thing typed out, and I told Alan it was done to that point, and he told me it would be a good idea for me to take the manuscript to him, otherwise I would only pick at it and worry about it uselessly, as I cannot see it clearly enough now to do anything. So I did, then paced the floor for 5 days, and then he phoned and said he liked it, and I still do not really believe this can be so, but I know it needs a good deal of work, yet, and also Alan feels (and one other reader who has seen it) that it gets off to a slow start, and that, as A says, in the first few chapters, I 'grind the reader,' which I think is true. I don't know, Adele – at one time I thought everything would have to be extensively re-written and re-re-written in order to be any good, but the feeling I have about this novel is that either it has come across to some extent, more or less as it stands, or it hasn't. It is a kind of tour-de-force, in a way, and I think that whatever I do to it, apart from some necessary cutting, would not make very much difference one way or another. I don't think I feel this just because I'm tired. I *am* tired – I am so goddamn beat that I can hardly drag myself around – but I think the way I feel about this novel does not hang on my present depleted state of mind. Some things come all-of-a-piece, and they either work the first time or they don't. I did a lot of re-shaping while I was typing this out, but now I feel – what? Either it is reasonably competent or it is a flop, and I do not in myself know which, right now. But whichever it is, I can't do anything very much about it. It has taken its own form, and apart from the obvious things which need doing to it, I can't alter it much. All I can do is leave it, and write another, God willing. I went through a time of feeling absolutely sick about it, because I felt that parts of it were written by a lunatic, and now I just feel – what the hell? I can't help the way it turned out. I didn't know it would end like that, but it did.

I know what you mean by not knowing how it will work out. I had that feeling about this one. I knew roughly what direction it would take, but all the details and the ending surprised me. Maybe it is worthless – I honestly do not know what it is like.

I'm glad your novel is coming along,[2] and in a consecutive way – it doesn't matter if it comes like this, but it is easier to cope with, I think, if it happens so. I hope the summer has been relatively uncluttered for you. My God, how hard it is to get enough time to oneself – how is this? When I think of myself, supposedly leading a quiet life in the country, I could laugh. The bloody place is like Victoria Station. I cope with confusion so badly – when things get too hectic, I have about six stiff drinks and then I can take anything in my stride but afterwards I feel guilty as hell and worry lest I go the way of so many of our tribe, etc. I don't drink when I'm working, however, as that is always a delusion, something which I discovered many years ago with the first novel. What scares the hell out of me with this present novel is that when I read it over, it seems to me that it might appear as though parts of it were written when I was stoned, and in fact they weren't – this makes me wonder if I am more crazy than I want to believe? Not that this novel is far-out in any sense, because it unfortunately isn't. Better if it were. If anything, it is too far-in, being about (I honestly hate to say it) an unmarried schoolteacher in a prairie town, how corny can you get? She, is, however, real, and although she is an anachronism, she knows it, which is the whole thing. I have the feeling that it will be awful if it turns out to be no good, because the people (her, especially) are there, and I really wanted to say to her, 'I'm sorry, baby, maybe I haven't done so well by you.'

I'm going to Scotland next week, for a week's holiday, while the kids go to visit their pals (Fort X Gang) in Sussex, so I hope to do absolutely nothing.

Alice Frick wrote to me re: your play, and she likes it and cares about it and also feels it might have to be somewhat shortened to be produced, but anyway, she is going to write to you – she was terribly keen to write to you and also somewhat diffident and did not want to do so if you didn't want her to, etc etc, so I said I thought you would be glad to hear. PLEASE WRITE SOON. I'm sorry about my long silence – it won't happen again. So, write when you can. I wish I could talk with you.

Love,

Margaret

ps. Jocelyn's 13th birthday soon – I have bought her lipstick, powder, a new dress and her first brassiere – almost unbelievable, but there it is.

1 She was working on *A Jest of God*, which was published the following year.
2 Adele Wiseman had begun *Crackpot* (1974).

[Elm Cottage]
6 September [1965]

Dear Adele:

Very glad to get your letter, and also to hear re: your novel. Naturally you are scared at the prospect of the 2nd chapter, but as you point out yourself, so what? Maybe we always hope there will come a time when something can be done, can be begun, even, without having to be terrified. But it doesn't happen that way. I have the feeling with this novel of yours that it contains a great deal of complexity, and that when you think about its ambiguities and twists and turns, you can hardly bear it, thinking you can't possibly get them down – maybe I'm quite wrong, but your pattern of writing seems to me to [be] one of a great many layers, and yet what is there underneath must never obscure the real and living presence of the actual and immediate people. God, Adele, I can see that you must feel you can never write it that way by yourself – that it's too much; that you're a broken reed, etc etc. But the fact is, as you know and I know and everyone else knows who's ever done it to any degree, that one does *not* actually write it by oneself. I'm not being mystical – I only mean that, with you, your characters are set free because this is the only way it can ever be for you, and because of this, *they* do the talking, you don't. I have a feeling that a novel is partly an act of will (the writer has to put the pen to the page, or start typing, etc) and partly an act of faith – and if it works out, it is largely because one has been able to have that terrifying faith in the other people, the ones who aren't oneself and who are yet inside oneself. What am I rambling on about, for God's sake? Telling you things you know better than I do. Only that your novel will be complex, difficult, awful to cope with, and that it may nearly kill you, but I believe you have the inner strength to let the people go free. You know? You know, naturally. If I could write on as many levels as you can, and could at the same time mingle with so many characters and allow them all their independence, I would – what? Get down on my knees, maybe, and pray to be allowed to do it once more. I can't do anything as complex and as broad in scope as you can, and this does not bother me, because I know that what I can do (granted some grace) is a very few people at a time. But because I've recently come to some terms with my own score (I'm not running myself down – I don't mean what I can do is less; it is just different) I can see to some extent what must be bugging you. If I had to deal with something with the scope and yet individual focus of your play, I would quite simply go out of my mind. So – you'll take time to do this novel. That doesn't matter. All that matters is that you let it be, which you will.

I wish sometimes that I could tackle things in a more broad way than I can. But I guess one can only write what is there – you can't write what isn't there. This novel I've just finished is bugging me to quite some extent, still. I don't really know if it is any good or not. All I know is that the few people who are in it are genuine – I'd stake my life on that. But really, Adele, it will go over like a lead balloon if it is ever published. It is a kind of tour-de-force, a single situation, an intensely personal dilemma (I don't mean personal to me – I mean personal to the central character). Have personal dilemmas any meaning any more? My most strong faith is that they have, and must. What, in a world sense, could matter less than the unhappiness of an unmarried woman teacher in a small town? But viewed in another way, what could matter more? I suppose it is a kind of study in ironies, and the ironies are those dealt by fate, but they can be liberating in the long run. My God, this sounds pretentious and awful. It isn't pretention, actually – it is a very simple story of a woman who wants to have kids and who does not have the opportunity, and who then does have the chance to have her children, and does have a brief affair, and thinks she is pregnant, and cannot for a time cope with the general community disapproval of unwedlocked kids, and finally can cope with it because she wants the child more than she fears the world, but in the end she isn't pregnant. The parallel (which seemed to be there, and I don't think I super-imposed it) is with Rachel (and the woman's name is Rachel) who for so long mourned for her children because they were not. If it is ever published, no one will see this Old Testament parallel, probably, and this does not matter. Enough. I feel I've said too much, and probably it will never come to anything, and even if it does, what I think is there won't be seen to be there, etc etc. I guess at this point I don't want to think about it so much, any more. If it has not come across, then it hasn't, and maybe the next one will be better. I don't know. All I can see in it at the moment are the awful flaws – the fact that there are so few characters, and that the thing takes too long to get going (inevitably, because she has to present herself as she is, before one sees what happens to her – my God, my viewpoints are so simple, are they?). And that the whole thing seems to be written in a kind of shorthand – very very brief, very cut-down, very much pared to the bone. Too much so? Honestly, I know you'll know how I feel. I feel like bloody hell. I want on the one hand to let this novel go, and not think about it. On the other hand, I want to explain it – this is what I meant. But one cannot. Either it says it, by itself, or it does not. How can you know? Alan says he likes the novel, and this means a good deal to me. But it would not surprise me if Jack McClelland and Alfred Knopf[1] said – take it away; it won't do. And yet, what I feel about it myself is absolutely not dependent upon what they feel. What I really feel, in myself, is this – she is genuine; that is the way she would be; but maybe very few people might be interested in the way she is. That's all.

Anyway, excuse all the blabber. And please write. All reasonably well here. Kids go back to school this week.

Love,

Margaret

1 Alfred Knopf (1892–1984) had established his New York publishing house in 1915. He was president from 1918 to 1957 and board chairman from 1957 to 1972. Knopf would be the American publisher for all the Manawaka cycle as well as for *Jason's Quest* (1970) and *The Christmas Birthday Story* (1981).

[1217 Drummond Street]
27 October 1965

Dear Margaret,

Just a quickly bashed out letter before I pop into the bath. I just had a phone call from the Penners in Wpg. They may be coming out during Easter or else in early May. It was good to hear their voices, and so nice of them to call. I guess my letters have been grim lately, though the last time I wrote them was awhile ago; I guess my letters have been grim for quite a while, hey? At the moment I'm feeling curiously cheerful. I seem to have fallen into a prolonged and scarcely interruptible reverie about this new book I want to write, and all kinds of odd little things are opening out and filling in for me. The result is that I keep walking in front of cars, tripping over obstacles I only vaguely notice and in general looking to first things first. As I've probably mentioned I have found this idea very disturbing because parts are coming into focus without the general picture being at all clear as yet, and I'm not used to this. I usually have a fair notion of the overall gestalt and have to find out how and why in the writing. Well, I don't care; if it will only come

I don't care how it goes about it; as long as I can have that strange pleasure again I'll put up with the insecurities. Those are always there anyway. How about you? I hope this writing is still coming smoothly, or as smoothly as we can ever hope; I know that novel will suddenly pop, too. Her voice or your voice, – ultimately it'll be the right voice, and you'll know it, and so will the rest of us. I guess if it wasn't so much pain it wouldn't be so much pleasure either, huh? And I'm no masochist. Did I tell you that funny story about how I accidentally discovered that I had forgotten to pick up my last cheque for $104. at Sir George last May? Some nut. You know, I'm secretly rather proud of myself. I was taught to despise money and the lesson sure seems to have interiorized itself ineradicably, in spite of my grim attempts to save and niggling stinginesses. But of course it's also self-destructive as hell, so what's to be proud of?

What do you hear from the Barons? I so often think of them, and keep telling myself I'm going to write, and will, too, soon. I'm annoyed with myself for letting the correspondence slide. I used to enjoy hearing from them so much.

It seems to me there's been so much I've been meaning to tell you. About Tom Boulton the other day I heard him playing his guitar and mouth organ simultaneously, and he's very good. He was playing a kind of Western style music. He's interested in what they call 'rank' music here, you know, the kind most people think stinks. It is the living folk music, after all, and he's interested in its sources, etc. I don't know how he'll do academically. As you say the intelligence is there; if he knew precisely what he wanted to do with it he'd have no difficulty. Anyway I hope he does well; I think he's a nice kid. Now I'm out of the bath; I'll finish this when I get back; see you later. Next day. Nothing much to report. I went to a party and baited a bunch of C.C.F'ers, – New Democrats, you know.[1] Told them their party had always played a cowardly role in relation to the communists, that they'd rather ditch a good issue than be associated with the commy's in it, that they lacked virility, (their party, though there were some rather flabby looking types present). What rage, what scorn, what contempt rained down on me! It's not really that I think they're insincere; it's that they're so bloody comfortable, so all-right. Anyway, there were some amusing moments even outside the argument. I think I must have drummed it up partly because I'm so bored with well bred entertainment. You know, it's not been so long since I discovered what boredom was. All my life I'd heard of boredom and never really known what it meant; and then a couple of years ago I found out. It was a terrifying discovery. I think to be really be bored when alone I'd have to be really depressed, because it's involved somehow with a failure of inner resources. To be bored with other people is a slightly different thing; it involves a recognition, which one hates to make because it seems to involve arrogance, that there are certain people who do not add much to one's world. This is an obvious enough thing. On a personal level everybody can't mean everything to you. Possibly it's hard to take because the obverse is true, and you have to recognize it; that you can't mean everything to everybody, and the human ego is so ridiculously ambitious. All this is one of those silly digressions from what I really meant to say, and that is that I had a couple of dates recently that bored me, and that it was rather depressing because though I had good cause to be bored, I feel, the tendency is to feel that it's somehow due to a failure in oneself. I don't like boredom. Seems like I've talked of this before. In a way it may be a good sign; maybe I'm getting ready to withdraw and do some work; certainly I felt withdrawn as I politely went through the social motions. But enough of this. Write me a long and detailed letter about what you're doing, what's happening, how the kids are and everything, please and about the work.

Love,

Adele

1 The Co-operative Commonwealth Federation had been founded in 1932 along social democratic principles. It was succeeded in 1961 by the New Democratic Party, a coalition of the old CCF and the Canadian Labour Congress.

Elm Cottage
24 January 1966

Dear Adele:

I guess our letters crossed. It was wonderful to have such a blowing-off-steam kind of letter from you, as I received it at a moment when I felt (and feel) like bloody hell, so in my selfish way I felt that misery loves company. This is not to say I don't sympathize with you – believe me, I sympathize like anything. At least you *want* to work – I mean, you don't want to but you really *do* want to. And you will. Don't panic – that is the main thing. I always panic in these situations and it certainly does no good. I can't understand this inability to work – I've been feeling that way since the end of July, really, but the difference is that I actively do not desire to do any type of work whatsoever. I must be sick. Mentally deranged. What I've been doing recently, to soothe the pangs of conscience, is to throw all my efforts into physical work such as housecleaning, which does at least get the house clean and also has the side-effect of making me feel, momentarily, that I've accomplished something. I feel very disorganized, somehow, although actually when I look at things more or less objectively, I'm not really disorganized at all. But I guess it is the fact that there is no external pressure to work, beyond the simple necessities of doing the laundry and ironing and getting meals, such as they are. And the pressures from within appear to be nil at the moment. I took on a job of editing and re-writing a really awful book on Canada, but I've chucked it because I just couldn't face doing it. I would've done a rotten job of it anyway. Now I am fed up and in semi-desperation over these scripts of West African literature. I wrote all four, as I think I told you, with enormous difficulty, and then Dennis, the guy I'm doing them for, told me they weren't what he wanted – he visualized a kind of 'impression of Africa,' through contemporary African writing but also with a commentary which made use of my personal experiences (ha ha, I nearly said to him, *what* personal experiences? I'm very fedup with this kind of phoney personal-experience type of thing – you know, 'I recall in Ghana once, the Asantehene[1] said to me ...' etc). Also, it seemed to me that Africa is kind of a big place ... you know? How do you give a picture of it? It's ludicrous. You have to tell pretty lies, that's all, and I seem to have lost my interest in that kind of challenge. Anyway, Dennis is a very nice guy and I like him, but I can see that his point of view and mine are not too close – mind you, I like his general approach to Africa, but he is an artist and is thinking of things in broad visual terms, as far as I can see, and I am left wondering how you get these sweeping effects in verbal terms without the whole thing sounding like the drivelling of an Africa-enchanted Peace Corps girl. Heaven forbid. I am getting sour in my old age, I guess. But I hate all these phoney generalizations. I sat down last night and wrote the first script, gritting my teeth. I put in as much as I could from the writings of Africans, and as little of my own comment as I thought I could get away with. I was determined to bash on and do the whole four this week, but Dennis phoned today and said 'Write no more until I've seen the first one.' So I spent the day copying it out and sent it to him with a letter which said, more or less, if he doesn't like this one, he can bugger off because I'm not going to spend my *entire* life re-writing scripts for him, damn his eyes. I feel so frustrated over this whole job that I could spit. I feel I will never be rid of it. I want now to get going on something else, or at least I *hope* I'll want to soon, but this job is like a dead hand on me or something. I can't chuck it unless he wants to because I've spent ever since last July working at it (more or less) – honestly, I'm embarrassed at how long I've been doing it. I feel I'm doing nothing but spending money. I'm not earning any. I feel life is passing me by. I feel a hundred years old. No, I'm NOT in love, although I damn well wish I were, but who would look twice at a beat-up old bitch like me? (Say, this self-pity really feels marvellous – for months now I have been sternly lecturing myself against this quality, but from time to time I must say it has a kind of therapeutic value). Also, it is cold as charity here and I spend my entire time stoking up the coal boiler, making up the wood fire in the livingroom, and turning on and off the gas and electric heaters, not to mention toting the kerosene stove out to the outdoor lavatory so the goddamn pipes won't freeze. Also, my typewriter doesn't like winter, either, and has been acting up and the keys sticking, etc. Also, I drink too much and can't lose weight because I don't stick to dieting for more than 24 hours at a time. In general, I feel like a mess, and I think I am simply frittering away my life. I'm not even working at a job, I mean an outside job.

I see from your letter you said please to tell you something nice. My God, and I've been going on like this! I can't think of anything nice to tell you at the moment, except what I told you in my last letter, that the kids and I are going to Greece at Easter, which is really wonderful. (I hope.) Re: Alex's book – it is called 'Strip Jack Naked,' and was published this week. I'm going to get it, so will send it to you when I've read it. It *is* a sequel to 'The Low Life.'

Yes, I saw 'Marat-de Sade'[2] in London, and thought it was a fascinating play. I want to get hold of it and read it, though, because I'm not sure yet what I really think of it.

The interview I did with B. Callaghan[3] was for TV. If possible, don't look at it when it's on – it will only embarrass you on my account.

I hope you re-establish the work pattern soon, because I know it is really really terrible when it's broken, and in this way you are really suffering whereas I'm not, in anything like the same way, as there isn't any pattern for me to break right now. But mentally I light candles for you. Please write and let me know what's happening.

Love,

Margaret

1 In Ghana, the head of the Asante people and keeper of the Golden Stool, the symbol of Asante
2 *Marat/Sade* is the abbreviated title of *The Persecution and Assassination of Jean-Paul Marat as Performed by the Inmates of the Asylum of Charenton under the Direction of the Marquis de Sade*, a play by the German writer Peter Weiss (1916–82). It was adapted by British playwright Adrian Mitchell (b. 1932) and produced in London in 1964 and in New York in 1965.
3 Barry Callaghan (b. 1937), Canadian writer and poet, was literary editor of the *Toronto Telegram* from 1966 to 1971.

[1217 Drummond Street]
7 July 1966

Dear Margaret,

Perhaps I'll be able to get a proper letter off to you now. I worked last night and again this morning, so the perpetual anxiety is somewhat allayed. I can allow myself to sit and type a letter. My nephew, sweet boy,[1] as you shall see, is sitting in his corner of the study at his table and building an extraordinarily intricate little model car, which he designed himself. We're back from the weekend up north, though I haven't recovered. I still itch madly and look ghastly, but feel that I know a little bit more of my native land and its inhabitants, perhaps more intimately than I would have wished, oh Canada! but let me not carp. The north country does have extraordinary beauty. I'd love to spend some time there when the insects ... July 10, – aren't in season. As you can see it's several days later. That's the way things have been with me lately, a lot of running around, flitting from one thing to another absent mindedly. But it's not bad. Ch. 4 is also trying to struggle itself out of my mind. Can one struggle oneself? ... into being? I'm so looking forward to having you here.[2] Mom has made proper drapes and door curtain for my study, and a new couch cover, so the place is looking really snazzy. There is nothing like tatty elegance. Elegance itself can hardly compare. Where you see elegance you know there must be a certain hefty minimum of lucre. But tatty elegance is an accomplishment. It has mystery, bouquet. Who's to tell whether it's an aspect of aristocratic decay or super sophisticated indifference which has cachet in spite of itself? Let me tell you I can tell. Who'm I kidding? All this is a roundabout way of telling you you'll be comfortable and I won't be sensitive if you laugh a little at my assay at homemaking. Just hurry up and get here. I want to know about Africa. I want to see the book.[3] July

12, – have just re-read the above and am embarrassed by the house-proud nonsense. Feel tied down to this accretion of stuff. Did I tell you even my great gesture of emancipation for the year has been limited, comfortably, thanks to the extreme kindness of my boss, who managed to get me a leave of absence from McGill, which reintroduces the promise of security into my vision of the future, and the harness, as well. But I try to think only of that lovely year stretching ahead, of total freedom, and what I may get done. I'm going to really try to finish this letter now and mail it on our way to my sister's. My parents are flying home to Wpg. this aft. We were going to go to the farm a friend has left me with for July, but Mom isn't feeling well enough and refuses to get checked up till she gets to Wpg. So Arnold and I will probably only get out there briefly if I get a lift. I had been intending to rent a car from someone for the month. Now I'll just coast. My brother isn't anxious for me to take Arnold into the country alone, away from possibilities of contact with other children, for any length of time. I'd love a stretch in the country but don't really mind not having it at the moment. As long as I can work I'm not being fussy about other things at present, though there are one or two, – (wistful note) that I wish would look up for me. Dry season, though not utter desert.

There are so many things I wanted to say to you, but all I can think of at the moment is a catalogue of questions, re Africa, re McClelland's plans for you, re the book, and I hope you have an MS with you. Did I tell you I'm fascinated by the idea of your critical book. I've always wanted to do some really close literary criticism, – have a go at it anyway. Since I've been teaching I've been even more struck than ever by the reading problems, – of professors. Well, we'll probably talk about that too. Please write and tell me the latest plans. See you soon! My God, to say that and know that it really will be soon, after all this time!

love,

Adele

– How little I've managed to say, – & this is supposed to be a decent letter for a change!

1 Arnold Wiseman, son of Harry and Esther. Esther had died the previous month.
2 Laurence stayed in Montreal with Wiseman in late August/early September during her extended trip to Canada from 30 July to 15 October. Much of the trip was a promotional tour to publicize the appearance of A Jest of God.

3 *Long Drums and Cannons: Nigerian Novelists and Dramatists, 1952–1966* was published
two years later in London and New York.

Elm Cottage
14 March [1967]

Dear Adele:

Further to my letter of last night – I've been sitting here in front of this
bloody typewriter for three quarters of an hour, trying to write to Prof.
Jensen,[1] and I CAN'T. You see, I think it is a bit different for you, as they
would only have to pay your fare from Montreal, but for me it looks
like a hell of a nerve to write and say 'Yes, I'm interested in coming,'
before they've said anything to me about it, and more or less ask them
to pay my air fare from England. If you are writing to Sid Warhaft,[2] you
might mention that I *would* be interested, but I think in my case it
would be better, as I live so damn far away, to wait and let them
approach me. Otherwise it may put them in a kind of embarrassing
position.

I *know* I am neurotic about protecting myself from the possibility of
being rejected. Etc. Etc. But I can't help it.

I have been wondering why I can't seem to get down to any work
ever since I finished the 2 articles on Egypt,[3] but I think maybe it is
because I have a feeling of 'Alone at last, thank God!' You know, this
past year has been a very odd one – I mean, from last April until now.
I was away for four months of that time, and when I was home, a
friend (Ann – I told you about her) was here for four months and ended
up in a state of mental breakdown (not due to me!). For another two
months, Jack was here, before he got a job and was very depressed,
naturally, about the job question.[4] So out of the past 12 months, I've
only been here on my own for the past two months, during which time
I've been going slightly mad trying to re-organize the house and to
write these articles. When I look at it that way, my present lethargy
doesn't seem so peculiar. I spent most of today wandering around my
garden, looking at the crocuses and daffodils, and toying with the idea
of weeding the rose beds (nothing came of it). I hope I can write this
story, but honestly, at the moment I would love to do just nothing. I
always think of your phrase, 'creative laziness.'

I hope you don't think I'm nuts not to have written to Jensen, but it seems more politic under the circumstances to do it in this sneaky roundabout way.

Love,

Margaret

1 Christian Jensen, Department of French, University of Manitoba, and program chair, Manitoba Festival of the Arts Committee. Wiseman had urged Laurence to ask Jensen if she might participate in the panel on 'The Creative Writer in Canada, 1867–1967' that was scheduled for 24 October.
2 Warhaft was at this time head of the Department of English, University of Manitoba.
3 Over the previous Christmas break, Laurence had gone to Egypt with her children on a one-month assignment commissioned by *Holiday* magazine. The articles were never published in *Holiday* but were collected as two chapters of *Heart of a Stranger*: 'Good Morning to the Grandson of Ramesses the Second' and 'Captain Pilot Shawkat and Kipling's Ghost.'
4 Jack Laurence had been hired as irrigation consultant for the British Overseas Development Ministry. He was based in Surrey and had taken a flat in Surbiton, a suburb of London.

22 March 1967 – CP night cable

CONGRATS. GOV. GEN. AWARD[1]   TRIED PHONING   COULDNT LOCATE YOUR NUMBER   BANISH FINANCIAL CARES   WORK PLAY WHOOPEE
love,

Adele[2]

1 For *A Jest of God*
2 This holograph draft of Wiseman's cable was printed by her on a blank page of Laurence's airmail letter to her dated 14 March 1967.

Elm Cottage
24 March 1967

Dear Adele:

Well, you were right! I got the letter today – my God, am I astounded and stunned! They pay my way over to Ottawa, apparently, so that is really marvellous. I don't really want to go to Toronto, even though I'd like in some ways to see people there, because it would be too hectic and I don't much feel like hectic evenings at this point. But I thought what I would do, if it is okay with you, would be to go from Ottawa to Montreal and stay with you for a couple of days – the only thing is, how much would this interrupt your novel? I *don't* think in terms of late nights, and wouldn't want any parties or anything like that – I would really just like to see you, only, and as you work late at night, that might still be possible. Only for God's sake level with me, and if it wouldn't be too good at this point, don't think I'd misunderstand, because I wouldn't.

Adele, do you remember when we were both still in Winnipeg and both somewhat younger, how we used to say, 'Wait until we've both got the Gov-General's?' Well. And what one sees now, at this distance, is that one used to believe once, naively, in external proofs of one's value, in terms of work, and now the only thing one can really believe in is the work itself, whatever anyone thinks of it. How strange. It doesn't get easier to do, does it? It gets more difficult, and now that my own particular decks are nearly cleared to begin another novel, and I can see my way financially for about a year and a half, the only useful thing I can think of doing is to pray – to pray that the novel will come, will be given. It looks simple from the outside, doesn't it? I wish I weren't so easily terrified by life.

Anyway, let me know if it will be okay re: my coming to your place for a few days – possibly around the middle or end of April. The difficulty appears to be that they don't know when the presentation thing will take place until a new Gov-Gen has been appointed.

You know, it was absolutely right, wasn't it, that I learned first about it from you? Thanks for cabling. Jocelyn took the cable over the phone, initially (they always send a copy later to the house), and she said it was amusing when elderly Miss Wright at the Post Office read the words – 'Work – Play – Whoopee' ...!!

I got a cable today from Pat Grosskurth,[1] saying congratulations and much love – too bad re: her, in a sense, because she didn't like my novel and gave it a horrible review and then proceeded to apologize to me for this fact – I wanted to say to her, look, it doesn't matter that you didn't like it, but please don't expect me to reassure you about it. Odd. See you soon – hallelujah!

Love,

Margaret

p.s. *Holiday* has accepted both articles – my God, what luck.

1 Phyllis Grosskurth (b. 1924), member of the Department of English, University of Toronto, and recipient of the Governor General's Award for her biography *John Addington Symons* (1964). Her review of *A Jest of God*, 'Pathos Not Quite Enough,' appeared in the *Globe and Mail Magazine*, 10 September 1966, 18.

Elm Cottage
2 May 1967

Dear Adele:

PROBLEMS! PROBLEMS! The Gov. Gen. Award ceremony is in Ottawa on June 2nd, and yesterday I got a letter from the C. Council, giving details. So I phoned Air Canada and also BOAC, only to discover that there is NO POSSIBILITY of a flight either June 1 or June 2. Because of Expo.[1] So what I have done is this – I have booked a flight to Montreal on May 26, so I can go to your place first, rather than after Ottawa. I do hope this is okay with you. I realize I ought to have consulted you first, but honestly, I didn't dare not book right away, as they are really getting sold out on flights rapidly. Thousands must be going to Expo from this country. I am quite astonished.

So, if all is okay with you, I shall be arriving in Montreal on Friday, May 26, at 12.10 noon, Flight AC/841. Don't bother meeting me, unless you really and truly do have the spare time, because I know my way around reasonably (which means I know how to summon a cab!). I can come in on the airport bus and then get a taxi to your place. No problem re: suitcase – I've just bought a new small one. If Air Canada loses it this time, I'll have hysterics.

What I've done is to book a flight from Montreal to Ottawa on June 2nd, which will get me in about noon, and the ceremony is at 6 p.m. So that will give me enough time in Montreal for us to do quite a bit of talking, plus maybe a quick look at Expo. We've seen TV programs on it recently, and it looks fascinating although a bit overpowering.

I am feeling horrible at the moment. Think I've got flu again. Temperature; streaming cold; the lot. Woke up this morning with ghastly stiff jaw, sore throat, swollen glands, and really was convinced I had mumps. (Lots of mumps around just now). However, I've decided it isn't mumps. I hate going to the doctor, but I guess I really should. Jocelyn also home with sick stomach. So we are looking after each other. I tottered up out of bed about 10.30, figuring I wouldn't feel any worse up, but now I feel so grim I think I'll go back to bed again. Wouldn't you know – I finished the *final* work on the Nigeria book yesterday, and handed it over last night to Alan Maclean, who was out here for dinner. It never fails. As soon as something is finished, I immediately get sick. Really physically sick. How can I control this psycho-somatic business? I wish I knew.

I am terrified about starting a novel. I feel like throwing up every time I think of it. I want to start it so badly that it is nearly killing me. I have been writing page after page in my head. I know so clearly what I want to do – all I don't know is how to do it. Everything is so complex.

How good it will be to talk to you!

Love,

Margaret

p.s. I have a book for Jim Ross[2] – the Oxford book of essays from *Can. Lit.* which includes the one of Warren Tallman's[3] which is partially an analysis of AS FOR ME AND MY HOUSE. It was obtained for Ross by a young Canadian friend of mine who is a great admirer of Jim. Shall I bring it, instead of posting, and maybe he could come around one evening? Would like to see: Jim Ross, Alvin,[4] your sister. That's all. Will phone some other people. I don't mean to be anti-social. It's just that what I need most of all is to talk to you – not *about* this novel, but about methods, neuroses, and other fascinating matters.
P.S. It is snowing here.

1 The Universal and International Exhibition of 1967 (Expo '67) was held in Montreal from 28 April to 27 October 1967.
2 The Canadian novelist Sinclair Ross (1908–96), whom Laurence greatly admired and who was living in Montreal
3 Warren Tallman (1921–94), a member of the English department at the University of British Columbia. His essay 'Wolf in the Snow' had been republished in the collection *A Choice of Critics: Selections from 'Canadian Literature'* (1966), edited by George Woodcock. His critical essay discussed *As for Me and My House* by Ross, *The Mountain and the Valley* by Ernest Buckler, *Who Has Seen the Wind* by W.O. Mitchell, and *The Apprenticeship of Duddy Kravitz* by Mordecai Richler.
4 Alvin Goldman

[1217 Drummond Street]
5 May 1967

Dear Margaret,

Even better. The sooner the better, & we'll have more time to talk if you come the 26th. So I'll be there to meet you with bells on, kid! I hope you've seen the Dr. & are over your ailment. There's so much going around all the time nowadays. I worked most of the night (don't commiserate, – a pleasure), – & woke up with a cold this morning myself, – nothing severe, but a nuisance. So I'm coddling me a couple of eggs in a Royal Worcester egg coddler I picked up at the junk shop for just such a time; when you really want to feel a bit coddled, it's such a pretty thing to coddle yourself with. Later on I'm going to drink brandy out of a snifter glass. If you're going to be sick, I figure you should get *some* satisfaction out of it.

You were very sensible to get booked up. Expo seems to be on its way to becoming a smashing success. You'll see when you get here; in fact we may be able to go more than once if you're not too tired. It can be pretty exhausting to go wandering around all day . But it's fun, too. I haven't seen Roman Kroitor's 'Labyrinth'[1] yet, but it's supposed to be very good.

Of course, bring Jim Ross' book. I haven't seen him since I got back, though I've been wanting to, & Alvin & I were just talking about getting together with him the other day.

Best news of all of course is the novel squirming through the symptoms. How I know those horrible symptoms, & how I shall miss them when I enter the barrens when this book is done. Bear with them, kid. They're way up there among the best things that are ever likely to happen to you. The 'how to do it' is tough, isn't it? But it's the key, & worth sweating over. It's so lovely when you finally know, & it begins to shape. If the 'how to do' ever stopped bugging one it would be a sure sign that something had gone wrong, – a numbness of sensitivity had set in at the nerve ends, – the beginning of artistic death. The substitute for it is the sterile virtuosity, form without substance, personality ploy, on which one can coast for awhile, I suppose, to ease the dying.

No girl, suffer! And at least we can talk together to ease that part of it somewhat; – & soon! Good!

See you,
love,

Adele

1 Roman Kroitor was the project director of 'Labyrinth,' the exhibit mounted by the National Film Board of Canada at Expo '67. The Labyrinth building was a structure of unusual architectural form designed to set off new developments in cinematography.

Elm Cottage
6 June 1967

Dear Adele:

I'm still not quite back home again, mentally, but probably soon will be. It was marvellous to hear your good news – congratulations, kid, on the Associate-Professorship – that is really fine. Don't worry about the good things happening, eh? We're crazy – things go horribly and we worry because we think we're accident-prone, and things go well and we worry because we wonder when the bill will come in. Nonsense. Take whatever is going, in the way of joy, and ask no questions.

Thanks several million times for a wonderful week, about the best week I've had in a long time. It was so relaxed and good and without anxieties of any kind, and even though I poured out my repetitive tale once more, it helped to do so. One doesn't always know what is operating under the surface. It seems curious to me that at the precise moment when consciously I thought I'd made some kind of renewed contact in the same old area, I also felt compelled to drag up the seaweed of the past, verbally, to you. It is, as you pointed out, an attempt to salvage whatever is salvagable (sp?) but it is also, as I recognize, a kind of naive desire to have everything all right, to create happy endings (which I myself believe in only momentarily and sporadically). Never mind. The week with you was very very good, and I feel human again, although still not working. But at least I don't feel I'm due for a mental hospital.

Ottawa, as I told you on the phone, was much better than I had thought it would be. The ceremony with the Gov. General[1] was short and unstrained. He got up and gave a touching speech on how brilliant we all were, and then Roy Daniels[2] presented each of us to him, and H.E. handed us beautifully hand-bound copies of our books. Madame Claire Martin,[3] who won the fiction award in French, was an absolute honey. She sat next to me, and before Michener came in, she got out her compact and dabbed away at her face. Finally she gave a massive charming shrug and said, 'Oh well, it's not a beauty contest.' She whispered to me, 'Do you intend to make a reverence?' I said heaven forbid, I'd never learned how to curtsy and understood it wasn't essential any more. She said she had learned once in convent school, but would much prefer not to, as her joints weren't as flexible as they once were. The dinner was okay, too, and the highlight of the evening for me was when Martineau, chairman of the C. Council,[4] proposed the Loyal Toast – 'To Her Majesty, the King!' I sat next to him, and thought he was delightful – he kept telling me how impossible it was to get good wine in Ontario. After the dinner, some of us congregated in Bob's[5] hotel room, and I was about ready to begin the serious drinking, as I had been so restrained all through the evening, but as nearly everyone else was stoned, the party wasn't all that long. Al Purdy[6] appeared at the pre-dinner drinks session at the Country Club, and when this enormous man shambled in, I thought 'My God, he looks like a cowboy,' which he does, but not to be deceived – he knows exactly what's going on, at any moment. He also isn't the kind of guy who goes around stabbing people in the back – he's aware of the reality of other people, and this is uncommon enough to be noticed.

When I got back, there was a really fantastic letter waiting for me, from a guy in California who apparently is doing a film script for A JEST OF GOD.[7] Not that this necessarily means a thing, except that the process has advanced one step more. But the letter was really weird. He wanted to know the sources for the hymns I'd used, and had apparently dug up a lot of exotic sources (Thomas of Celano's *Dies Irae*, etc), little knowing that I'd only taken the hymns from the Book of Common Prayer, nothing difficult at all. He seems like a nice enough person, and serious, although to my mind a little over-enthusiastic (which always makes me suspicious). But what slayed me was the following statement ... 'Rachel is built up of so much else, so many darting mysteries – as hard to catch as the bluebottle flies you mention, whose eggs, I discover (as I plunge through yet another reference – this one, 'Undertaking Science') are the ones those maggots come from that flourish best in the ears of unembalmed corpses.' Adele – can anyone really write that seriously? Does this nitwit think I read books on how to become an undertaker, before writing the novel? And yet, touchingly, he ends the letter by saying 'I have tried not to betray you.' I find this very strange, and in a way appealing, because what he doesn't realize is that in film terms I am unbetrayable. Nothing he can do with the novel will change it, in the only terms which matter to me, namely the printed word. Yet I also realize that *he* takes it seriously, and if (by a long stretch of the imagination) a film were to be made, and made well, it might be a good film. But this isn't my country. The sheer lunacy of the bluebottle bit, though, astonishes me. (I can't even remember where in the novel I mentioned bluebottle flies – strangely, I can remember where I mentioned the same species in The Stone Angel.)

Please write soon. It was so good to talk with you again, and I'm so damn glad that things are going well for you. Isn't it odd how many things can't be said in letters, even though one isn't at the time aware of this? People need to meet, from time to time, to get caught up on what has really happened.

Love,

Margaret

p.s. almost missed my plane when leaving Ottawa, and filled with more affectionate feelings towards Canada than I have harboured in many a long year, so naturally began thinking 'Could I live here again?' Don't think so, really, at this point, and can't get over the way in which I love my house etc here. But strange that reactions were so different from last summer, when I arrived back here gasping with relief. As I said on phone, *Canada* obviously hasn't changed that much. Or am I really talking about Canada, as such, at all?

1 Roland Michener (1900–91), governor general of Canada, 1967–74
2 Roy Daniels (1902–79), member of the Department of English, University of British Columbia, and chair of the adjudication committee for the Governor General's Awards
3 Claire Martin (b. 1914) had won the Governor General's Award for her autobiographical work *La joue droite*.
4 Jean Martineau, QC, chair from 1964 to 1969
5 Robert Weaver
6 Al Purdy (b. 1918) won the Governor General's Award for poetry the previous year for *The Cariboo Horses* (1965) and had come to Ottawa to meet Laurence, with whom he had recently begun corresponding.
7 Stuart Stern (b. 1922), whose credits included *Rebel without a Cause* (1955) and *The Ugly American* (1963)

Elm Cottage
29 June [1967]

Dear Adele:

I am a pyromaniac ... i.e. firebug, or so I begin to think. I have just gone out into my garden and have burned all the hundreds and hundreds of pages which I wrote on this novel about 3 years ago. How can I have ever thought I could sort out the good bits? It is the character who is there, not the individual words. And she is still there, but I can't seem to reach her, or not yet. All this delving into what was written before was only an evasion, I guess. If any bits are worth putting in, they will be in my memory. I've also destroyed all the plans for the novel – ie. the intricate setting-down of plot, etc etc, which was another evasion I've indulged in with this one for some six years now. All gone. Consumed in flames. I don't need a bloody plan – either it will come by itself or it won't, and I certainly ought to know the people, as I've lived with them trampling around inside my skull for so many years. But do you think it is possible to crack up without knowing it? I feel very strange, Adele. I think that if I can't write this one, I can't write. But sometimes I feel I just won't ever be able to get through to it. So help me, it isn't for lack of trying. I think it was at one time lack of comprehension. Now it is lack of faith. It isn't any hell of a great expedition, in external terms – just another novel. But for me, crucial. This time I *have* to see it through. But can I? Honestly, Adele, I feel like hell. As Paul Hiebert[1] said in WILLOWS REVISITED, a sequel to SARAH BINKS, published this year ... 'Who woos the Muse woos ooze' ... I can't disagree with that one.

PLEASE WRITE.

Love,

Margaret

p.s.   I have to give a talk on Can. Lit. at Oxford, to some students, tomorrow. What an irony. I feel at the moment disinclined to speak on the subject at all.[2]

p.s.2.   God, I am shameless ... sending out these appeals for reassurance. Wouldn't do it if you didn't know why, etc. At the moment, your credit is extremely high, as I hope you will remember the next time you are in need of cheering words. What stuns me about this kind of thing is that life does go on, and I make peanut butter sandwiches and all kinds of enquiries about my kids' exams and I worry because the cat has diarrhoea again and so on – how is this possible? Did I ever tell you that when I once read about 'role conflict' in an anthropological book, in reference to African chiefs who had been educated at Oxford, I really had to laugh – it seemed to me that 'role conflict' was the story of my life. And then one thinks – tut, tut ... self-pity; self-dramatization. Which also is true.

1 Paul Hiebert (1892–1987) was a chemistry professor at the University of Manitoba. He had won the Leacock Award for Humour for his *Sarah Binks* (1947), a life of the 'Sweet Songstress of Saskatchewan.'
2 As part of Canadian Centennial celebrations in England, Laurence had agreed to give a lecture, 'Canadian Novels: Changes in the Past Decade.'

                              [1217 Drummond Street]
                              17 July 1967
Dear Margaret,

This is the first chance I've had to get near the machine in ages, but I have been writing you mental letters ever since I rec'd your last. It may seem strange, but it isn't at all, that everything you've done in relation to your new novel seems to me precisely right as soon as I hear about it. Thus it was right for you to try to glean what material you could from the old notes, and it was equally right for you, a little later, to make a grand bonfire of the lot! (Wish I'd been there; pragmatic as ever, I'd have thrown in a few potatoes.) You ask if I think it's possible to crack up without knowing it. Not for you. You can't even not crack up without knowing that you're cracking up. There must be a very close similarity between the pre-integrative and the pre-disintegrative states of the human mind, is all I can figure out. It's the point when one is conscious of the fissures, and one is incapable of knowing whether they're there because things are falling apart or because they're just coming together. So what's happening now? Of course you must realize you're stuck. You can't go back because there is no back to go to. One way or another you're going to have to complete this novel. Is it possible to suffer with equanimity? My God I sound smug and pompous. That's what comes of asking a rhetorical question of a fellow writer. You get a rhetorical answer. So what is happening? Have you felt any of the pleasures yet? Myself I have written one sentence of Ch. 14. Luckily it's rather an amusing one, so that I can delude myself when I think of it, into imagining I have a toe hold on the chapter. There just hasn't been time. I saw the Penners off this morning. My kid brother Mo left Saturday, my aunt Thursday and my parents Wednesday. My brother Harry should be coming into town in about a week. He and Arnold are going to Europe on the 1st of August. They'll be spending a few days in London in early September. If there's any chance that you'll be coming into town any time the 6th and the 10th, let me know; I'm sure Harry would be delighted to see you. Don't misunderstand, please, this is not a request for you to do so, just an in case you are. They will have plenty of touristing to do, so they won't need any looking after, and except for a side visit to Oxford and Stonehenge, they will stick to the City. I'm writing Miss Gerson to ask if she'll let them stay in the Hampstead apartment. Meanwhile, Arnold just called to say he's through for the day at Expo, and will be coming home shortly. His best friend and family (4 altogether) are coming into town this weekend so the kid will have a break, someone his own age to go to Expo with for a change. It's rather lonely for him here otherwise. I'll move in with Dmitry[1] for the time they're here, as he's leaving on another trip after the weekend, and let them have the run of the apartment. His son[2] will be coming here at the end of the month. Des Cole[3] will be escorting him from Vancouver. Dmitry will actually still be out of town when he arrives, so I'll look after him for a couple of days on my own. He sounds like a very nice kid.

So, maybe in the next few days I'll be able to add something to the first sentence. I'm going to have to, or begin to feel (and act) spooked.

From the accounts here you gave a good talk at Oxford. Do you want me to send you the clipping? There's a very good picture of you with the article.[4] By the way, thanks for returning the article on Hugo.[5] They've moved into town already, and on Sat. night we had a big reunion of the Penners, McPhersons, Alvin Goldman, Noel Stone, and a few other ex-Wpg'ers and ex-Vancouverites. It was touching, really, to see Alvin and Adie Penner, who had been in grade ten together and hadn't seen each other for about twenty years; a pleasant party.

I hope all is as well as it can be with you working at the novel in spite of everything including yourself and the novel. By the way, hope you're not annoyed; I had a phone call from Jack Ludwig.[6] He and his family were on board ship, – or just getting on board. They're spending *a year*? or all summer? in London. I gave him your address and phone number. I know you've told me you're rather shy of him, but if you feel up to it when he calls, you can always give him another try. He's rather fun, – has enormous vitality. I also gave him George Lamming's address; he's an admirer of George's. His own book is coming out at the beginning of '68. And oh yes, he's been invited to be Writer-in-Residence at the U. of Toronto next year. I remembered afterwards that I could have given him Alex Baron's address too; well, maybe later.

I'd better go now. Be strong. You can't help being, really. And WRITE!

love,

Adele

1 Wiseman had met and fallen in love with Dmitry Stone (b. 1929), chief biologist with Beak Consultants in Montreal.
2 Sergei Stone
3 Professor Desmond Cole, chair, Department of English, Macdonald College
4 A description of Laurence's lecture and her photo were included in an article by Boyce Richardson in the *Montreal Star*, 15 July 1967, Entertainment section, 4.
5 Hugo McPherson (b. 1921) had moved to Montreal to become government film commissioner and chair of the National Film Board of Canada. The article has not been traced.
6 Jack Ludwig (b. 1922) was a professor of English at the State University of New York at Stony Brook. He was the author of the comic novel *Confusions* (1963). *Above Ground* appeared in 1968.

[1217 Drummond Street]
27 August 1967

Dear Margaret,

I am so sorry! Things have been so absolutely wildly hectic here that only this minute, the first I've had a chance in simply ages, and only because I've forced myself, to sit down to write a couple of absolutely crucial letters, have I taken a look again at your letter of July 16, and to my horror discovered that there was a request in it for copies of Chatelaine that had completely slipped my fuddled addled brain.[1] I am going to write to Chatelaine immediately and ask for issues, and hope it isn't too bloody late to do you any good. I am sorry. My God! For five days early this month we didn't have Expo visitors, and that's because Dmitry, his son Sergei who's been staying with us, and I took advantage of a few days Dmitry had off and beat it out of town and did some camping in New Hampshire and Vermont. Long distance calls galore, – I had to put off my friend Amy and David[2] her husband, who were already in New York, and wanted to come up, because the Reaneys[3] were in Dmitry's aptmnt, – (I think they left this morning), and with the three of us in mine there was simply no room. And at the same time I had to put off my old friend Miriam Selchen-Dorn,[4] and get them accommodated at other friends' because we were loaded. Hannah Green just called from Sugar Loaf, no, Breadloaf, that she and a friend are coming up tomorrow.[5] There have been old friends literally popping up from all corners of the world. So please, please forgive me for my stupidity in forgetting your request. What with all this, you can imagine I haven't done much writing lately. And yet the darn thing is there, bulging out of my forehead it feels like sometimes, so sometimes in spite of everything I sit down for two hours and bash away. So at least am a few pages into the chapter. But I will have to be back at work in less than two weeks, and Dmitry and I are househunting, as we'll both have to be out of our apartments by the end of October, so? I still have this funny feeling that I'll have the draft done before long. What of you? Your friend Clare Slater[6] was over one evening a couple of weeks ago, and we had a very pleasant talk. She has no doubt given you regards from me, as I frequently requested her to do. I hadn't realized that I had met her before in London, though when you talked of her she always seemed to be a terribly familiar name, and I even had the feeling in my mind of a rotund configuration of some sort. She seems a very nice gal. And I was very delighted to hear that you were really at work on the book. Not that I was surprised; I figured it was about ready to begin to flow properly last time I heard from you. How's it really going?

While we were on our camping trip we got as far south as Peter-borough, N.H., and I visited the Macdowell Colony with Dmitry and Sergei. Hannah Green was there, and in fact that very evening they were throwing a farewell party for her and someone else who was leaving. So we stayed for the party. Don't know why I'm impelled to retail this bit of gossip, but it's the kind of thing that is well nigh irresistible, at least to ingrained gossips like myself, and no one at Macdowell seemed able to resist repeating the story either. One of the artists there at the time was a poet called Isabel Gardner,[7] who is, I gather, quite a well known poet, though I don't know her work myself. She seemed a very nice middle aged woman, a few years older than ourselves. The story is about her husband, Allan Tate, who impregnated and ran off with a young nun recently. That's it, the story. Sad, humiliating for the wife, and yet something comical about the whole action. These poets simply will not grow old, and if grow old they must, they will at least go on being naughty.

Has Jack Ludwig called you yet? What was Claire Slater telling me about you putting up a whole big family from Canada for the summer? What is happening? Hannah Green, in her call, mentioned that Norman Mailer[8] had been at Breadloaf for a day or two. She sounded quite en-chanted with him. I guess I'll hear all about it tomorrow. She's bor-rowing a car and driving up with a friend, – I've already told you that.

Anyway, I'd better leave off now. The boys are back and Dmitry's on the phone with prospective landlords, so I'd better go be moral support. I'm glad he's doing the calling, as I hate making that kind of phone call. I always feel at a disadvantage, as though I were asking a favour.

Was saddened to hear of the death of David's friend.[9] It must have been pretty grim. Hard on a kid to have to face that kind of thing so early in life. By the way, this is going from something serious to something somewhat frivolous, but what reminded me was the business of the maturation process of children. Roman Kroitor, the chap who did Labyrinth at Expo, who was a year behind me at Manitoba, and also a protegee of Malcolm Ross, invited us and the Macphersons and Alvin and the Reaneys over last night, when he heard the Reaneys were in town. At one point in the evening I had to go up to the john, and as I sat there I was struck by a tiny little hole which somebody had obviously pretty freshly drilled through a beautiful, solid oak door. It was done at an angle which was very precisely beaded in on the genitals of anyone who happened to be sitting on the john. I also noticed that the keyhole was stuffed full of paper. So when I came down I asked Roman who had drilled the hole. Sure enough, he had just had a long and understanding heart to heart with his eleven year old as a result, all about what happens to a boy at a certain age. He had also rec'd confession of a youthful passion for a statuesque 18 yr old girl neighbour. Roman was a little disturbed because the hole was also, & should theoretically, presumably after the understanding heart to heart, have remained, stuffed with paper too. I guess the hormones are stronger than mere understanding.

love, write,

Adele

1 Laurence's short story 'Horses of the Night' had appeared in *Chatelaine*, July 1967, 46, 70–7.
2 Wiseman's old friend Amy Zahl and her husband David Gottlieb
3 James and Colleen Reaney. James Reaney (b. 1926), poet and playwright, was a professor of English at the University of Western Ontario.
4 An old friend from Winnipeg who was living with her husband, Harold Dorn, and their two children in Princeton, New Jersey
5 Hannah Green, American novelist and short-story writer, had been a MacDowell Colony fellow in 1960 and 1964. The Bread Loaf Writers' School was founded in 1920 at Middlebury College in Vermont, and the annual summer conference was initiated in 1925.
6 Clare Slater had been a colleague of Alice Frick at the CBC. She lived in England for several years, worked at the new theatre in Chichester, and was connected with the theatrical agent Elspeth Cochrane in London.
7 Isabella Stewart Gardner (1915–81), American poet, actress, and author, was the second wife of poet Allen Tate (1899–1979). They were married in 1959 and divorced in 1966.

8 Norman Mailer (b. 1923), American writer, whose most recent work was the novel
  Why Are We in Vietnam? (1967)
9 A young friend of David Laurence had been killed in a car accident.

Elm Cottage
27 September [1967]

Dear Adele:

Gosh, it was nice of you to phone this morning! I was slightly dazed
with sleep, or I wouldn't have talked for so long before considering how
much money it was costing you. I hope it didn't amount to a small
fortune.

Never mind whether your suggestions re: me in job of writer-in-
residence actually do work out or not – I'm damned grateful to you in
any event.[1] Don't quite know what that sort of thing would involve, do
you? I must phone Jack Ludwig and ask him and his family out here
one Sunday. I invited them awhile ago, but they were going to Paris at
that time, and haven't phoned since. I think, however, that he told me
he was going to be w-in-r next year at U of Toronto.[2] In fact, I'm pretty
sure of it. How many bards etc do they usually accommodate? I don't
know whether I would be so hot at the job, as I have never taught in
my life and haven't been involved with academic life since I was a
student. Never mind – with *Plotto* in one hand and the *Concise Oxford*
in the other, I would be prepared to live dangerously and make a stab
at it.

There would still be terrible complications. I think the whole idea
would not be greeted with joy by Jack, especially as he knows me well
enough to know that if I took the kids out of school here and put them
into school there, I wouldn't really be prepared to change them to
school here again – too many changes. I'd have to consider all this very
carefully, as I really don't think they ought to change schools more than
once more before university. Also, would Building Society (whose
mortgage I have) allow me to rent house?[3] Mind you, I think it is
unlikely that a university in Canada would consider me, anyhow. I
don't have much of a public personality, not like Ludwig. Also,
someone like that has had so much experience of academic life – he
knows his way around. I really and truly don't. However, if they'd
chance me, I'd try, simply because I feel so damn isolated here and
know I need to live in Canada again, just at the grassroots level, to hear
Canadian voices – one forgets the inflection, the idiom, stuff like that.

I don't know about this novel. I still believe it is there, if only I could reach it. But I think the real reason I broke off after Chapter 2 was that something is still drastically wrong with the way I've been doing it, and I'm damned if I know how to do it right. I know what's wrong, though, so maybe that's something. It is plainly a personal fear of some kind that is blocking me. This kids' book,[4] in a way, was a good thing – like, God gives you a consolation prize, although in some ways I feel I put in what I thought was a legitimate requisition for a novel, and instead I got this one – something wrong with the office system Up There. The heavenly IBM has flipped its lid. The celestial computers need to be overhauled. But at least I've been able to do something, which is a lot better than doing nothing and has probably saved at least a portion of my sanity. Funny the way the kids' book came – all in a piece, complete, package deal. Come to think of it, nearly everything I've ever written has come that way. Except this ill-fated novel – maybe that's what's wrong with it; contrived. When I got my last instalment of $$ from the Can. Council, I felt like a worm. However, some novel or other may be completed some time or other. What I really need is a kind of gift from my personal protector-god (my concepts of this become progressively more African as the years go by) – what I need is grace, I guess, and this I do not at all have at the moment.

Actually, I feel like hell. I feel as though I have been battling for 5 years, only to find myself now back in the same situation exactly, personally and in writing, as I was 5 years ago. Except then I had the nearly completed manuscript of The Stone Angel. Now what have I got? A book about moles and Flower Power pigeons, for Chrissake. Damn it, I *know* that novel is there, lurking in some other dimension. Why why is it not given to me to be able to see it?

Enough of this self-pity. Honestly, I wonder how many times I would have been carted off to a mental hospital, throughout the years if I hadn't been able to pour out my woes on your shoulder, through letters? I can do this with one or two other people, to some extent, but precious few. Another irony has just struck me – had I decided last summer to move, I could have done so with practically none of my present complications – I wouldn't have owned the house, and Jack then hadn't decided what job to take and so wasn't committed to staying here. But I simply could not have moved then, as I wasn't mentally ready. Still don't want to move until I get this novel done – unless I just don't get it done. Also I would like to hang onto this house if I could make it pay for itself. That might not be possible.

My dichotomy is obvious even to myself – I keep saying I cannot move back because of the many unsolvable problems, and yet I keep talking as though I were going to do so.

Thanks very very much for all your help and moral support. I'm so glad you and Dimitry have found a place. Tell me all about it. An apartment?

Love,

Margaret

1 Wiseman was pushing for Laurence to be writer-in-residence at the University of Toronto.
2 Ludwig was writer-in-residence in 1968–9.
3 Laurence had bought Elm Cottage the previous April with money from the sale of film rights to *A Jest of God*. She was paid $7000 for the movie option and an additional $23,000 for film rights.
4 Faced with a block about her next novel, Laurence had just finished the draft of *Jason's Quest*, which would be published three years later.

[1217 Drummond Street]
8 October 1967

Dear Margaret,

I've been trying to get this letter off to you for the last several days. More things keep happening; nice things on the whole, for a change. Dmitry finally got back from the West coast after three weeks. We're doing all kinds of things preparatory to the great move over at the end of the month. Yesterday I authorized my sister to pick up our first piece of furniture bought for the new place. I'd spotted it a month or so ago, and my sister happens to be friends with the junk shop dealer and his wife. Dmitry, who hadn't seen it, nevertheless said if I liked it I could get it, though he did look a little startled, and afterwards told me that somehow he would never have thought of an umbrella stand as an item of furniture to rush out and buy first thing when you're setting up house. But I know he'll like it. It's tooled leather, and if not antique, at least decrepit looking, which is the poor man's substitute for antique.

But what I have been dying to tell you, – they're such nice men! I had a letter from John Gray very soon after I'd spoken to him about the writer-in-residence idea. He had immediately got in touch with

Robertson Davies,[1] though he was only in Toronto for a day, who told him that Don Forster[2] is handling such matters since Claude Bissell[3] is away for this year. Apparently, they're not having a writer in res. this year, and are partially committed for next year. Forster, whom he called, was very pleasant and agreed with him that you would be a good choice, – as did Davies. Somewhere along the line somebody's wife was your teacher – at United?[4] – and thinks highly of you. Anyway, John said the way might be blocked for next year. Now, don't despair. I was going to talk to Malcolm Ross when he came here, – but as I think I told you, he didn't come because of gout in his left foot, – with possible osteo-arthritic complications. But here's the fantastic thing. I wrote to him, and suggested the w-in-r idea, and said that it needn't be the U. of T. There are several new U's recently opened in the area, – York, etc. etc. Also, there's Queen's, so I made the request more general. AND the other night I got a long distance phone call, from Malcolm, who, in spite of the fact that he was suffering from pneumonia, took the trouble to call and tell me that he'd been thinking, and working on the idea. Apparently the holdup in Toronto is that Jack Ludwig asked for a year's delay in taking up his appointment, which is why there'll be no one this year and they've a commitment for next year. However, Malcolm said that his idea is to try to get the Canada Council to help out so that he can bring you to Trinity! Isn't he marvellous? And here is a quotation from John Gray's letter, which would amuse (?) you. John didn't know who the other guy was. 'Perhaps Malcolm can do something if there isn't a real commitment, or perhaps Margaret can be wait-listed in case the other guy breaks his leg.' Now, I know that Hugo McPherson is also asking around too, and I saw John Marshall when I talked to his Library School kids[5] last week and he's very enthusiastic about the idea of you coming. So, kid, it looks like a good possibility. By the way, you seem to have some misconceptions regarding what will be demanded of you. Those jobs are really very simple, and designed to enable you to work. You have to do very little prepared work, just be there, occasionally, to talk to the students. It's your presence that they want, so don't worry. Malcolm told me you did a terrific job when you spoke to his students.

The talk went off all right. Regards from both John and Chris Marshall. John is thinking of going back to school for his Ph.D., which seems like a very good idea. He's such a 'young' and enthusiastic and gentle kind of guy. By a happy coincidence I was able to spend an hour and a half with my brother Harry while I was in Toronto that day. He was waiting for a plane to take him on to Vancouver, where he was giving a talk. Mom & Dad are in Miami, and they phoned me the night before I was flying in to try to connect with Harry, so I was able to arrange my reservations. It was a pleasure to see him. He will be coming through here next week and we'll have a few days together. He's never met Dmitry, though Arnold has, and I'm anxious for you to meet. It's interesting, Harry seems to have had a similar effect on a lot of people. Miss Gerson stayed over 8 of the 10 days that Harry & Arnold were in London, at her flat, and insisted on taking them around and looking after them, in spite of the fact that she's been having terrible staffing problems, and simply hardly ever sleeps over at the place at all, normally. Amy's sister Sosh, who visited me here for the first week of Expo, just wrote that he's the nicest man she's met in a long time and she wished she could have spent more time with him. I hope some good things will come to him soon; it would be a change all right. God I'm glad he's a fighter. And Arnold seems to like his new High School, and, from what Harry tells me, has matured enormously over the course of the trip. They're spending a good deal of time together now, which Arnold really needs. So, I'm hoping it will be a better year for all of them. My Dad spent a month in the hospital when he and Mom got home this summer. His arteriosclerosis has affected the circulation in his legs rather badly, but at the moment the condition is not considered dangerous. He'll enjoy being in the warm climate. Mom won't, but she's Mom, and she's needed, so she'll deliver. All else is okay, – Mary & Arnold & the kids, Mo and his boat, etc. I showed the photos of Jocelyn & David to everyone, and took them to Toronto to show the Marshalls. They're lovely kids. Will write more.

love,

Adele

P.S. Re: your story in 'Chatelaine,' I wrote requesting copies. Got one copy, & discovered, while I was reading it, that someone had cut out the second half of your story!! Will look around some more.

1 Robertson Davies (1913–95), novelist, playwright, editor, was from 1963 to 1981 founding master of Massey College, the location of the writer-in-residence at the University of Toronto.
2 Donald Frederick Forster (1934–83), a professor of political economy and at this time an executive assistant to the president and provost
3 Claude Bissell (b. 1916) was president of the University of Toronto from 1958 to 1971.

4 Constance Sword, wife of acting president John Sword, had taught French and
English at Neepawa High School.
5 John Marshall was a faculty member at the School of Library Science, University of
Toronto.

Elm Cottage
21 October 1967

Dear Adele:

How can I ever thank you? Re: Malcolm Ross and everything. Anyway,
I know I don't have to, so I won't.

Situation at present: got a letter today from Head of English Dept,
Dalhousie,[1] asking if I might be willing to go as Writer-in-residence
there for a year, and if so, would I make application? This was partly
because a young Canadian friend, Don Cameron,[2] who has recently
joined the Eng dept there, put up my name as w-in-r. So I've written to
Dalhousie saying I am interested, and would like to know more and
will forward letters of recommendation. (Sorry about typing errors –
yesterday I bought a new typewriter, the first new one in 10 years, and
it is a honey, but I'm not used to it yet). The thing is, Adele, if I could
move back to a relatively small city and to a university slightly less
imposing than Trinity Toronto, obviously in the beginning this would
be better for me, for small-town reasons which I need not explain. The
main thing is I wouldn't be quite so terrified as I would be at Trinity.

What I want to do is to move back to Canada – if possible, to a job
as w-in-r which would pay me enough to live for the year – and not to
pull out of England entirely just yet, but to wait for that year and see
how I and the kids feel about Canada, and then perhaps in the summer
of 69 move back here to settle up all my business – either rent this
house long-term or sell it; arrange transfer of money to Canada; arrange
transfer of income-tax from Eng to Can, etc. Halifax, if it possibly
worked out, would be a good foot-in, because not so large or intimidating as Toronto, and yet with the possibility of my visiting
Toronto to size up the situation and decide what to do. When I do move
back, will have to be either in Toronto or near. Best would be to buy
house in Rosedale, with accommodation for tenants, and flat always
available for self, and make that a base, if I can, then if I can arrange it,
and need to, move out to some old shack somewhere to write from time
to time. This may be a fantasy – I do not know. All I know is that

Toronto will have to be the ultimate base, for earning a living in terms of things peripheral to writing (in times of need) and also in terms of seeing people – this being also not too far from Montreal. What I'm *not* thinking of is a permanent series of sinecures and grants. If I could get on as Writer in residence for a year somewhere in a relatively small university, that would be fine, as it would allow me a foothold into Canada with no worry about transfer of money from England, and it would allow me to see what it offered me and what (more uncertain) I could offer it. Having spent many years being bugged by what means we can devise to penetrate more deeply and also more instantly into the human dilemma, verbally, it would interest me to know what the young writers 20 years my junior have to say. Of style, they must of necessity be more certain than I am, and probably they must know some things which it may benefit me to learn from them – I believe so with all my heart. What they cannot, however, know, is the unmeasurable – the way the pain feels twenty years after when you never thought there would be a twenty years after or that the indignities could ever happen to you (the silences between people who had vowed communication; the astonishment with which one finally sees that one's kids can't be talked to, really, any more than you in your generation could talk to your parents – I am the mother now; all this bugs me, to some extent, which is to say it breaks my bloody heart and I have to try to put it down even though I think I have picked this time a fine loser, someone who won't speak to anyone except me – but you know, Adele, fuck all of *them*, if this is so – so one thinks, speak to me, and if you can't speak to anyone else, never mind, that's a hazard of life, baby. Am I right? I've got to be, in this). Well, my dilemma is not complex. I am bound up at the moment with this novel, which I intend to do whatever it may be like, and if it says sweet bugger-all to everyone else, I do not bloody care.

Anyway, I have written today to Jack, asking him if he might be willing for me to take the kids to Canada for a year, with the possibility of their staying on there somewhere, and I think he will try to work out something with me. We are not really on opposite sides, exactly, but it is difficult because (a) for him – what a shock to find your wife may possibly be able to hold a job and/or earn money in some way or other maybe more money than you are earning; one doesn't want the dollars to be the deciding factor, but in the end, alas, he who pays the piper calls the tune, as I bitterly wrote to him some years ago when I was dead broke and had to rely on him for sustenance for self and kids – money doesn't matter a damn, Adele, but it matters if you are the one who hasn't got it and is therefore dependent on someone else – and if you *have* got it, you have to consider what the (maybe temporary) having of it may mean to the other person. In my case, I can at the moment afford to take on the kids – do I say to him, look, I don't need and I don't want your money for them? No, I don't do it that way. I say – look, if by any fluke of circumstance I happen to get on somewhere in Canada as writer-in-res., then I would be earning money and it would be silly for you to pay an allowance which you need more than I do, so if that happened, we would sensibly have to consider who could afford to do what. I.E. ... I would keep the kids, and would pay our fares over here to England in the summer holidays, and might go halves with him for him to go to Canada at Xmas, because he is on an English salary and at that point I could afford to do this more than he could. Adele, in the end, what will happen is that he will go back sometime to Canada because he will not be able to bear the fact that I make more money than he does. This is ironic, because as you know, what I've made is a kind of fluke and it may stop tomorrow, and probably will – I feel no security except my own ability to hire out my labour to a magazine which wants me at any point. And even this might disintegrate as of next year. I'm willing to take on responsibility for my life and even (with some reservations) for the kids' lives, but how do I get around the problem of somehow always for his sake to pretend that all this with my work is some kind of meaningless hobby which doesn't affect him? The money that I've earned (quite gratuitously, without effort, in things like this film) mean nothing to me except that I am with this money enabled to maybe move where I want and not to have to worry too much about the next month's payments. But still, for him, it hurts and I haven't even told him what I got out of the film – all this is crap, you know, doesn't mean tuppence, means only a fluke that permits one to stash away a little for the future when perhaps the writing isn't coming well. But I suspect that this is not the way he sees it, and so in a sense I am not levelling with him – I am not daring to tell him that the financial position for me is pretty okay just at the *moment*, and I know what to do and am doing it. I don't want to make him feel he is not needed. He wrote last time and said that if he were to die tomorrow, at least it would be a good thing to feel he wasn't essential to anyone. I almost broke my heart over that one. I *know* it's emotional blackmail – God, Adele, I know, but he doesn't know he is doing that. So my first reaction is to say to him – look, you *are* needed – which is really true, in many ways, especially where the kids are concerned. I can't bear his loneliness. I really just can't. He says 'I am of course profoundly lonely' and goes on to say that he is glad we could relate for some years and sorry that it couldn't go on for all our lives. This leaves me almost suicidal. Because, actually, he is a good man (as good as any of us) who didn't deserve what happened to him with me. On the other hand, it is difficult for me to have work which I want to do and which may at this point extend beyond myself and my kids. For 15 years of my life, I have done my writing and attempted in some fashion to bring up my kids. Now I would like, if it is not too late, to divert myself in some slightly different direction.

But I have to consider the kids' schooling, and at this point I am not too perturbed, as I think both of them may do better in a Canadian university. I also have to consider whether Jack will be willing to have me take them back to Canada, and I have to get his consent on this because they aren't just my kids.

If one were a male writer, things would (maybe) be easier. Then one would take jobs where they were indicated, and either the family would go with one, or the wife would remain with the kids and the established schooling, as in the case of Norman Levine,[3] moving to Fredrickton for a year as W-in-R. But I am not in quite that position. I have to consider 2 kids and they must go along with me, and yet I must also consider how often and where their father is going to see them, although his job may take him to W. & E. Africa etc.

Well, we'll see. I've written to Malcolm Ross, asking him to write to Dalhousie for me, and explaining that I'd rather go to a small university first, with my total lack of experience, and consider Toronto later. If I can work all this out in personal ways, so much the better. We will see. I don't feel that the right solution is to give in and say *Your work means more than mine*. But on the other hand, I can't with any honesty say *My work means more than yours*. The man's work, of course, socially, tends to be taken as more valuable by everybody. This is partly why I feel so goddam guilty at wanting to do my own work despite Jack and even despite the children's educational needs. A mother is not supposed to feel this way. Repeat three times and underline, eh? And yet I love them terribly, so what the hell am I to do?

Well, we'll see. Anyway, many thanks for all your moral encouragement. I hope this letter reaches you – before you move to the new establishment. I can see Dimitry's point of view: I, also, would not actually have thought of an umbrella stand as the first piece of furniture for a new home – but I feel tenderly towards you for feeling so, as I am sure he does, even much more.

Love to you both,

Margaret

ps. YOU HAVE NOT TOLD ME YOUR NEW ADDRESS. PLEASE INFORM IN-STANTLY.

1 Allan Rees Bevan was head of the Department of English from 1958 to 1969.
2 Donald Cameron (b. 1937) was a Killam post-doctoral fellow in the Department of English at Dalhousie. A recently completed PhD at the University of London, he had first met Laurence in the summer of 1965.
3 Norman Levine (b. 1924), Canadian writer best known for his short fiction, was the first writer-in-residence at the University of New Brunswick, in 1965–6.

[2234 Girouard
Montreal 28
Quebec]
2 February 1968

Dear Margaret,

Forgive me for not writing for so long. I hadn't quite got the draft done by the time the Xmas holidays were over, so I determined that I would pay no attention to any other but the barest minimum of tasks till I got through the thing. So, while the dust balls gathered and went bowling along the corridors of the house, Dmitry cheerfully banged away at making & converting furniture & I banged away at the book every chance I got. At school I ad libbed through lectures. Luckily, the outrageous things I said had about as much probability of sinking in as my usual pearls of wisdom, so not much harm can have been done. I warned Des that I was going to be more non compos than usual around the place, & he was very good about it, – even refrained from making up the duty roster; (we each have a week of having to be 'in' during the whole working day, to take calls, etc.) – since my turn happened to be coming up. Well, about a week ago I completed the draft. Eureka? Quasi Eureka? I don't know. I've put it away till the term is over, as it's most unlikely I'll have much chance to do anything with it before them. As it stands the thing is bloody long – nearly 500 pages of 1½ spacing, which makes each page about equivalent to a printed one. As for what it's like, I can't really say yet; I haven't read it through. But this stage is past anyway.

And none too soon. Tomorrow Dmitry's mother & her husband are coming to visit us for two weeks. She has never been this far East, & has just finished a course prior to beginning a new job, so we're bringing them out for a breather. But the place is hardly in shape for visitors. Luckily, Dmitry says she's not the type to go in for microscopic examination. Unfortunately, this week has been my duty week, so I've been pretty tired when I got home, & haven't done much to improve the shape of things. Dmitry, thank God, is as feckless as I am about these little crises, so as yet we haven't been able to work up that hysterical frame of mind between us, which gets things done.

At the moment I'm sitting & overseeing a test I've just set for one of my classes. I should be reading *Vanity Fair*, which I must begin to teach on Monday, I'm on page 105, of 728 pages. I'm such a bloody slow reader, & can't resist the urge to annotate. But I want to get this off so that you shouldn't think anything is wrong.

How are things your way? How is the book coming? Any news of the children's book? or didn't you submit it anywhere? Is the Africa book out yet? I know this is a silly thing to say; it's the sort of thing one says knowing full well that one is incapable of taking one's own advice when the need arises, but isn't it possible at some point to simply accept oneself & one's rel'nsh'ps, – provided one is doing the best one can? Don't we in fact find reasons in the new order to feel over again the dominant anxieties, that have somehow become necessary to us? What started off this train of thought was something you said in your last letter. It's something I've been trying to muddle through for a long time anyway, – but you were saying something about your distress because you feel you're perhaps not able to give enough to this new relationship with Jack. It reminded me that early in your marriage you worried about not being good enough for him. During your separation you worried about a variety of things which had reference to, usually, your feeling that you were not being fair to him, in one way or another, and now you're worrying about not being able to give enough. What's kind of interesting is that I'll bet that the *feeling* behind the concepts & words during all these stages was very similar, though the words appear to be related to vastly dissimilar situations & times. The anxiety & inadequacy feelings put on these guises without changing their own inner nature. It's the many headed Hydra. Specific situation is simply a shape, a form, a disguise. So are these feelings, stripped from situation, simply anarchic? How relevant is specific situation? Simply as outlet? I suppose madness is the alternative. More on this another time. Please write.

love,

Adele & Dmitry

P.S.   I suppose you've seen Marjorie[1] since her return? How is she? Regards to Jack & the kids.

---

1 Marjory Whitelaw had been fiction editor in Montreal of *Weekend Magazine* and had come to know many Canadian writers. At this time she was with CBC Public Affairs in Halifax, and made frequent and extended trips to England.

2234 Girouard
31 March 1968

Dear Margaret,

Hi! *April 6.* Forgive, I've been juggling duties, pleasures, responsibilities, the gestures of habit, and a confusion, if not plethora, of mental activities. I'm not complaining, mind you. Every moment is a gift of late. I held off writing at first because Malcolm Ross was coming & I wanted to give first hand news. He came. We had a party for his old friends. It was very pleasant indeed, Ross hadn't seen Alvin Goldman for fifteen years! He looks fine, seems to be over his last summer's ailments, though has to cut his meat intake to guard against a return of the gout. He's Provost as well as Dean of Arts & Vice Chancellor of Trinity this year. But next year (several hours later, hours during which we took Vivian Bliss & J.J., Mary's kids[1] & their housekeeper from Barbados, to the Sugaring-Off party at Macdonald College, in the Arboretum. You know, that's the maple-sugar party. We had snow cooled, maple syrup candy & hot dogs. A tractor dragging a large, flat, open trailer, took us (shades of the old tally-ho) to the sugaring house area. Needless to say the kids loved it. Anyway, back now.) Malcolm will be getting next year off, & will be visiting Prof. – at Dalhousie? – for part of next year.[2] But he'll also be in England for 3 mos. All of this will give him a chance to finish his book – on 19th century aesthetics, Ruskin, Pater, etc.[3] Very interesting. I realized again how much I owe to the man. Anyway, it was a nice party, & we got a sweet letter from him a couple of days later, in which he noted especially that he liked Dmitry *very* much. He's always dead-on-the-mark. He told me what you'd hinted at, – about the invitation to you for Toronto next year. He says it's a very definite invitation. I guess now that you & Jack have stabilized things, that you will be able to work out a way to come if you want to. I hope you do, I guess just because time is so short & life is so short & things so awful all around, the air gets denser & I sometimes feel that Dmitry & I are kind of crazy, and yet thank God for this craziness. He actually believes that we should be good to each other, though the policy has brought him a hell of a knocking around in the past. What have I ever done to have a lovely, warm, sentient, human, loving, intelligent rock to hang onto? I don't know, but I'm hanging on. If there were nothing more, – every day is a gift. And it would be nice to have you within calling-on distance for a change.

But meanwhile I've still not told you how glad I am the first draft is done. By now (I hope) you're well into the (no doubt exquisite) torments of the second. I was very struck by something you said in your last letter, that you have an idea of a direction in which the novel can go in the future. That sounds like an exciting breakthrough. Is it describable? Part of my own fuss these past few weeks has been the problem of getting together eight legible chapters to send to an agent who wrote to me on Hannah Green's advice, (Random House has taken her book – hooray!)[4] I'm told she's a top notch agent, Candida Donadio, with Russell Volkening. Anyway, I've finally sent her the ch's. to see if she really would be interested. Easter weekend we're going to N.Y. City, unless this hideous sit'n in the U.S. grows even worse.[5] God. Write.

love,

Adele

[P.S.] This letter doesn't seem very legible, but I hope you'll be able to make something of it. What an awful summer the U.S. has to look forward to. Poor King. Poor all of us stupid humanity. But don't let me succumb to the temptation to strike poses. Our fate is a triumph of logic. WRITE!

1 Children of Mary and Arnold Distler, Wiseman's sister and brother-in-law
2 Ross was to remain at Dalhousie for the rest of his career.
3 The book was never published.
4 Perhaps *The Dead of the House* (1972), which was ultimately published by Doubleday

5 Martin Luther King, American civil rights activist, had been assassinated on 4 April
in Memphis, Tennessee.

                                    Elm Cottage
                                    16 April [1968]
Dear Adele:

Thanks for your letter, which was tremendously welcome as I had been
feeling kind of low. Post-novel depression, mainly, but complicated by
physical symptoms of an unusually bizarre nature. I always get ill after
finishing a book but this time I really out-did myself. I got flu (or
something) about 4 weeks ago, just after finishing first draft,[1] and finally
when it lodged painfully in my sinuses, I went to doctor and he gave
me some kind of antibiotic. Flu and sinus cleared quickly and then –
horrors – I woke one morning and found myself absolutely covered
with a red rash. Doctor said it was an allergy rash caused by antibiotic.
I was damned relieved that I wasn't contagious, and thought it was
rather a joke, believing it would go in a few days. It didn't. It has lasted
now for 2 grim and ghastly weeks of itching day and night. Have been
on some kind of pills for it, and they make me so sleepy I can hardly
keep awake. Now it is getting better, thank God, but for awhile I was
beginning to feel like a lesser and ludicrous Job. Also got exhausted
through waking dozens of times per night and staggering up to put on
high-powered anti-itch lotion which worked beautifully for about 10
minutes. Full of self-pity, etc. Also I felt like a leper because I really
looked as though I had some terrible disease. Also felt guilty for feeling
sorry for myself when world in such an awful mess, but the cries of
one's own stinging flesh are humiliatingly loud. Anyway, I am more or
less recovered now.

America seems to me to be open now to the maelstrom, with Dr.
King's death. The passing of panic legislation for human rights seems
to me to be too little and too late and too obvious in its motivation –
nothing done until the white community as a whole begins trembling
with fear. I can only try to keep on reminding myself that the ancient
Christian doctrine that despair is a sin is a correct one. It seems difficult
sometimes to continue one's work in good faith. Why in hell write
novels now, one sometimes feels. But this just absolutely is not true. It
is more important than ever, now, to keep on, it seems to me – and to
keep on right to the moment when the physical blow falls, if it does.

Interested to hear about Malcolm Ross's visit. I'm so glad he is feeling better now. He is a wonderful guy. I'm glad he told you about the possibility of the U of T job next year for me – I have been too superstitious to mention it to anyone except Jack. We have discussed it all very thoroughly, and he feels strongly that I ought to take it, and we will try to work out domestic arrangements. He will try to arrange his job so that he will be in England at the time, if necessary telling the Ministry his reasons for needing to be here then. God, Adele – does that indicate anything to you? To me, it indicates just how much both Jack and I have changed. Five years ago I would have been scared stiff to contemplate such a job, and if I had, Jack would certainly never have agreed to put himself out in any way to make it possible, as he then believed a woman's place was etc etc. He has been marvellous about this, and I am very touched by his helpfulness. The only problem will be – what to do about a housekeeper? Jack could be home weekends, but cannot be here during the week, as Surbiton is just too far to commute without all kinds of difficulty. I am considering asking my younger aunt to come over for the period, but don't know if she would. The Charletts, who housekept when I was in Canada and again this year when Jack and I were in Spain, might do it, but 6 months is a long time. Anyway, I told Jack Sword that it would really depend upon my being able to make arrangements for the kids. It would be a great wrench to leave them for so long, especially as Jocelyn is at such a tricky point in her life, with (at that time) her university-entrance exams coming up, and also now she has her first boyfriend and is emotionally very up-and-down. But I would love to do the job, if it proves possible. Anyway, I am trying not to think of it right now, until I get done this year's program, which is to finish this novel and to do 3 short stories to complete a series of 10. So we'll see.

I'm glad you've sent some chapters to an agent, and cannot see that she could fail to be interested unless she is a complete nit. Let me know immediately anything happens, eh? Will you submit it simultaneously to Canadian, Eng and Amer publishers? That seems the best plan, in many ways, to me. God, it's wonderful that you're finished it. My novel is very thin-textured in comparison, but then we write so very differently – I can't cover as much territory and in as great depth in one novel as you can, so have to do slighter and more novels. I haven't got far with typing this one – have kept on re-writing and picking away at it, but really must leave it now and try to get it typed out, however it may be. I care about it so damn much, and yet I want to throw up every time I look at it.

Re: possible new areas – I wasn't thinking of anything new, as such, only something new for me, namely the area of myth. Don't think I can write (or want to) any more anything set in specific contemporary country (geographical or spiritual). But have some idea of semi-historical setting, although very vague, but based on an aspect of Can. history. WRITE!

Much love,

Margaret

ps. so damn glad at the tone of your letter – you and Dmitry are *not* crazy although I see what you mean – in this present world, to love one another and act with comprehension and tenderness places you among the far-out cases.

P.S. Please don't say anything much about the Writer-in-Residence job in case it doesn't work out.

1 Of *The Fire-Dwellers* (1969)

Elm Cottage
4 May [1968]

Dear Adele –

Am so damn fed up with typing that godawful manuscript so have decided to take a few minutes off and write to you – only please don't think I am doing same only because bored with typing! I wanted to tell you about our trip to Scotland, and intended writing this weekend anyway. But this damn typing, Adele – I can see the problem now. I have never before typed a book which I had so recently written. Both This Side Jordan and The Stone Angel were typed at least a year after writing. The Nigerian book was also typed a year later, and was much shorter. A Jest Of God was typed by a typist. So this is why I feel so grim about this one. Every word is too familiar, and I still agonise over it as I type. That, plus the anxiety – is it any good? I know – we both know all about that bit. In the end, it had to be written for myself, whether or not it ever gets published, and I am well aware of it. But can't help feeling that I would type it now with more verve if I only knew – even a little – how it affected even one other human being whose judgement I trust. That is, provided it affected them in some measure. If it didn't, I would be tempted to shove it into a trunk or something. This is the bad time for me. Remember how I practically tried to get rid of The Stone Angel by packing it up at your place with a lot of old tennis shoes in an uncertain cardboard box and mailing it to England? Am suffering the same neurotic anguish over this one.

How goes your typing of novel? With more balance than mine, I hope, although probably not. Yours is much longer and has more layers of reality than this of mine, and I wonder if your typescript is legible enough for you to get help with the typing? I hope so. I think this stage is hell. Aren't they all? Yet there is some kind of tremendous sense of release and joy, almost, in actually having the thing written, for better or worse.

The kids and I had a marvellous week in Scotland. Stayed at the house of a friend, in a village in Perthshire – a friend of Marjory Whitelaw's, really, and she drives so we rented a car and drove all over the central highlands. I will tell you only about the real highlights of the trip, as the whole thing was terrific. First, we went to Burntisland, the village in Fifeshire where my people came from, and this was a kind of sentimental journey for me. Secondly, in a junk shop in Dundee, David found a REAL SWORD for £2.10.0 (I advanced him the money on his lawn-cutting) – it later proved to be the sword-cum-bayonet type of thing used in mid-19th century, and we found on the blade a name inscribed – de something, a French name, and Avril 1848!! David was in absolute heaven, although he said he felt like a nitwit when we returned on the train, carrying a sword into the restaurant car! Third, we drove to the now-deserted house of James 'Ossian' Macpherson, the man who translated old Gaelic poetry and epics in the late 18th century and known in histories of Eng. Lit. only as the perpetrator of a literary hoax exposed by Dr. Johnson.[1] Have now read Dr. Johnson on the subject, and feel quite strongly that although Macpherson may possibly have added bits of his own, or not translated quite accurately, what he was doing was to take down poetry from the still-surviving oral literature of the Highlands, and Dr. Johnson just did not know bugger all about oral literature. Anyway, all this fascinates me very much, as I know quite a bit about African oral literature, but nothing yet about Scots, and that literature came out of the same conditions, roughly, as the African – i.e. a tribal situation in a non-mechanized but culturally highly developed area. So up we drove to this huge deserted house, greyish pink granite, high on a hill, resplendent with towers but otherwise quite austere in the Scottish baronial manner. David, miraculously, managed to discover a door which could be pried open, so we all explored the mansion from top to bottom. Beautiful old rooms with high simply ornamented ceilings and gorgeous simply designed fireplaces. Grotesque stags' heads hanging in the great hall. No heating or plumbing. An air of intense occupation by ghosts. Some very lovely William Morris-type wallpaper, now much faded. On one fireplace, some tiles were missing, so for the first time in my life I committed vandalism – I pried off a charming tile with the Scots thistle and bluebell on it, and brought it home, where it now rests on my brass table in my livingroom. Got a letter from a bookshop in Edinburgh today, that they have found for me a 2-vol work of Ossian's poetry, with original Gaelic (not much use to me) plus Macpherson's translations plus a more modern translation plus an essay on authenticity of Macpherson. I'm terribly excited about it. It will cost me £7, which seems mad extravagance, but I don't care.

Well, back to the old grind. Jack doing fine in Br. Honduras and hopes to be home end of May. David and pals working on strange electronic projects. Jocelyn fluctuating between happiness and utter gloom re: boyfriend. Today is gloom day, unfortunately, but I am learning not to get too personally upset, either by her unhappiness or by her natural (but to me hard to take) tendency to say Go away to me – she's right; I can't do anything; but it's difficult to learn.

I had a letter yesterday from Bob Weaver, who said he'd seen you and that Harry had been visiting. Please write!! Much love to you and Dmitry,

Margaret

1 Macpherson (1736–96), a Scot, had become wildly popular through large sales of his volumes of 'translations' of epic and other poems by 'Ossian,' the son of the legendary Celtic hero Fingal. *Fingal* (1762) and *Temora* (1763) were quickly republished as the two-volume *Works of Ossian* (1765). In *Journey to the Western Isles* (1775), Samuel Johnson (1709–84) described Ossian's poetry as a forgery and the product of Macpherson's imagination. See Fiona J. Stafford's *The Sublime Savage: A Study of James Macpherson and the Poems of Ossian* (1988).

[2234 Girouard]
8 May 1968

Dear Margaret,

Some intuition must have told me to hold off writing you last night because my head would be clearer this morning. My head's no clearer, the usual fuddle, but this morning I have a letter from you, so for the moment, this grand sense of power-in-clairvoyance. Funny also that you should be writing about the problem of typing up your M.S. More evidence for E.S.P. That's been holding me up for a couple of months already, that and exams to mark & school business to clear up. But the typing business really bugs me. That's why I sent the agent about half the book (over 200 pages), in an M.S. that had been photocopied from my M.S., (the one you saw) on about 5 different occasions & 3 different kinds of machines, in varying degrees of legibility, – a couple of chapters are even photo-stated, – the printing is white on a mushy grey background. This does not prevent me from being very annoyed be-cause it's a month already & I haven't heard from her. I feel like sending her a stinging note & ordering my scraps n' leavings back from her ungrateful table. All she's supposed to do is tell me whether she's interested in taking the book on. I'm using this, I can feel it, as an excuse to delay getting down to typing the final draft. The fact is I don't want to type all that out again. There are some changes to be made in some of it, but they hardly seem to justify the retyping of about 500 pages at 1½ spacing. At least you're a speed typist. You can agonize at a better clip, suffer faster as it were. At the rate I type I'll be a broken woman by the time, if ever, I reach the end. It'll take me months. I hesitate to give the thing out to be typed partly because it makes me nervous, but partly also because then I'd have to proof read, which I find a pain in the neck. Of course I hesitate also because it will cost a fair whack too. So meanwhile I'm concentrating my wrath on the agent & avoiding my manuscript. I've just finished with school so I feel I can take a few days, – but woe is her if I don't hear soon! Meanwhile the house is in an awful mess & I'm trying to work up the housewifely enthusiasm to scrub & wax floors. I just had a call from Dmitry's office that he won't be back till tomorrow night instead of tonight, because of same trouble with the boats. He's been in N.B. since Monday. I worry about him when he's away, which probably sounds silly, and I miss him. Who'da thought it would come to this? I'm hoping to go on some of his jobs with him this summer. It'll be a great chance to get to see some of this country. I'm also hoping to get to Vancouver when he goes that way, – if we can connect. The 'Learned Societies'[1] are meeting in June, & if I can get them to give me a travel grant it'll take care of much of my fare. If only Dmitry will have his assignment out there at the same time he can show me his home territory. I have little desire to go by myself at this time.

I would really love to do a lot of reading this summer. After every book I feel this great void in my mind & want to read & loaf & vice versa. I have been promising myself as soon as this book is finished to take some kind of concentrated French course in the summer, but now that the time is nearing I feel so drained mentally. I just want to stoke up without the huge effort of learning to articulate another language. I am wrong and I know it. If I were simply taken & put into a force-fed French situation, it would probably be a great idea, but my own fat lazy mind just wants to curl round a book.

Your interest in Ossian, & your idea linking him to the oral traditions sounds great to me. I hope you'll follow it up further. We are really far too rigidly trained in our 'academic' traditions. Here's a recent experience which helped open my eyes. I've told you about the quotation on which the title of my novel depends at least in part.[2] Well, I've been unable to track the quotation down, – know only that it's from the Caballah somewhere. So, when the time came I sent out a call via the grapevine, to all the Hebrew scholars around. Dmitry & I spent an evening at the Jewish Public Library; telephone calls started pouring in, quotations, references, discussions, but no exact lead-in on the quot'n I'd seen. And some of these people are formidable scholars, know the stuff in the original. Was the problem in the original? in the translation? Who knows? Finally I was given some advice. Make up your own version. There are thousands of interpretations. That's how they came to be. And attribute it to the Kabbalah: Legends of Creation. So, at least for the time being, I reproduced a quotation as close to the sense of what I'd seen as I could remember and now I'm trying to figure out whether I've just become a serious contributor to the tradition as well as a frivolous writer of fiction. So go ahead, reinstate Ossian & give us all more elbow room!

It sounds like a lovely holiday you had, & the tile you took is not a vandalized item, it's a literary relic. Macpherson himself would be glad that you have it. Don't let the values of the daily world obscure the existence of higher values, more profoundly significant metempsychoses, as it were. On a less exalted plane, have you tried garbage picking? Seriously, Dmitry & I have several times driven along the lanes ahead of the garbage van & picked up some very useful items. By the way, we had a lovely time in New York, really a joy. Even the civil disturbances were in abeyance that weekend, thank goodness. Regards to the kids, – & Jack when he returns. Did Marjorie Whitelaw get her grant? Please write. Sight unseen, I can tell you to go ahead & publish that book!

love,

Dmitry & Adele

1 The annual meeting in May and June of Canadian academic associations
2 Wiseman attributed the epigraph to *Crackpot* to 'Ari: Kabbalistic legends of creation': 'He stored the Divine Light in a Vessel, but the Vessel, unable to contain the Holy Radiance, burst, and its shards, permeated with sparks of the Divine, scattered through the Universe.'

Elm Cottage
13 May [1968]

Dear Adele –

I agree – it's ESP! Got your letter this morning, and while I am not glad to hear of your troubles re: typing, I have to admit in a purely selfish way it makes me feel heartened to know I am not alone in my agony. At the moment I am not suffering faster, either! I got to the point when I recognized that I was setting myself unreal goals and then feeling awful when I failed to achieve them – like, say, telling myself I would type 25 pages in a day, and then only doing 12. So now I am trying to do a steady 10 pages on allocated days, until the end of the month, and see how I get on. At least I can do 10 pages without spending the entire day over it, and really, at this point I am just not capable of spending 6 or 8 hours a day at the typewriter – I get so fed up I want to chuck the whole novel away. It really is hell, and I sympathize 100% with you. I think that for myself, the 10 pages a day method (makes it sound like a diet) is the only one which will work. Sure, I can do a lot more than that, but if I do, then the next day I can't even look at the manuscript without wanting to throw up. It's odd – I find the typing terribly boring, yet at the same time I can't help suffering through the whole damn thing myself all over again, and I just don't feel like thinking about the novel any more, at this stage. Could you get even some parts of your novel typed for you? I agree – I feel nervous, too, when I've only got 1 copy of a manuscript and it is out of my hands. That was the great thing about A Jest Of God – I had the handwritten version, so would have been able to reconstruct it even if the typist had lost it. Actually, however, she made such a mess of typing it that I had to go through it and make corrections on every page, so I might as well have saved myself £20.

I certainly hope you can go with Dmitry on some of his trips this summer – it would be marvellous to see the country together, and I am damn sure you could do with a holiday. The amount of psychic energy which is used up in writing a novel is tremendous. Personally, I don't intend to do anything much this summer except read and do gardening and maybe rewrite a kids' book which I don't have many hopes for but would like to finish. Jack and I intend to take the kids somewhere in Europe for a week or so in the holidays, also.

I love your story about the quotation from the Caballah. And why not? If there are many different versions and interpretations, as there always are with this sort of thing, why not add yours? I've just received my 2 volumes of Ossian, which is fascinating – contains the translation of Macpherson, plus a later translation (1870) of Rev. Archibald Clerk, plus Dissertation by said Mr. Clerk on the authenticity of the Gaelic version, which is also included. Poor old Macpherson got a raw deal from Dr. Johnson, I'm convinced of that. Rev. Clerk thinks that some of the Gaelic goes back to the 10th century. I'm not contemplating getting hooked on Gaelic epics, by the way, as I did on Nigerian writing. I'm really interested in it for another reason – nothing specific, but just a general feeling that it will come into something, sometime. The Nigerian book comes out in the autumn – did I tell you? It will sell about 5 copies. Panther Books are doing A Jest Of God in paperback, but calling it by the film title – NOW I LAY ME DOWN (!).[1] I couldn't care less. I hope it sells a million copies. I'd care if the book had never been published under my title, but as it is, I feel quite remote about it. Did I tell you McC & S brought out The Stone Angel in the New Can. Library? And that the pic of me looks like I am a heroin addict with 15 chins and 2 black eyes? Jim Ross's stories also came out same time[2] and it is a very nice looking book, apart from being a good collection – I'm so damn pleased to see it at last. Jim's picture is much better than mine, although probably he doesn't think so.

I am sitting here drinking (sipping, rather, thinking of the price) costly sherry which I had no business buying, but got reckless the other day and thought – oh hell, what if I go broke? Etc. As I get older, I lose my taste for cheap booze, which is really unfortunate. Cheap red wine

I don't mind, but feel I've had Cyprus sherry. The trip to Spain ruined me for life – drank nothing but good sherry, and now I KNOW, so will never be quite the same again. My unreasonable justification for buying good booze lately has been that I am saving £20 by typing my manuscript myself!

Got a letter from Jack the other day, describing riots in Belize – stone through his hotel window; tear gas (he said 'I can assure you it does cause tears') ... sounds awful. I don't suppose he is in actual danger, but it sounds unpleasant. I'm sure you worry about Dmitry when he's away – I don't think it is silly at all. I don't any longer worry about J's physical safety, as I long ago learned not to think about that aspect of things, as he has always been away a lot, often on quite dangerous jobs as bridges etc. For some years I used to worry dreadfully, then somehow without actually realizing it, I came to a kind of mental state in which the thought of any accident was subconsciously suppressed. After that, funnily enough, the years I used to worry most about him were when we were separated and things were kind of grim – I guess I felt with part of my mind that it would be awful if he were killed or died faraway and everything was terrible between us. Now I don't worry so much. But I think it is perfectly understandable and inevitable, to some extent, that you worry, if only because superstition comes into it and you probably feel afraid in some ways because you're happy – but don't be afraid. It's marvellous. Write.

Love,

M

p.s. didn't have room at end of letter, but meant to say Love to you and Dmitry. Would so much like to fly over and drop in on you (at a convenient moment, of course). Well, maybe I will actually get there next yr.

1 The Panther edition was published on 5 September 1968, but was withdrawn shortly after its appearance and reissued as *Rachel, Rachel*, the title of the movie version of Laurence's novel. The film, starring Joanne Woodward and directed by Paul Newman, opened on 26 August 1968. Knopf reissued the novel as *Rachel, Rachel* in 1975.
2 *The Lamp at Noon* (1968), with an introduction by Margaret Laurence

29 May 1968

Dear Margaret,

The non-stop jet for Vancouver is just about to take off. We (Mom, Dad, Big Julie[1] & I) arrived in Wpg. Sat. night. Now I'm on my way to meet Dmitry. He's taking a week off while he's out West on some jobs, & I'll get to see the area for the first time. After our holiday I'll stop off in Calgary while he goes on to Oregon & Northern B.C. to do some of his work. The Learned Societies are meeting in Calgary this year. I got a travel grant from McGill to attend, which has helped make the whole junket possible. It's been rather a happy trip so far, because I was able to attend my cousin Larry's wedding. I don't know if you remember the little boy I used to dote on. He's still a sweet boy, & married a very cute little girl. It was a delightful wedding. I didn't even cry, which for me is extraordinary. Of course I was busy taking flash-camera shots in the synagogue, & refusing to pay attention to the rabbi's signals to stop, so there wasn't much time to cry too.

We're taking off now. I will not panic. I will not panic. The engines are making funny unnatural sounds. I will not panic. They've just demonstrated the oxygen mask. I can't breathe. I will not panic. Thunka thunka chukachucka ningy ningy whine chucka chucka – If we fall & this scrap (charred) is recovered from the wreckage it may help the investigators. We're moving along. We're off the ground. _It's not for humans_!!

Gee the prairie looks pretty from above. Are you finished typing? Have you sent the M.S. off? Have you heard from the agent? the publisher? Did you hear what happened to the agent I'd been in touch with? I sent her a variously photo'd copy of about half the book, April 4th. Over a month later I still hadn't heard from her, but Hannah Green wrote me that on April 8th she'd left the agency & gone into a new partnership. (Pause while I check all the rivets in the wing.) Finally I heard from her, very enthusiastic. So when I get back home I'll have to sit down to the M.S. and clean it up. The agent, Candida Donadio, is the one who pushed Catch 22, – which I haven't read, – (Oh God, we're travelling over water now. It says, 'Use bottom cushion for flotation.' Bottom of what, for Godsake?) Anyway, she has already begun to talk the partial M.S. up to various editors, she says. Before I left Mt'l I wrote to outline previous commitments, & to explain that I'd like to retain the connection with John Gray of Macmillan in Canada. So, we'll see what happens. (Does it mean float on your arse?)

We had regards for you from Noel Stone,[2] who said he had dinner with you in London when he was over recently. He's a nice guy, isn't he? I hope his play does well when he gets it done. Donadio is now hooked up with a man who's supposed to be a good play agent, Robert Lantz, so maybe he may turn out to be useful to Noel too. I let Donadio know that I have written a 'splendid' play. Funny how some you have to be modest about because they really don't need you, & some you have to shout & scream & yell about. It's an indignity, because they really don't need you, either. Oh well.

Regards from Mary & Bill Mindess. I spent a couple of hours with them the other day. They seemed fine, & were glad to know that you & Jack are together again.[3] Are you putting out a new book of short stories? Somebody wrote or called Mary for some biographical material on you for an introduction to a book, but she didn't find out what book. Regards also from the Penners who are fine. I really didn't get much chance to see people. Maybe I'll stop in W'p'g. for a day or so on the way back. The Mindesses want to know about Ken Black.[4] How is he? What's he doing? Women? etc. Also, I would like to know whether Marjorie Whitelaw got a Canada Council grant. How is she, etc? And you? Is Jack back? What are your plans now the book is done? Did I write you when we were in N.Y. we saw Wole Soyinka's 'Kongi's Harvest?'[5] and found it quite fascinating. But what a problem to try to integrate all the elements he's juggling with! We met a young woman at a party recently who spent a year teaching in Nigeria & is very much interested in Africa & wants to write. She knew Soyinka & some of the other Nigerian writers. She'll be in England this summer so I gave her your address. Did I do wrong? I thought there might be some mutual benefit. Hope all is well with the kids & Jocelyn's love life is proceeding happily. Please write.

love,

Adele

P.S. Regards from Dmitry & my folks & everyone.

1 Adele Wiseman's dog
2 A freelance writer and friend of Adele and Dmitry
3 The Laurences were attempting a reconciliation.
4 Ken Black had worked for the CBC in Winnipeg and since 1964 had been working for the CBC in London.

5 Wole Soyinka (b. 1934), Nigerian playwright, poet, and novelist. His sombre satire was first performed in Lagos in the summer of 1965.

[2234 Girouard]
26 June 1968

Dear Margaret,

Am beginning this while waiting for a train to take me out to do my final 'duty day' at Mac. It's some kind of formal thing; each of us has had to do a two or three afternoon stint this month, to remind us, I guess, that we're being paid on a yearly basis. I don't mind; it's no great hardship.

I must tell you how delighted, if unsurprised I was, that your publisher likes the book. And of course the fact that he likes it better than *A Jest of God* is really great, because one loves to feel, even though it's not always possible, that one is moving forward somehow. (It's not even logical, because qualities are not crudely time-tied), but when it happens there's a kind of satisfaction that points up how embattled one really is in this world & its tick tocks, – 'I'll get better & better & better & better ... ' Someone may, I suppose, someday. Is that what's behind Jesus? When was he at his best? But before I spindle off the thread entirely, the fact is one does feel that some are better than others; I do at this moment about my current one, that it's better, more mature, more complex, etc. Maybe that's because it's closer. But about yours I'm not at all surprised at its being better, because it seems to me it's been in the marinade of the emotions for so much longer, (pardon the culinary image). It seems to me you've suffered it longer & harder, & it's meant more. I'm really very anxious to see it. Is there any chance before long? What will you be doing for the rest of the summer? Any news of plans for the '69 term? I met the Head of the Dalhousie Eng. Dept. & chatted to him for a while. He was very disappointed you couldn't come this year. Malcolm Ross will be there all this next school year, & I think he's hoping to persuade him to stay longer. Lloyd Wheeler is already on his staff. He himself used to teach Eng. students at the U. of M.

Was very happy to receive yours & the Barons' joint card. I must & will write to them as soon as I'm over the big push I'm just setting out on. When I got back from out West, – (we had a lovely holiday), – Arnold my nephew was in M't'l. He'll be spending the rest of the summer in W'p'g. He's grown very much this year, – is as tall as his

Dad now. Harry, by the way, is due in town any day now. He's going to England for a meeting of some sort. You'll probably hear from him. Anyway, I just last night pulled my M.S. out of the drawer & read a couple of ch's, & made a few corrections. From now on I'd better work solidly. Dmitry's two younger sons will be spending the latter part of the summer with us probably, and I doubt whether I'll be getting much work done then, so it's July or nothing to do the final revisions.

It's such a *fat* book. The agent hasn't written me after that initial response. She hasn't answered any of my questions, which is irritating. One of them was, 'do I have to retype completely, or can I just zerox a clearly corrected copy?' The retyping is such a chore, & I'm already tired of those parts which I won't be doing much else with. So why should I have to work on them, – or even re-read & correct typist's copies? Proofs are bad enough. So let me be querulous. As long as I can get myself to work, I would like to be done on time to be able to take a work trip with Dmitry towards the end of the month.

Other news. Mary & Arnold may go to Israel with the kids this fall. The daughter of a cousin of Arnold's, is getting married there. Arnold survived the bunker with this particular cousin, & so it would really be nice, since their family has shrunk so, for them to be able to go. My parents are not doing badly. Dmitry managed to spend a day in W'p'g & got acquainted with all the relatives, on his way back from the West. He picked me up there & we travelled home together. He should be home later this aft. He's in & out all the time during the summer. It's sure nice when he gets back.

Now I'm on duty. Several hours later. Duty over. Shortly I'll be off to catch the train. I'll be carrying a caseload of fresh new books that'll have to get read & marked up before the teaching begins again come Sept. I successfully avoided having to read Lawrence's *The Rainbow* last year but it looks like a must for this year. Many of these books are get re-acquainted texts, like *To the Lighthouse*, which I look forward to re-reading. I can't remember if I ever read *Jude the Obscure* before, – or *Bleak House*, though both sound terribly familiar. I may have devoured them in my omnivorous days. We'll see. I have to make a choice of which of the two to teach, since we have options. I'll also have to choose between *Tristram Shandy* & *Emma*. But at this point I'm just going to put them aside till my own work is done. I'd like to teach Shandy, but it may be too difficult for the 1st year kids. They balk at reading the simplest & most formally constructed stuff, & Tristram is a bit, what is the current phase? – 'unstructured?' for them? – Nerts!

Anyway, I just called Dmitry. He's at his office. I'd better take off now. Please write & cheer me up during the next few weeks (I spelled it 'weaks' first) of earnest grind. Let me know how things are with you. Is Jack back? How are the kids? How were Alex & Delores? I'm so fond of them. You're right; she does take care of him. But as for men writers having it easier, I guess you're right, but you know I used to think men had more energy than women. But women seem to go on so much longer that I wonder. WRITE!

love,

Adele

Elm Cottage
30 June 1968

Dear Adele –

I was so damn glad to get your letter yesterday – in a work sense, all is more or less okay, but in a personal sense we had a hell of a scare this week, so somehow one is even more glad to hear from friends. On Wednesday, Jocelyn wasn't feeling well, but I thought it might be largely due to nerves over exams which she has been writing all this month. She had 2 more to go, at that point. She got worse during the morning, and I phoned doctor, who said after examination that it was probably gastro-enteritis, but might just possibly be appendix, and to phone him if anything further developed. Late afternoon she began vomiting at frequent intervals, and about 6 p.m. the pain which had until then been very diffuse seemed suddenly to localize in right side, so I phoned doctor again. I must say, he was marvellous – was here within half an hour, and said he thought it was appendix and she ought to go into hospital at least for observation. He made all arrangements, including ambulance, and finally ambulance bowled up and I took Jocelyn to High Wycombe General. The surgeon examined her and said he intended to operate as soon as he could get hold of the anaesthetist. I came home and phoned about 11 p.m, as they had told me to do, and the op was done and she was back in the ward, apparently okay. 'Her condition is satisfactory,' the nurse said, and I spent the next hour or so wondering how satisfactory that might or might not mean. Anyhow, I went in the following morning, as early as I could, and she was really okay – pretty wan, of course, and still very sick-feeling, but okay. I later learned from our doctor that the surgeon phoned him that night and said it was lucky he had diagnosed appendix and had her taken to hospital then, because the appendix was just on the point of bursting when they operated. When I heard that, I began to shake more than somewhat for awhile. It did not at the time seem that acute – she was obviously in pain, and when the vomiting got more frequent, I realized it was likely not gastro-enteritis, as no diarrhoea, but thank God I did phone the doctor when I did – my God, so much depends on luck – it doesn't bear thinking about. That evening I felt dreadfully alone and I certainly wished Jack were back in England. Sent him a cable, and he cabled Jocelyn next day, which was nice. I waited until I knew she was okay before cabling him, as this sort of thing can be so frightening at a distance. But in any real crisis, the scales fall away from the eyes – I sat here by myself that evening and knew all over again that he really is the only human being upon whom I can really really call in crises affecting my children, and also how damned unimportant my work seems when related to the lives of my kids. Naturally, when the crisis had passed, I recognized how terribly good so many neighbors had been – and they really were – and also, the work became important again when I knew Jocelyn was okay. But how odd it all was – how damn terrifying to me, and yet (now that she is okay) how much it has restored me to some kind of mental balance. I had been pacing the floor for weeks, re: verdicts on the novel, and that night I knew so terribly clearly how little any of it mattered in comparison to her. I did not, I may say, reproach myself for past neglect of kids – I don't do this any longer, as I now know that I suffer more or less permanently from what is anthropologically called 'role conflict,' and when the conflict gets less it will be too late to do me any good, as I will then be in the position of having grownup kids at a time when my own work is terminating as well, but none of that can be helped and it could have been a hell of a lot worse in every way and I really think how goddamn lucky I have been to be able to do both, although both less well than I would have liked. Anyway, Jocelyn now complains that her side hurts when she laughs, so that is pretty cheering! With luck, she will be home on Tuesday. The whole hospital experience has been a very thought-making one for her, as she is at an age when she can perceive many of the undercurrents. She said one day 'You know, mum, you think how awful you feel yourself, and then you see people who have been here for ages and won't be going home for a long time, and you see things differently.' Just so. The hospital is new and very nice, and apart from boredom and loneliness, she seems okay now. She is too shy to do much talking to the other patients, as most are much older and some quite elderly, but she seems to have at least traded magazines, etc. Some friends drove here yesterday all the way from the New Forest to see her, so that was much appreciated by me. I also shamelessly phoned (partly for my own reassurance) nearly everyone in England whom I know, and in passing suggested they drop her a card, so in fact she has had rafts of mail. She hasn't been in hospital since she was terribly ill that time when she was 1 month old, and David has never been in hospital except when he was born, so fate has so far been pretty good to us.

The work now returns. I got a cable this week from Jack McClelland, saying he liked novel, and thought it was pretty nice of him to cable, as he knows how neurotic I am at this stage. Later this week got a letter from him, which among other things stated his criticisms of novel – basically only one, and one which I agree with, so that is good. Got this week, also, a letter from Macmillan's stating the criticisms of their readers, which boil down basically to one point, and they are not being insistent at all, but although I know I cannot change novel in structure (they don't suggest that I should), I think they have a point re: a few things to be clarified, things very clear in my mind but not rendered sufficiently clearly to readers. However, I am pretty glad about all this, as the only thing I worry about is – do the characters come across? If they do, all these minor points can either be clarified or left as they are, which is only to say that I recognize only too well the structural weaknesses but cannot necessarily do anything about them – they are inbuilt, and it isn't a perfect work but so what? I think at this point, all one can say is – if I were a better writer I would have written a better novel, but this is the one I wrote and now it is on its own.

I can say quite truthfully that I think with this particular novel that it begins slowly – but for reasons which I believe valid – and it accelerates almost too much in the last 3 chapters, so everything bowls along at a terrific speed, and one would have liked to check the pace somewhat in that section, but to do so would have been to manipulate – that is the way it happened; sometimes life happens all at once and too fast; I can't alter it and won't try. What I will do is to go back and try to make a little more comprehensible some of the things which are perfectly comprehensible to me but not necessarily so to a reader coming to the novel cold. Haven't yet heard from Knopf, but do not expect to hear for another few weeks. They will be more detailed in criticism than either Macmillan or McC & S, but they will also be (if they like the novel at all) quite open to my explanations of why I did it that way. Maybe one ought not to have to go through this period of various people saying their say about it, but I think it is okay, really – it's like the diplomatic world must be, in a way; a certain amount of dickering must go on. But it seems to me that the only thing a writer can do is to seriously consider the criticisms, which do, after all, come from mainly intelligent and concerned people, and to act on those which strike an immediate bell, and to parry the others as tactfully as possible. The publisher, or so it seems to me, isn't the enemy – they want the book to be as good as possible, and they are really only anticipating in their criticisms what the critics will say about it. The writer is in the isolated position of not knowing, until some other person has read it, how it may affect any other human being except him-or-herself. I know perfectly well that if I wrote to Macmillan's or to Jack McClelland and said I was not able to do any revision, they would still publish the novel, and to know this, at last, is a vast reassurance, because it means I can now consider what they have to say about it, and select the criticisms which seem to me to make sense and to be things which I can do something about, while at the same time being able to turn down the criticisms which are either mistaken or which relate to aspects of the novel about which nothing can be done although one might have wished it had come out slightly differently. Does all this sound like nonsense? Maybe I'm only trying to express for my own purposes the process which I'm now involved with – the damn thing is nearly off my neck, but not quite, and I wish it were entirely off, but have to see it through although I would really like never to have to look at it again. You are dead right, kid – this one was in the marinade a long time, and I guess it matters to me a lot, and I found it so bloody hard to write that I really thought I was going to end up in a mental hospital, as you know from my letters over the past year, and now I really want to forget it, and can't yet – hell hell.

I DO know how awful it is for you, re: the typing, etc. Your novel is a hell of a lot longer and also more complex than this one of mine, and it must be terrible to have to type it at all. I really felt like throwing up when I was typing mine, and I know that it is not nearly so complex in structure as yours and also I am a very speedy typist, which is my good luck, so can sometimes bash away almost automatically. But when I think of how easy the basic typing process is for me – sex and typing are the only physical acts which I am good at – I really feel for you, kid. The 300-odd pages of this goddamn novel nearly knocked me out, but I can when pressed do about 30 pp a day. I can't lecture on English lit; I don't think I have read *any* of the novels which you mention; I feel bloody illiterate; but I am a good typist – put it on my tombstone. Cannot you get someone to take the corrected copy and type it? It will cost you the earth, but the stress on yourself will be so much less. I know you don't want it out of your sight, but on the other hand, you NEED HELP with the straight physical process of transferring a novel from your own typescript to three or whatever carbon copies. So – get help, if you possibly can. Nothing is to be gained by sitting on the manuscript for months and feeling guilty that you haven't typed it. Take the chance, if you can, and try to get somebody to type it out for you in triplicate (costs not much more than 1 copy) ... I have a vested interest; I want to see the novel, and I can't bear to think of you sweating away about the typing of it. So pawn the family jewels, kid, and hire a typist. It'll be okay – her house won't catch fire, etc. It is too good a novel to hang around waiting for an uncertain typist (you) to type it. So you're a good writer – do you have to be a good typist as well? Get help – what you need is to get the novel typed up in good shape and sent out. (I once felt it was immoral to get a woman in to clean my house each week – but you know, it isn't!) GET THE GODDAMN NOVEL OUT AND TO THE PUBLISHERS – <u>NOW</u>! I would not say any of this, knowing how presumptuous it might seem to anyone except you, but really, I do know how awfully discouraging it is to have the damn thing done and yet not done, not yet able to be sent off. As I say, this is a straight physical job which I am able to do, not having spent any of my life in acquiring skills such as the ability to lecture in Eng. Lit. or address the Learned Societies (you don't really know, I sometimes think, how near-illiterate I am). So – accept the fact that you can write an intricate and beautifully structured novel and you can earn a living in an academic world which is all mystery to me, but when it comes to typing – HIRE SOMEBODY, you nit.

Don't know re: U of T in 1969. Want to go, but remains to be seen what family arrangements can be made. Much love to you and Dmitry, and please WRITE SOON.

Love,

Margaret

P.S. Jack's job has delayed him, & he now hopes to be back end of July. ps.   Nearly forgot to tell you one very nice thing – we bought a secondhand pedal organ from a Scots MP friend and had it shipped from Portshire to here – it is very Victorian and in its way lovely, and kids are delighted with it. It turns out to have been made in Guelph,

Ontario, and has (as the metal letters proclaim) a 'MOUSE-PROOF PEDAL.'
It is HUGE and fills playroom.

2234 Girouard
14 August 1968

Dear Margaret,

Strike's over, at last in M't'l too, and I got my first mail today. Some
mail! Pause while I gnash teeth and tear hair, – only not my hair. I had
a letter from my agent. She'd rec'd the rest of the book which Dmitry
had got someone to mail across the border, and ' ... I read it with great
pleasure. It is a good good book!' Nice, eh? But perforce she had to go
on. 'But there is not splendid news from Marshall Best,' (Viking)[1] 'There
is a letter from him today, very kindly in intent, though he is formally
rejecting the book.' Herewith, Marshall: 'To have this new script arrive
was tantalizing. It is apparent that she has been working away at it
slowly for years. (Shit!) The material is as authentic as it was before and
the central characters are moving and effective. Meanwhile, however,
times have changed for this kind of story, which might have seemed
fresh and important a decade or so ago, now seems too familiar. The
painstaking and leisurely style also seems somewhat out-of-date.' Then
he goes on to say that if Macmillan take it, and I do 'a good deal of
cutting, we would be glad to see it again.'

I don't give a damn about Viking, but the grounds of the rejection!
Wow! I remember when John Gray was talking about Jim Ross' book
sounding somehow old fashioned and 'dated,' and giving it as one of
the reasons why they rejected it. That book was written, say, thirty years
after his first one, and presumably in the same style, the style of the
man. Perhaps it was the style of the era too, and I think we discussed
the question of literary out-of-dateness, and how authentic a criterion
it was. What is fascinating here is that not thirty years, but about twelve
years have elapsed, the pace has apparently tripled, and yours truly is
a has-been without hardly even having was'd! The agent still seems
pretty confident that she can place it elsewhere, but I am really chilled
to the marry-bones. Why bother writing? Why go to all the trouble to
try to find my voice, when it's been heard before and no longer seems
as fresh and N.B. as it seemed before? And yet his response is true to
the tenor of the age, isn't it? I can't help thinking 'You shmuck'! but it
is somewhat disheartening. With such criteria, it could be.

Other things have happened since the surprise and pleasure of your telephone call. Dmitry and I were out in New Brunswick; I was on the job with him and enjoyed it, though it's terribly depressing to see a great, beautiful river that's dead, as the St. John River is, for a very long stretch. Black, stinking, no fish life evident, except for the occasional dead mudsucker, the species that survives longest, floating by. The death of nature, on that scale, is appalling. One has such deep feelings about water as a life giver, that it really shakes one to see the godly creature dead. Man, we are a mess.

[—] very likeable youngsters. If it comes to it I hope we can provide them with a good home. We had just had the two younger ones with us and they'd gone off home a day or so before I joined Dmitry in New Brunswick.

So we've had a fair share of excitement around this way. I still have an enormous amount of reading to do for next year's teaching, but this news today threw me off my stint for the day. I had better collect myself and go to it before long, since all those rosy dreams of maybe making something on this book have receded summat. I had better make sure I continue at least as a satisfactory, (if, as I've been told, somewhat too rigid as to literary standards) teacher.

The main thing, one lives. And there's not all that much time left. Are you still thinking of maybe being writer-in-residence in Canada next year? Dalhousie? Toronto? If the former, I picked up a place mat while we were out East that will give you a local view of the importance of the province, which I'll include here.

Harry was through briefly while we were still out East. I told you he'd talked about what a lovely time he'd had with you. I'm sure he'd be delighted if David were to come down to learn to skin dive. His boy Arnold will probably be back here next week, and will stay a while before he has to go back to school. Mary's husband Arnold is giving him some draughting training. The youngster is very good at it.

God, I was delighted to hear your voice, and to hear your news. Any additional dividends which will serve to keep you independent while you write what you want are a blessing.

Love to you, the kids, and Jack. Please write. Love from Dmitry.

Your out-of-date pal,

Adele

1 Editor with Viking Press in New York, which had published *The Sacrifice* in 1956

Elm Cottage
3 September 1968

Dear Adele:

Got your letter of Aug 14 when we returned from holiday a couple of days ago. All I can say is that I personally believe that Viking are out of their minds. Don't mistake me – I am not saying this just because I care about you and I care about your writing. In fact, the whole question of idiom and of writing the language of one's contemporaries is one which I know we don't entirely feel the same about. For myself, I feel and have felt for some years now that I was the kind of writer who had to speak mainly to my contemporaries and when I had out-lived my own idiom, to shut up. This is partly because all I have written has been in some way or other much concerned with the current social patterns, even though the characters themselves represented what I valued most in the writing, and what I cared most about. But where have my books been set? Ghana, at the time of Independence; a prairie town in the thirties but also the current social background of Vancouver and an old woman there; a prairie town sometime in the past 10 years; and now, Vancouver and a middleaged housewife and mum. In fact, it has all been an expression of my own scene in some way – I mean in an outer way; whatever it may be inside, which is an expression of some of the ways one feels about various aspects of life, and oneself and etc etc. What I am trying to get at, in my hamfisted way, is that with my last novel, THE FIRE-DWELLERS, I realized very very clearly that I had come to the end of the road in terms of expressing things through my own generation's idiom, not necessarily because that idiom isn't understood any more (it *is*, at least by people my age) but because I don't think I have any more to say in that genre. Therefore, the next novel, if there is one (D.V.) will be something quite different, and maybe the last one I have to write. I have always had – or thought I had – this slight clairvoyance re: my own writing.

BUT – AND HERE IS THE IMPORTANT THING – I have, as you know, always felt about your writing (and have said so many times) that it works on many different levels; that it has a quality of interwovedness (is that the word?); that people appear and inhabit the reader's mind not only as themselves but also as archetypes; that the echoes are not the ones made from yodelling at a mountain but rather the voices heard in the caves, the things about ourselves that we would frequently rather not know, or the things about ourselves and others which we perceive only dimly and from time to time, here made real and undeniable. You see, I don't believe and never have believed that you were writing for any one generation, Adele. That is what has made it so much more difficult for you than for me, and why the quick rewards which I have had (and let's face it, have mightily enjoyed) have not been open in the same way to you. It must have been seventeen years ago when I first really realized this about both of us. Neither of us had then published a novel. It was in Rome, and you were working on THE SACRIFICE, and I was pregnant with Jocelyn. Again, don't mistake me – it wasn't that I thought my work was superficial; I didn't, and don't think so. It was just that I knew then that you had committed yourself to the god more than I could – more than it was given to me to do, because really it has nothing to do with what one wants, one way or another. (Incidentally, I wouldn't use that phrase ... 'committed yourself to the god' to anyone else, and never have before, but you'll know what I mean – maybe every writer thinks it, but it shouldn't be spoken, or only when really necessary, as now). When you had all that mishmash-of-mentors difficulty, re: THE SACRIFICE, I felt very strongly about it then, that you might have hellish difficulty with everything you wrote, but had to keep on regardless, because your writing is the kind that people do react strongly towards, if not pro then con, and you mustn't be conned by the cons, kid, because what you do is too valuable in the long run. Same thing happened with THE LOVEBOUND, and it will one day be published in its own form, as itself, as a play, or as I always tend to think of it, as a novel in play form, but published it will be. What angers me terribly is that it should have been published already. Adele, the same goddamn thing is true of your new novel. The patterns haven't changed. This is where Viking is so terribly terribly wrong. OF COURSE you are not writing in a totally contemporary idiom – you never have.

SOME WRITING IS DATELESS AND UNDATEABLE. IT DOESN'T SPEAK TO ONE AGE ABOUT ITSELF. IT SPEAKS TO MAN ABOUT HIMSELF.

And in this kind of writing, idiom and even style are capable of bridging many generations. Your writing is like this. Quite simply, that is it.

Adele, I've never consciously *tried* to write in the idiom of my generation – it has simply happened, because that is the only way I can write. With Rachel, in A JEST OF GOD, I knew only too well that I had not lived in a prairie town for many years, but I carefully (I hope) covered myself by updating certain external details and by leaving others vague – that was easy enough to do, in a book which was largely an inner view anyway. Same thing with THE FIRE-DWELLERS. I was on firm ground, really, because the main character is a middleaged woman (close enough in age to myself) who *knows* her speech quirks are out of date because her teenage daughter is always telling her so (as mine does with me) – Stacey is completely contemporary in one sense because she is a middleaged woman bothered by the fact of middleage, still in some ways dwelling in her own past while at the same time being faced with herself as mother-figure by a new generation. In other words, what I was trying to get at, in this new novel, was a dilemma which I have personally felt and that's why I wanted to do it, but which I also recognize as one which very many women of my age must experience. I didn't pick it because it would have a wide appeal – I don't even know if it will, and I don't much care. I wrote it because it was there to be written.

BUT DON'T YOU THINK I KNOW THE DIFFERENCE BETWEEN THIS KIND OF INTIMATE CHARACTER PORTRAYAL, HOWEVER WELL DONE IT MAY OR MAY NOT BE, AND THE KIND OF WRITING YOU DO?

In about twenty years time, every book I've ever written will be out of print or on the remainder barrow. One or two will survive a little longer in Canada, but not much longer. Again, don't mistake me – this is NOT something which I regret or which I feel badly about. I don't. I have the same kind of feeling which African carvers used to have about their work – the doing of it is the important thing, and the speaking to some people of one's own time; after that, if the termites eat the wood, it really and truly does not matter. I have been extraordinarily lucky in my lifetime; I'm grateful.

It's not the same for you; it never has been, and I suppose it may never be. Because you are trying to do that most difficult thing – to write with a kind of total commitment about whatever you could see, however terrifying it might be. And for that kind of writing, believe me, the question of current idiom is totally and utterly and forever irrelevant.

However, it is one thing to see quite clearly (as you probably don't but I think I do) that your work will be seen and comprehended some time, and quite another to think about the present situation, where the practical and gawdawful elements enter in. Could you suggest to your agent that she tries the book with a publisher such as Knopf? Also, with English publishers such as Macmillan, MacGibbon & Kee, Gollancz, even maybe Heinemann? The far-out and stylish publishers such as Calder (London) are out, it seems to me, as they are only interested in what is go-

go-going at this precise moment. In the long run, it is a novel which should ultimately be translated into Ukrainian, Russian and maybe (you should forgive the expression) German. What I am trying to convey is that there are parts of the world which would understand maybe better than the present North America the roots and conflicts of this novel.

I don't know what I could do in a practical way. There is a woman I know slightly here, who is a kind of agent for Knopf and who does a lot re: translation of novels, but I must add mainly into German, and also if you thought it might be of any interest to you, maybe to write to Judith Jones[1] who is an editor at Knopf. GOD, ADELE, DON'T MISUNDER- STAND ME. All this kind of crap should not be necessary; I know it only too well. It's an insult – not to you personally, but to what you serve – that there should be this kind of massive uncomprehension on the part of a publisher, this kind of necessity to fiddle about with the existing setups.

Anyway, the old ladies of Rome were right, in the end. CORRAGIO; AVANTI. [...]

Much love to you and D,

Margaret

ps. we've recently acquired a book (pamphlet) on British coins which we'll send to Harry's Arnold. It was so damn good to have Harry here for a few days – maybe I'd never really seen him as himself before, only as your brother. He rates high with my family.
P.S. have just decided this letter will be too slow, so have cabled – hope you got it okay.

1 Jones had edited Laurence's books at Knopf beginning with *A Jest of God* and possibly with *The Stone Angel*.

[2334 Girouard]
4 (or 5) September 1968

Dear Margaret,

Hi! What a delight to get your cable! A rather smug sounding female voice read it to me over the phone yesterday, & when I asked her, – being somewhat dazed, having just got out of bed, to repeat, & then spell some of it, she did seem injured that I should appear to imagine that just because she was French Canadian she couldn't read perfectly simple English. All day, in my subsequent euphoria, I was tempted to write you, for fear that when I received the actual message in the mail it would disappoint me, and plunge me into gloom again by making more sense. But no, telegraph operators being what they are, I needn't have worried. This morning, in the mail, the priceless message:

'VIKING IS IN SPAIN TRANOPF LETTER FOLLOWS LOVE MARGARET.'[1]

No, don't spoil it by trying to explain. I know what you really said, but it's perfect this way. I got the IN SPAIN part yesterday, & it made my day. The TRANOPF, which she spelled in such tones of injury I had to see, this morning, to understand. Two days with laughter in them. And when Dmitry gets home tomorrow, one for him too. Thank you! What better comfort?

Don't worry. After my first spasm of rage, injured pride, perhaps a little despair, I've rallied. So much for taking it for granted that it's obvious you've written a good book. What right do I have to take such for granted? Few of my colleagues, for instance, agree with my literary judgments, so why, in this least objective of cases, should I imagine instant acceptance? I suppose because I got it once, & only now do I realize that that was not based on literary judgment, that literary criteria had nothing to do with Viking's great joy in finding me. How naive one continues to be. Now I find it rather funny. As for Knopf, I think I'll leave the peddling part to the agent. I suspect someone at Knopf has already had an unofficial look at some of it, from something she wrote me, & since she suggested she try Harper next, I suspect, logically that whoever did see the part was not as enthusiastic as she had hoped. So I think I'll just let her make the rounds as she sees fit. She did ask if I had any preferences among publishers, but I know very little about them, so I'll leave it to her.

Please don't worry about my state of mind in all this. After the first outraged yell, I've settled down to the odd grumble, and a fair amount of giggling, of a sometimes subacid nature, but what the hell. Life is too interesting at the moment for me to waste what little I've got left of it on other people's reactions to my work. If it's good it's good & will, presumably, catch on somewhere; if not, no amount of wailing & ranting will help.

I've just finished going over Sergei's first day's spelling with him. He's very eager to learn. Don't know if I told you, for awhile it looked as though we'd have all three boys for the winter, but things turned out apparently not as desperate as we'd gathered, and their mother was unwilling, so Sergei, the eldest is with us as planned. He's a nice kid – popping corn at the moment. Anyway, will write again shortly. Just wanted you to know I got the wire, and thanks! Write soon! Love to you, the kids, & Jack, from us all,

Adele

1 The cable ought to have read: Viking is insane   Try Knopf   Letter follows   Love
  Margaret

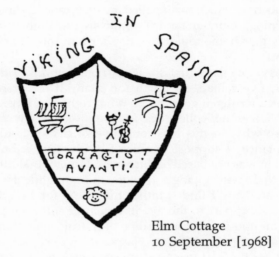

Elm Cottage
10 September [1968]

Dear Adele:

The above is submitted for your approval as your new coat-of-arms. Wow! When I got your letter yesterday, I laughed most of the morning. And to think I carefully had the girl here read back the cable to me, and had even spelled out various words! God knows how it got mixed up, but as you say, it is so much better in this version. I suppose the telegraph people thought Tranopf was a province of Spain. As a war cry, however, VIKING IS IN SPAIN seems to me nearly as good as some of the old Scots ones such as the Camerons, 'Sons of the hound, come here and get flesh'! What is especially [—] caught on almost instantly to my intended message [—] shall henceforth murmur it to myself, just as I have for so long done – 'Corragio, Avanti'!

I had lunch yesterday with Alan Maclean of Macmillan's, and could not help telling him about the cable. Mentioned what had sparked it off, saying only it was a dear friend of mine and the novel was bloody good. I honestly intended nothing more. But Alan immediately guessed who it was, and said 'Should we see the manuscript?,' so I said Yes, he should. If you're handling it all through an agent, could you get a copy sent to Macmillan, maybe? Mr. A.D. Maclean, Macmillan & Co. Ltd., Little Essex Street, London, W.C. 2. Better still, send a copy right now yourself.

After my little outburst of self-pity to you in last letter, I feel much restored and ready to go back to work as soon as my kids go back school (this week, praise heaven). My only trouble, really, is the same old one I've had for many years – the tension after awhile affects me in physical ways. It appears I've got colitis, which I've had (I now think) off and on for years – stomach cramps, diarrhoea, etc. My doctor said 'You've got most of the classic gallbladder symptoms – the only trouble is, you haven't got a gallbladder.' Probably my goddamn gallbladder was taken out under just such circumstances (it *was*: I read the proofs for my first novel while in hospital waiting for them to decide what was the matter with me; they settled on the gallbladder for lack of anything else definite, and even that wasn't very damn definite – I always felt it didn't need to come out). Never mind. The doc has me on some lovely pills now, which I am highly suspicious about because I know they contain barbiturates, but will stay on them for 1 week more and hope all will be well. What is difficult is that one's family does not, in general, see any reason why one has been under some tension, so tends to think that one is malingering or else has some incurable disease, and if you say 'don't worry – I'm improving, and it's only tension,' they say 'Tension over what?' Which is not their fault, any of them – who could really explain such ridiculous symptoms? Remember the time I nearly went bald? 'You have,' my doc in Vancouver once said to me, 'bizarre symptoms.' He wasn't kidding! I wish to heaven it didn't all hit me this way, but it does and I'm going to stop apologizing for it. It is certainly tough on the rest of the family, but I have come to the conclusion that they would – bless them – rather have me as I am than not have me at all, so I must try to accept that basic fact. Only twice in Italy did we have to sprint for the nearest john – that's good going, really. Later, Jocelyn said 'I thought it was rather funny, actually,' and in a way, it was – me, puffing along the main drag of Milan, past Milan Cathedral, thinking 'The hell with all that lovely medieval architecture – where is the nearest underground station where they have that beautiful door marked WC?' Somebody wrote a Good Loo Guide for Britain – I could write nearly a world-wide one. I have an instinct for finding lavatories just like some alcoholics have an instinct for finding parties. And I must try to stop feeling apologetic towards Jack – ie. also resentful – poor guy, it's not *his* fault he's so healthy. (Incidentally, zanily, Harry had a view of me at my relatively poorest – when we went to Oxford, I suddenly said in the middle of an antique shop, 'Sorry – got to find a Ladies,' and later, when the kids made fun of me, Harry said 'Oh don't worry – she's just free and easy on the go,' for which I really was grateful).

Glad to hear about how well you seem to get on with D's kids. Not that I am surprised. Also glad that you are back in reasonably fighting mood re: the novel. Personally, I think the n.b. thing is to get it taken by an Eng or Amer publisher, and then Toronto will not be worried about finances, which always worries them.

Much love,

Margaret

[2334 Girouard
23 September 1968]

Dear Margaret,

I've had such a hard time trying to bring myself to write letters lately. Really, I want to talk face to face. If you were in Canada & it were after midnight I could phone you & it would only cost one buck for three minutes, – new rates. I phoned home the other night, & had an unhurried chat with Mom, & even spoke to Dad, who has a hearing aid and is doggedly trying to stick with it this time. The other times he wasn't able to bear the static. Now he actually decided on his own to try again. Good for him!

Thanks for your letters. I appreciate them, need I say how much? I accept the coat of arms gladly. Do you think, I know I'm being greedy, but do you think maybe I could ask for one small addition, – a tasteful bar sinister added somewhere? Or is that called gilding the lily? What I think is marvelous is that you leap to my defense and insist it's a good book even though you haven't read more than a couple of ch's. yet. Well, I'm glad. I don't think you'll find you were mistaken. That sounds vain, but it's not, I think. Mind you I haven't looked at it lately. Maybe I should go back & read it. Anyway, what I do think is wrong, inaccurate, & really nothing you or I can judge anyway thank goodness, is the relative value of either of our works; the degree of one's own seriousness, depth, value, staying power, honesty, grasp, complexity, all that jazz, how can one measure it against another's? particularly a contemporary's? Yes, one can measure all kinds of things, but what relevance do they have? *The Stone Angel* is an absolute, a being. Is *A Jest of God* there to run races? Will *The Sacrifice* run ten years longer in the eternity stakes? I know you are paying me an enormous compliment, but at the same time you are unfairly denigrating yourself, as you've always done. You too can be a hostile depressive rebellious paranoid. Put them all together & they spell my particular kind of DEDICATION. But who needs it? Honestly, the fits & spasms of rage come quite infrequently now. I haven't heard from the agent again, so I assume things aren't going very spankingly. I can't deny I'm a little disheartened at times, – in between those infrequent spasms of rage. But I have Dmitry. And Sergei, his oldest boy, is a lovable sort of kid who seems to be settling in here quite happily. He & I get on quite well together. Dmitry's been away a lot lately so we keep each other fairly easy going company. Dmitry left this morning again, for the West Coast, where he'll be for about two weeks. He just got back from the East Coast. I must say my gloomier periods tend to coincide with his absences.

I haven't written to thank Jocelyn for the sweet naming of Theodore book,[1] & letter, but I will. Partly, I'm frozen in my letter writing juices because this past week & a half was beginning of term chaos, straightening out of timetables, etc. I have to go out to Mac five afternoons a week, – makes an awfully long week, & there's the constant worry about cadging lifts in & out of town. For years there has been a kind of halfhearted attempt on the part of the powers-that-be to get us to teach some 'composition.' They keep putting fat, indigestible comp. books on the syllabus & we manage to ignore them. This year the Comp. Committee not only picked a relatively slender volume, but set out a few assignments in advance, for all of us to follow through on. Result: most depressing, I have two sets of timely, topical 'paragraphs' to correct. I've read them through & can't for the life of me figure out how to grade them. Oh phooey!

And yet it's an easier way to earn a living than having to constantly submit material as a writer, at least for me. But how depressing, 5 days a week for the next 8 months, trek out, trek back. Never mind. I'm actually quite well off, as at least I'm not being frustrated. There's nothing I want to write now. Nothing.

I spent an interesting evening with your friend Nadine Asante, who's just recently arrived in town & came over a couple of evenings ago for a drink. Several things, – remind me to talk about it when I see you. I had got your briefing of years ago all mixed up. I thought she was a negro, till she walked in. She didn't, apparently, know that I wasn't on my own any more, and was very curious – almost disappointed; I think because she was feeling a bit disgruntled with the married state. Anyway, she several times asked about my marriage, how long I'd known Dmitry, whether you knew him, when I'd met him, etc., & somewhat to my amusement, everytime she came back to the subject she'd got something or other slightly skewed, – just like any newspaper person who's ever interviewed me. What I say & what eventually gets printed never quite coincide. We had really a very interesting talk. I imagine she's led quite a life, & I can understand why the current situation makes her very uneasy, – (after this stint, when he gets his fellowship, her Tojo² wants to go back & work off his debt to his govt. at a pittance per week. What she would like, naturally, is for him to stay on here, earn enough to pay Ghana off in money, then go back as a free man.) Anyway, we'll probably be seeing more of them, once Dmitry settles down in town for the winter. Her Tojo sounds like an interesting guy. Do you know him? And she seems like a very bright, dynamic sort of gal, & very fond of you.

I have not yet written to the agent about your suggestion that she send my M.S. to Alan Maclean, – out of simple lethargy. I haven't even written to John Gray to ask what it's all about. Des showed me an advertising blurb in a Macmillan book folder which said they were putting out *The Sacrifice* in pocket edition. But no one's ever mentioned it to me. I don't think that's right, somehow.

What a dull letter, sorry. I am intrigued by your mention of the new approach you're thinking of using in further work. You've mentioned it before, & I'd love to see how it works out. When will you be able to talk about it? Or is it still just a glimmer of idea that you want to develop before you can describe it?

Noel Stone called the other day to say he saw the Newman film of your *Jest of God* very favourably reviewed. Have you seen it? It will be showing here within the next few weeks.

Well ducks, like they say, I must chase Sergei off to bed. I think I'll do it by example. Forgive me for writing such a terribly dull letter. It *feels* dull, not at all as I'd like it to be. I would love to have a hearty laugh with you.

[In the] Sat. Montreal Star I read a review of a book written by all the latest way-out thinkers, the new age popularizers, & to me the review just didn't make sense, a sort of hysterical mouth to mouthing of tag ends of unbelievable jargon.[3] And in yesterday's paper was news of near riots on Wall street where a crowd of 5,000 gathered for several days to watch a young computer operator, in red miniskirt & yellow sweater, – measurements 43", 26", 34", walk, or try to walk, from the subway to her job. (The police had to rescue her). The triumph of mass what? Someone had happened to notice this babe, & word of mouth did the rest. The public are now their own advertising & publicity people. They make their own instant sensations. Boy! By the way, have you heard anything about the financial sit'n of McClelland & Stewart?[4] Keep hearing rumours.

love, write,

Adele

P.S. The reason I mention having to write to the agent to send an M.S. is that I only have the one – I made one zerox copy which I sent her.

1 A reference to the mouse, Theodore, created for the Manchester *Guardian* by the British illustrator and political cartoonist, William Papas (b. 1927).
2 Asante's husband's name was, in fact, Kojo.
3 Under the heading 'Primer for Proselytizing of Friendly "Squares,"' C.D. Cecil reviewed *Innovations*, edited by Bernard Bergonzi (*Montreal Star*, 21 September 1968, Entertainment section, 7).
4 The publishing firm was reported to be deep in debt. In the spring of 1971 the Ontario government provided a loan of $1 million to prevent the sale of McClelland and Stewart to American interests.

[2334 Girouard
12 October 1968]

Dear Margaret,

Got your letter this morning & am beginning this on the train on my way out to school. I'm very sorry that the role definition thing still causes so much active pain. I wish you didn't blame yourself so. Maybe there is no blame. Maybe the human organism is just so, & under the circumstances you respond in such & such a way. All right, that's the way it is. Accept it. Sound great don't I? Just like that. I've been trying to do it lately with responses that I feel might tend toward making me lose those few hours & days which I know are the best that will be given me as a human being. It isn't easy, with the spectre of failure, the smart of rejection in the sphere in which I'd concentrated all my half a lifetime plus. Nevertheless, madness & disintegration are so potential in me, that these days of optimal life are a real miracle, and it seems I would do anything, even accept the horror of self, to protect them. We talk very casually (& inaccurately, I'm told) about how many camels can pass through the eye of a needle. What about that poor needle, balancing there precariously, with herds of camels tramping through its head? This is to say that I don't understand the process of life, but I have caught on to the fact that it is a process I am passing through & that is passing through me & that I've decided to acquiesce not because I have no choice, as indeed I haven't, but because the rape is inevitable, and at times even enjoyable, & if you acquiesce life may even be induced to do it again. As usual, these little metaphysical rambles lead to nonsense, back to home base. Dmitry is enormously tender & protective of me in these areas of professional stress, for which I am very grateful. And yet I have the feeling that his sympathy is for me as a human, that though he has great respect for me as a writer, he really cares about me as me. Indicative of how closely I myself have based my value on my writing, it puzzles me, rather. What does he see in me, bless him? Funny, this is several hours later, & on re-reading the above I remember that I was even so being evasive, because I found it difficult to say that he loves me as a woman, which I know is true, & yet find so hard to believe possible. But how nice, how very thoroughly completely nice in the undebased sense, nice enough to completely change the atmosphere of my life.

Now it's the next day, last night Mom, Dad, & my boxer Big Julie arrived by plane. Mom & Dad will be here for a week, & then down to Miami to look after Harry's household. They are well, Dad considerably slowed down, but says he feels well, & voluntarily wearing a hearing aid, Mom as vital & gutsy as ever, though she claims her memory's going. It hasn't gone very far – now it's about a week later, Fri Oct. eleventh, to be exact. Much has happened in this short week. God! Has it! First of all Dmitry called last Fri. night from Vancouver, to say that he's bringing the other two boys home with him.[1] Their mother has decided to give them up & devote herself to her painting, her zen, her yoga, her hippy idealism, her recorder, etc. etc. We've been expecting that this may happen, so, weren't utterly surprised. On Sat. night they arrived, & now we're a considerably augmented family. They're sweet kids, not without scars or problems, as you can imagine, but very responsive to affection & attention. Mom & Dad stayed over with us & met them. Sweet to see my mother put her arms around the youngest, from behind & say 'Would you mind to have a grandmother who loves you & hugs you?' And the kid almost paralysed with pleasure, grinning with open mouth, saying no, he wouldn't mind. Dmitry's mother, by the way, is one enormously relieved grandmother now. She has been very worried about the kids. Anyway, to continue running over the week, on Monday I arrived home from work to find my charlady sprawled on the kitchen floor; looking as though she'd had a stroke, Big Julie looking very puzzled, I called the police. What a fright! The cops took one look & started to ask what she'd been taking. It turns out, as far as we can figure, that she'd got into the overproof rum. I've been, & seen people in, all kinds & conditions of intoxication, but for the first time now I know what 'stoned' is. She was paralysed! Henceforth I guess I'll have to lock up the liquor. Well, on Tuesday Dmitry left for Newfoundland. He just called he'll be back tomorrow night. Then on Monday he goes to Michigan. By the end of the month things should let up, though, & we'll have him home more. Meanwhile, the other day I got a letter with the Harper & Row rejection quoted: 'There are some very nice things in *Crackpot* & some very crazy things, & finally the craziness simply overpowers the nice things & one worries about the success of the novel.' Are they reading the same novel as Viking? I phoned her today, my agent, Candida Donadio, because her letter baffled me; it implied she'd only been sending bits of the novel out. But it turns out no, they've both had the complete M.S. she says, & says she's had this kind of varied reaction from publishers before when they get a script that's out of the ordinary. She seems quite cheerful about it, & claims Alan Maclean is an old & dear friend & she'd be delighted to have him to take the thing, but neither of us really think an English publisher will want to publish it first. I'm going to make copies & she'll send one out to him. Will write again shortly.

love,

Adele

1 Marshall (Winnie) and Michael Stone, two of Dimitry's three sons. They lived with Adele and Dmitry until the summer of 1970.

[2334 Girouard]
24 November 1968

Dear Margaret,

I'm puzzled and worried because I haven't heard from you in so long. Is everything all right? What is happening? Are the kids o.k.? You? Jack? Why haven't you written? I can understand why I haven't written. The change to a family totalling five is a rather drastic one, & what with rather a full schedule at school this year, – not more classes, but *daily* classes, so that I have to go out every day, I haven't had much time. The kids are settling in gradually. They have difficulties, & there have been some trying moments, but we're hoping they'll relax and accept things. What choice do they have? I've no idea what is likely to happen re them & their mother in the future, though I can make a few grim guesses, which would be pointless. Current problems are adequate for me. It's no point depressing oneself in advance. I am grateful that I've got my book off my hands at least. At my rate of gestation I won't have to worry about beginning a new one for awhile, so this situation will have some time to stabilize itself I hope. They are really nice kids. It's a pity to see them having to wrestle with problems they're not fit to cope with yet.

The latest from my agent, after I sent her my precious original for her to xerox & return, was the xeroxed copy, with a note from her secretary that they were keeping the original because it's clearer. I kept calm, clarified the xeroxed copy, & am sending it back to her & demanding my original back. No other news.

One very pleasant evening we had recently. After trying to see 'Rachel Rachel' on a previous weekend, & being turned away because it was sold out, we finally got in. It's not your book but a very nice job of what it is. I won't even go into my detailed quarrels with their reading of it. I know you don't care, so it doesn't matter. It was a pleasant evening in the theatre, & of course I kept thinking that now your work will be in demand for the medium and you'll be able to make a hell of a lot more money next time, which is important. And at least they didn't *absolutely* screw it up, as is done so often to good books on the screen.

What news of the new one? There was a big article in the paper this weekend about Jack Ludwig being writer-in-residence at Toronto this year. Anything further for you re next year?

I still intend to write to Jocelyn, – before Xmas anyway. Have not done anything else socially, so haven't contacted your friend. We've been intending to invite people but are just a bit harassed at the moment, partly because I've had an internal upset too, – nothing serious, – will write about it later, – but enough to weaken me somewhat.

So that's it, & I still don't know why you haven't written. Please write & let me know at least that all is well. Love to Jack & the kids. Love from Dmitry & me. Be strong.

Adele

Elm Cottage
27 November 1968

Dear Adele –

I haven't answered your last letter for a long time, but not because I haven't thought of you (how is that for an excuse?) – I did write once, but tore the letter up as it was filled with what I recognized as a momentary depression – not momentary, exactly, but the black Celt in me that rises up sometimes and has to be fought all over again. God knows it is not that I am complaining about my life, which has been damn lucky these past few years. I think, really, that the gloom of my ancestors is perhaps closer to me than I once thought, and also that about this time of life, my childhood nightmares tend to rise up all over again and have to be dealt with. One can't alter the past – one can only try to accept it and let it go. I do agree with what you said in your letter, about acquiescing – sure, some battles have to be fought, but why fight unnecessary ones? Why go over the same old ground a million times? It is this that I'm now trying not to do.

I can understand, I think, how you must feel re: your evaluation of yourself – ie that one tends to evaluate oneself in relation to work, rather than in relation to oneself as a person and woman, because (at least this is true for me) one is very apprehensive about the latter kind of evaluation. Scared. And I think it is a damn good thing that you can now admit *in words* something of what your relationship with Dmitry means to you and to him. I call that progress!

I'm glad the boys are with you now – it must be a tremendous change to have such a large family, more or less all at once, but if anyone can cope with it, you certainly can. I was very touched by your description of your Mom with the kids – it was so like her!

I hope you've either got a lock on the liquor cupboard or a new cleaning lady! What an experience. Isn't it peculiar how things sometimes seem to happen all at once, too many crises converging? And yet, these are the times when one tends to cope best, I find. It's the interim periods, when domestic life is quiet and I am not writing and don't know what to do with myself that I find difficult.

I cannot at all understand Harper's reaction to your novel. As you say, they cannot have been reading the same novel as Viking. I wouldn't really agree re: the possibility of finding an English publisher. I think it is definitely worth a considerable try. 'Craziness' may not be quite so strange here as it still is popularly supposed to be in N. Amer. Anyway, what the hell do they mean by that word? I think they have a nerve to use it – or utter lack of knowledge of what goes on in the world and in the skull. I think myself they were simply and ignorantly mis-interpreting your title. By the way, Alex Baron has just left Collins and joined Macmillan's writers, as he wrote me the other day to tell me. I am delighted. Is this an omen? Please get your agent to send a copy here.

My Nigerian book, LONG DRUMS AND CANNONS, has been published but remains unreviewed, as I suspected it would. Never mind. I've sent you a copy, but don't feel duty-bound to read it! I have finished re-writing my kids' book, and am getting it typed – I kind of like those little characters in it, but have a feeling that the publishers may feel otherwise. Odd, isn't it – I rather dreaded going back trying to re-write it, but when I began, the old pattern reasserted itself, and I couldn't wait to get at it in the mornings. I can get involved even in a story of the quest of a mole, an owl and 2 cats; I must be nuts. I sometimes have the feeling that however much I love my kids and find involvement with husband, friends, etc, in some peculiar way I exist only as an extension of my typewriter. I know that isn't true, but I sometimes feel as though it were true. In fact, often. The letters to friends are the same, really – the typewriter is my radio set, from which I send out messages – this is in some way my main contact with life, however crowded and real my real life. I guess it is this which sometimes makes me feel as though I must be insane in some way. Don't worry, kid – disintegration is very potential in me, too. And I read an interview with V.S. Naipaul[1] the other day, in which he said 'I *became* my typewriter, my apartment, the page I as writing,' and I thought – oh brother, do I ever know what you mean. I am always making mighty stabs to lessen the isolation, but then I create it around myself all over again. I recall with minimal amusement the two (two!) bedsitters in London, at various times, thinking I would entertain all kinds of scintillating acquaintances and lovers there. All I ever did in those damn bedsitters was to sleep there by myself, at huge expense. One must expect to pay high for one's fantasies, eh? It's the same about my recurring problem about returning to Canada – I visualize myself living (with all domestic problems – kids and J – somehow sorted out intelligently, to everyone's satisfaction) in a lovely little A-frame on the edge of a Canadian lake, where (somehow) all my buddies will be able to get there very easily, and I (not being able to drive, but never mind) will also be able to get to Toronto, Montreal etc, whenever I want. And we will all live happily ever after, in the garden of Eden, when we are all young again. Well, I guess this is the reason I don't see myself making any very great efforts to split my household and disrupt everyone and return permanently to Canada – at least I can still tell the difference between (some) fantasy and (some) reality. And what I've got here isn't ideal but it is *real*.

I was assessing the situation the other day, and I realized all over again how much I love this goddamn ramshackle house, which causes me so much worry sometimes but is like no other house on earth. The elm tree has turned golden, and the leaves are still on it, and against the blue of the sky last weekend, it was so terrific I had to stop raking leaves and just stand and stare at it. I've planted 10 new rosebushes this fall, and I guess in some ways I've planted myself as well. Jocelyn said the other day that she reckoned this place was a good investment because of the property value. Good, I said, I'm glad you think so. 'But we likely won't sell it when you kick off,' she said casually. It made me realize that over the years it has become their home, and although they don't know whether they're English or Canadian and don't have the same kind of sense of belonging as I did (both for worse and for better) when I was a kid, they do belong here, in this two-thirds of an acre of English jungle. Jocelyn thinks Penn is Endsville, which indeed it is, but at the same time it gives her a place to escape from and also to return to, sometimes, when she may want to, in the future. David at this point quite simply loves the place. It has everything he needs, for now. He and a pal have built a four-storey fort (I jest not – four storeys including the 10 foot tunnel underneath the place, built because they had both read THE WOODEN HORSE) and have also built 2 very fancy vehicles from old planks and wheels they got at the local garbage dump, and are now busily engaged in building a large underground garage for same, the top being concealed with old boughs, etc. He has about a third of an acre to do this sort of thing with, and where else could I find that in a hurry? I guess it amounts to this – we've made a home here, and we must accept it and be true to it. I'm never likely to be entirely at home anywhere, but my restlessness has nothing to do with external things, and I do love this place more than I can remember loving any other place except the house I was born in.

Of course we do have some drawbacks. Thank God I have a little more money than previously, because within the past fortnight I learn that I have to have 2 new water tanks (old ones about to expire any moment and pour water all over house); the Gas Ascot heater in the kitchen is on the blink and the Gas Board has to be phoned bi-weekly to remind them they are supposed to be putting in a new part soon; my washing machine needs a new gear-box (£15 – what a Christmas present). And so on. Also, I haven't yet been told what my income tax for last year (with the film) will be, and am in a constant state of neurotic anxiety about that. So yesterday, just to live dangerously, I went to Wycombe and bought a new bike (£24) for David's Christmas present. He needs one very much, as his old one is packing in, despite very good care (he maintains his equipment very well, thank goodness). Finances aren't really a worry right now, which is damn lucky. Jack pays me an allowance for the kids but does not actually have much idea how much it costs us to live and repair house, etc, and for the moment this works best, as it saves argument and also I am able to do it and he has a depression background which forces him to worry about money even more than I do, plus an austerity outlook which enables him by himself to live for very little indeed – if he really knew how much it takes me to keep this house going, he would think I was madly reckless, as in his terms I am, and maybe in many people's terms, but in others' terms I probably live pretty simply – it seems to me that my main extravagances are books, cigarettes and wine, plus a large meat bill and telephone bill. (How boring all this must be – sorry!)

What did I start out to say? Like you, I get sidetracked. I really want to talk to you, I guess, and this is an imperfect substitute.

Anyway, I will be taking the kids to Canada next summer – plan to go mainly to BC with them, as that is where their friends and relatives are. I will then go on to Toronto by myself, end of August. I have already rented a house in Toronto, or at least agreed to rent it, as a person from the U of T, who is in charge of floaters like myself, wrote and said a house was available for that year, and even sent coloured snaps. It sounds okay, and reasonable rent. I still can't believe I will actually get there, but maybe I will. Am trying, with Dave Godfrey's help,[2] to find a young Canadian couple, man a writer, wife agreeable, to come and live here for that year, expenses paid, and keep an eye on things for me – I want to find some guy who seriously wants to have a year to write a novel, and someone who is known to someone I trust. It all sounds impossible, but maybe it will happen.

Got a letter from Harry not long ago, enclosing pictures he took the day we went to Oxford with him. It was so nice of him to send them. Haven't replied yet. In the pic, the kids look wonderful and I look like a cow, but never mind.

Must go and do the laundry – a job I hate and always put off until I can't delay it any longer.

Much love,

Margaret

1 The novelist Vidiadhar Surajprasad Naipaul, born in 1932 in Trinidad, had been living in England since 1950.
2 Dave Godfrey (b. 1938), writer and publisher, was co-founder with Dennis Lee of House of Anansi Press in Toronto in 1966. He was teaching English at Trinity College, University of Toronto, and had published a collection of short stories, *Death Goes Better with Coca Cola* (1966).

Elm Cottage
29 November 1968

Dear Adele –

Got your letter the same morning I posted several to you – mental telepathy, I guess. I'm afraid my letters were slightly rambling (Carried-Away-By-Sound-Of-Own-Voice dept) and may have conveyed the impression that I am suffering as usual – in fact, things are pretty reasonably okay. I guess I have a real, if despicable, streak of spiritual masochism in me. If there isn't much to agonize about, I can always invent something. I think, as I implied in my letters, that it is really only the old divided personality bit – one part of me is very practical and sensible; the other part is black Celt. I am more and more drawn to trying to understand something about my ancestors – odd.

Your household must be fascinating, difficult at times, hectic, and as you say, quite a change. It certainly is good that you aren't finishing the book at the moment – there are times when work is physically impossible. I can never work very well during the summer holidays, even though my kids are accustomed to being told not to disturb me unless they break their necks. But just the presence of a lot of people, plus having to prepare large meals, is enough to make me unable to concentrate. Winter is my best time, and here it is winter, and all I've done is re-write that idiotic kid's book. I dread starting the short stories – I guess because I haven't done one in that series for about 2 years and will have to re-think myself back into the situation. But maybe it will be okay when I make a beginning.

I'm getting the kids' book typed by a typist, as couldn't face doing it, and she keeps phoning me, asking me all sorts of peculiar questions – the manuscript will probably turn out looking like hell. It's crazy to be spending money to get it typed, as I do not anticipate making much, if anything, on it, but after typing THE FIRE-DWELLERS, I felt nauseated every time I considered doing this one. How I wish I were an artist – wouldn't it be fun to illustrate a kids' book that you'd written? I can visualize exactly how the drawings should go, but cannot do them, naturally.

Did I tell you I've rented a house in Toronto already?[1] It seems crazy, but I had a chance to rent one – member of the univ staff going away for just the right period, so thought it seemed indicated by fate. I hope I can get some agreeable lady to share it with me. (Too bad I can't get some agreeable man, but I suppose the univ would not approve – also, how to find same?) I still cannot believe it will all actually work out, my being in Toronto, but maybe it will. As Amos Tutuola says, 'If God is good.'[2]

LONG DRUMS AND CANNONS has had no reviews – a friend of mine has recently published a new translation of BEOWULF,[3] which also has had no reviews. We are thinking of starting a club.

Jack arrived home this morning from Malawi – terrible fog, so I thought for sure the plane would be about 10 hours late, but it wasn't. He seems very well and had a good month in Africa. He stopped off in Nairobi, on business, and was impressed with Kenyatta's Kenya.[4]

I'm glad you thought the film was reasonably okay. I liked it pretty well, to tell you the truth. I was so damn glad (even tho I thought I wouldn't care) that they did an acceptable interpretation of the whole thing, and I thought Joanne Woodward was excellent. It was kind of weird to see it, but also rather exciting.

Do you think they would let me register for a course or two at the univ of Toronto, not for credit but just for interest? Have decided I need to broaden my scope of interests. Would like to take a course in early Canadian history, although in a way maybe it is better just to read what

I want to know about. Am beginning to see what I want to find out about. I would love to learn Gaelic, odd as it may sound, but do not think I have sufficient ability with languages.

Must go and make some pies – I make them so seldom that my kids nearly faint with surprise when one appears. I used to be a better housekeeper, but can't bring myself to feel too sorry.

I thought I had solved the smoking problem – a friend told me about Honeyrose, a smoking mixture of rose petals soaked in honey and fruit juices, and I tried one at her place and thought it wasn't bad. So, determinedly, I ordered no less than 16 oz of the stuff, like a fool, and got all the equipment – cigarette rolling machine, etc. Well, one is fine, but after smoking about ten one morning, the livingroom smelled like an oriental whorehouse with incense and I felt sick at my stomach.

Much love to all,

Margaret

1 At 9 Westgrove Crescent
2 Amos Tutuola (b. 1920), the Nigerian novelist. Laurence is paraphrasing the expression that the protagonist and narrator of his second novel, *My Life in the Bush of Ghosts* (1954), repeats throughout the narrative.
3 Kevin Crossley-Holland's translation had been published by D.S. Brewer Ltd. of Cambridge.
4 Jomo Kenyetta (1890–1978), national leader and first president of Kenya from 1964 to his death

[2234 Girouard]
28 December 1968

Dear Margaret,

I have hesitated to write you the news, as I've been having a fairly rough time of it, but the other day I saw the Dr again and it looks as though my pregnancy is fairly normalized. So I'm expecting (with luck) in July. Add that to the picture kid. The canvas has become fairly crowded, wot? So far I'm only letting a few close friends & relatives know. I'm still not sure I'll be able to carry it through, & will feel securer when a couple of more months have passed. Meanwhile I'm dutifully taking sustaining pills, – thyroid & hormones, – & hoping this ghastly period will begin to let-up soon. It has been grim. I've never quite felt so-out-of-myself, possessed, usurped before. My whole mechanism seems to have gone wonky. Food, hitherto my solace & sustenance, has turned prime enemy, & I have to overcome revulsion in order to eat, which I do periodically, nevertheless, for fear of starving the guest. But ugh, the odor! Anyway, it is kind of funny, at my age,[1] & a part of me is enjoying the long delayed primal experience, when it can believe it. Nevertheless, I would like to be able to feel myself again. I suppose it's a good thing that I'm asleep as often as I can get into a comfortable position; it cuts down the periods of conscious nausea. It's funny, this is something I've always wanted, & yet I had reached the point when I'd come to see it as being a kind of vanity, & had reconciled myself to the relinquishment of this particular vanity, – for the sake of the unborn. Now I must cope with a vanity come-to-pass for the sake of the unborn. That is, I hope it will come to pass after all this bruhaha. So, we'll have to play it as it comes. Dmitry is delighted; we're both naturally very curious about what we're likely to produce. I begin to understand the anxieties of prenatal women. Just let it be normal, is all I ask. The other kids don't know yet. There may be some complications, particularly with the youngest, but we'll have to take those as they come too. Meanwhile, very shortly nature will no doubt be forcing an explanation; and I hope it'll work out all right. There are really so many problems to be worked out, but at the moment I'm waiting to make sure I'll really be able to carry the thing through before I worry about them; and besides I'm so sleepy!

Thanks for the Africa book. I'm so glad it's out at last! And so far I like & am enjoying your approach. I haven't read very far yet, as I just finished marking exams & late essays yesterday, but it is interesting to read & I'm looking forward to getting into it properly. I really was relieved to hear from you finally. I had been worried. Am very glad you're all set up for a Toronto visit next year. God it'll be nice having you close enough to see & talk to occasionally.

We ran into Mordy Richler at a party at the Macphersons' a couple of weeks ago. He's still at work on the Penguin Anthology,[2] as well as his own novel. He had some trenchant things to say about what a waste of time the Sir George set-up has been, mainly because they haven't known how to make use of him sensibly. He's given Neil Compton[3] some suggestions about what to do for, or rather with, future creative people they bring in. Certainly they demanded nothing difficult, just nothing intelligent. I think the Toronto set-up is more advanced & you'll have a chance to contact the kids at a better level. I think you'll find it interesting.

I was very much struck by what you said about your house, & particularly about how good the grounds were for David. We sure could do with some space for ours to play in. We find they spend most of their time indoors watching T.V. Yet, when we took them into the mountains for a few days they were always outdoors, – as I recall kids used to be. We're going to have to think seriously about these things very soon.

Well Dmitry is waiting to mail this! Answer soon. I still have more to say, but will save it for next time.

Much love,

Adele

1 Wiseman was forty-one when she gave birth to her daughter, Tamara Stone, on 26 June 1969.
2 *Canadian Writing Today*, edited by Mordecai Richler, was published by Penguin Books in 1970. It included excerpts from *Crackpot* and *A Jest of God*.
3 Neil Compton was head of the English Department at Sir George Williams University, where Richler was writer-in-residence for 1968–9.

Elm Cottage
1 January 1969

Dear Adele –

Just got your letter – this is the best news I've heard in a long time! I am so tremendously happy for you and Dmitry, and I really and truly pray with everything I've got that it will all go well and both you and the baby will be fine fine fine. I know what you mean about pre-natal anxieties – I could never understand people who really cared whether it was a boy or a girl, just so it was okay. Don't let your age bother you – it happens all the time, and I don't believe the risks are that much more; it may be a bit more uncomfortable for you, that's all, but it's worth it. Anyway, just try to RELAX and have faith and sleep as much as possible (I am a great believer in sleep!), and all will be well. And don't get too energetic, eh? So the hell with other responsibilities at the moment. Gosh, it really is WONDERFUL! I'm sorry you are having such a grim time re: eating, etc – some people are damn unlucky that way. However, the guest will take what it needs and you will probably be beautiful and slim afterwards, unlike me, who put on about 15 pounds each pregnancy and never completely took it off. I wonder if you find your mind is kind of vacant? I remember feeling that way – I couldn't seem to think very straight, and did no writing at all; read for preference any kind of feeble who-dun-it I could get my hands on. Also read very boring books at night in an attempt to get to sleep – ARABIA DESERTA was a dandy;[1] no one could read more than a page without dozing off. I can't help repeating it – I am SO DAMN GLAD FOR YOU!!!.

At the moment I seem to have five cats, 25 fuschia plants and no booze. Wait, I can explain – I haven't flipped my lid. A friend is moving house, so I offered to have her 3 cats for a month until she finds a new place to live – at the moment the three are lurking in the old livingroom here (recently vacated, fortunately, by my young tenants who now have their own house) and refusing even to put a foot outdoors. They hate my cats and my cats hate them. All very jolly. The 25 potted fuschias also belong to the friend (Clare Slater – I think she looked you up in Montreal; she is a dear) and they are reposing quietly in the back bedroom, so that is not any difficulty. The booze aspect – I decided I had to quit totally, so am now on some lovely pills which make you vomit and turn black in the face or something if you take even one drink. I have been sufficiently wary not to risk it for about 3 weeks now, so I suppose that is progress of a sort. Got through Xmas and N.Years on grape juice, which really isn't bad stuff. I suppose it was an idiotic time of year to begin program, but thought I better do it now before I changed my mind. I can't say I feel all that cheery about the whole thing, but perhaps it will have benefits in the end. Anyway, it has to be done or at least attempted.

The kids' book has been accepted by Macmillan, and I am quite ridiculously pleased about that. I have to do some revisions, but not too many at this point. I am longing to see what kind of illustrations they get.[2] I haven't begun work on the short stories I want to do, because I haven't yet had sufficient inner reserve. One battle at a time, I say. Would like to get them done in the next few months, though. Then – this sounds stupid, but it isn't – I've only got one more book to write. I know I sound too pessimistic, etc etc, but it is just that I *know*. It will (if I'm lucky and given the grace to do it at all) not be done for a few years yet. I've always known exactly what to tackle next, and I know now. At one time it seemed I would never get them done, but now I can see the end of it. I don't even feel badly – in some odd way, it is a kind of relief. I can't really explain. I have a strange feeling that some other kind of work will present itself when the time comes. At one time I felt horrible about all this, and thought it was like becoming middleaged or old, something I couldn't accept – but it isn't that way at all, and actually, becoming middleaged or old isn't that way, either – a lot of things have changed recently in my point of view, I guess. I just think I am undergoing some kind of metamorphosis, that's all, and I'm not sure what's going to emerge, but I'm curiously optimistic.

Once again, do take care of yourself, and I pray everything will go smoothly – actually, it should get easier and easier, from now on, and the nausea will probably diminish soon (that's probably cold comfort at the moment). I know what you mean about not believing it is real – I felt that even with David; couldn't believe I actually had borne a child until I saw it and held it. Even all this time later, I still find it kind of surprising sometimes! I know it won't be easy for you, with the other kids, but you and Dmitry are both loving people, and I still have faith that that is what matters the most.

Best love to *all*, seen and as yet unseen,

Margaret

1 *Travels in Arabia Deserta* (1888) by the English poet and traveller Charles Montagu
   Doughty (1843–1926) described his solitary journey among the Bedouin tribes.
2 The illustrator of *Jason's Quest* (1970) was the Swedish artist Staffan Torell.

[2234 Girouard]
13 January 1969

Dear Margaret,

Got your letter this morning. Thank God the mails are relatively swift. I'm in much need of reassurance nowadays, one way or another. Primarily, to be frank, I feel myself so inadequate in my function as ersatz mother to the boys these days; in fact, even as simple housekeeper I've kind of fallen apart, & Dmitry is coping heroically, almost all by himself. Normally I am relatively even tempered, except the occasional spasm of irritability. Now I am irritable except for the occasional spasm of good temper. I am asleep most of the time, – best tempered then too, I suppose, though I *feel* drugged & completely helpless. Underlying, I am haunted by characteristically obsessive thoughts. What was it like for a woman like me in the concentration camps? Answer, simple, she didn't survive long. Here I am, cushioned by Dmitry in every way, – cushioned even by the children, who get used to seeing a sleeping lump lying around, & are (the eldest), even a little tenderly amused, though they still don't know what it's all about. But I'm not coping with the problems, & there are problems. The youngest could become a disaster. He already is a very disturbed, spiky child, more than I feel, particularly now, but even at any time, I can cope with. I just don't know enough, & he has already settled into what he is pretty thoroughly. We are going to have to get help. Hardly a day passes without some eruption from him, & that frighteningly empty bellowing and wailing, – desolate – it's really strangely depersonalized; – with most kids you sense pain when they cry, with him it's surrender to rage & chaos & cold empty places, – anyway it's very trying because there's something so cold about it. As I say, we're trying to figure out what to do about getting help. He's only eight for Godsake, & to look at an adorable cherub, but there seems to be no way of making rational contact in crucial areas. He already has his world of defenses so systematized. Oh well, who said it would be easy? Of course the role I'm to play is difficult for me to define anyway. They are fond of their mother. She *is* their mother, & in her own erratic way is fond of them. I certainly am not going to jockey for that position. Where precisely does it put me? What to give? What to expect? Even in a normal state it's not easy, but now I think the problems themselves contribute to the desire to curl up & sleep instead. The foregoing was written while I was under the dryer at the hairdressers, – my first time in a couple of months. What a morale boost! I was looking, & feeling, like an old rag. I'm learning, in middle age, to deny a little less the vanities. I used to think that even to be caught glancing in a mirror would reveal in me the abysmal depths of egotism. So I suppressed the impulse & allowed the egotism to burgeon elsewhere, & not unseen, either, no doubt! Anyway, I arrived home & even young Mike, with unexpected gallantry, – he's usually murderously frank, denied, when I told him I wouldn't come tobogganing because a fat old lady would hold them up, that I was either fat or old. Of course he then went on to explain what was old, & thank God from his description, at least with my hair done, I'm not quite. God, I wish I were in a more normal frame more often. Maybe you're right, & once the internal discomfort eases more, I'll feel more like I can cope. I'll remember more that this really is a very happy time, with good things happening. The discomfort & anxiety tends to blur the real & important things.

I remember your letters when you were pregnant, in fact looked in myself for the symptoms you described. You're right, I have a little game I've been playing, trying to think of a short story I'd like to write. Damned if I can think of anything. I've gone through all kinds of things but nothing wants to be written. Of course with me it's partly the complete drain of the book I just finished. I'm usually quite drained for quite awhile. For all I know I may never fill up again, – something you always have to face. In a way it's a good thing, – one anxiety less. Can you imagine how it would be to have something you want to write as well as be in this state? Best if I somehow reached a more stable equilibrium with my domestic situation first. At the moment it doesn't even seem to matter whether or not I'll ever write again.

Re your comments on the one novel you feel you still have to write, & what will follow, it's not something I can comment on. All it means is that you don't know what you'll write after. In a sense you're saying that your present cycle will be drained. That doesn't mean by then you won't see another cycle coming up. What I do know is that you're not to worry. There's nothing to worry about. This is perhaps fatalism rather than faith talking, from experience, though.

Meanwhile I'm delighted that Macmillan's will be doing the children's book. It sounds, from the hints I've got, a delightful thing & I'm looking forward to it. Is the Africa book going to be published here? I'd like to review it but chances are slim of finding an outlet unless the book will be available here.[1] I've been reading it in my word-by-word way. I'm on John Pepper Clark[2] at the moment. I found Soyinka, in your account, utterly fascinating, – a beautiful, stark, complex mind. I'd like to see more of his plays performed. As you know we saw *Kongi's Harvest* in New York last year. So far I'm enjoying the book very much. You'll have to put my slowness in reading down to present condition, but as you know I'm a slow reader anyway. It's the enjoyment that counts. As you said about Lamming a while back, thank God there are people doing it.

Well no news re my book. I did get the zeroxed copy of it off to Malcolm Ross the other day, so I can expect some straight comment from someone I respect, who will have read the whole thing. Other than the agent & whoever she's shown it to, only one other person has read it through as yet, & though I respect her opinion, – (she liked it) I feel it's got to face more opinions. Obviously they'll be varied, judging by publisher's reactions to-date. Anyway, write soon.

Love to all at home. Love from us all.

Adele

1 She did not review it.
2 John Pepper Clark (b. 1935), Nigerian playwright and writer

[2334 Girouard]
3 March 1969

Dear Margaret,

How about giving me a chance to reply before you change your mind?
August would provide no difficulty at all as far as we can see, unless
you worry about joining a rather hectic household. The boys are very
affectionate & love company. The baby, if all goes well, should be
spending much time asleep at that point of its life, so what's to worry?
There's plenty of room. It's rather a large apartment, & I know you
don't expect first class accommodation under the circumstances, so what
are you worried about? I'd be delighted to see the kids again, & Dmitry,
to meet you all properly. Again what's the worry? It would be such a
pity if the kids missed the chance of seeing Montreal. How often do
they get the chance? Please reconsider, hey?[1]

About Nadine Asante and her article,[2] there you've got a real
problem, as D. agrees. I don't know what to say. My immediate reaction
is 'Oh God, don't let her! Not if it has that effect on you! I know that
kind of embarrassment and even friendship doesn't seem worth it.' On
the other hand there's the equally excruciating problem of *how* to tell
her please you'd rather not, and so you feel like just giving in and
letting it get written and be published by default. I don't know. Dmitry
says can't you edit, approve or disapprove the article? Is this too much
to ask of Nadine? Would she take it wrong? – or rather, right? What a
bind! On the other hand does it really matter what is said in articles?
Whether your friends write them, your enemies, or neutral parties, they
seldom sound other than idiotic to you. I personally, don't think you are
being too sensitive because I know just how you feel. However, I
suppose it would be just as well if we desensitized ourselves somewhat,
for strictly practical purposes. Which all adds up to no advice at all
because I don't know what to say, or how to cope. My own response
would be similar to yours. I don't see why, whatever you decide to do,
you should feel compelled to answer silly questions, though, just
because they're there. Couldn't you just be evasive & general &
comment about what you feel like commenting about? Either way, let

me know what happens. I was asked by David Legate[3] to do an article for The Star; he gave me a pretty general choice re topic, – anything re the lively arts. I wrote what I thought was an amusing piece about how I hate being asked to write articles, & he turned it down on the grounds that he didn't think readers would be interested. So much for my latest venture into journalism. It taught me one thing though, not to submit stuff on spec. I didn't realize it was on spec at the time. Next time I make sure.

I heard from Malcolm Ross. Since the new barbaric rule in the Post Office has come into effect, we get no mail on Saturday. The result was that by some fluke I got the M.S. on Friday and had to wait till Monday to get the letter. His response was on the whole very positive. He says he was hit by the novel. He had some interesting criticism. The sex seemed to bother him considerably where he is most fastidious. I can't gauge the degree of validity of the crit. on that score; anyway was glad to get it to get some response, & in this case there was enough positive in the response to reassure me that everything I'd tried to do wasn't a dead bust. I haven't heard from the agent for three months. It does seem rather a long time. And meanwhile the thing has just lain dormant. Very disheartening.

I am at last beginning to take an interest in things pertaining to childbirth. Until now I simply haven't felt chipper enough to care. Now I have begun to read books on the Pavlovian method of painless child-birth and am thinking of taking exercises. God knows, I can't see myself as one of those painless cases. That sort of thing I couldn't get off with, – too easy for such as me, – but I had better do something to combat the simple, stark terror I see waiting to grip me as the time approaches.

Tomorrow morning I'm meeting John Gray for coffee for an hour before I go to school. It'll be nice to see him again. I think I mentioned that he hasn't seen the M.S. because the agent hasn't contacted him yet. I don't know what she's at, but I guess here too one must have faith. For how long? Should I write her? I'll write again. You too, please.

Love,

Adele

1 Laurence and her children did stay with Wiseman at the end of August 1969.
2 Asante's article appeared as 'Margaret (Rachel, Rachel) Laurence' in the *Montrealer*, June 1969, 30–3.
3 David Legate was book review editor of the *Montreal Star*.

[2234 Girouard]
25 March 1969

Dear Margaret

I'm glad it's settled that you'll be coming here. We're looking forward to having you. Don't worry about anything. Everything will be taken care of. No big parties, but lots of talk and any friends you feel like having up.

This letter is by way of being a warning & a disclosure. I got a call from the Bureau Chief here of Time magazine. They wanted to interview me re you, sort of a friend's view for a piece they're doing on you & *The Fire Dwellers*.[1] At first I was very suspicious & unwilling, told the guy bluntly I didn't trust Time, & didn't want to jeopardize a friendship because of their tendency to distort. He assured me the article was very positive in intention & that since there was nothing political involved there would not be the danger of distortion – (an interesting admission). Finally, because I didn't want to refuse to help when publicity might be useful, I agreed to let him send a reporter down. This young girl came & stayed most of the morning. I disclaim any responsibility for what comes out because, as she admitted, what she gets down will get sent to New York to be worked on. I can just imagine what it'll be like when they're through selecting & patching & finding clever angles. Fooey. But it'll be publicity. Forgive me in advance. Whatever I did say was well meant. In fact she kept trying to get me to tell anecdotes or an anecdote that would make you seem perhaps a little less perfect, perhaps a little humanly ridiculous. The only ones I could think of made me the Charley, which I usually am. Anyway, I hope the result isn't too ghastly.

I didn't realize *The Fire Dwellers* was coming out so soon. I'm anxious to see it. She said it might be out this week. It sounded as though Time Mag. was very positively disposed in general. Of course you can never tell with them, but it won't hurt if it's so. They can sell books.

Nothing much new otherwise. I'm still struggling along with work, an up-& down-situation with particularly the one boy at home, & the strange feelings inside. All seems to be coming along. I get very fatigued if I expend much more than a modicum of energy, & go dragging around looking for a bed. The baby is kicking madly these days. It's kind of fun though last night it was hard to get to bed, what with not knowing whether it was complaining about every position I happened to get into, or just frolicking, & also what with having to urinate every couple of minutes. I guess all this is par. My school term is going to be longer than usual this year because of the particular courses I'm teaching. I'll be teaching till the end of April & marking papers into May. But the single course I'll have to carry on with won't be too strenuous I hope. Everybody is very careful of me around here; I am handled with a certain amount of amusedly affectionate concern. I feel something like a monstrous glass-blown cupie doll.

Re my book, I got the copy back from Des. He was quite enthusiastic.

26 March 1969

Next day. Yes, Des seemed to like the book a lot. And he's a close reader, so it was very gratifying to hear his comments. I sent the M.S. off to John Gray. In spite of the fact that it's over a week & a half since I wrote to remind the agent of my existence, I still haven't heard from her. All this on top of an over three month dead silence. I really don't know what if anything, is going on. You'd think she'd at least be capable of a polite reply, – a reply of any sort. Right at the moment I've finished cleaning up the supper things, so I've popped into bed with some papers to try & get marked. The job of getting the boys to bed is Dmitry's, & better so, as he's far more patient about their delaying tactics than I am. He also reads to them, and in general gets bedtime over with very smoothly. All of these things I do when he's out of town, but don't mind turning over to him when he's here, particularly since he doesn't mind either. He's very good with the kids. I'm more erratic, particularly now when I'm yearning for bed most of the time.

The latest long range news is that Dmitry's Dept. may be moved from Montreal in the fall. We may be moving to Ontario – in the Burlington-Hamilton area. It's all still up in the air but it seems a likelihood. In that case we'll try to get a place in the country with some land attached. If only we could get something like a big farmhouse, it would be good for the kids, & I'm tired of the city, & also it would be convenient for Dmitry, since his work place will be probably on the outskirts of town so we could as easily be commuter's distance in the country. I don't know, but we're kind of daydreaming. We'll see. I won't be working next year anyway. If only something would happen with the book we might even be able to think of buying something. Anyway, we'll be closer to where you'll be, if it comes to pass. This, by the way, won't interfere with summer plans, – it's for the fall. Write soon.

love,

Adele

1 'Rachel's Sister,' *Time*, 28 March 1969, 13

Elm Cottage
17 April 1969

Dear Adele –

Sleep on, sleep on in majesty! Don't feel guilty about wanting to sleep. Golly, when I was pregnant with both kids I nearly hibernated for 9 months – I simply could not get enough sleep. I was amused at your description of the natural childbirth classes – of course, you *would* think you needed twice as much instruction and exercise! You are probably in much better shape (metaphorically speaking, of course) than you think you are. Incidentally, could I ask you one small favour? When the child is born, could Dmitry send me a cable? I feel like I'm its aunt, somehow! It must be very trying when Dmitry is away – of course you feel the weight of the responsibility, and would feel it under any circumstances, but it must be worse when you're really concentrating all your forces on what is going on inside you. All one can say, really, is – hang on, things will get better. Even with D's boys, they will get better, as kids do (thank god) get older and one is increasingly less responsible for them. Personally, I am delighted that my kids are becoming more and more responsible for themselves – I am not at all tempted to hang onto them; the decrease in my responsibility is like a weight lifted from my mind.

The novel (mine, ie – one always says 'the novel' as though there were only 1 in the world) isn't out yet – won't be until beginning of May. I think TIME did the piece because in some sinister way they are hooked up with the LADIES HOME JOURNAL, who serialized a very chopped version of it[1] just at the time when the TIME piece came out. But you mention a review in the Montreal Star, I now see from your letter.[2] Could the novel be out already in Canada?[3] I just do not know. I know what most of the Canadian reviews will say, though. They will say what a pity it is that M.L. hasn't written THE STONE ANGEL all over again. That old lady, you know, hit into quite a few Canadians' own back-grounds, and nothing I ever write will be the same as that. It touched (I realized only much later, when I saw what response the book got) a lot of raw places in the Can consciousness. So naturally every book afterwards will seem like an anti-climax. I can't help it. One cannot repeat oneself. In fact, I care equally about all my characters, just as one does with one's children, and the last 2 novels have (or so I like to think) been a kind of advance, in methods of my own personal way of communicating. The English and American reviews of A JEST OF GOD were better than the Can ones, and it would not greatly surprise me if the same is true of this novel. (Superstitious thought – I should not have made that prediction; now the Amer and Eng reviews will be disastrous.)

The TIME piece was pretty terrible, but I suppose it may help sales. I went into London to be interviewed because the guy had broken his leg and could not come out here. Would it had been his neck. The writeup described me as 'slightly mannish without being unmotherly' ... God in Heaven, how do you like that? I was sorry I hadn't appeared in a black nylon nightie. They also mentioned my short brown hair, which upset me so much that I have lately taken to wearing it shoulder-length, which really does not suit me very well but satisfies my femininity. I could murder the bastards, but what can you do? It isn't really worth thinking about. But they did another awful thing – they sneakily suggested throughout that the whole novel is autobiographical. Which it is NOT. Except in inner ways, but that is too subtle to com-municate to TIME, and in fact when asked about this, I denied that there was anything autobiographical about it at all. Stacey is Stacey – she isn't me, although we know one another pretty well. But TIME suggests she is me, from beginning to end. But the hell with it.

I took David and one of his pals to N. Scotland for a week, while Jocelyn is in Italy with her class. We just got back yesterday. It turned out to be slightly more exciting than we had bargained for – Dave had a terrible attack of pain in the left side (appendix is on the right) and I called the doctor, who said it might be a small obstruction of the urinary duct, or maybe a kidney stone. Kidney stone! Ye gods. I was nearly out of my mind with worry. We were in Cromarty, small village 40 miles from Inverness, and the doctor got the hospital car and driver, and Dave and I drove to Inverness hospital through (as luck would have it) a blinding snowstorm. He stayed 2 days in hospital, and the trouble turned out to be nothing more than severe constipation – I wouldn't have believed it possible. Anyway, massive relief that it wasn't serious. They did x-rays and the whole bit. Dave thought he was there for life. When they gave him an enema, he said he thought his guts were dropping out! He was in the Men's surgical ward and there was a half-insane Pole there, who had had an ulcer op – he was an alcoholic, which the hospital had not known, and when he came to, he had D.T.'s – David's description was lurid in the extreme. The chap tore out the needle which had been in his wrist for intravenous feeding, and got out of bed and swore at the nurses and thought he was in a car and was crashing. Charming. But I think it made David think of things he'd never considered before.

Much love,

Margaret

p.s. You didn't misread between the lines of my last letter – it was a strain in some ways to have the Purdys here, although it was great to talk writing with Al.[4] Maybe, paradoxically, that was part of the strain. All slightly complicated, but okay. I did find it hard to plan decent meals, though! I've become lazy in this way. My poor kids!

p.s.2 Will send *The Fire-Dwellers*

1 A much abridged version of the novel was published as 'The Fire-Dwellers' in *Ladies' Home Journal*, March 1969, 127–34, 136, 138. It appeared as the *Ladies' Home Journal* Book Bonus.

2 David Legate's review, 'She Pines amid the Firs,' *Montreal Star*, 5 April 1969, Entertainment section, 6

3 It was published in Canada on 3 May.

4 Cutting short a vacation in Greece, Eurithe and Al Purdy had come unexpectedly to London when Eurithe required emergency surgery. Laurence recommended a doctor and afterward invited them to Elm Cottage where they stayed for most of March and into early April while Eurithe recuperated. Laurence had written Wiseman on 25 March 1969 while the Purdys were still with her.

Elm Cottage
26 April [1969]

Dear Adele –

Got your letter this morning. I'm sorry to hear you've been having further upchucking and heartburn etc. Inconsiderate little Kid! I do hope you're still improving and won't have any more unpleasant symptoms.

When exactly, is the baby due? I can't remember. One thing about your letter bothered me – my God, girl, don't worry about falling to pieces and being utterly undignified!!! So what if you're undignified? It is not a very dignified process, birth, not physically anyhow, but that doesn't matter. Kid, if you feel like yelling, YELL! No one will mind. I certainly sympathize with you re: the exercises. Some of us are just not the athletic type. But probably you'll find when the time comes that the exercises have helped.

Thanks for your sympathy re: the Time piece. It's true, they do always seem to get at people where they're most vulnerable, in my case my appearance, which I have always privately considered to be pretty terrible anyway. I do agree with you about autobiographical fiction – it usually has to be rendered very much before it can be good fiction, and this is not just to avoid hurting one's nearest and dearest, either. If it is put down more or less directly, it doesn't seem to work. Even the short stories which I've done which are based on my childhood family are actually rendered quite a lot.

Did I tell you I saw David Legate's review of THE FIRE-DWELLERS in the Montreal Star? You mentioned it in a letter, but I think I hadn't seen it then. Well, he does not seem to have read the novel I wrote – the old old story, eh? You know, it seems to me that one can criticize a novel for being dull or badly written etc, but one simply cannot criticize it for not being the kind of novel you would have written if you'd been the author. Which is more or less what Legate does. He obviously wants to be kind, but ends up damning with faint praise. Never mind.

I'm beginning to get colder and colder feet re: the U of T job. What will I be able to say to young writers? What if no young writers turn up to talk to me, anyway? I can see myself pacing an office for 8 months and NOBODY EVEN KNOCKING AT THE DOOR! Also, I have to give 3 or 4 lectures – on WHAT? Have I got anything to say, I ask myself. And I reply, no, I haven't. Etc. etc. But no doubt I'll stumble through somehow. Jack Ludwig has given readings from his new novel. Well, I cannot do that. I probably won't have a work in progress anyway, but even if I do, I don't want to get up and read from my own writing. That is okay with poetry, but not with prose. How would you do the conversation bits if you've quit using 'he said' and 'she said'? Anyway, I am too superstitious to read from something that isn't finished yet. I feel the god would desert me forever, in outrage. So I shall be reduced to whomping up little talks on the CREATIVE PROCESS (I Was A Middleage Madwoman; Writing As An LSD Substitute; etc).

Must go as a friend is coming for dinner and I haven't got anything ready yet. Dinner can wait – have thought of a few things I wanted to say. If John Gray is so absolutely off his head as to reject CRACKPOT, for pete's sake send it to Macmillan in England. Honestly, John is a dear man but very very conservative and traditional. Also, try Jack McClelland. I believe he has been having financial difficulties and hence may have a smaller list than usual for a few years, but I think you really ought to try him anyway, should the need arise. Any word from America? I become so enraged when I think of your being held up like this over the novel that I want to fire off angry cables to all those concerned. (Don't panic – I won't!)

Really must go. Please write soon.

Love,

Margaret

p.s. My God, the crises we are living through with Jocelyn's boyfriend. He did not phone the other evening when he was supposed to, and instantly she assumed that all was over. Was inconsolable. In despair. The next day he went around to the school and presented her with a beautiful carnation and invited her to a pop concert last night. So we breathe again. How much more of this will my frayed old nerves stand, I wonder!

[2334 Girouard
3] May 1969

Dear Margaret,

At last I can write a letter with practically no guilt attached. Usually I have essays to correct, or exams, or lectures to prepare in the background. Now I've just finished the last of the essays; the last set of exams doesn't come in till Thursday, so I'm free of school worries. I've even set supper to cooking, so the only guilt is how come I've got a few minutes free of guilt? Recklessly I've put some records on the player, removed part of the dog's blanket from his bed, (our best couch), & am reclining anyway, as though all this luxury were coming to me. The weather has improved considerably, so the kids are spending more time out-of-doors. At the moment, having received their allowances today, I notice the older ones making periodic pilgrimages to the corner store to buy crap (chips, etc) to stuff themselves with. Oh well, it's their guts, & their allowances too. Dmitry has had to go to the office to put in a couple of extra hours' work on a special job. He spent most of the morning doing chores, – like taking about five machineloads of laundry to the laundromat, & doing a week's shopping for staples. Actually those chores will be somewhat eased for him in the future as we've just agreed to buy a friend's washer & dryer & stove. She's going to England for her Phd work. I used to help with these weekend chores but for the past few weeks have been immobilized mornings, what with my various (real or imagined) physical infirmities. Yesterday of all things I caught a cold, just a cold, but I seem to not have the excess energy left to put up much resistance, so I'm practically invalided by the sniffles. The monster inside seems to be perfectly healthy & active, judging by the almost constant drumming that goes on. Anyway, at least I got those essays done today, though I'd hate to have to answer for my judgment. Just think those may be the last essays I have to mark, – maybe even forever! – though I can hardly believe it. I've been marking essays since about 4th year. How I've hated it!

Yesterday I was at my exercise class, but the cold that was just coming on had drained me so much I could hardly drag through the (very mild) routine. I take such good care of myself, & get such good care taken of me I can't help thinking of what happened to all those pregnant women during the war and feeling guilty and scared. How come I'm so lucky (bitch that I do), & for how long? Life at this moment is such a melange of good & bad luck that it's hard for my psyche to pick its way in & out of the ramifications. I still haven't heard from John Gray about the book, & in this case it's pretty certain that no news is bad news. About the agent I can be sure she's steadily at it, chalking up rejections. Against all this it seems vain in more than one sense to continue convinced that I've written a good book. And yet that's what the inner certainty, for what it's worth, says. Not that it makes much difference. Remember how we were always girding ourselves against rejection from the powers that be? So, one can still grouse.

Did I write you we saw an amateur group here do a couple of Soyinka plays? One was 'The Strong Breed,' terribly amateurishly done, – painfully, so Soyinka hardly had a chance. The other was 'The Trials of Brother Jero,' which was redeemed because one of the actors, – the trader woman's husband, was a natural for the part.

You ask when the baby is due, – around July 11th. Don't worry, you'll hear as soon as it happens. I still have enormous misgivings, in

spite of all the reassurance I demand & get. For Gawd's sake, at the
moment I can't even seem to produce a bowel movement!

I sympathize with Jocelyn's trials & traumas. Hope all is going well
with her romance. Oh those sharp aching days! Who'd want to live
through them again?

Please write. Tell me how the reviews have stacked up on the whole.
The references I've seen here have been mostly complimentary. Never
mind Legate's non-review. Can't tell you how we're looking forward to
seeing you again. Things still up in the air re Dmitry's firm's prospective move. Oh well, who knows what the next few years will bring? I've
seldom had so much in question at once. Let's ask for survival first.
And then? Write!

love,

Adele

[2234 Girouard]
18 May 1969

Dear Margaret,

Have just received, & now read, *The Fire Dwellers*. Thanks for sending
it to me. I like it. I found it a very moving book. It certainly worked for
me, so much so that I was doubly irritated to remember Legate's
pointless review in the Star a couple of weeks ago. I am particularly
annoyed now, remembering the condescending references to the problems of 'the little woman.' What an arsole! (*The enclosed clipping, by
the way, refers to a book *about* you, which I thought you might find
interesting. Have you seen it? I haven't as yet, but it's good to know
there's one out.)[1] There are a lot of things I wanted to ask you about *The
Fire Dwellers*, but they're not things to write down, so I'll wait till I see
you this summer. The main things I did want to say were in reference
to the feeling of absolute authenticity, the ringing true of the book, &
the way the tone was maintained throughout, without false notes. I was
very much affected by it. It was such a truthful, & in ways frightening
picture of marriage, – a particular marriage, very specific it's true, but
with an enormous amount to say about marriage in general, about relationships in general, not only between husbands & wives but parents &
children. I also liked the technique of partial fragmentation of speech
very much, the unfinished sentences, the way people actually speak. It's
very effective, & you managed it so that there was a kind of poetic

rhythm to it which made it doubly effective. All in all I like the book very much. I think it really comes off. Also, I get the feeling from it that there's more coming. I don't share your fears that you've used up what you had to say. There's far too much power there for anyone to say the engine's run down. Thanks again for sending it to me. Dmitry's going to read it now, & we'll get a genuine male reaction. I think he'll like it all right. Have you had much other critical reaction? Surely the honesty of the book is a rare enough phenomenon to attract plenty of notice. How has the U.S. press reacted? What of the English literary papers? Let me know. I don't get to see many literary mags, nowadays. My God, I can still feel Stacey's anguish! And another thing, it's interesting the way the end of the book dovetails with the pending arrival of Rachel & her mother. It gives the thing a kind of Faulknerian spread.

I want to get this off to you now, so will save other things till I write again shortly. This is most important for now, that you've written a damn fine book and you've got to know it.

love,

Adele

* I believe the woman was in touch with you.

1 McClelland and Stewart had just published Clara Thomas's monograph, *Margaret Laurence*, in its New Canadian Library's Canadian Writers Series. Thomas (b. 1919) was a member of the Department of English, York University.

Elm Cottage
25 May 1969

Dear Adele –

Many many thanks for your letter. Like you were when I first read THE LOVE-BOUND, I was suspicious about your comments, on account of knowing you would want to comfort me for dreadful reception of THE FIRE-DWELLERS in some quarters – but as I read your letter, I knew (as you did with mine re: the play) that it was all okay and meant and so on. So – thanks, kid. I'm glad Stacey communicated to you. She seems an odd kind of character – either she communicates quite a lot with a reader or not at all (and arouses a kind of fury, it seems). Well – reaction of the gentlemen of the press? In England, a resounding silence, except for favourable but totally unperceptive reviews in The Listener[1] and a few other places. Who needs a favourable review that doesn't see what the book is about? Alan Maclean phoned me the other day to declare Macmillan's intention of taking a half-page ad in the Times Lit. Sup, saying they don't often disagree with reviewers but want to declare their faith in this novel – well, I think that is bloody nice of them, although of course quite useless.[2] In America – so far, only 2 reviews, both good. There is a lady on the Cleveland Plain-Dealer who loves me! And she goes overboard, so of course that is nearly as bad as a bad review.[3] Anyway, most of the reviews from Amer (supposing there will be some more) not yet in. But in Canada – migawd, what an odd reaction. Guess I told you about some of it in my last letter. Reviews absolutely split. So far not too many, but either in sympathy with Stacey and knowing what the novel intended, or absolutely *hating* her – vehemently, passionately, almost wanting to kill her. Adele, this is so astonishing. To see these reviews (all by middleaged males who might have wives like Stacey, I think – I really do believe this) which indicate that whatever a woman like that thinks, they DO NOT WANT TO KNOW. So they do all kinds of quite strange things, like saying she is empty-headed (she is *not*, whatever else you may say about her), or she does nothing but drink (who do they think gets the meals in the Mac-Aindra house?), etc. etc. One cannot help but feel that the novel in some ways is being judged on grounds other than literary. The message I get from some (especially Canadian) reviews is of enormous male hostility, which I guess I am naive enough to be surprised about. The same reviewers do not, apparently, notice the humour of the novel, nor the (I would have hoped) attention paid to the form, which gave me a lot of bother but in the end (although it is not anything very new, only new to me) I think fit the people and the material. There are exceptions, thank God. As I told you, Bill French in the Globe gave it a very perceptive review,[4] and now Philip Sykes in Macleans has given it a pretty decent review,[5] not all uproused male ego, so that is marvellous. The reaction in Can has really astonished me. Apparently Jack Scott in the Van Sun has done a hatchet job, too,[6] although I have not yet seen his review. Well well well. One is prepared to have a novel attacked on professional grounds, kid – like, how is its characterization, its form, its selectivity, and all the other things. But hardly to have it attacked on sexual grounds (Our women are not like that – or if they are, they bloody well ought not to be –). I'm encouraged by the few straightfor-ward male reviews which look on it as a novel to be reviewed as a novel, not as something touching their maleness. Jesus – I never meant to threaten anybody!!!.

Re: myself – I suspect I will tomorrow (Monday) or the next day get a letter from you, worried-like, after that letter I last wrote you. Well, don't worry. I am really okay. Now have realized why the whole bit flung me into emotional disturbance[7] – it took me years after getting to Eng to see myself as myself, and someone who could cope on her own and also be a professional writer. Then, when J and I decided to try to make a go of it again, I reverted abruptly to trying to see myself as the compleat housewife once more, although I knew I wasn't – and decided the only way to make the situation work was to never discuss or reveal how I really thought or felt about anything, at least not within the confines of the family. Well, none of this was his fault in the very slightest – only the fact that we *were* really at that point too different and not likely again to relate except in terms of what we had meant to one another in the past. Result was that the outer and inner were in constant conflict, and result of that was the bottle, never before such a bad problem. Things improved when I quit drinking, but only because I could then suppress all and be what I wasn't. So now – once again, change of self-image, back to what one might term cornily my real self, and yet enormous panic for awhile, as no one changes their self-image instantly without some kind of reaction. However, this time it is, I hope, for keeps. Even if he does not go through with it (although God knows for all our sakes I hope he does) I shall have to. We both have tried, for the past 2 yrs, and it does not work. I really wish him only well, and would like to think he could be happy with someone, because I know he can't be with me, nor I with him. I also do really want to be freed at last from this enormous guilt for not having been his kind of wife. Write, please.

Love,

Margaret

1 Stuart Hood, 'Post-Freudian, Pre-Freudian,' *Listener*, 1 May 1969, 618

2 The following notice occupied one-third of page 718 of the *Times Literary Supplement* of 3 July 1969: 'It is very seldom that we feel that a book has been seriously underrated by literary editors and reviewers. We believe this to be so in the case of Margaret Laurence's The Fire-Dwellers. Please read it. 35s'

3 Eugenia Thornton, 'This Worn Theme Is a Gem,' *Cleveland Plain Dealer*, 11 May 1969

4 'A Compassion for Flesh and Blood,' *Globe and Mail*, 3 May 1969, 17. French (b. 1923) was literary editor of the *Globe and Mail*.

5 *Maclean's*, June 1969, 98
6 'Some Arsenic on the Old Lace,' *Vancouver Sun*, 16 May 1969, 29
7 Jack Laurence had asked Margaret for a divorce. She had immediately written
  Adele who, as instructed, had read and destroyed Margaret's letter.

[2234 Girouard]
5 June 1969

Dear Margaret,

Am writing this in the laundromat, where I've managed to drag my cart with a couple of loads full. Our bathroom was getting to be a mess. Unfortunately I couldn't bring everything so there's still more to do at home. D. & I have recently acquired a washer & a dryer, but they're not connected yet, & the landlady's machine, which she lets us use, is hardly ever free. They've a small baby in the house, so keeping up with the laundry is kind of a nightmare. Pardon me for boring you with domestic details. I suppose it's a question of venting small irritations before I get round to big ones. The big one at the moment is really an irritation and a half. I rec'd my M.S. from Macmillan's a week ago, but have rec'd no covering letter at all, just the bare M.S. I have waited this full week with what I consider exemplary patience and calm, except for a nagging feeling of depression which tells me that somewhere deep down I'm pretty upset. Today I will write to John Gray (calmly, with only a hint of what shall it be? gentle irony?) I don't know, frankly, quite how to cope. I know there are numerous forgiveable reasons for this to have accidentally happened, but I also know that it should not have been allowed to happen to anyone, & this kind of thing happens all too frequently with publishers. I guess I am really very angry, but I am also rather heartsick too, I suppose. Anyway, all this should not be happening now, while I am gravid and uncomfortable and not at all confident of what's in store for me in the next little while and seem to be surrounded by responsibilities I'm not superbly equipped to cope with. It's Dmitry's travel season and he's off again, this time for Vancouver & B.C., on Sat. for anywhere between 1 & 2 weeks. Luckily, Mom & Dad are coming in tonight so Mom will keep me company some of that time, but one thing I can't fob off on her is the work & responsibility of looking after those three kids, not at her age. By the way, I'm really sorry you're not coming here a couple of months sooner. Mom & Dad are celebrating their 50th Wedding Anniversary this month, & Mary & I are throwing a big do for them. Mary is doing all the arranging, thank goodness, and it promises to be fun. We've already had acceptances of invitations from relatives in N.Y. & L.A. Of course the boys will come up from Miami. Our granduncle, from L.A., will be coming, the patriarch of the house.

I'm now supposed to see the Dr. every week. He told me yesterday that I'm carrying a big baby. It certainly is an active one. I hope all goes well.

Listen, I hope Leslie Adamson will be looking you up before you come over. She's been a good friend. I think you'll like her. She's originally from W'p'g., was divorced last year. I think you met at my place once. Anyway, she's got regards for you. She's gone over to do her Phd in History, (with some qualms about what she'll do afterwards.) Once you reach a certain age, (and are a woman, too,) jobs in colleges are not easy to come by, & she's had no assurance from McGill that they'll take her on again. I guess if I ever want to go back to teaching I'll have similar problems, particularly since I have no Phd, and since my 'acceptable' contribution to the creative world is an ever receding issue of the past. I know Des didn't want me to quit. He's given me every opportunity to hang on, but I just don't believe it would be right for the tot. Besides, the Ontario move seems more & more likely.

You mention Godfrey & the Anansi Press. It's a problem. Macmillan may have rejected the M.S. but I am still not (technically) trying to peddle it in Canada. My agent still hasn't responded to my query about showing it to Macmillan in the first place, so I don't know whether to go ahead & show it elsewhere or not, till I get something more definite from her. I'm sure this Godfrey is good, as you say, but have my reservations about people in their capacity as editors & publishers. Godfrey recently did something to Alec Lucas that gave him an unnecessarily unhappy weekend.[1] Remind me to tell you about it. Not that this is by any means a rejection of your idea. Frankly, at this point I just don't know what to do.

I'm back home now. My boys & man have had lunch & are off about their business. I've put a load of washing in the landlady's machine, & will be up & down the backstairs a few more times before I can have me a proper lie down. Sorry this is such a glum, egocentric letter. I am thinking of you & hoping you're feeling better about things. Let me know how things are.

love,

Adele

1 Alec Lucas (b. 1913), professor of English at McGill University, was writing *Hugh MacLennan* for the Canadian Writer Series in McClelland and Stewart's New Canadian Library. Godfrey was the editor of the series.

[2234 Girouard]
12 June 1969

Dear Margaret,

Well, the Macmillan axe fell the other day, about 1½ weeks after the M.S. was returned. The original letter was somehow delayed in the post, so they sent me photostats. Included were two reports, one supposedly favorable, the other not. All the others were unfavorable. Here are some excerpts from John Gray's letter: 'The first two reports were pretty strongly unfavourable; the first because it was felt to be grotesque & incredible and, in spite of brilliant flashes, beyond fixing; the second thought it might be fixed but was unenthusiastic for the same sort of reasons as the above. Both felt that whatever was done, the book would really need substantial cuts.'

The two reports that he did send me were, well, as far as I was concerned, there was not much to choose between them, so far off the mark were they both. John goes on to say that he agrees with the reports. There is one bit of gross presumption in his letter. 'As it is, I suspect you don't yourself now like the book enough to enjoy revision.' How should I respond to such arrant stupidity? I can't help his response or his readers', but the assumption that I would agree with them in their obtuseness floors me. It does not seem to occur to them, or to him, that I could possibly go on thinking that I've written a good book. Anyway, John is of course full of commiseration. I've no doubt he's upset to have to deliver such a verdict, though he agrees with it, & if that's their reaction, okay. I would like you to see the actual reports. Talk of hatchet jobs! And a curious personal note prevails in both. The world of the book is not seen as such. It's 'I like this sort of thing and I can't stand that sort of thing.' Well, that's that. I find it very difficult not to think of myself as in large part a writer. I am afraid if that aspect of my identity is to survive it will have to go private. I'm afraid I'm incurably pig headed about my own literary judgment. I am not incapable of responding to someone whose judgment I respect, but nothing I read in the reports or John's letter aroused much by way of respect. I am still stunned, for instance, to find that my characters are grotesque.

Meanwhile, let me not go on cavilling. What good will it do? I must simply gird myself to what may turn out to be the total response of publishers, in which case tant pis. We always thought it might turn out this way.

Mom & Dad are now in Montreal, & Mom is staying with me & helping me out, since Dmitry's on the West Coast & will be for 8 or 9 days more possibly. The weather's turned hot & muggy. The Dr. tells me I'm expecting on July 5th, rather than on July 11th as I'd thought, so there's about three weeks to go & I'm trying to prepare myself. It's good to have Mom here. As it is I feel now the sooner the baby comes the better. The carrying has become a chore. But the baby hasn't dropped yet so I'll have to be patient.

Yes, I was going to send you the M.S. of *Crackpot*, but figure now that I'll just wait till you're in Canada, & sometime when you're settled in & ready you can read it if you like. By the time it got to you now you'd be just about on your way here anyway. One thing I remain adamant about, though I realize it may ruin my prospects as a possible success. I'll write, when I'm working seriously, what & how I feel I have to, even if only for the closet.

Well kid, I'd better close for now. Hope things are better with you. Write when you get the chance.

love,

Adele

Elm Cottage
26 June [1969]

Dear Adele –

I was so distressed about what John Gray said about the novel that I could not bring myself to write for a few days. He really has shown no perception at all about either the novel or you. I think one must now accept the fact, though, that his judgement is more and more an overly traditional one. I don't think that Macmillan's in England is one tenth as traditional these days as Macmillan's of Toronto, to tell you the truth. I was at Brighton last weekend, visiting Alex and Delores – Alex and I talked about you – I hope you do not mind. It is just that we both care so much not only about you, but in this context principally about your writing. Alex said an astonishing thing ... he said he thought the play was 'like a novel in theatre form' and that it should be published as such. As you know, this has been my view for several years now. Anyway, he also said 'Adele is a prophetic writer, and in the deepest sense her work may not be dated but actually too far-out for many publishers.' I think this is dead right, and I think it is true about those parts of the novel which I have read. Anyway, one does not expect you to be a great PR woman for yourself, and you are not. Alex and I, who are both less penetrating writers than you (and we both feel this and acknowledge it, and this has no emotional connotation – it is just a statement of fact) are both more practical when it comes to dealing with publishers. Would you, then, at some point, agree to let me have a copy of the novel (I already have the play) and to give Alex and myself more or less a free hand to let them be seen by publishers who we would consider to have slightly more depth and understanding of your sort of work than any publishers who have so far seen the 2 manuscripts? This would not mean that either of us want to interfere, Adele – and any further communications would naturally be between yourself and a publisher only, but we both feel that an attempt must be made to find a comprehending publisher, in the interests, quite frankly, of literature. Don't decide right away – but we can talk of this when I see you. In the meantime, concentrate only on the immediate events (very soon, now, I guess) and simply keep in the back of your mind the fact that there are people whose opinion I hope you trust to some extent, namely Alex and myself, who have an intense faith and belief in your work.

If I don't write before we leave, my address from 14 July to about 15 August will be: c/o Mrs. Mona Hickman,[1] 1569 Jefferson, West Vancouver. If the baby is born after we leave England, could Dmitry let me know in Vancouver?

God bless, Adele, and all the luck in the world when the time comes. May it all be easy and joyful.

Much love,

Margaret

ps. my young couple[2] are here and are very very nice.
ps. the great news is that Delores is pregnant! She is three months, so hopes the danger period is over. She feels nauseated all the time, but thinks it is beginning to improve a little. They are both very pleased about the whole thing, and she was much heartened when I told her you were expecting a baby, as she has been having the same kind of qualms as you did in the beginning.

ps. re: your being a kind of prophetic writer, it seemed to me that for a publisher to say CRACKPOT was not sufficiently with-it in terms of today's literary fashions is rather like a publisher saying to John of Patmos ... 'This book, REVELATIONS, now, baby – it might just have possibilities, but, like, it's not really groovy, see? If you can take it back and turn it into a swinger, we might just consider it again.'

1 Mona Hickman (née Spratt), Laurence's childhood friend
2 Dave Godfrey had recommended Ian and Sandy Cameron to Laurence as house-sitters for the academic year 1969–70, when she was writer-in-residence at University of Toronto.

[2234 Girouard]
28 July 1969

Dear Margaret,

Hi! It was good to get your note, with a forwarding address, today. After our last talk on the phone I felt as though you were off there in limbo somewhere for the next month, with no point of contact. About meeting you at the airport, if Dmitry's in town we will certainly do so. If you don't see us there, call me before you take a bus or cab. If you do have to take one, we actually live on the way into town, so you might get let off without having to go all the way downtown. Anyway, I hope we'll, or one of us will, be there to meet you.

Tamara is fine. I had her in to see her pediatrician this week, for her one month's old check-up. She'd grown 1½ inches and gained 2 lbs. 10 oz. from her birth weight. Unfortunately she's a bit colicky for periods during the day. Poor little kid is very gassy, – gets it from her mother I guess, so we get some pitiful wailing. But on the whole she's very good, very sweet natured, very lovable.

I was going to wait till I saw you to discuss John Gray & the things you'd written about, & actually I will. But I had another letter from him today, and I have to give vent somewhere. I'd replied to a letter from him, in which he'd asked why he hadn't heard from me, by telling him that there didn't seem to be anything to say in response to his & his readers' crits. of my novel, that I disagreed heartily with them & found their level of comprehension inadequate, & that it was pointless engaging in argument at that level. Comes back a letter, which I'll show you, which indicates clearly that John is certainly not unsure of this verdict, – & he's got *four* and *not only one* reader, – unanimous – behind him. And not only that, but he's determined that I too shall see the blinding light.

First of all he points out that I'm not being calmly reasonable. Then, re the readers, 'you should recognize that their level of comprehension (which you deplore) is better than you can expect from the reading public. If they have misunderstood the book, the public will do the same, & more. Those were good intelligent readers – & admirers of Adele Wiseman.'

– So much for the reading public, & a sop for Adele. But he goes on. 'You wouldn't quarrel with the proposition that the onus is on the writer to interest, & to be understood by "average" readers. So – ? I don't ask you to like the verdict but I think you must face it & recognize that there is a good deal about the book that is less than the best you can do. It may seem to you an over-simple approach but the fact is that large segments of the book go on too long, don't hold the interest & become boring. And large sections do not convince on their own terms – or any other. All readers felt this & I think you should count ten before saying they are all wrong.'

– And he goes on tossing in another little sop or two, but firmly sticking to his guns.

What is excruciating is that it's all done with earnest good will and sincere friendship. Only by God, I'd better accept their verdict, because the book's getting longer & duller by the minute. What can one say? I don't agree with his premises re the 'average' reader, or readers in general. I don't know whether the book is too long & too dull. It's the way it had to be.

I find his letter killingly depressing, but I guess I'll get over that. Anyway, must go now; I hear Tamara complaining. I hope you're having fun. Much love, and will see you soon thank God!

Adele

[29 Monclova Road
Downsview, Ontario]
September 1970

Dear Margaret,

A quiet moment; the baby asleep, Sergei out with his friends, Dmitry just flown off to Alberta, & I sitting here, watching the dishwasher somebody gave us flood the kitchen floor. It's no use getting hysterical. I might as well let it at least finish doing the dishes before I start mopping up. These have been a very crowded few months. Did you know before you left that we had to move by the end of August?[1] So we found a place just in the nick, a really great place, though it's just got a bare open backyard & we'll have to manufacture some privacy and garden next year. But it's only about 4½ years old, and it's got _eleven_ rooms! Interruption. Sergei came in, insisted on peeking into the machine while it was working, & elicited an even greater flood. Then when it was finished its cycle, I found it was full of soapsuds, so I have to put it through the whole deal again. And I've hardly got any dishes in there! I just wanted to get the hang of working it. Feh! Machines! Anyway, this place will cost us slightly less to rent than the old one, mainly because the Italian owner has rented it on condition we won't rent out rooms. I guess he's afraid that just about anybody would be tempted to rent a room or two. What else would you do with eleven rooms? There's even an extra kitchen downstairs, a big one. Apparently that's a feature of Italian built homes around here; upstairs for show, downstairs to live in. So we've plenty of place to spread out in, though the family has diminished. Winnie, the middle boy, opted to stay with his Mother in Vancouver this year. Sergei is back home with us though, & rather happy, I think, to be the only son. He's always wanted to be. I hope things go well for Winnie in Vancouver, & that he's not in for another rejection in that quarter.

Tamara is beautiful: walking, climbing, falling, & getting bumped, but getting up again & very quickly turning on the sunshine after each mishap. She's still such a darling. Have you seen or spoken to the Barons? How are they and how is their baby? I hope everything is okay. How was Alec's book received? the one about 19th c. East End London? I'd love to read it.

We are far from settled in this place. We would never have got this far had it not been for an old friend from Stepney days, Billee Rothe, who stayed and helped us pack & move. Dmitry was out of town much of the time & I wouldn't have been able to do it on my own, _and_ continue work on the book, without her. She not only packed & cleaned, but was marvelous with Tamara. What a godsend!

The agent tells me that she & Longmans are close to an agreement, & that the contract should be ready any day now.[2] I've done all I want to do on the book, so there is a real possibility I'll be rid of it soon! Now I've got to prepare for the talk in W'p'g next month. I'm looking forward to it.

Sorry this is rather a pedestrian note. I'll write more next time. I'm still tired after the move. And there's so much to do!

From the sound of it you do have a novel on the way. Good! I hope you'll be into it soon, – if you're not already. How are the kids? Please write & let me know what's happening. Are you enjoying being back? My new phone no is: area code 416. Tel. no. 247-9617.

Love from us all.

Adele

1 Laurence had returned to England in July after her year as writer-in-residence at University of Toronto.
2 Longman initially agreed to publish *Crackpot* and paid Wiseman an advance on royalties of $2000. However, it subsequently withdrew the offer.

Elm Cottage
6 October [1970]

Dear Adele:

Thanks for your letter – no, I didn't realize you were having to move. What a drag for you. But your new house sounds great. Marvellous news about the novel!!!! HURRAH! Did you have to do very much work on it? Anyway, it's wonderful that it is finished and Longmans are producing a contract. Next thing is to persuade them to publish the play.

I was very pleased to see that Mordecai had used a portion of your novel in the Penguin Canadian Writing. I thought the whole collection was pretty interesting, didn't you?

I sympathize profoundly re: your dishwasher ... hell, that kind of crisis isn't trivial! It's nerve-wracking. We have had a short crisis here this morning. Dave is home with a cold, and this morning all our lights started flickering, so he fortunately thought to look at the main switchbox, and found that part of it was getting extremely hot. We switched all power off, phoned local electrician and he came and said he couldn't deal with it, because it was part of the mains arrangement and had to be done by the Southern Electricity Board. He also said that when the house was rewired, some 7 years ago, one part of the switchbox was left in its old state (that is, part of it should've been replaced and wasn't) and that it was a distinct fire hazard. Charming. The place might have gone up in smoke anytime these past years. I phoned the Elec Board, and the guy is here now, replacing the box that should've been replaced 7 yrs ago. I am somewhat shaken and also somewhat angry.

Our house repairs and decoration nearly finished now, thank goodness. It only remains to have several more bedrooms carpeted, and I'm going to paint the back bedroom myself (oh joy). Now I've spent so much dough on the house that I feel panic stricken and think I'll never earn another penny. Of course the more panic stricken I feel, the less I can get down to writing again. I am trying to relax and quietly tell myself I can survive for the next two years, but so far I really have not written one word since getting back here. I feel quite terrified at the thought of this next novel – I don't yet know how to tackle it, and although I'm sure it is *there*, I seem to have no confidence in my ability to get it down. I wish I didn't scare so easily.

I spent a weekend with Alex and Delores not very long ago. Their son, Nicholas, is a honey – huge dark brown eyes like Delores, and the most concentrated stare ... he really sizes one up. It's lovely to see Alex and Delores with him ... naturally they are absolutely crazy about him. He's very sturdy and well-built.

Tamara sounds absolutely wonderful ... what about sending a snapshot of her? Gee, I'd like to drop in on you all again! Maybe next summer, if God is good.

Jocelyn left last week for university and seems to be getting on okay, although she is still very lonely. She has quite a nice room and her landlady seems a pretty reasonable sort of woman. She is reading for a degree in Sociology. Guess who teaches in the Social Sciences at Birmingham and will be teaching Joc (I think) Political Science? Harry Ferns. Remember him from Winnipeg? He taught at United and I worked for him for awhile when he was getting the old Winnipeg Citizen organized. Small world.[1]

Elec power is now back on, thank God, and the man assures me all is now safe. Must go and do the laundry, which couldn't do this morning on account of no power.

If I don't get myself back to writing soon, I will probably be in a mental hospital ere long. I wish I found it easier to begin. I wish the whole thing were easier! Why didn't I take up some other profession? Much love to you all, and PLEASE WRITE SOON.

Margaret

ps. Alex's novel, KING DIDO, got v. good reviews here. It is an extremely good book, in my opinion. I'll get a copy for you.

1 Henry Stanley Ferns (b. 1913) had taught history at United College (1944–7) and economic history at the University of Manitoba (1947–9). In 1946–7, he was founder and first president of the Winnipeg Citizen Co-operative Publishing Company. He had been a professor of political science at Birmingham since 1950.

[29 Monclova Road]
11 November 1970

Dear Margaret,

And about time, I know. Since I received your last we have been a week in W'p'g., & Dmitry has been away most of the time since then. He should be home very early Fri. morning, which means sometime during the middle of the night, – from the West Coast. Then he'll sleep a couple of hours & go in to the office. That's the way it's been lately. The poor guy's been run off his feet, – or is it flown off his wings? Anyway, pollution is big nowadays, and suddenly all the sinners want salvation simultaneously. Which is just fine from all points of view, only I'm going to have to see to it that Mitia takes his holidays and gets away periodically. The week in W'p'g. at least took his mind off work, & it was hard to get at him there. Last spring when he took a week off, the office came to the house, or he was at the office, all the time.

The week in W'p'g was good all round. The weather was golden blue Manitoba autumn, crisp and fresh. My talk, on Creativity and Mom's dolls, went over well and was a pleasure to give. Dmitry & Sergei were behind screens putting up the doll exhibit on stands they'd made and tables, while I talked, using just a few dolls as examples. Then, at the climax, since I'd held back the identity of the 'artist' till then, I signalled Dmitry & they unveiled the mass of dolls. All those vital creatures, (I had over seventy there), have quite an impact. What a ham I am. I said, 'It's a world. It's my mother's world,' & they pulled aside the screens. The audience stared, struck dumb. Dead silence. 'I still don't know what art's all about, but I know that this is it.' Then they applauded & came rushing down to the stage to get a closer look. The room held about 200; – it all took place in the morning, during classes. I can't say that everyone there got the point, but I think that the majority caught on that something was there, & some few got a new view of what it's all about. And of course it was good to see friends & family again, and it was Tamara's first visit to the ancestral, so that was fun.

How is the new novel coming? Are you well into it already? How does it feel? It sounds as though you're moving into a new sphere, from the way you write, though you haven't as yet said anything specific. Will you be coming here next summer? Do you think you'll be able to work, as planned; I mean on the new book, in the Peterborough 'shack'?[1] It sounds as though you've done some considerable work on Elm Cottage too, recently. From what I've heard, not only from you, that's a very lovely old place. Surroundings become so important. I suppose it's the feeling of having at least achieved some small kind of harmony with immediate surroundings, however fleeting, that's so important. I literally spend days wondering where a picture should hang, to give the right feeling, whatever that is.

Sergei is at the moment designing a stained glass window for a school competition. He is evolving a beautiful design. Tamara is playing & singing on the kitchen floor. Of course she not only walks, but runs, or I should say, hurtles zig-zaggily, already, & we go for walks outdoors, these last two days in the drizzle, even, which she seems to enjoy.

Mort Forer[2] has had another heart attack. He has been working madly, in a kind of frenzy, whipping himself up to euphoria, as though unconsciously trying to challenge fate. He has been writing two screenplays simultaneously, working with an ambitious, egocentric man who eggs him on. Now he's out of Intensive Care & back at work, still in the hospital. Marion is terribly upset, but what can she do?

love,

Adele

P.S. Love to the kids. How are they? And to Alex, Delores & Paul. And to you. Please write! Adele

1 Laurence had bought a cottage on the Otonabee River, near Peterborough, Ontario, in November 1969.
2 Mort Forer (1922–82), author of the prairie novel *The Humback* (1969), was a Toronto-based freelance radio and film script writer. He had been best man at Adele Wiseman and Dmitry Stone's wedding.

Elm Cottage
7 January 1971

Dear Adele:

Gosh! It can't be this long since I last wrote, but I see yr letter is dated
Nov 11! Will explain presently my long silence. Your talk in Winnipeg
sounds absolutely great, and I don't think you're a ham actor at all ...
I thought it was lovely, the way you revealed that it was your mum
who had made the dolls. I wish I'd been there.

The pic of Tamara with yr Christmas card is absolutely beautiful. She
really does look like a little girl-bird being fed. I wish I could swoop in
and visit you for a few days. Never mind ... I'll be back in June, I hope.

I was very sorry to hear that Mort Forer had had another heart
attack. I do so much hope he is better now and not driving himself.
That must be terrible, tho – to be forced to take it easy and to find it
almost impossible to do so. I still feel so upset every time I think of his
novel not being published in Amer or Eng. Has there been any change
about that? I did a review of it which came out in the last issue of
Tamarack, by the way.[1]

What about your novel? When is Longmans publishing? Please give
me all the news.

Reason for my silence – for about 2 months, after finishing getting
house fixed up and repaired, I did nothing except brood about novel.
Made about 10 false starts. Worked religiously every day, and later
ripped up all I'd written. Really no good. However, just recently I think
I may have begun to find the right voice for it. I did feel very low about
it, but am feeling better now, as I think the way may open up if I try to
learn patience. I couldn't think of anything else, so wrote no letters at
all. Then Christmas, with its usual hectic quality. However, Jocelyn goes
back to Birmingham on the 15th, so I will be able to settle down then,
I hope. In the meantime, am trying to communicate with friends, as the
pile of letters on my desk reached alarming proportions. I just feel with
this novel that there's no way I can drive myself to do it ... it either
comes, relatively quietly, or it doesn't. I think maybe now it will. At
least I discovered about a thousand different ways it *couldn't* be done.

Christmas was good, but v. busy. We had 4 houseguests for that
whole weekend; 10 people for Christmas dinner and 14 for Boxing Day.
Then, on the Monday, Jocelyn's boyfriend from Belfast arrived and will
be with us until the 11th. She is not quite so sure now that she's crazy
about him, as he is v. possessive and she resents this, so the atmosphere

has been slightly tricky. New Yrs Eve was fantastic ... Joc invited a lot of her friends and didn't know how many would turn up, so I was trying to prepare a casserole which would do for somewhere between 8 and 14 people! Martyn (J's boyfriend) got into one of his depressive phases, and spent day in his room, drinking British sherry (poison), so by eve was sloshed and was sick all over my new upstairs carpets. David decided to smoke Martyn's pipe and was also sick on ditto. By the time the New Year rolled in, I felt (and smelled) like a nurse's aide! Meantime, guests all over kitchen and liv. room. Martyn, sobering, decided he had disgraced himself and tried to phone B.E.A. to book first flight back to Ireland and Joc frantically said to me, '*Do* something!' ... well, it was a kind of different N. Yrs Eve, anyway.

We had snow for Christmas, and it was gorgeous and I felt very homesick for Canada as I tramped around the woods here. It has melted now and we are back to the dreary old rain.

I've managed to find a young Can couple who are going to come in June so I can go to Canada. I don't think the kids will come. Martyn and Jocelyn wanted to come, especially Martyn, I think, in Sept, altho I was not too sure I really yearned to have them there! However, I think now that it likely will not work out that way. Joc would love to go over for summer and work in Toronto, but I don't know how good her chances would be of a job ... not marvellous, I think.

It would be nice, tho, if she could, and then could come to the shack for some weekends. We'll see. David is saving for a motorbike, and I think he'd rather stay here and get the bike than go to Canada for summer.

Alas, I have to go out into the stormy wind now and go to London. Would rather stay home on a day like this.

Please write sooner than I did ... and I will reply quickly this time. I was simply in such a depressed state over novel that I could not bear even to talk to anyone, but I think the cloud has somewhat lifted now.

Much love to you all,

Margaret

ps. we drove to Birmingham the other day to see the univ, and to the flat where Joc will live next term with 3 other girls. The univ is very redbrick, but not bad. The flat looks like a mess, but that's her problem ... at least she has her own room, and I think she'll be happier there than in a boarding house as before.

ps. through my literary frustrations, I have become a bird-watcher ...
now have a tame robin, name of Charlie, who is a people-watcher ... we
stare at one another for long periods of time; maybe he is writing a
novel, too.

1 'Stubborn Pride,' *Tamarack Review* 55 (Spring 1970): 77–9

[29 Monclova Road]
15 January 1971

Dear Margaret,

I am just paranoid enough, to wonder, when I haven't heard for a long
time, whether it means something personal. That is my natural,
ingrown, selfish response. My next one is to wonder, Is there anything
wrong? Reaction to the first is to stop writing so as not to impose an
unwanted presence. Benefits are all the joys of self pity and the taste of
martyrdom. Reaction to the second is anxiety, apology, selfabasement,
worry, guilt, & finally the impulse to write, write, write, offer services,
help, reassurance, whatever is needed that is within one's provenance.
Having been through both states, I've decided now to try to avoid
egocentricity & pessimism both, and just to say 'Hi! Longtime no hear.
Why?' It's just not like you not to write. I hope it's just something
simple like you never felt like it, which it seems to me is a most
legitimate reason. Nevertheless it is time you dropped us a word, if only
to say you don't feel like writing.

   We here are all fine. The baby has had a bout of high fever, some
sort of infection, which she's more or less over, though she's still on
sulfa to prevent recurrence. Dmitry should fly in from M't'l tonight.
Sergei has just gone off to the Science Centre for his Fri. evening's
entertainment, with a buddy.

   We spent a quiet festive season. Saw Hugo & Louise[1] once when they
were in town. A couple of days ago Leslie Adamson stopped over, on
her way back to England. She promised to look you up this time. She's
a very fine person, a hell of a lot of fun, too. I hope you do get together.

   As I write it's grown darker & darker in the living room, so I can
hardly see the pen marks, but I'm looking out on a striking sunset.
We're on a hill here, directly facing some monolithic apartment houses,
& a good, prairie type expanse of sky, & lights over towards the airport.
It's a daily pleasure, this sunset. When I'm finished writing I'll give

Tamara her bath & supper, & perhaps, after she's in bed, get down to completing a report for Naim Kattan.[2] I've been doing a bit of reading for the C.C. Interesting. I wish it paid better. Are you still planning to be here this summer? We may go to a conference in Leningrad, & if we do I hope we'll be able to spend a few days in England. But that'll be in late August.

How are the kids? Anything in the work line you can talk about? Health okay?

Love, as ever,

Adele

1 McPherson
2 Naim Kattan (b. 1928), head of the Writing and Publishing Section, Canada Council

Elm Cottage
[30 April 1971]
Tomorrow is May 1st – good omen.

Dear Adele:

Brief note, to let you know things are changing, maybe for the better. I seem to have begun writing again, and am still so bloody scared that it will all go away that I hardly dare mention it, and indeed will not, except to you and also to Al. A quite different novel from the one I so carefully planned and then had to throw out. I dunno where this is going to go, except in a general way, but I don't *want* to know yet, either. I would like, if God is good, to find out as I go along. I do not think this is likely to have much appeal to anyone but myself, because the reasons I'm doing it are not valid, I suspect, for very many people. However, that is not important. Even if it is not published, I would like to set it down somehow. The one I threw out, you know, was really great as a theory; as a novel it was dead before it even began. So, who knows? All I know is that I feel better than I have since I finished The Fire-Dwellers, which was in 1968, and for the first time since then, I want to get up in the mornings. What I would like you to do, please, is pray for me. I am not at all joking, as no doubt you know.

Domestic life is simmering down somewhat. Only Dave and self here now, praise the lord, for a change. Joc and Peter okay, but Peter unwell again ... he is far from robust, and in my worse moments I get frantic with worry, seeing Joc supporting an invalid, but I *know* I am inclined to gloomy imaginings. I find it harder than I thought I would, to let her go. I mean, to *really* let her go and not worry about whether she's getting the right things to eat and if her job is tiring her, etc. We all think these things are going to be easier for *us*, because we are more enlightened than some parents, and then we discover nothing is ever easier for anyone, and we are no more enlightened than most. I'm having to re-learn all my responses to her, and she to me. She came over the other day and looked *awful*, tired and depressed, and my heart turned over, and she began to pour out her difficulties, and then, quite soon, we both saw that it was too damn easy for both of us to fall back into the old patterns ... me as protective mum, her as child. So we tried to discuss that one, and it certainly isn't an easy one. She *has* problems, real ones, but they are *hers*. I have my own. When I think I have to go through this in about 1 or 2 yrs time with Dave, I feel weak. But maybe the experience with Joc will help me with David.

See you soon, God be praised!

Love to all,

Margaret

Elm Cottage
13 January 1972

Dear Adele –

A note in haste, while I wait for the dinner to cook and Dave to change out of his motorbike gear. How is your *health*? I have been kind of worried, and hope the damn infection has cleared now.

Christmas was great here, tho exhausting. We had no less than 10 for meals for about 2 weeks. One of the young writers from that year in Tor (Paul Mutton, one of the 2 best) and his girl were here for Christmas, and that was very nice. Eight of us living here, and others coming and going, so it was hectic, but everyone pitched in and helped, so it wasn't really much of a strain for me, except that various people felt the need of talking about either their writing or songs or personal dilemmas, so I was slightly drained by the time the hols were over. Various Can friends visited – Lyall and Jean Powers (I know they are Amer citizens, but I can't think of them as such) who are in Rome for a year, came over to Eng for Christmas and came out one day. Good to see them again. Lyall is working hard on a book on Faulkner.[1]

After Christmas, the usual winter domestic crises – old lead water pipes in back hall about to burst; six tiles blown off roof; plaster falling in front hall; washing machine conked out, etc. Me on phone to plumbers, builders etc, BEGGING them to come and *do* something. Finally they all converged upon house, and now we are more or less back to normal. One day we had 3 builders and 2 plumbers here all day, and I spent about four hours making tea for them all, at least half a dozen times. However, I was so glad to see them I didn't begrudge the time.

Back to work this week, and novel mushrooms horribly. Adele, I'm in trouble and I have to let you know about it. I dunno what to do. The thing is, people are going to call this novel highly autobiographical, and in some ways it *is*, altho the main character's background pretty different from my own (altho Scots and in the same bloody town for heaven's sake!) But odd things are happening. The main character's best friend, coming into this last chapter for the first time, talks awfully like you, I regret to say. I mean, she does and she doesn't. She *isn't* you, I need hardly say – but any fool who knows both of us would never believe I didn't base the character on you. ADELE, I'M SORRY!!! I NEVER MEANT TO! It happened. What to do? Of course, the character in the story *has* auburn hair (dyed, tho – no, not dyed, but that kind of process like that friend of yours in Rome had that time, years ago, so it comes out the natural colour which is underneath). Also has 2 sisters. And a great mama, ho ho. *Her* mum is *very tall and thin!* Also a Marxist, the ma, I mean. Ploys ploys. ? The portrait of the friend isn't done in great depth, and is loving, of course, but ... some of the wisecrack talk between her and Morag could be you and me, when about 21, or even now for that matter. What shall I do? I didn't mean it to happen. No beastly secrets are revealed, I need hardly say, but it all bothers me, all the same. Also, it bothers me about the guy Morag marries – I swear to God he is not Jack; he really is much different in every way, but of course some of the underneath emotional things are the same. I quite often think that altho I have to write it, I may not want it published. On the other hand, how many people know me? I mean, would say – Aha! Not that many. Also, the main character, Morag, is not me, but alas is a writer about my age and certainly talks in one of my voices. Of course, I haven't had an illegitimate daughter by a Manitoba Métis whom I'd known since childhood, but let it pass.

Well, I don't really know what to do, Adele. I know I have to go on and write it the way it wants to be written, but it bothers me. The echoes reaching into one's own life, I mean. I don't seem to have done such a good camouflage job this time. They've all been there before, but better painted. But I can't help it. Of course, Morag's childhood is UTTERLY different from mine, and in fact she goes to school with Vanessa MacLeod, who was me as a young girl, so it is all rather spooky. What comes into her childhood, tho, is the parents who died when she was very young, and her need for them ... so even there, some similarities do exist, altho the couple who bring her up are the town scavenger and his wife (did you have that term, *scavenger*, for garbage collector? In my town, that was what he was called, and the town dump was The Nuisance Grounds ... migawd!). Anyway, a word of advice, admonition or reassurance, would be much appreciated. I feel a bit insane.

I think I'll be over in Can about mid-May. Everything very complicated here – Joc doing okay with her course, but Peter still has no job and is on social assistance, which is okay but demoralizing.

Please write when you can, and I do hope you're feeling okay. Love to Dmitry, Sergei, Gorgeous Tamara, and Julie.

And to you,

Margaret

ps. what news of yr novel?
ps.2. what news of the house situation?

1 Lyall Powers (b. 1924) had been Laurence's classmate at United College and was professor of English at the University of Michigan. *Faulkner's Yoknapatawpha Comedy* was published in 1980.

[29 Monclova Road]
31 January 1972

Dear Margaret,

So you're going to put me in a book! Ha ha! I guess I'm just one of those people; sculptors itch to sculpt me; painters to paint me; musicians orchestrate me; the very substance of life, food itself, fulfills its function joyously in me, on a gargantuan scale. So what else is new? You don't need comforting, girl; you're working. Just do your job well. What am I supposed to say?

And what else is new? You sound as though you're anything but isolated out there. We've had a spate of recurring flus here; everyone, including Julie, but excepting me, kept coming down with it. Harry's son, Arnold, was up from Penn State, & his girl came up too, from Miami, & Arn. got very ill for awhile. However, everyone's up & fine, now. This morning Dmitry left for the West Coast, where he'll be for a couple of weeks. Sergei has won his orange belt at karaté, & Tamara, who was entranced when she saw the little Japanese girls dancing in native costume at the Canadian Japanese Culture Centre, now does Japanese dancing impromptu and has told her Dad very frequently that she really needs a black fan, though she makes do with an accordion white paper one temporarily.

Myself am fine, dithering about as usual. We're finally getting our books unpacked. Dmitry's knocked up a few shelves in the library. We figure even if they sell this place in the next few months, it'll be just as easy for us to pack them anew as to re-pack those collapsed cartons. And meanwhile we'll have them around. Such a pleasure to see one's tattered old friends.

Well, Tamara & I are going to mail this note now. I put off replying to your letter because I thought I had better wait & see whether my immediate reaction would change any. But it's essentially the same. Ultimately, one does what one has to do, I suppose. You should concentrate on what you're doing, I guess, & not worry so much about reactions, which you'll have time to worry about later on, if you're so inclined. But I suppose you have to do it all simultaneously, so go to it, write, suffer, worry, & keep on writing!

I'm sorry Joc's Peter still is without a job. It is demoralizing. Sergei just came home from an afternoon at the Youth Theatre, which is touring the high schools. He was all excited & pleased, informed me it was all about the violence that's everywhere nowadays, 'sort of symbolically,' – & he thought it was very good. I don't know how we got along before we began to get these lessons in our own violence. It is in itself a brutalizing exercise. We will accept violence much more readily, our own & others', now that we're so familiar with it. So it goes. Do write & tell me how I'm getting on.

Yours,

Adele

Elm Cottage
24 February 1972

Dear Adele –

Thanks thanks for yr letter. I mean, for responding to my blatant
request for reassurance. So you did exactly what was right – not to
reassure, but to say, in effect, we all do what we have to do. Which I
knew. But good to hear, all the same. Adele, I dunno which or what
parts of this first draft will finally find their way into a novel (if ever).
I just do not know. I do know I am trying to cope with too many things
at the same time, but cannot seem to help it. I also know that it may all
turn out to be a load of fatuous rubbish, in which case I won't want it
published. But in the end, I have to go ahead and try to put it down, in
all its detail, all its verbosity. It isn't that it has *no form*. It has. And I
think the form is basically not too bad, but there is too much flesh
around the skeleton, or so it seems at the moment. I guess all I can do
is just write it the way it comes, and then see what I can do with it. It
comes in fits and starts. I don't work at it every day – wish to God I
could, but I can't. It is partly the presence of a lot of people here, but
mainly it is the hesitance in myself about getting into any particular part
of it, plus the goddamn feeling I have more and more here now – I am
so split between the external and the internal life. I am so involved with
both, but can't any longer manage to be totally involved with both at
the same time, somehow. I dunno – I think it was easier when the kids
were younger. Their problems and their stance towards life was somehow simpler; they went to bed early and then I wrote etc. But now it is
different. They are both adults (David nearly so, if not quite, at almost
17), and one is involved not only in their hassles with the world but
also in a very *good* way in their interests, opinions, etc. I find with both
of them now that I am enormously anxious about their physical survival
in this terrifying world, but am also kind of astonished and grateful at
the way we do sometimes manage to connect. Joc and Peter are here
most weekends, and the house is full of young Can visitors as often as
not, and now David has got to the point of confidence with his guitar
that he will play accompaniment to Peter's one unworded composition
– P mainly composes songs, but this one is a kind of orchestral-guitar
piece, and the two of them improvise and do lots of strange things
which I can only listen to, with wonder, but not with real comprehension. I always thought that when one's kids were adults, one would be
much less involved, but it does not seem to be quite so. When J & P

come for the wkend, Joc makes all the meals, because she wants to and believe you me, she is one fine cook. But she also has many worries – she will finish her Secretarial course and can get employment; but she wants to go back to university as well, in Eng Lit. What about Peter? I have become very fond of my son-out-of-law, and think he has musical and indeed verbal talent, but don't much relish J supporting him throughout. Maybe I worry needlessly, but you know, Adele, I some-times feel that with the very many young Canadians who come here, and whom I have known, their concepts agree with mine to a very great extent, but the whole relationship between men and women really has not changed as much as I had always hoped it would, in my kids' generation. I really worry, in some ways, that Jocelyn, knowing Peter's needs and indeed frailties, will subdue her *own* needs and expressions.

Dave had an accident with his motorbike last week, which turned my hair nearly white overnight, but luckily it was only minor cuts and bruises. It was fairly awful, tho. A middleaged driver and his wife, so who is to prove who was (if anyone) wrong? The driver has a witness – who would believe a 16-yr old? Apart from D's cuts etc (he grazed the car), there were some scratches on the guy's car's paint, and I took the easy and maybe cowardly way out – just said 'Get your garage to give you an estimate and I will send you a cheque.' I don't think D was really in the wrong, but I did not feel capable of dealing with all the hassles with both insurance companies. Money seemed so dreadfully irrelevant, beside the fact that my son was alive.

Am going to Can about May 15, and will phone as soon as I get there. Staying with C. Thomas because her house is so central and also she has a flat in the basement. Want to get to shack about May 20. But have several things to do – U of T giving me hon degree June 1st, and I have to give convocation address (Vic College) – have written damn thing and it sounds like fatuous rubbish to me; the staff (or some) will think it too radical, whilst the kids (or some) will think it too conserva-tive. The hell with it all. Have had various hassles re: this whole idiotic bit about Companion, Order of Canada. Oh heavens. They wrote to me and said the Investiture was April 12, so I wrote back and said no way I could be there. They then wrote and said next Investiture was going to be end of Oct. I wrote back and said what did one do if one could not be there, *ever*? Got a letter this morn, saying they did not post the pretty brooches (they did not put it quite that way), so if I could not be there, maybe a private Investiture could be arranged – they sounded kind of sour, I thought, and don't blame them.

Well, Adele, I had about five bad minutes, in which Authority threatened. I thought – heavens; must be there when the Gov-Gen wants me to be there, etc. Then I thought – what matters most? I can't be in Ottawa the end of Oct, for heaven's sake. Am I willing to leave D on his own in this huge dump for maybe 2 months? Of course not. And what if anything happened, I mean another accident with the bike? It isn't going to be good enough that maybe Joc and Peter are somewhere in England. I had a long thought about it all this morn, but not a *very* long thought. Odd. With my inbuilt (and much-resented) fear of Authority, I still seem to be able to know what I have to do, at least most times. Came to one firm conclusion. If anyone has to be INCONVENIENCED AND TO SOME EXTENT PUT OUT, better it should be the Governor-General of Canada, rather than a member of my family. Actually, they can keep their bloody brooch, as far as I'm concerned. So I wrote back today and said – no way I can attend yr official functions, très sorry. So we will see.[1] I wish they would just post the damn thing to me (I am now beginning to regret having accepted it, but how did I know it would create all these problems?). You know, of course, what this sort of thing means, in our tribal terms – as we say in England, with euphemism, SWEET FANNY ADAMS.

What I really need and am looking forward to, is 3 months in the shack. To work, hopefully, and see dear ones on weekends. I guess this is basically a way out of my situation with the kids at the moment – I love them and worry so much about them that I become well-nigh paralysed, and they are so good and understanding, and *they* worry about *me*, and quite a lot of the time we can go on quite well, here, with also the many young Can visitors. But one is so much entrenched into NOW, Adele, that it is difficult to write. This is both good and not so good. When I see the way our house is, which is what Joc not so long ago referred to as 'The Elmcot community,' I feel such a sense of gratitude. These kids are really *something*, you know? But I still feel split, and would just like to be able to complete this one more novel before I totally hand over to the kids, which I will and will want to do, altho with no demands on their part.

Yr letter – yes, about the violence. I have split feelings. Joc decided that she could not bear to look at the film A CLOCKWORK ORANGE,[2] so Peter and a young Irish friend (once a boyfriend of Joc's, who is briefly in London and staying with P & J) went to it, while Joc came along to Alice Frick's, where I was for the eve, and we talked. Violence has to be explored, I would guess, in fiction and film. But also, and this is a real qualification to the previous statement, I would guess that a kind of tenderness and affection also have to be explored, more and more. There may not be that much time left to us, so what are we going to do with it? Last night, at dinner, Dave made the laconic statement, 'I have to face the fact that I may not see forty.' The violence bit seems to me, just from personal experience, to mean less and less. What can you do, except love the people who matter to you, while you can? We live at such risk, everyone. The children live at such enormous risk. Every day, when I see Dave go off on his motorbike, my heart turns over.

I think we have to live as though we had forever.

Much much love to all,

Margaret

ps. hope Tamara gets her real genuine black Japanese fan!

1 Laurence was invested on 27 June when she was in Ottawa.
2 The film was released in 1971. Written and directed by Stanley Kubrick, it was based on the novel by Anthony Burgess.

[P.O. Box 193
Kleinburg, Ontario
6 December 1972][1]

Dear Margaret,

My opportunities to write letters have diminished somewhat since I am becoming a familiar face around Kleinburg. Now when I sit in the library during Tamara's story hour, or up in the church while the young mothers are being given ideas for Xmas decorations, I am engaged in conversations & can no longer sit quietly & write notes to my friends. I don't mind, really, but it's hard to find another quiet time. At the moment it's hardly quiet. We're at the library again, & they're showing a film, 'The Little Drummer Boy.' Still, no conversation, & I'm getting used to working amid great noise & hullabaloo. Tamara no longer sleeps in the afternoons, so I do my own work in the mornings, when Tamara may or may not feel like watching her programs on T.V. Sometimes I feel as though I am in the middle of a Chinese classroom. They used to tell us that Chinese kids study out loud simultaneously in their classrooms, each doing his own particular lesson. And you know, it can be done. It can be done. Of course other things are neglected, like housework, etc., never of prime importance anyway. The child is not neglected, however, though she may have to compete a bit with the machine. Still, she manages to assert her preeminence. *Dec. 6, '72.* I called Sergei in to take a snapshot of a typical scene, with Tamara & me at the typewriter. I'll send it along as soon as it's developed. Let's face it, she is pre-eminent. What other writing-mother has the privilege of watching leaps & fouettés and pliés while she works? We tend to be fearful of losing the precious word; actually what we, (at least I) have to say is not playing footsy with me, coyly eager to disappear at the least disturbance. It's rather a lusty type, only unpleasant when misrepresented. It goes on kicking to come out right. So that I look on myself at the moment, not as a victim of the impositions attendant, supposedly, on motherhood, but as the lucky recipient of multiple gratifications. This does not prevent me from being riddled with anxieties, of course, but why should it? There are realities & realities. It is now some, oh, seven or eight days since I began this letter. I wish our chickie were in shape to do some dancing at the moment. She's got some kind of stomach flu, has been chucking-up for two days & at present is asleep, exhausted. The Dr. says she should be coming out of it, so I hover & hope. She was so upset when she discovered she wouldn't be able to go ice skating with an 102° temp. We'd been once with her nursery group, & though she spent most of the first half hour slithering on all fours on the ice, 'She's still smiling,' as one of the women remarked, & in fact she kept telling me, 'I *love* ice skating,' & it was obvious, she could see herself doing pliés & fouettés here too. By the time we left she could at least take a few steps without losing her balance, & we were both looking forward to this trip. Oh well, there will be plenty of opportunity during the winter. Otherwise all is well. Dmitry took 'Monique' to work to show her off today. Sergei has made me drive her already. When his dad's out of town he always manages to miss his bus, & then tells me blandly he'll hitch-hike, knowing damn well that if I have to bicycle him to school I won't let him hitch-hike. I also know damn well he does anyway. So, I found myself pumping Monique, not having operated a shift gear for years. She's really rather nice, – *won't* go over 50 except down a steep grade with a high wind behind her, & is the kind of machine you want to grunt & groan along with, not one of your soulless wonders. In a way she's a bit like Julie, sits there incontinently dripping oil in the garage, – but it's only seepage, nothing serious. – more –

6 December 1972

Just popped in to see the babe. Still sleeping, & so beautiful.

Mitia has been working very very hard, long hours & an awful lot of travelling, one deadline crisis after another. The holiday break will do him good. We're just going to stay put & give him a chance to relax & putter. The Forers had proposed, two years ago, when the Penners bought some property in the Lake of the Woods area, on a lake, that this Xmas we all go there for the holidays. The Penners have built a winterized cabin & a road & it sounds great. Only none of us can afford the plane fare right now, & though we toyed with the idea of driving out (6 days driving to & fro, & 3 days' stay), we all chickened out at the prospect. Can you imagine, 8 of us in our van, 3 adolescents, one babe, & three adults, for 6 days?, with 3 taking turns driving, of which three one has already had 2 heart attacks, one is a neurotic who hates driving anyway, & can't keep her mind on the road, & one is exhausted & over-worked to begin with? All this at dead of winter? So we'll stay home, & like it, I think.

Have been reading Miriam Waddington's 'Driving Home,' – a very good title, I think. I also think she is a much underrated poet in this country, as you know, & have been delighted to have my opinion strengthened by this book, or rather underlined.[2] Also read *Survival*,[3] which Joy was kind enough to send me. It was fun to read, an interesting thesis engagingly developed. I'm a little wary of seeing these observations rigidified and codified as 'tradition,' though, something the book seems to imply. We're still a bit too young in this country, I hope, for the 'this is how we write, & these are the patterns to look for' approach to be rammed down the intellectual gullets of our kids. In that sense I was made somewhat uneasy by the obviously classroom context which appears to be at least one of its aims. I can already see the exam questions, (oh how well I know!) 'Trace patterns of victimization in Can. Writing, with particular stress on, a) victimiz'n by man of nature b) victimiz'n by nature of man c) by man of man d) by men of man e) by women of man, ... etc., and illustrate your points by specific refs to the texts you have studied.' The book is a mine of potential exam questions. But interesting & stimulating; she's obviously a very bright gal. The danger of so much critical writing is that it is so easy to misuse, 'this is how to' rather than 'this is something often found.' But I've always enjoyed it, as you know, & was very glad Joy sent it me.

And now to what really counts in writing, – *writing*. How are you doing? From the sound of your letter you certainly will have more peace & quiet in which to pursue your work than is usual at Elmcot. I hope this means you've already made enormous strides since you got back. I know you may occasionally be more lonely, though. Are you getting to see some people? Of our own generation? Have you seen Delores & Alex? What has been happening? Don't worry about publication. Have I said this before? A thousand times. Am I right? You might well say that I am one who should really worry a little more, (about public'n). But not so. Anyway, you'll worry your due amount of worry regardless, won't you? It's in the system. Be of good cheer natheless. And have a Very Happy Xmas & a Great & Bountiful New Year. Much love from us all.

Adele, Dmitry, Sergei, Tamara,
Big Julie, & Monique

1 The previous October, the Stones had moved to Kleinburg, a village on the outskirts of Toronto.
2 Miriam Waddington (b. 1917) was a professor of English at York University.
3 *Survival: A Thematic Guide to Canadian Literature* (1972) by Margaret Atwood (b. 1939)

Elm Cottage
18 December 1972

Dear Adele –

Got the 2nd of yr 2 letters today – the 1st came yesterday – Christmas mail is the reason, no doubt. You will probably curse me for replying so soon, but don't imagine I expect you to do the same – I know how hard it is to have enough time even for your own work, never mind letters. But of course you are right re: kids – when mine were little, I sometimes resented things like housework and ironing (both of which bore me) but I never resented the kids. Naturally I got mad at them from time to time, but not because of my writing. Even now, if Dave is ill (as he is at the moment) I find it hard to write, because then one always sees which really has priority, and that is the kids, of course.

I do hope Tamara is quite better by now. Little kids seem to be able to run high temps and then recover very quickly, unlike adults. But at the time it is worrying to the point of near-neurosis. Honestly, for me it still is. If either Joc or Dave are ill, I can't focus on any other thing until they're okay again. I was supposed to go and see the Barons tomorrow, but Dave has flu and I very much fear I have it, too, as my stomach feels very peculiar and I ache all over as tho with rheumatism. So I phoned and talked to Alex today – I'll go in early in the new year. He has a cold and feels awful, so perhaps it is just as well I'm not going. Otherwise, they are all fine, Nicholas going to nursery school and loving it. I am so furious at getting flu right now, but I guess it is better than getting it on Christmas day. I'm incapable of staying in bed all day, even tho God knows I'm not an early riser, but I get bored and irritable when ill. It's not a terribly bad attack and have only upchucked once, unlike David who has been v. pale and wan for 3 days, poor guy. I must try to clean the house before the weekend, but no way I'm going to do it right now.

Your work seems to be coming along just fine – that is *great*. Never mind if it proceeds slowly – it's proceeding. The Big News with me is – wait for it! – I've written 3 songs and am about to write a 4th and maybe 5th. Did I mention this in my last letter? I don't think so, as it was about 1½ weeks ago when I began, thus slowing up the typing procedure with the novel, but not to worry. The songs are for the novel. One of the characters composes them. I made up a tune for the first one, which is about old Jules Tonnerre, who fought with Riel at Batoche when young. Songs are written by Skinner (real name Jules also) Tonnerre, old Jules' grandson, who is a major person in this novel. Ian Cameron got the tune, and sang the song with accompaniment on his guitar. I was ecstatic! Songs! Wow! Then, so much did his singing inspire me, I sat down the next day and wrote words to another song, Song of Lazarus, Skinner's father (Lazarus appears in Stone Angel; Bird In The House; Fire-Dwellers; briefly, but much more in this novel.) Well, Adele, a miraculous thing occurred. Ian took words and composed a really great tune, kind of country & western, and just right. I was absolutely stunned! Made him sing it about 14 times! Songs! Ye gods! Hence, becoming again inspired, a few days later I wrote words for Song For Piquette, who was Skinner's sister who burned to death when the Tonnerre shack caught fire one winter in the valley – her 2 young children also died. This has to be the most repeated death in fiction – it is told in The Fire-Dwellers, A Bird In The House, and again in this novel. Wonder why it haunts me so much? Anyway Ian & Sandy were over last weekend, and Ian suddenly got tune for this song as well. I've only heard it that one evening, but it sounded just splendid. Ian and I are all excited over possibility of a novel being issued with a 45-record included. This is Top Secret – tell No One except yr family!! If I could persuade publishers, it would be really nice, and not a gimmick, either – those songs really belong, and it would add another dimension, to be able to hear them.[1] Well, this may sound as tho I have slipped a cog at last, but we will see. Meantime, the novel proceeds and am at page 285 in the typescript – have ceased worrying about the length; the hell with it; if it is long, then it's long. Haven't made as good progress with typing this month, partly because of songs and partly because of Christmas, which is an inevitable slowdown. Also have had some fairly nasty sessions with the dentist, which always is traumatic for me. Last week I completed the sessions, but the freezing didn't take, and as I sat there suffering, I had what I later considered to be the perfect Irish-type thought – 'My God, I hope I have a painless death – it'll kill me if I don't!' That seemed so funny to me that it cheered me up no end in the dentist's chair. Nothing like laughing at yr own jokes.

God bless you all, and all the BEST for 1973.

Much love,

Margaret

ps. I am so glad you decided against going to the Penners for Christmas ... that trip in winter sounds really hazardous, not to say insane. P.S. I read *Survival* – I think it's brilliant, but I *do* hope teachers, especially, realize that this is only *one* way of perceiving our literature – there are valid other ways.

1 The record was produced by McClelland and Stewart in association with Heorte Music, but sold separately from the novel.

Elm Cottage
18 February 1973

Dear Adele –

Brief communication. How *are* you? Is everyone okay? How is the princess?

I have finished this novel. Well, not really finished it, but finished it for the moment. Have to distance myself from it. Have to let at least one other person (preferably my editor in Amer)[1] see it, and see what reaction is – I *know* what she will say; it will be only a confirmation of my own feelings about what is wrong with damn thing. It is far too long – 500 pp and more, but that is not main problem. Main problem is that some sections aren't written well enough yet. Maybe can work on these during summer, but I feel I just cannot do more now. Jocelyn is typing it for me in fair copy – wow! the fact that she wants to type it (which means reading it) is pretty strange and new, and probably pretty good. Anyhow, I'll be back in Can end May, I hope, and at shack for most of summer, finishing revisions. Also would like to go to N. Manitoba – I have this sense of wanting to go places and see things, having been inside this bloody book for some 3 years now. Will spend that whole year (September 73 to May 74) in Can, w-in-r at Western and then Trent, trying to whomp up as much money as I can, for buying house in Peterborough. I can sell Elmcot (which I will have to do in Summer 74) for a lot of bread, but am caught up now in trying to find out how I get out of such cheery things as Capital Gains Tax (which could take 30% of what I sell Elmcot for), and Emigrant Tax (by which I have to fill out lots of forms, to return to Canada as a repatriated Canadian, when I decide to do so, or else I will lose another 25% of all my assets to Brit. Gov.) I have to leap only once, now, obviously, and must leap with great caution, in order not to give the goddamn government here almost all my hard-earned and insecure assets. Thank God I have a bright accountant. Will see you end May, hopefully. By the way, this will make yr day, I hope – I recently got a letter from a Canadian lady who admiringly told me she wished she could write like me or Pierre Berton.[2] Hm hm. Makes me feel I oughta take the vow of silence.

  Please write. Much love to all,

Margaret

1 Judith Jones
2 Pierre Berton (b. 1920), popular historian, best-selling author, and Canadian nationalist, for whom Laurence later developed a deep respect

[Kleinburg, Ontario]
2 March 1973

Dear Margaret,

Wow! Zowie! and Kazow! I can hardly believe it. Just yesterday it seems you were moaning that you weren't going to make it, and it's finished!

It may be just the draft but it's first base, and probably second and third too. If you're willing to let your ed. see it you must be pretty sure way down. Polishing is secondary. At least you've got what to polish. Not that the moaning will stop for a while, but never mind. It's very good to be able to change the precise tone of the moan occasionally. I'm sure the tones are different at the different stages. One could orchestrate the tones of moans of writers at different stages of works in progress, and get a very effective modern work. Speaking of music, what's happened with the ballads? I have been chuckling over that ever since I got your news of it. Any[way] why not? If a work is fully imagined why shouldn't it include the songs of the characters? It would be a very nice break-through if the publishers did go for it. I have kept mum about it, except to Dmitry, as you asked, but have wondered if you kept on with it. Of course, I could have written to find out before this, which brings me to the nit I mean to pick. Please, never tell me that I don't have to answer immediately. I usually don't anyway, but to have written permission has a curious effect on me. It baffles the anxiety-to-respond mechanism, confuses the sense of time, and finally arouses a defensive, 'Whassamatter, she doesn't want to hear from me? So what if I'm busy?'

It's really very touching that Joc wants to type, – has probably almost completed typing the m.s. by now. I don't imagine it's an easy job at all. Bless her. I hope her personal affairs are going well. And I hope David is okay too.

When we were in London, Ont., recently, – (I gave a doll talk and show), Colleen and Jamie[1] mentioned the fact that they were looking forward to having you as Writer in Res. next term. We stayed with them, Dmitry & Tamara & I, and they were really very kind. Colleen is a very warm person as well as a gifted poet. And Jamie is tops to my mind, an extraordinary creative vitality. I think you should enjoy your time there. There seems to be a lot going on.

Well, Tamara has taken two French lessons, 20 minutes each. I was told she could join the class of 5–7 year olds if I signed her up as four and a half instead of three and a half. So I did, having made the mistake of warning her she was to pretend to be four and a half. I guess it made her anxious, because halfway through the first class she burst out suddenly, 'You know how old I am? I'm three and a half years old, three and a half, I'm three and a half years old.' Luckily the teacher chose to ignore the information. The mothers sit in the rear pews of the United Church while the kids are being taught up front, and I noticed that he sat her beside him on the steps for most of the lesson, so I thought that she must be inattentive, or something. I could only see heads. But afterwards he told the gal who arranged the classes that 'That little Tamara, she certainly absorbed a lot today.' I was relieved, I had been somewhat reluctant to accept her report on the lesson that 'he let me sit on the steps with him for a very long time because he likes me,' (unsolicited, the latter).

I gather that her class will be taking part in a recital to be given by all the ballet classes in the 'school.' Tamara and her mates will be 'galloping ponies.' I can hardly wait.

In about a week or so Dmitry will go to New York to testify for Vermont, which is suing N.Y. State and one of the big paper mill co's for polluting Lake Champlain. He's been working very hard. Sergei is back to school today after a couple of days lay-up with a cold. Terrible disappointment when, on the second afternoon, his temp. goes down from 101 to 97. Poor lad had to go back today.

My work is coming along; at least I move from page to page, accompanied by the concomitant luck of pleasure quite frequently, well, frequently enough for me to briefly nurse the illusion that it is a necessary concomitant; no, not illusion; for all the misery, when it's right it is pleasure. Let's keep our values straight for all our moaning.

I have just looked up that Can. Council app. form. It's due March 15th! I'll mail you the referee sheet under separate cover. What a dolt I am! No! You already have your sheet, – you took it with you. No! You didn't! I'll fill them out tonight and mail your copy. As Jamie is the only one who's seen the doll show, I've asked him too. He was very positive. Oh God, ... Oh well. We'll try.

love,

Adele

P.S. Forgot to tell you about Godfrey & 'The Lovebound' – We're in correspondence. All about how he was blocked & couldn't respond because of you & his feelings for you, warm, grateful, etc. etc ... So I reassured him & we may get on with it, wherever it's going.[2] More later. – God, how confused this! I mean he apologized for not writing me sooner about the play, – said he was probably blocked, etc ...
[P.S.] Oh help, I can't understand this damn C.C. form. How can I fill it out?

1 Reaney
2 House of Anansi Press did not publish the play.

[Elm Cottage]
15 May 1973

[Dear Adele –]

[—]¹

Macmillan of England have taken my book, but I have not yet heard from Knopf or M & S. I'm very glad about Macmillan, tho, as I had been very doubtful about them. Now I think, naturally, that the reason I haven't heard from Knopf yet is that they hate the book and are trying to think of some tactful way of telling me. Well, we can only wait and see.

I am getting really panicky about the house move – have got so much to attend to, and only 2 months to do it all. However, no doubt I'll get it done somehow.²

This is a brief letter because I have a stack of letters to answer – last week couldn't do a thing except think of wedding reception.³ Also, 2 friends from Vancouver staying with me – they had to move out over weekend, as some wedding guests from Somerset had to stay over. Kind of hectic. They're still here (Van couple) but leave in 2 days time.

Please write very soon. I pray things are okay.

Much love to you all,

Margaret

1 Only this fragment of the letter remains.
2 Laurence had sold Elm Cottage, and was moving back to Canada on 22 July.
3 Jocelyn Laurence had been married on 12 May.

[Kleinburg, Ontario]
26 May 1973

Dear Margaret,

I didn't know Joc was getting married! Last I heard she felt Peter was the man whose babies she would like to bear, but I didn't realize she was going to do it formally! I am delighted, & Dmitry too. Please let Joc know, & her Peter, that this is one wedding we would have loved to attend, & please let them know, as you do, that all our very best wishes go with them. Is there any chance that they might come out this way? Joc married, gee. It feels strange. Marriage really is a demarcation point.

Now that she's over the line I hope she will find it a lovely place to live. I'm sure she'll have lovely babies at any rate.

Glad you destroyed my letter. I don't believe my anxieties are unrealistic. It keeps on happening to people, so nervous people anticipate unpleasantness. This time I'm o.k. I can avoid an op. if I can hold out against these attacks till after the menopause, if nothing gets worse. So I'm holding out. The Dr. has given me pills to take to combat the symptoms, bloody paralysing pain, but preferable to an op. I've had my plenty of them.

The news that Macmillan of Eng. have taken the book is fantastically good. Didn't you say that this is only the first draft? It is pretty obvious that there is nothing whatever to worry about *at all*. What about the ballads? Have you mentioned them to them, – the record idea? Or is that just for the U.S.? There can be no doubt that the U.S. people will take it now, it seems to me. Wasn't one of your worries that there was too much of the specifically Canadian in the book? Obviously, if the Eng. people have snapped it up you've no problems to worry about over here. Is there a publication date set yet? By the way, you never told me the name of the book.

I've been having rather a pleasant series of pre-meeting calls & notes from the Anansi people. They're so cordial. I am working on a thread that may tighten up *Crackpot* some, & am trying to get it done before I actually meet Shirley Gibson[1] & Jim Polk,[2] who'll be coming out to see me soon. It's not a great deal of work, just a different way of getting where I want to go, which may have other advantages in strengthening the thing. Anyway, I'm anxious to get back to other interrupted work, which is tantalizingly near, yet so far, from completion. And if the C.C. comes through in the fall, I'd like to be able to begin on the doll book,[3] so I'm feeling all balls in the air at the moment. My in-laws arrive in a few days. Later on in the month my folks will be here for a few weeks, I hope. Sergei goes off West as soon as school ends, & there seems to be some likelihood that Marshall, & possibly afterwards Michael, may come to visit, during the summer. So things will be going on. I seem to be able to work when I determine to. The trouble is I'm afraid that my judgment won't serve me in all this hurry. No I'm not. It's a worry, but I'm not really afraid. If I slip up, so what? I don't think one's judgment necessarily improves with lengthy rumination anyway.

love,

Adele

P.S.   When are you coming? Will you be here for the meetings in mid June?[4]

1 Shirley Gibson (1927–97) was president and managing editor of House of Anansi Press.
2 James Polk (b. 1939), writer and editorial director, House of Anansi Press
3 *Old Woman at Play* was published by Clarke Irwin in 1978.
4 On the weekend of 15–17 June, a conference was to be held in Toronto to establish the guidelines for a union of Anglo-Canadian writers.

Elm Cottage
7 June 1973

Dear Adele –

I was very relieved to get your letter and learn you are more or less okay and won't need an op. I certainly hope the pain does not go on, though – that must be dreadful to have to cope with.

I'm glad you've made contact with Anansi – I don't know Shirley Gibson personally, but I know she is a very good editor. I hope you'll be able to do what you want with CRACKPOT without too much sweat. Also, that the CC will kick through so you can get cracking on the doll book. You've certainly got a lot on your plate, which is good.

My American editor, Judith Jones, is in Eng now and came out on Monday. Knopf are enthusiastic about the novel (the title of which is THE DIVINERS), so that is good news. Judith and I had a five-hour nonstop session – she came out bearing Macmillan's criticisms as well as her own, as we've agreed I'll only have the one editor for this book. Nothing she said surprised me in the least. I knew what the areas of weakness were, but when I handed in the 2nd draft I just could not at that moment face trying to cope with more re-writing. However, Judith and I (and Mac's) are in total agreement this time re: what areas need to be revised or rewritten, and after our session I think I can see more or less how to tackle most of the problems. It will, I think, mean about 2 months of concentrated work, which is kind of awkward at this point, what with moving back to Canada etc. I'll try to do the easier bits this month, then will go to Toronto on July 22. I hope my things which are being shipped will have arrived so I can get them through Customs and into storage. Will stay with Clara Thomas (15 Lewes Crescent, Toronto 12) for about a week, trying to organize various business things, and would love to go out to your place for a couple of days, if you're there at that time. Then I'll flash up to my shack for August, lock the door and work like hell. I've promised to try to get novel completed by beginning of Sept,[1] which is really cutting it fine, as I start work at Western the middle of Sept. Oh god. Will I be able to get it all done by then? I sometimes get rather panicky, thinking I won't be able to get moved out and get novel done, etc. But in fact I'm pretty well organized re: house. I have nearly all the million cupboards cleared of old rubbish. The movers will come on July 6th to get my books and other things which I'm shipping, and after that all I really have to do is clean the place thoroughly and try to get financial business wound up before July 22. Actually, my morale is pretty high right now, despite all that I have to do in the next couple of months. It's just that from time to time it gets to me, and I think I'll be sitting here on July 22 surrounded by chaos. Which is silly, because I know I won't. Dave is writing his A-levels now, which is awful for him, and also there is no way he can clear his room and the toolshed and garage until he finishes on June 21st. Still, all will work out, no doubt. I keep making endless lists of what remains to be done! Selling the house furnished, however, is an enormous help. If I can just KEEP CALM everything will be okay. Trouble is, there are so many details that cannot be attended to until nearly the last minute.

A friend whose marriage is on the rocks is coming from Can on June 28 for a couple of weeks. I just could not say no. But I think it'll be okay – I'll put her to work cleaning the house; it'll take her mind off her problems, or even if it doesn't, it will fill the time and will be a help to me.

I have new glasses – bifocals for the first time, and they are driving me crazy. I'm okay on the distance viewing – I don't trip on the stairs, as many people do when they first get bifocals. But the reading and typing are very difficult still. I haven't yet figured out how to get the angle of vision just right. But I paid £25 for the bloody things, so I *will* get used to them!

Must go and make a rhubarb pie – I promised David I'd make one final pie!

Much love to you all,

Margaret

ps. thanks for your good wishes to Joc, which I'll convey to her. Yeh, it seems odd that she's married. Doesn't seem 21 years since she was born – I always used to think parents were pretty corny when they made remarks like that, but I don't think so now.

1 In fact, she completed her revisions to *The Diviners* by 13 July, just prior to moving back to Canada.

[Kleinburg, Ontario]
9 [July] 1973[1]

Dear Margaret,

It's sheer sentiment, my last letter addressed to Elm Cottage, which I've never even seen, except in pictures, but about which I have that lived in feeling. I've known it so long & so well. So long, Elmcot!

Ave, old pal, & Welcome Home! Among many others, the entire complement of the new Canadian Writers' Union awaits you, – but entire! You were elected by acclamation, none more worthy nor more deserving![2] You've probably rec'd many versions of the recent conference by now, & we can talk about that anyway. More important now to kind of ease you out of England & back home. Much awaits you. By now you've probably got the book ready for the presses, sooner than expected because you always expect it to take longer, – or nearly ready anyway. It's good that you'll be kept busy once you're through – help you get over the slump. It'll be busy but pretty exciting, it seems to me. What's happening with the kids?

Myself have been very busy too. Got a new insight into a possibility for *Crackpot*, one day while I was standing at the sink, mulling over a telephone conversation I'd had with Margaret Atwood, & have promised them at Anansi I'd try to have it done by the end of the month.[3] So I'm busting away at it. Have also had in-laws visiting, – till a week ago, & my parents are with us now till next week. Very pleasant. I may even make the deadline, am anxious to as I'd like to get back to what I was doing & finish it, – I'm about ⅔rds through, & get on to Mom & the doll book. Wow! Balls in the air! I can hardly wait to see you & talk. Let me know when you'll be staying with us. We'll come & pick you up. Love from us all.

Dmitry, Adele, & Family,
inclusive.

1 Wiseman had misdated the letter, putting June instead of July.
2 Laurence was to be interim chair of the fledgling Writers' Union of Canada until its official establishment the following November.
3 In fact, *Crackpot* was ultimately published by McClelland and Stewart the following year.

[Kleinburg, Ontario]
5 January 1974

Dear Margaret,

The enclosed[1] arrived t'other day. How goes it? Dmitry returned from Edmonton & Calgary yesterday, & flew off to Ottawa this evening. He'll be back in a couple of days, then on to Michigan, & back before the week's out. Maybe then he'll stay put for awhile. At the end of the month he's leaving for Malawi. Sergei just now returned from a skiing weekend, so naturally I have to take him to the hospital to-morrow morning to get his leg x-rayed. Hey-ho! This week Tamara's various classes & entertainments begin again. Luckily, Dmitry has Monique back in fine shape. I could have done without having to spend a morning at the hospital. I've been back at work on the play, & it feels like progress, but these are life's (and especially Sergei's,) little accidents. I wish he'd get over this accident proneness. There's always the uneasy feeling that he might manage to really do himself permanent harm if he keeps it up.

Do I have to tell you it was great to have you here? I will anyway. It was great!! And great to read The Diviners & know it's great!! A big book, Margaret, big with what you know and what you feel and what is. And the recordings are more than just additions; – those ballads are extensions in dimension, another art form to give your world that much additional resonance, that much more space. 'Sei Arrivata,' – after all that 'su su corragio, avanti!' – You arrive!! You have arrived!! – Not that you haven't been before; mind you, – but this time it's the Royal Suite, kiddo!

Noo, the babe's asleep after a day of dancing, making things, and a leisurely bath. I too shall go to bed & read a detective story, blank out the surface mind till sleep comes.

Write when you have the chance. Ciao for now. Much love from us all.

Adele

1 Not identified

[Champlain College
Trent University
Peterborough, Ontario
K9J 7B8]
25 January 1974

Dear Adele –

At last you get to see the beautiful paper upon which I write my letters –
think I'll pinch a few tons of it when I leave here. It was great to hear that
the play is nearly finished, and that the editor from M & S[1] sounds
reasonable. Bash on, bash on in majesty! (to quote a song from Jason's
Quest, somewhat influenced by an old hymn).[2]

   I got another letter from that Parr[3] gal in Winnipeg, this time asking
permission to print, as part of a book, a program on me which contained,
among other idiocies, an interview with me, and which was run a couple
of years ago by the CBC in Wpg as part of a series called (of all things)
MAKING IT. They conned various people who'd known me into saying
things like 'We always knew she had it in her,' etc. Actually, Joan Parr
wrote this letter and just explained all over again about how they were a
non-profit organization and any royalties would go to paying printing
costs on other manuscripts. She then went on to say would I just please
sign the agreement form and return in the stamped envelope – all very
easy. Well, Adele – heavens, I don't know if I did the right thing or not,
but I wrote back yesterday, saying NO. I explained that (a) other people
than myself were involved, and I would not want it printed without their
consent; (b) as a member of the Writers' Union of Canada, I felt it was
setting dangerous precedents for any of us to give away our copyright
material ... assuming I hold copyright on the printing rights, whereas the
CBC holds copyright on broadcasting rights; (c) I do not believe, anyway,
that transcriptions from taped interviews print very well unless massively
edited ... it is one thing to have someone speaking and quite another to
read all the repetitions and ums and ers on the page, and I didn't think I
felt like editing a thing like that. So – very sorry, etc. Do you think I did
the right thing (query). (This fancy typewriter has such exotic signs as •
ñ ç © ¶ § ¨ ^ etc, – but NO QUESTION MARK!) I just don't know, but I felt it
was slightly a con game – makes all of us look bad if we say No, and we
can then be accused of having grown too big for our boots and forgetting
where we came from etc etc. (I didn't come from Wpg, anyway!) But I feel
that that is the intention – to make it very hard to refuse without looking
vain and cheap and mean. And anyway, I don't see why I should help to

finance 'Winnipeg writers' just because they are Winnipeg writers. If they're *good* writers, I'd go out of my way to help, altho not necessarily in that particular way. But how can we know what they're like (query). Also, I really do NOT like to see a transcription of a tape printed, unless with very careful editing. Don Cameron's book of interviews with Can novelists reads very well,[4] because Don himself edited it very skilfully and all the people involved were then consulted before it was printed – a very professional piece of work. So – in Wpg they will probably hate me, at least those particular people, but it can't be helped.[5]

On with the horror stories! Had a horrific experience this week. I had agreed, probably foolishly, for Saturday Night to do an article on me. Actually, Bob Fulford[6] had wanted Don Stainsby (an old Vancouver acquaintance of mine) to do one last winter when Don was in England with his third wife [...] He [Don Stainsby] did not mention the article ... but later (about a few days before they were due to come) phoned and said, 'Oh, and by the way, can we more or less spend the weekend interviewing you ... Sat Nite wants an article.' So I said, 'No, I'm afraid you can't,' more or less implying that weekends were social visits, and if he didn't view it that way, the hell. I then phoned back to say I was terribly busy getting Elmcot sold, so could they just not come at all right now, please. I put it more tactfully that that, but I guess they got the message. So when this gal phoned and said could she do a piece which Sat Nite had commissioned, I said Yes. More fool I, or me. Her name is Valerie Miner-Johnson, and I hope she isn't a friend (hell, I KNOW she isn't a *friend*, but maybe an acquaintance) of yours. Not that it would matter, of course. She came out this week and I talked with her for a couple of hours. She is quite a nice young woman, and I didn't actually dislike her, but I just felt I was not at all getting through to her. She had a tape recorder, so all my babblings (and at times I was really struggling, as one does when there is a sense of total non-communication with the other person) are there, and I can't stop her using any of them. HOWEVER. She had read THE DIVINERS in page proof, from M & S, and had obviously made up her mind about the angle the article was going to take ... MARGARET LAURENCE WRITES TOTALLY AUTOBIOGRAPHICAL NOVEL HA HA KIDDIES IT'S ALL HERE. I tried to explain the basic nature of fiction, at least my kind of fiction. I also said it was all in the novel ... ie. the nature of fiction, but I guess she missed those parts. I told her, obviously, that a character like Morag, just as with Stacey and even Rachel, is both me and not me ... but NOT me in the external sense *at all*. She is *herself*, of course. She represents many of my stances towards life, yes. Some of the material (I did not say which bits, natch) are based on or drawn from my own experience, but a great deal is not. (There are dozens of bits which are in some complex way based on my own experience but rendered fictionally – bits which naturally you spotted, but Valerie didn't, and I sure as hell didn't enlighten her!) All this about fiction was too much for the poor girl. She had made up her mind. She kept saying things like 'Well, *you*'ve got a grownup daughter ...' and I would say 'Yeh, but she isn't the illegitimate daughter of a Manitoba Métis.' And on and on and on. Finally she said 'Now, can I just ask you about your *own* marriage and divorce ...' And I said 'No, as a matter of fact, you can't.' By this time I was growing hostile. I asked if she would let me see the article before it was printed, and she refused. Said it was unprofessional. Well, she's probably right. But Peggy Atwood has done a really good article on me (and on the new novel) for Macleans,[7] and she read it to me over the phone, to check facts and also she said if I really hated any of the personal bits, she'd remove them. But of course she is a friend, and also a writer, and she knows about the complex and subtle questions of how fiction relates to personal experience and yet doesn't in other ways. So – the agreement had been that Valerie should return in a couple of weeks. I spent the night wide awake for most of the time, firing off furious mental letters ... GET LOST! STAY AWAY! etc. But decided that it would probably be better to let her come here again, and have my plan of approach well thought-out in advance, because she really caught me off-guard. There is more than 1 way of skinning a cat, and two can play at that game, and other old cliches which happen to be true. So – we'll see. I anticipate that the article will be awful,[8] even tho perhaps on the surface not hostile, but I sensed an awful hostility in her, which took me by surprise, and I just didn't know how to cope with it at that moment. I can now see that any attempt at a reasonable discussion and explanation about Fiction In General is out of the question. She isn't hearing what I'm saying. Peggy Atwood was concerned about getting somewhere near the truth, both about my approach to my work, and her own responses. But I have the feeling that Valerie is concerned about her reputation as a writer of snappy articles, and that is *all*. Well, never mind – I can stand anything, as long as Barry Callaghan doesn't give the book a good review!

Went to 3 CanLit classes this week – very small seminar groups of about 8 kids. It really does work better with small groups. I like this university for that. It is small, and people do get to know one another. A number of the senior students in the residence (my apartment is attached to a residence) have dropped in ... not to talk writing, just to say hello and generally shoot the breeze. I really like that.

Amber[9] is well, and mischievous. She made off with Valerie's wool hat, which only turned up today! She says to give her love to Tamara, and hopes to see Tamara when we are in the Lakefield house and all of you come up to visit.

It's 5.30 p.m., so guess I should think about dinner. Oddly enough, I don't mind dinner for one – it's awfully easy. But I miss making huge meals for a lot of hungry youngsters.

Much love to you all,

Margaret

ps. have rented already a post-office box in Lakefield, as I was told they are in short supply. It is only $10 per year, so it is worth it to me to have one assured.

p.s.2. there was a writeup of me in the Peterborough Examiner, with a picture of me and Amber. Mrs. Wakefield, from the farm, phoned to say that her little girls, Linda and Susan, had rushed in saying 'Hey, Amber's FAMOUS!'

ps.3. an hour later – Steve Veale, the young reporter from the Examiner, has just been here, to bring me extra copies of his article on me, bless him.[10] He has worked for the paper for precisely 2 weeks now! I told him the strangely nice story about my house having been a Funeral Home, and he then informed me that – wait for it, kids! – his father is an undertaker!!! He told me of one time, very moving really, when his dad came in to a gathering of Steve and his buddies, when Steve was at university here at Trent, and said, 'Look, I wouldn't ordinarily do this, but if you agree, I'd like to show you a part of life – which is death.' Steve, like me, doesn't think it is bizarre. He thinks it is a part of life, and that the people who pretend it does not exist and cannot face it on any terms are the ones who are in a way morbid. How odd life is, though – full of revelations. And mysteries. What his father said could have been said by Niall Cameron.[11]

1 Possibly Anna Porter, vice-president and editor-in-chief of McClelland and Stewart

2 *Jason's Quest* (1970), Laurence's children's novel about a questing mole. The title of the original Palm Sunday hymn is 'Ride on, ride on in Majesty.'

3 Joan Parr (b. 1929) had recently edited *Winnipeg Stories* (1974).

4 *Conversations with Canadian Novelists* (1973)

5 The interview, however, was eventually published in *Speaking of Winnipeg*, edited and introduced by John Parr (1974), 66–79.

6 Robert Fulford (b. 1932) was editor of *Saturday Night*.

7 'Face to Face,' *Maclean's*, May 1974, 38–9, 43–6

8 'The Matriarch of Manawaka,' *Saturday Night*, May 1974, 17–20
9 Laurence's pet cat
10 Steve Veale, 'Laurence Wants Greater Opportunity for Authors,' *Peterborough Examiner*, 21 January 1974, 3
11 Rachel Cameron's father in *A Jest of God*

[8 Regent Street]
Box 609
Lakefield, Ontario
12 November 1974

Dear Adele –

You've probably seen the review in WAVES,[1] but I got it this morning and just have to send it to you on the off-chance that you've not seen it. WAVES is very uneven (ho ho, as why wouldn't waves be?) but is sometimes very good, and I think this is once when they've been very good. I don't know Kenneth Sherman, but his review of CRACKPOT makes accessible to me whole areas of the book which my background and heritage haven't equipped me for. It's the kind of critical article which illuminates, in my view, and I felt so excited by it when I read it. Admittedly, he's dealing mainly with one aspect of the book, but that is an aspect which people who don't know much or anything about the Kabbalah will, I trust, find enormously helpful and good. Clara Thomas always says there are two kinds of critics ... one is the academic-analytical, the other is an 'illuminator,' someone who can open doors into a particular work. I've had that kind of article about some of my work very rarely, but when it happens, it is great. George Bowering once wrote an article about the use of the English language in A JEST OF GOD, and pointed out things I'd thought probably no one would ever really see.[2] This article of Sherman's struck me the same way. I could see, in my own terms (and NO, I don't think of Hoda as the Virgin Mary!) some of the broken vessel symbolism, because true symbolism is organic and archetypal and doesn't depend upon particular special knowledge, and yours in CRACKPOT is that. But this article gives me a view which I hadn't had before, and I find that very good. A work of art contains itself, and can't have footnotes. The job of an illuminator is to provide the footnotes out of the perceptions which the critic has had. I wish this article could be reprinted, as maybe it will be, because I think it is *a good thing*. I was also moved by Joe Rosenthal's line sketches of Hoda and Danile. I don't usually approve of pictorial representations of characters, but there are exceptions. If a real artist reads a novel and feels strongly about it, it may be possible to achieve a sensitive and also kind of flexible interpretation of a character, and I think Rosenthal has done it here. There is something very loving in these portrayals – the sense of Hoda thinking her own thoughts, the veiled eyes of Danile weaving his baskets. I wonder if Rosenthal would part with the originals? You should have them – that is, if you feel a sense of sympathy with what he's done with Hoda and Danile. I think he hasn't gone too far – he hasn't been overly specific – he still leaves to the reader's imagination all the necessary things. He's made, in a few quite beautiful lines, some suggestions. He hasn't overstepped what an artist could do under those circumstances. Maybe he couldn't have done it if he hadn't worked with you before.[3] He obviously has read CRACKPOT with love and understanding. Incidentally, I was sent 2 copies of this issue of WAVES, so I'm only parting with one. I really want to keep this review, and Rosenthal's drawings. I hope J.G.McC[4] sees this – should be ample backup of the rightness of your title, not that any backup was needed, God knows, but nice that someone else has seen it and put it into words.

I'd forgotten (of course) when you were to be in Montreal, so phoned you today without result. I'd written down when you'll be going to Wpg, but not Montreal. And can't remember when you'll be back from Montreal, so maybe you could ring me.

Two more things. First, I'm also enclosing a review from the recent issue of Quill & Quire, which no doubt you'll get from M & S but may not have got yet.[5] This review is a classic example of what I call the favourable but stupid reviews. She loves the book; she doesn't see what it is all about, except that Hoda comes across (as how could she fail to?) loud and strong. But since when is Hoda 'obnoxious?' I must have been reading a different book. And to make comparisons with other writers is at best ignorant, at worst insulting. Does this young lady (why do I say *young*? maybe she isn't) think that Gabrielle Roy[6] invented descriptive prose (whatever that means), or I invented internal monologue? Good heavens. But these are people who don't know what fiction is all about, or where it comes from. I guess we just have to be glad if they give us 'favourable' reviews, however idiotic. And yet, you know, in a way it's these favourable but stupid reviews which annoy me the most. I don't think I really mind if someone hates a book of mine. Even the lady in Austin, Texas, who said about THE DIVINERS, 'A Violent And Obscene Childhood'[7] doesn't really bother me as much as those who seem to like the book and yet not to have read it.

Two kids were here on Sunday for lunch – a young couple, about 20 yrs old, who wrote to me rather touchingly and said they'd like to come up from Grimsby, Ont, and see me. I wouldn't ordinarily have invited them, but they sounded really kind of nice, so I did. And of course, like so many of the kids, they *are* nice – touchingly young, but intelligent, rather shy but also very positive about themselves. She's going to university at York U, he is a cabinet maker (I really like that) in Grimsby. They live together when they can. Martha, the girl, looked at my Study and said 'I see you have CRACKPOT on a shelf by itself' as I'd displayed on the top shelves (a) CRACKPOT on a shelf by itself, and (b) Dennis Lee's two new books of kids' poetry,[8] plus Al Purdy's new book, IN SEARCH OF OWEN ROBLIN, as kind of evangelical things which I wanted people to notice. I said Yes, I did, and said a bit about how I felt. I didn't tell her I knew you. She then said that she had just read it and was knocked out by the character of Hoda – these kids get kind of incoherent ... but the message was plain ... 'She's so terrific, I mean, like, she's so much, she *says* so much, like ...' I said Yep, right on. And then told her I knew you. She said she was too shy to write to you (it had been her boyfriend Mike who wrote to me asking if they could come and see me), but could I please tell you. I said I would.

A guy from Wpg CBC-Radio is coming here next week;[9] apparently they've got you roped in, too, for their program. He says there is an honorarium. Good. I think it's probably in a good cause.

All okay here, by me. Haven't heard recently from Dave & Jane,[10] but they should be back here by the end of this month. It'll be so good to see them. It's really odd, Adele, but in so many ways Dave reminds me of my brother, whose blood relation he isn't.[11] A quiet man, who in his own way will live his life the way he wants to, not dictated to.

Much love,

Margaret

1 Kenneth Sherman, '*Crackpot*: A Lurianic Myth,' *Waves* 3, 1 (Autumn 1974): 5–11. It was accompanied by two illustrations by Joe Rosenthal.
2 'That Fool of a Fear: Notes on *A Jest of God*,' *Canadian Literature* 50 (Autumn 1971): 41–56
3 Rosenthal's illustrations had been featured in *Old Markets, New World*.
4 Jack McClelland of McClelland and Stewart Publishers
5 Carol Finlay, 'Book Reviews: Fiction,' *Quill and Quire*, November 1974, 20.
6 Gabrielle Roy (1909–83), French-Canadian novelist and short-story writer
7 Luella Edgar, 'A Vulgar, Obscene Childhood,' *Austin American-Statesman*, 8 September 1974

8 Dennis Lee (b. 1939) had just published *Alligator Pie* and *Nicholas Knock and other People: Poems*. Both were illustrated by Frank Newfeld. Laurence had reviewed them in the *Globe and Mail*, 5 October 1974, 35.
9 Not traced
10 David Laurence and his girlfriend, Jane Gadd
11 Laurence's brother had been adopted.

Writer in Residence
Massey College
University of Toronto[1]
Toronto 5, Ontario
7 January 1976

Dear Margaret,

It was great having you with us. I hope you enjoyed it as much as we did. And I hope you enjoyed the rest of your visit too. I *know* how glad you are to get back home.

Enclosed are some of the little mag. lists, & also your elegant cigarettes, which you'd left behind.

New term started off very busily. I've actually got several undergrads lined up, as well as a no. of other people. There will be much in-&-outing this term. Tonight I'm going to be working on my end-term report for the Pres., as I want to show it to Pat[2] tomorrow.

The young chap who's doing the doll display design will be coming in again tomorrow to show me his final design, after which we try to get the Ont. Arts Council to move quickly, so we can get it built in a hurry. He seems to have a nice feeling for the dolls, & showed me some intriguing sketches yesterday.

Had a note from Jane Rule,[3] declaring a stand-off, & insisting on her continued good humour & goodwill. So be it. So may it be.

What a lovely Xmas dinner that was at Jocelyn's![4] Memorable, somehow. I was so glad to be able to be there, actually *felt* the turning over of history.

Dmitry's in Ottawa for a couple of days, the house rather empty without him evenings. The babe had a last, (I hope) bout of tummy upset a couple of nights ago, & seems to be feeling much better. What fun she is. My inner life is compounded of acute anxiety & the sense of being blessed.

Mom & Dad arrive next week, & the week after I'll give the doll show, the week after that will be the W'p'g reading.

Yes, there seems to be a definite possibility I'll be offered something at York for next year.[5] If I could only manage to get the doll book done before then, & if it were something at a good enough level (of salary) it might be real luck. Did you know our moving date, is now set at April 18th? The owner's other plans didn't work out. But I'm not going to think about it till February.[6]

Much love from us all. Will be talking to you soon.

Adele

1 Wiseman's appointment was for the 1975–6 academic year.
2 Phyllis ('Pat') Grosskurth
3 Jane Rule (b. 1931), novelist and short-story writer, had written Wiseman the previous November to protest Wiseman's review of Rule's *Lesbian Images* and *Theme for Diverse Instruments, Books in Canada*, September 1975, 3–6. Their epistolary exchange lasted into January.
4 Jocelyn Laurence was living in Toronto.
5 The projected appointment did not materialize.
6 They were moving to 324 Rushton Road, Toronto.

[8 Regent Street
16 February 1976]

Dear Adele –

I re-typed the letter, because it seemed to me that the 'declaring interest' bit should go in the body of the letter, not as an afterthought. I'm sending the original copy to you so you can see what I said. I hope it's okay. It seemed to me I had to deal with both aspects … ie. the critical side, re: your work, and the personal, re: you. I hope the committee will understand what I'm talking about.

Love to all,

Margaret

ps. Just received the Ban story from the Star, in which Margaret Tanner, who used to write The Lakefield Leader nearly single-handed but who does not (thank goodness) work there now, says that The Diviners goes against the laws of God![1] My, my.

1 Elaine Carey, 'Prize-winning Novel under Attack: Teachers and Students Defend It,' *Toronto Star*, 14 February 1976, A13. In early February, *The Diviners* had been removed

from the Grade 13 English curriculum at Lakefield District Secondary School
pending a decision by the Textbook Review Committee of the Peterborough Board
of Education.

8 Regent Street
16 February 1976

Professor Eli Mandel,
Chairman, Recruiting Committee,
Division of Humanities
Faculty of Arts,
York University,
4700 Keele Street,
Downsview, Ontario,
M3J 1P3

Dear Eli Mandel:

I can think of no Canadian writer who would be better qualified than
Adele Wiseman to fill the post in Creative Writing at York University. She
is unquestionably one of our senior writers of prose fiction. Her two
novels, THE SACRIFICE and CRACKPOT are works of great scope and depth,
works which by their presence add immeasurably to Canadian literature.

Adele Wiseman has an extensive knowledge of the theatre, and is
familiar with the whole area of contemporary drama over the past twenty-
odd years. She has herself written two plays, which hopefully will soon
be published and available in book form. She has a very wide knowledge
of literature, both English and European, and has taught literature at
Macdonald College, McGill University.

One thing that I believe should be stressed is her great gift for
communication with young people. She is able to establish a strong
rapport with students, and the warmth of her own personality inspires
greater self-confidence in them – she is hence able to draw out their
enthusiasms and talents to a remarkable degree.

I suppose I should, in the phrase which is used in England, 'declare
interest.' I have known Adele Wiseman for nearly thirty years, and she
has been a close friend during all that long period of time. This whole
question, however, seems to me to centre on what I can only call pro-
fessionalism. No serious writer would allow considerations of friendship
to affect critical judgements of fellow-writers' work. If I did not profoundly believe, through reading and therefore personal experiencing of Adele

Wiseman's work, that it is of a very high order indeed, then I would maintain silence. I cannot, of course, prove my artistic integrity – I can only trust that it will be accepted. We do not tell lies in the areas of our own dedication, in this case the writing of prose fiction. My knowledge of Adele Wiseman throughout so many years does, I would think, place me in a rather unique position to speak of her character and personality. When I say that she relates extraordinarily well to the young, I know because I have seen this happening. Her deep concern with the whole creative process in terms of words is one I know awfully well, and my knowledge is the result of our many years of correspondence and talk on these matters. I have witnessed her generosity of spirit and her concern with mankind's dilemmas, both in her writing and in her life.

In conclusion, I can only say that I think York University would be fortunate indeed to have on staff a writer of Adele Wiseman's capabilities and professional stature.

Sincerely,

Margaret Laurence

8 Regent Street
Later on Saturday
[13 March 1976]

Dear Adele –

Leonard's, the local miraculous hardware store, did indeed (as they had promised) get in the correct staples for my stapler, so here is Chester Duncan's book,[1] for which many thanks.

In the *Examiner* today, the school Trustee James Telford once again held forth.[2] I am beginning to be scared by that man, not personally but in a wider way. He is, as I told you, a member of the Pentecostal church. Today, in an interview he said, among other things: 1) as a Christian (and I suspect here he means Pentecostal, not including even Anglicans) he knows that Christians have insights and good judgements not given to others – he personally has been given wisdom by the grace of God (he appears to believe that people who do not share his particular religious denomination are, per se, denied the grace of God ... ye gods, can you imagine what God would think of that???). 2) Only true Christians should be allowed to choose the books on school courses. (Don't ever run for school Trustee in P'borough County, kid. I jest, but the implications are very frightening). 3) He doesn't trust any high school teachers to choose books, because they are too 'liberal-minded.' 4) He has not read either THE DIVINERS or LIVES OF GIRLS AND WOMEN,[3] and doesn't intend to, because 'you don't have to wade in the muck to know what it's all about'; 5) He limits his own reading to the Bible, religious writings, and the science texts he teaches at our local community college ... oh ye heavenly host! He *does* teach there. 6) Adam & Eve & snake/apple syndrome should be taught in science courses, if they're going to teach the theory of evolution – as another view of creation, and he means a factual view, because mythology he doesn't grasp, of course. 7) The right path for society would be a merger of church & state, as long as the church was the true Christian church, ie his, which would then have power to direct people's thoughts in the right ways – shades of the Inquisition?? The terrible thing is that this guy is *sincere*; he believes himself to be a good man – he doesn't beat his wife or his kids ... neither did Hermann Goering.[4] And politically, Adele, he is, like all such people, smart. He has been taught how to convert people. The man who will be opposing him on the textbook review committee is our local high school Eng Dept head[5] – a very good guy, much in favour of THE DIVINERS, but a man who is afraid of offending the local School Board, a man who is afraid of losing his job, a man who did a radical thing probably for the first time in his life when he rallied the support of other high school Eng teachers for my novel and Alice's, but a man who is politically a child, who hopes the two books can be reinstated quietly, without a fuss. One doesn't have to have Celtic second sight to see what will happen. I find the implications just appalling. I've kept silent because I don't think I should have to defend my own book, but if this guy wins out, I think I will have to take the whole file to the union, for publicity, and also make a personal statement. It goes far beyond the question of my book and Alice's. Among other aspects, it is the racial/religious one that scares me the most – he would, of course, deny that it was racial prejudice, but how in hell can one interpret his statement otherwise? Racial/relig prejudice it is, and of a very nasty nature. I must say I'm much less amused by all this fuss than I was initially. Well, we'll see what happens. I really hope that Telford raves and rants a whole lot more – if he keeps on, there is just a chance that the other members of the committee, several prim ladies among them (who have already made statements vs the novels – not exactly an unprejudiced jury with open minds) may decide to vote not so much for the books as against Telford.[6] It's all very upsetting.

Much love to you all,

Margaret

1 The humorous memoir, *Wanna Fight, Kid?* (1975). Chester Duncan (b. 1913) was a professor of English at the University of Manitoba and well known as a pianist and composer.
2 John Goddard, 'Only True Christians Can Set Standards: Telford,' *Peterborough Examiner*, 13 March 1976, 3
3 The collection of short stories by Alice Munro (b. 1931) was published in 1971. It had been removed from the curriculum of Kenner Collegiate and Vocational Institute in Peterborough.
4 Hermann Goering (1893–1946), Nazi politician and field marshall
5 Robert J. Buchanan
6 At its meeting of 22 April, the Peterborough School Board voted 10–6 in favour of retaining *The Diviners*.

8 Regent Street
20 January [1979][1]

Dear Adele:

I have flu and I feel so utterly lousy that I can't summon energy to phone, but wanted to let you see the enclosed clipping (how could you see it if I *did* phone? Obviously I am not myself). Do not worry – I will be better in a few days. I have dosed myself with aspirin – don't think there is much else one can do. It is partly my own fault. I felt it coming on yesterday but nonetheless went out shopping ... did my village rounds, and found the weather colder by far than I had realized, and wasn't sufficiently warmly dressed, so by the time I got home I was chilled to the bone. Now I've got three layers of clothing on and feel freezing! Never mind – it will pass.

I wish I could agree with Frye re: the would be banning-of-books people,[2] but I'm afraid they won't just go away if we ignore them. (Incidentally, I think we should call them something other than book 'banners' ... I like the word banners in its other meaning too much to use it for those slobs!)

Heard from Joc yesterday. They got back from Cyprus on Jan 7th. She decided to go back with Saro, rather than stay on a week longer, then was sorry she hadn't spent more time with Jack, after all.[3] She hopes to get over again. She took your book to show to him, and he was very interested and impressed. She said he might write to you to enquire if he could get a copy. (Just give him the address of the Longhouse[4] or ask him to send $14.95 plus postage – I am sure he would want to pay for a copy).

Got a letter from Marian the other day. She is going to review your book for BRANCHING OUT ... (feminist mag, v. good, based in Edmonton).[5]

Joc also wants a copy (which I am sending her) for her friend Marleis, a German woman. She also wants me to send a copy to Gran Laurence,[6] which I am also doing (I got some extra copies from Longhouse).

All for now ho ho! It is only 1:30 p.m. and I want to write to Joc, but after that I am going to bed.

Snags (real, not imagined) with novel. I am going to have to set it aside temporarily and work on memoirs. I have batted my brains out for two weeks (ho ho, I hear you say, *that* little a time!) on the damn thing, and now realize that several assumptions have been totally wrong. Mostly, I *cannot* go back into Manawaka country, because that would be pushing it. The five books out of that territory were all necessary and demanded to be written, and together they form some kind of whole. But this time, I think I latched onto that background not because I really wanted to write out of it again, but as a kind of *refuge*, which isn't the right reason for doing anything like this. The revelation last summer that I wanted to attempt some kind of memoirs also makes me question whether I *really* want to write *fictionally* about the Old Left in Wpg – I think I'd rather write what I truly know, which is my own (very limited) experience. I want to do something, sometime, with the evangelist thing, but I wonder if at this point in my life it would come out sounding like a desire for revenge. I had to re-write all the sections of my first novel that dealt with the Brits in W. Africa because I had treated them so unsympathetically. Also, a danger at this point would of course be the opposite ... that I would lean over backwards to be fair to the pentecostals, thus soft-soaping their very real dangers. Actually, in just over a year of thought about this darn novel, I find that there *are* some things I genuinely want to attempt ... characters and themes, and these are not the ones I originally saw as the most n.b. at all. I'm not abandoning the idea of a novel ... but I must try to have further patience and to let it grow as it will. In thinking of it, and planning it, I have perpetuated too many pre-conceived notions of it. I've got to start afresh, but am too close to the old ideas as yet. I came to these conclusions early this week and was quite depressed for a time, but don't feel that way now. The memoirs idea is a godsend ... without that to work on, I would feel pretty down. I have gone through similar crises before, heaven knows. After I finished writing the stories later collected as The Tomorrow-Tamer, I had an entire novel planned, set in Africa. A beautiful plan it was, too. But I could not write it. I had really said everything about Africa that I had to say. Some guiding spirit has always prevented me, thank God, from writing a mock-up. There are other backgrounds, after all, that I know a good deal about, other than the prairie one. I sometimes forget that I have in effect lived in a small community in Ontario for ten years! (I bought the shack in 1969 ... it hardly seems possible.) Of course, one's childhood background is a special one and nothing is ever quite that strong again, but I feel that this time I want to find another quite different direction in fiction ... not that my basic methods are ever likely to change much, nor do I want them to. By which I mean I am not suddenly going to begin writing avante garde stuff ... whatever *that* means!

Once I burned 100 pp of manuscript when I got off to a false start with The Fire-Dwellers. I then realized I had to write A Jest Of God first. (Reading Woodcock's article on the Earth Air Fire Water thing[7] actually made me wonder if some mysterious something had indeed made me write those 4 novels in that particular order, but of this we can know little, nor does it matter). So I know this period of hiatus only too well. One never learns to love misery, however. But I will put away the notes etc for the novel and let it simmer on the back burner, and will go on with memoirs. I feel a strong hunch that this is the right way to go about it.

I read SILENCES[8] this week, and was tremendously moved and impressed. There was far more that deeply connected with me than I had at first thought from a superficial glance at the beginning of the book. I also felt it was telling me some very important things re: writing any kind of memoir. One can choose to leave some things out, as indeed Olsen certainly does in writing of herself, but what one puts in has to be as true as one's fiction and that is pretty darn true, as we know!

I see now the reason for writing not phoning was to say all this on paper, partly for you and partly for myself.

Much love to you all,

Margaret

P.S. did you notice that Olsen mentions you, me and Alice Munro, among a bunch of others, in a footnote? Will return book to you next week.

1 Laurence and Wiseman had exchanged only a handful of letters since March 1976.
2 Context not traced
3 Jocelyn Laurence had spent Christmas with her father, who was working in Cyprus.
4 The Longhouse Bookshop in Toronto handled only Canadian books and was co-owned by Beth Appeldoorn and Susan Sandler.
5 Marian Engel (1933–85), novelist and short-story writer. 'The Dollmaker,' *Branching Out: Canadian Magazine for Women* 6, 3 (1979): 42

6 Elsie Fry Laurence (1893–1982)
7 George Woodcock (1912–95), author, critic, poet, editor, and founder of the critical
quarterly *Canadian Literature* (est. 1959). His article was 'The Human Elements:
Margaret Laurence's Fiction' in *The Human Elements: Critical Essays*, edited by David
Helwig (1978), 134–61.
8 Tillie Olsen (b. 1912) had published her memoir in 1978.

[8 Regent Street]
10 February 1980

Dear Adele:

First, I hope you don't think I was too negative re: TWUC in our phone
conversation. Truly, I *do* share some of your concerns, while not able to
share all of them. I know $17,000 seems a lot, but I just don't see how we
can get anyone capable unless we pay that.[1] Believe me, I do realize the
irony in the fact that few writers make that much from their writing. I just
don't know what the answer is. I feel so damn depressed about the state
of the world, plus the overwhelming need to do my writing – I guess these
things render me relatively useless in other ways just now. These 2 factors
set up, of course, horrible tensions in me ... not new ones, heaven knows;
I've been struggling with this dilemma for more than 30 years ... is it
worthwhile to write, when the world is falling to pieces? I must believe it
is, but sometimes I truly wonder. Then, also, the fact that my own
financial situation, although at present okay, is so damn insecure.
However, it has always been so, and I've managed thus far. I had just
completed my income tax when you phoned, and I have to admit that the
day I do my income tax is usually the low point of the year for me!
Perhaps foolishly, I keep a year-by-year comparative list of basic expenses
(not food ... if I did that, I'd probably have a nervous breakdown!) When
I see how expenses such as fuel and Hydro etc keep rising, I get nervous.
I also go through agonies of self-reproach when I see my phone bill, which
last year was out of sight, but then I reminded myself that Joc was in
Corfu and I phoned her about 4 times. I swear to write letters, not phone,
but of course within about 2 weeks I've forgotten my good resolve ... and
why not? I simultaneously curse and bless the phone daily. If I couldn't
talk to you and Marian[2] and Joc and Dave and a few others, I'd go up the
wall. Anyway, June[3] phoned yesterday as I had known she would when
she found I wasn't going to attend the AGM. I told her with perfect truth

that a) I *had* to concentrate on writing or I would be both off my rocker and broke, and b) that I thought it was time I quit taking on the earth-mother role – it's not good for me, and I don't think it's good for the union either. She asked me to write a note to be read at the banquet, and I agreed, but now I don't know. What could it be but a motherhood statement? Also, it would seem, I think, to be assigning to myself an influence that I don't have and don't want. Anyway, old friend, I just wanted to set down some of these views, and I know you will understand. Yesterday I got back to the writing. What I wrote on Jan 2 was garbage but has provided a teeing-off point ... I tore it up and started again, in the correct assumption (this has happened before) that if anything was worthwhile there, it would still be in my mind. I get off to such a slow and *boring* start, always, and always have to re-write the first 30 pp or so totally, later on. I have not yet learned, after all these years, that one doesn't have to get in *all* the salient facts about a character in Chapter One! However, I have resolved now just to press on, however repetitive, bor-ing, or just plain awful it may be at present. One doesn't have anything to work with unless you have a first draft, after all. You know that feeling you have when you think you're probably going crazy? I have it, and take it to be a good sign! Please send up the odd prayer or two.

I'm enclosing a copy of a letter I wrote to my friend Budge Wilson,[4] and her reply to me. It is strange how things sometimes reach out in ways we least expect. I thought you would like to know that in mysterious ways, OLD WOMAN AT PLAY and then my own responses to your mother, had somehow comforted Budge's sister over the death of her husband.

I hope you do not consider it presumptuous of me to have written this letter to Budge. I needed to write it out, but also to send it to someone I love and trust. She is truly a person who speaks our language. She and her husband are on a sabbatical this year in N.S., where they originally hail from. Alan teaches Can Studies at Trent. My ref to Budge's RC sisters is that she taught a class of *very* elderly nuns here, for some years – a class in physical fitness, really dance movements!

I mention your exhaustion, Adele, but not your grief.[5] This is because Budge would understand without my having to say, and also, because I can speak of my own grief, but another person's is too private for me to speak about. As we know well, also, although one does not keep on *mourning* for the rest of one's life, the real grief never ceases, and it is right that this should be so, I think. At least, this has been my own experience. As you know, my own mother died 50 years ago, when I was only 4, and yet there are times when I still grieve for her, as I do for my stepmother who died 22 years ago. I don't even think of them that often, but when I do, it is still with a sharp sense of loss. I think that is why I was so moved by the letter my aunt Norma sent me, from my young parents, written to her in 1922 ... four years before my birth.

All for now, except I want to share with you a very funny thing that happened this morning. I went to church, and the Sunday School kids took part in the first part of the service (Valentine's Day on the 14th being the reason). The teachers ushered in the children just before the service started – kids from about 3 or 4 to about 12, I'd say. As Jack Patterson, the minister, entered (in his cream coloured robe trimmed with green) one tiny tad's voice rang out loud and clear. 'Hi, God!' The congregation, to their credit, chortled. And Jack, taken completely off guard, was great. He just bent down to the tad and said, 'Hi! That's a nice valentine for me, eh?' Presumably the theological niceties can be dealt with later, and gently! I hope God got a laugh out of it, too. I think He/She could probably use a few.

Love to all,

Margaret

P.S. Am reading Elie Wiesel's 'A Beggar In Jerusalem.' He has the rare ability to come right to the heart of things right away, a great gift. How unlike my meanderings. However, we press on!

1 The Writers' Union of Canada was looking for an executive director.
2 Marian Engel
3 June Callwood (b. 1924), writer, chair, Writers' Union of Canada, 1978–80
4 Budge Wilson (b. 1927), short-story writer and children's writer. Laurence had come
   to know her and her husband, Alan, who taught history and Canadian studies at
   Trent University. Excerpts from the letter were published in *Dance on the Earth* (1989),
   239–44.
5 Adele's mother, Chaika Waisman, had died on 2 January.

[8 Regent Street
December 1980]

LETTER FROM LAKEFIELD.[1]

The bus trip from Peterborough to Toronto is two hours. It's a trip I take frequently, more frequently than I would like, because the demands of my profession require me to be in the V.M. (Vile Metropolis) for meetings,

book-signings, worthy causes and the like. The bonus is that I get to see
my friends and my daughter and son, who live there. Being a non-driver,
I'm an old hand at bus travel. I'm organized. I go from my village to
Peterborough, only a few miles away, by local taxi. I get there early, and
I'm first or second in the bus lineup. I sit near the back, seats for smokers,
window seat, just opposite the lavatory, *in case*. I have never yet had to use
the facility on the bus, but proximity gives me peace of mind. I haul out
my paperback, usually a who-dun-it, aggressively light a cigarette, hunch
towards the window, and hope no one will sit beside me. Bus travel is a
time for light reading and meditation, for looking at the land, not for
gabby exchanges. I'm lucky sometimes, and sometimes I'm not.

This time was the worst ever.

It was the 11 a.m. bus, which is usually not crowded. This time it was,
because it was shortly before Christmas 1980. The lady came stumbling
down the aisle and sat beside me. Her husband took the unoccupied seat
opposite, next to a young man who already had *his* paperback out and *his*
cigarette aggressively lit. If only that young man and I had come to some
tacit agreement, beforehand, to share a seat. But then, all us experienced
bus travellers go for the window seats.

Off we groan, the bus rumbling and snorting.

The lady is possibly in her late 60s, wearing a checked trouser suit,
sunglasses and a whole lot of lipstick. She is also sloshed. She has
numerous shopping bags and purses and other gear, which she stows
around her feet and mine.

Lady: Damn bus damn bus damn bus. I jus' don' know how I can *demean* myself to go by this damn bus. Listen here, if you'd of bought a
new car, instead of being so damn tight-fisted ... hell, I *knew* the car was
gonna pack it in, but would you buy a new one? Oh no. Not you. Too
much money, you said. Too much goddamn money. So we have to
travel by. BUS. For godsakes. How I can *demean* myself ...
Husband: Sh, Bertha. It's okay. It's only two hours. Sh, please, eh?
Lady: (fumbling in one of innumerable bags) Oh shit oh shit oh shit.
I've lost my cigarette holder. John – JAWN – It was a bran new one! I
musta dropped it when I got on this damn bus. Jawn! You just go and
ask the driver!
Husband: Sh, Bertha. It's okay. You'll find it.
Lady: I will *not* find it because it is *not* here. I dropped it. Sure, I know.
I bet the goddamn driver picked it up and he'll keep it, too. I know
those guys. Buses! If you'd of bought a new car ...

Husband: (low, but not so low that he could not be heard) If you could leave the house just once without having six drinks first ...

Lady: Don't you talk to me like that! Don't you dare! Don't you bloody dare!

Husband: Okay dear okay dear okay dear. I'll go and ask the driver.

Lady: (struggling up) Oh no you won't. You damn well won't. I will go myself.

Husband: (terrified) No, dear, it's okay. I'm going. Right now.

(Husband climbs out of seat and shuffles to front of bus. Returns.)

Husband: Here it is, Bertha. The driver did pick it up. He was going to ask people when they got off.

Lady: Well, now. Well, isn't that the nicest thing. Well, he sure is a nice person, that driver. Haven't I always said that these bus drivers were really nice guys?

(She lights a cigarette, eats a salmon sandwich from her baggage, announces that she thinks she'll just have a little snooze. I, a smoker, am suddenly aware of the dangers of allowing smoking on public transport. I am eating cough drops. Sure as anything, this bus is going to be set afire by this lady.)

Lady: (mumbling to herself, cig in holder in her hand) Goddamn bus. What a way to travel. How I can *demean* myself by travelling by bus, I jus' don' know. I just DO NOT KNOW.

(Miles and miles of this. I read, hardly seeing a word. The fiction writer in me says that this is a life of awesome complexity. Another part of me just wishes she would shut up.)

Lady: (suddenly leaning towards me) *You* seem awfully interested in that book. How come yer reading? You don' wanna *talk*? You a student or something? Are you learning English?

Me: (taken aback and by surprise) Well ... uh ... no.

Lady: (scrutinizing me closely; I have high cheekbones and slightly slanted eyes inherited from my long-ago Pictish and Celtic ancestors.) I know what *you* are! You are one of those damn people from Vietnam or Taiwan! Tha's what you are. Boat people! One of *them*. Why did we let you all in? Wha language you speak, parn my curiosity? Chinese? Vie – man – eez? Yer trying to learn English, eh?

Me: No. Actually, I speak English pretty well.

Lady: Then why the hell you're *reading*? Don' deny it. Yer one of the foreigners we let in. You don' fool me any. Where you from, then? Jus' all I ask is one simple question – where you *from*? You too ashamed to say, or what?

Me: (*Thinking* – what if I *were* from elsewhere? How would I feel about this lady?) I'm from here. Canada.

Lady: Ha ha. I bet. You cernly aren't from Canada. Where you say you came from, jus' answer me that.

Me: Manitoba.

Lady: Manitoba! Jeez! Well, now I know what *you* are. I shoulda' known. Yer a halfbreed, one of those goddamn halfbreeds. Admit it! You are!

Husband: (quietly, desperately) Bertha, the lady wants to read her book.

Lady: Book! She's a halfbreed and she won't admit it!

(How can you talk to somebody who can't be talked to? She could have been sober as a judge and I still couldn't have talked to her. But in the confined space of a bus, and a captive, what to do? I don't think I handled this especially well, but would there have been a good way to handle it? I doubt it. A pitched yelling match on a bus is not my style).

Me: Madam, if I were a Métis, I would certainly not deny it. I would be proud.

Lady: (snorting, lighting another cig) *Madam*, she says. Madam! My gooness, you trying to be fancy, eh? Halfbreeds.

Husband: Bertha – for pete's sake – she wants to read her book!

Lady: Okay then, whatcha think of Louis Riel, then? A devil. A devil. The worst. Part Indian, I ask you. Whatcha think of *him*, then? I was born and raised on the prairies, myself. Saskatchewan.

Me: He was a great man.

(But to my shame, I did not say this *loudly*.)

Lady: (face close to mine) Lemme tell you something, jus' lemme tell you! Nothing but trouble, tha's what I tell you. We lived in Montreal for *years*. Had a nice house, good dis'rict, the whole bit. Did those goddamn Frenchies ever *appreciate* us? No bloody way. We moved to Ontario. But I tell you, people here don' realize how bad it was in the West. My father worked for a bank ... yessir ... in the old days in Saskatchewan. Gee, I used to go out with him when I was just a kid, and I'd hold the dog inside the car while he talked to the farmers. None of those farms was ever foreclosed on. *None*, I tell you. You better believe it. Of course, people *said* different, but *we* know.

Me: (Mumble, mumble.)

Lady: Now you jus' tell me what you think about the goddamn French Canadians! Those damn buggers ...

Husband: (whispering) Bertha ... Bertha ...

Lady: Oh you, shut up! Jus' shut up!

(She turns to me once more.)

Lady: What you *do* eh? I mean, what do you *do*? You a student or something? What do you (this said with dignity) *intend to do with your life*? Nothing? Nothing?

(Nightmare proportions seem to be taking over. I want earnestly to tell her something quite untrue, but I find I can't. One isn't permitted to tell lies in vital areas.)

Me: (unhappily) I'm a writer.

Lady: Well, my heavens, think of that. And jus' what *do* you write? Is your whatchacallit in the *papers*, pray tell?

Me: (Thinking – she obviously does not believe me, so maybe we are home free) I write books.

Lady: Reely? Books, eh? Well, now, isn' that jus' so *interesting*. What kind of books?

Me: (Thinking – oh hell, is she beginning to believe me, alas?) Novels.

Lady: (Rummaging in one of her innumerable bags) Jus' a minute, here. Where's my pen and a bit of paper? Where? Hm. Wha's this? No. Oh, here we are. Now you jus' write down the names of your books, and your name, so I can jus' go and *read* them.

(Trapped. At this point, I don't know what to do. So I write my name and the name of one of my books. There is not much chance that she will have heard of me.)

Lady: (peering through her tinted specs) Who? Margaret Laurence? Yer Margaret Laurence? Well, I jus' cannot believe it. I HAVE SEEN YOU ON THE TV! Well, isn't that something, now!

Me: (Mumble)

Lady: Well, it cernly has been *such a pleasure* to meet you and have this *nice frenly talk* here on the bus.

Me: (Cough)

Lady: Well, I sure will tell my frens. Well, I know where you live – in Lakefield! Maybe I'll jus' drive up and drop in on you some day. I'd reely enjoy that. That would be very nice. You gotta meet my husband. John!

(She reaches across the aisle. He is not there.)

Lady: JAWN! Where the hell *are* you?

Me: I think he's in the lavatory.

Lady: (pounding on lavatory door) Jawn! Are you there? Come out! I want you to meet a *famous* person! She is sitting right here, right beside me. I have seen her on the TV!!

Sepulchral Voice From Bus Toilet: Bertha, quit it. I'll be out in a minute.

(The bus is drawing into the Toronto station at Bay & Dundas. It halts. I step across the Lady and her baggage, and grab my coat from the rack above. The procession in the aisle, as always, takes awhile to get moving, but when it does, it moves briskly. John, poor refugee, is still in the can.)

Lady: Wait! You gotta meet my husband! He's so literary!

Me: (now telling lies with comfortable abandon) Maybe outside. Gotta get a taxi.

I'm middleaged, but by heaven I can still sprint when the motivation is strong enough. I sprinted. There was a cab there. Freedom.

I didn't look back.

*****

– Margaret Laurence

1 This story was included in a 'Cheery Package' that Laurence had sent after Wiseman's operation in early December. It was published in *NeWest ReView* 6, 8 (April 1981), 11–12

[324 Rushton Road
Toronto, Ontario
M6C 2X9]
Saturday
10 January (I think) 1981

Dear Margaret,

Right I should whang off my first letter to you. Dmitry's taken Tamara to her drama class. The living room is now filled with dining room furniture. We're sleeping upstairs. But I've cleared a space on the grey couch & have found this lined, easy-to-follow paper. Of course, the minute I sat down, with record album cover & paper on my lap, pen poised, Osker appeared & offered me something more important to do, – his paws, – one after the other. Tongue lolling, much yawning & sighing. Who could doubt that a dog's paw in hand beats poised-pen hands down? However, he's gone off to scratch now, so I may proceed awhile.

I am so sorry about your flu. No, no guilt trip, just very sorry, having just been through it, with still an irritating cough, I know it for such a drag. Try to sit it out at home. One of the workmen, Miguel's daughter had it recur. Don't risk it; I'm trying not to. (Just did another paw. A lot of swift chop licking, a yawn or so, & now he's appeared on my left side, so I can write *and* play with his paw. Well, my handwriting may be slightly affected, but women should know how to do more than one thing at once, n'est-ce pas?) Punning in French yet. What's to become of us? That little rascal can't bear the pen as rival. The minute I stop coughing (damn fit, writing about it probably reminded me) & begin to write, out comes a re-straining, hopeful paw. Well, no more about Oskie. Just know he's in the picture.

I will not embarrass you by dwelling unduly on my, – on *our* – grati-tude for the time you have spent nursing me. It's there, – always will be. You must know it. So I'll simply play the other angle, – boast all over about how I was looked after by the Chancellor of Trent.[1] I told you about what Hoseh said when I told him who you were. He said the really big people, the ones who really had something, didn't worry about little things like their surroundings. (I'd been saying I hated to see you up in the sordid surroundings of the third floor). He said it was only the smaller spirited people who were trying to pretend to classiness who made a big thing of such. He was, of course, so right. And one nice thing, you really can't deny it. That is one compliment you'll just have to learn to swallow head on, like the plucky Pict you are.

In my determination to begin to write letters again, I had forgotten that one of the reasons one had let the habit slip in these days of swift contact, was to spare busy friends the boredom of having to skim much semi-legible script, which turns out not to be saying much anyway. Also, if one were only a letter writer of the scintillating kind, whose epistles were guaranteed to be Woolfed down by the hungry Canlit essayists of the future, with some little shocks of *pleasure*, it would allay perhaps the uneasiness of knowing this is scheduled for the 1981 file marked 'Writer Friends.' Unfortunately, Osker gives me neither the time, nor has nature given me the gifts required to charm & scintillate with the natural wit & elegance, not to speak of the naughty indiscretions of my epistolatory style. Margaret, do you realize that one now has to address at least one level of one's letters to the 'unknown reader?' Either that or ask you to tear it up. And I'll certainly not do that while there's a chance of you get-ting paid for this stuff.[2] I'll tell you, as a friend of mine used to say, 'It's all balls & dances this year my dear.' (Said, of course, with an English accent.)

By the way, your brown-letter-envelope, the second one, sent to the hospital, still hasn't arrived. I assume it may yet be returned to you someday, in which case I'd love to see it. Better late than ... etc.

Otherwise not much new. Yes, we did go to the pictures last night, – saw a touching film of the genre I guess they'd call docu-drama nowadays. It's called 'Best Boy,' & is about a retarded adult of 52, who's been looked after by his parents, now ageing, & the process by which their cousin, the film-maker, encourages them to allow him to join the world of his peers, & prepare himself for the inevitable future.[3] The filming was actually done as the process was taking place. It was, as I say, touching & often very depressing & at times rather beautiful. There was also in me a certain amount of probably unjustifiable uneasiness about an element of exploitation, in spite of the sincerity of intention of those involved, & the very positive results. On balance my uneasiness must be the least relevant thing. This will probably do much good, & is very laudable. Still, well, fiction is different. But it's not at issue here. Anyway, much love to you. Best to Audrey.[4] Don't do anything to strain yourself in any way for a few days.

love from us all,

Dmitry, Tamara & Adele

1 Laurence had just begun her term as chancellor, a position she was to hold until the end of 1983. She had been staying with the Wisemans to help care for Adele, who had recently returned home from hospital.
2 In anticipation of a possible sale to York University, Laurence had deposited her papers and personal correspondence in York's archives the previous summer.
3 American documentary (1979), written, directed, and produced by Ira Wohl
4 Audrey Schultz, the Trent student who lived in the self-contained apartment attached to Laurence's house

[324 Rushton Road]
20 January 1981

Dear Margaret,

Hi! I am enclosing Tillie's letter.[1] Note the address. I think she must have received my letter, though mis-addressed, because I had a sweet note, full of commiseration from her today. On Saturday evening, when Tamara & her young friend went to see 'Dracula' at the Young People's Theatre,[2] Dmitry & I went to see the film of 'Tell Me a Riddle.'[3] As a film it is a touching piece of work. But of course, as we knew in advance, it is not _THE_ 'Tell Me a Riddle.' It not only coarsens, it destroys all the fine balances; the delicate strings, in the story tuned just so, now twang out their notes without the subtleties of nuance by which she builds to her precise effects. The result is that the film doesn't say quite what she was saying, though it clearly makes some stabs in that direction. Since the dramatic focus is on the husband largely, because he is acting out, & she a passive recipient of memories, her own emotions, & other people's responses, the focus is shifted, & indeed tends to swing about so that the crucial climaxes get fudged. Remember the really important one in which he responds with something like 'Still you believed?' That was hair raising when Tillie read it. Here it was so placed that it couldn't gather the full force of the story into itself as it does in the prose; & so missed that tremendously concentrated effect. Anyway, as a film in itself it had some interesting things worth seeing. _I hope it makes her a lot of money_! Somewhere in some small album I have a picture she sent for you. I discover I'd 'lightened' my handbag by putting those albums away somewhere. As soon as it turns up I'll mail it to you.

Work on the house proceeds. I find it rather thrilling to contemplate the prospect of a future with the house actually in order. That, of course, will not be till sometime after the workmen are through. Nevertheless, Dmitry is working very hard on the fine finishing. He's been sanding & scraping & painting windows & doors, painting heating pipes, & doing a thousand & one jobs. Wait till you see some of the innovations in Morag's suite. Mr. Freed was in to look at the job this morning, & suggested a more radical alteration on the third floor still, which I'll mention to Dmitry, but I doubt he'll go for it at this point.

Did I tell you Miguel & Hosé came in one morning & told me how thrilled & unbelieving their kids were that they had actually been in contact with you. It appears that Miguel has a daughter of 20 & a son of 16. His daughter loved _The Stone Angel_, & thinks you're terrific. Hosé has a daughter of 9 & a younger little boy. So what I did, when they went home that aft., I gave them each one of the copies of your _Christmas Story_ that you & Helen Lucas[4] signed. I told Miguel that he'd no doubt have a grandchild in due order, & Hosé's (sp?)[5] kids are still young enough to enjoy it for themselves. I doubt somehow that it will make much difference to them, even though they are probably Catholic, that your version of the story is not according to their orthodoxy.

Oh yes, '_Dracula_.' Tamara was not at all frightened by it. 'It was fun.' But when we got home & Dmitry & I took Osker for a walk, as we came homeward, there was Tamara, coat over nightwear, coming toward us in the snow. 'Footsteps' in the house. And sure enough in the middle of the night 'a bad dream,' so that I ended up sleeping with her, naturally. Nothing to do with Dracula, of course. Oh well, how much longer will I have the privilege?

Well Chancellor, I would like to see your reply to your – ahem, – colleague the Chancellor. You move in elevated circles, my dear, – though the expression that comes simultaneously to mind is, 'You cruise in shark-filled waters, my dear.' Write.

Love,

Adele

P.S.   Tamara received, & immediately set-to to translate some of the Hebrew in the little book you sent her. It's a very nice little book, a very good idea. The illustrations are quite amazing, particularly considering the medium.

1 The Laurence papers contain an undated postcard from Olsen with New Year's greetings for 1981. The address is 3420 Hardin Way, Soquel, California.
2 Toronto theatre, established in 1966, specializing in plays for children and adolescents. *Count Dracula* was adapted by Ted Piller.
3 American film (1980), adapted from Tillie Olsen's work of the same name
4 Helen Lucas (b. 1931), Canadian painter and illustrator of *The Christmas Birthday Story* (1980)
5 Wiseman has consistently spelled his name 'Hoseh,' and then had struck off the final 'h' and put an accent on the 'e.'

[8 Regent Street]
27 January 1981

Dear Adele:

HI! Back to the pleasures of letter writing! I'm sure we will not be able entirely to avoid the temptation of the phone, but even sometimes will ease the phone bills, add to the pleasure of receiving the mail (after all, what is more pleasant, when the mail arrives, than seeing a letter from a friend?), and in general restore us to the civilized living of a bygone age. Thanks for your 2 letters – written under incredible difficulties (for which read 'beloved Osker's demands for affection'), and also for sending the things from Tillie. Gosh, what a wonderful lady she is! She sent me one of those lovely little Japanese calendars. (What the hell is the matter with my typing?[1] Do I save my non-mistakes letters for business? Is that like kids saving their good manners for company?) I'm interested to hear your impression of the film of TELL ME A RIDDLE. Actually, I guess one can feel it is fortunate that at least it's a decent film, even if many of the subtleties of the writing aren't there – couldn't be there, really, when you think of it. I will never forget Tillie reading it.

Was really touched by what Hosé and Miguel said about me. I'm really glad you gave them the Christmas story. I accept Hosé's compliment about the third floor with this proviso – I'm not kidding when I say I love that little room ... I really do! When I see it all gussied up, in all its finery, I may be just the teeniest bit shy for awhile!

Re: my reply to – ahem – you know who. I decided it would not be proper to *send copies* to friends, but what I said was ... 'Thank you for your letter of January 12th, and for your good wishes to me in my new appointment as Chancellor of Trent University. I did not, of course, know that you were Chancellor of W— University, when I remarked that "as far as we know" I was the first Canadian writer to be appointed a Chancellor.[2] Please accept my apologies for any embarrassment this statement may have caused you. It was, I assure you, done unwittingly. I will naturally take care to correct this erroneous impression in my future dealings with the media. Yours sincerely ...'

I also put in the lower left corner: ML/ml. I reckon that from the tone of my letter he will not be able to figure out whether I'm being ironic or not! Heh! heh!

Here's the pic of the kid I told you about. What a sweetheart ... and the look on your face is so touching!

Also I enclose a pic of me taken by Doug Boult. He took black and whites also and I've bought a bunch from him to use when I need to send out a photo. Don't tell me – yes, I know I should get my son to do pics of me, and I plan to ask him sometime, if he will do so when not too busy, on the same kind of financial basis as a photographer like Boult. I would really like Dave to do a portrait of me, but somehow, I'm a little shy about asking him. He wouldn't, perhaps, feel free to say No if he'd prefer not to. I don't know. We must discuss this sometime.

It is 3 p.m. I have been writing letters for hours, but this is the first one I've really wanted to write. I have 2 ladies coming in at 4 for tea ... oh woe. One of them I've known for some time ... not a close friend or anything, and I like her, altho she is a bit overpowering. But she phoned in some embarrassment, saying there is this woman who is (an artist? a ... I can't recall) who wanted to meet me, and knew that *she* knew me, and ... yeh. The heart sinks, but can you say NO? You cannot. So here we go with the tea and the store-boughten cookies. If they stay more than an hour, I will *faint*. Sometimes I think it would be lovely to be able to faint at will, as women once did, but I guess that was more because of their stays, etc, than anything. I've never fainted in my life, so guess I won't begin now.

About the 'Future Reader' bit ... isn't it peculiar? I'm damned if I will be inhibited, but of course we do know we have the option, as we always have done, of saying 'Please Eat This Or Flush Down Toilet' with letters we do not want preserved. I don't really think future critics and scholars are going to Woolf these letters down, but they'll sure as hell be disappointed if they want to, eh? I was so damn annoyed at myself when you told me on the phone that indeed, despite your admonition *not* to explain, because you *did* know what the cable had meant, that I in fact apparently explained VIKING IS IN SPAIN STOP TRANOPF. Could we, do you think, mischievously ink out the explanation in the relevant letter? Then, perhaps, long after both you and I have gone to our ancestors, there will appear in some critical mag an article which will read, in part, as follows;

'Although the Laurences were Margaret's family only by marriage, she long felt a deep sense of connection, possibly through her children, to these Highland Scots. The Laurences of the Shetland Isles were, of course, descended from the Vikings. There is strong evidence that ML was once considering writing a novel of early Viking times. It is known that the Vikings, those mighty seamen, ranged far and wide, and even had settlements in Russia. Spain was naturally one of their ports of call. In a most revealing cable to Adele Wiseman, Margaret Laurence announced her firm intention of dealing with this theme, and even states the name of her central character ... Tranopf. It is not known whether Tranopf was a man or a woman, but given the nature of much of ML's writing, the latter seems likely. The manuscript of this novel ... if, indeed, it was ever completed, has been lost.'

Last week was incredible. Never a dull, not to mention spare, moment. Mon – shopping and etc; evening, at Trent for dinner and to hear Bob Kroetsch[3] read; afterwards, Mike Peterman[4] drove me home, and Joyce M[5] and Bob came along ... I asked them in, and the session of talk lasted until midnight. Tues – finished cleaning house; Audrey had done floors, so I just had to dust, do woodwork, re-do hall floor tracked up with mud, do bathrooms, polish copper, etc. Afternoon ... 2 small friends, 9 yrs old each, came in to make mint patties. Wed ... on panel with Bob and Joyce at one of Peterman's Canlit classes. Audrey, who was there (but who just doesn't ask questions ... it is not her style and for this I do not fault her) said later ... 'Great questions ... at least Grade 10 level.'! This wasn't quite true, but there was kind of a lot of pauses, when B or J or myself rushed in and burbled. Wed eve ... John Frick phoned, saying he was in L'field to visit Dave and Vi Frick[6] and could he come for lunch Thur. Thurs ... John for lunch; stayed until 4:00 p.m. Dave and Vi also came in; by this time my 1 bottle of scotch was down to zero, after Mon night. Fri ... 2 couples, Eng dept, Trent, for dinner, plus Joyce plus Harold Horwood[7] who had intended coming Sat but came Fri instead, which was okay. Sat ... Harold left mid-aft; Jocelyn arrived 5:30 p.m. ... great to see her! Sun ... the christening at the Anglican church, of Ren and Michiel's[8] little daughter, Hilary, my god-daughter. Being unfamiliar with the Anglican order of service, I kept flipping through the wrong hymn books etc, but never mind ... the kid was wonderful! Didn't blink an eyelid as the minister splashed the water on her head, and then sensibly went to sleep in her mother's arms during the sermon! Lunch at Ren and Michiel's farm, then back here in time to make sandwiches and tea for John and Angela Graham, from London, Ont (he is Eng Dept; I went to college with both of them, and their daughter goes to Trent). End of yet another quiet week in the country. Enjoyable, but ye gods and little catfish!

I got the funniest invite yesterday, Adele. You will love this. There is a small group, MEN, called The Fortnightly Club. They meet every 2 weeks in a member's home, to discuss WEIGHTY MATTERS AND CULTURE. As it was put to me (by a dear good man, actually, who I respect and love; retired Eng prof from Trent), with some embarrassment ... for he had been detailed to phone me ... 'We are served dinner by our hostess, and then we have our meeting ... mostly professional men ...' (mumble, mumble). No doubt the 'hostess' (wife of a member) gets to eat in the kitchen. Once a year, however, they hold ... wait for it! ... A Ladies Night! They take all the 'hostesses' ... wives ... to dinner at the Peterborough Club! Yipee! And *this* year, they have decided that maybe they might actually, after dinner, have a Lady as Speaker!! Wow! Sound the trumpets! So guess who was to be that Lucky Lady? Yep. Yr friend. I said a very courteous but a VERY firm NO. What I wanted to say, but did not, was 'Why don't you ask one of the Lady Hostesses to give the after-dinner speech? You might find that more than one of them had more in her head than tuna-fish casserole recipes.' Oh Shades of Tillie Olsen! Oh Silences! It is to laugh but also to *rage*.

The other funny invite I recently received was to address a 'retreat/conference' (I can't remember where; I forget as soon as I answer these damn things), on the theme that so many women (housewives, mothers, etc) in our society do not have enough time to learn, meditate, think, etc. They are asking me to take 3 days out of my life to talk on this subject! I wrote back and said, in effect, it's a problem I have with my own life, but I don't think I have the time to attend this conference. I wanted to say ... your invite to me seems rather ironic; if guys like you would leave me alone I'd have more time to meditate, think, and maybe even write. However.

Heavenly days, no wonder when I talk with you on the phone, I go on and on for hours. When I write a real letter, I go on and on, too. But the stamps are cheaper than Ma Bell. Also, it really is a pleasure to *set things down*. I have too much grown out of that admirable habit. You're right – we must re-establish the habit.

Much love to you all,

Margaret

PS. 5 p.m.

Tea is over, and my visitors have departed. Once again, it turns out to be people who need much reassurance, contact with others, talk, warmth, etc etc, and oh Adele, they *are* good people and my shoulder is not wide enough for all those needs. We do what we can, but it can't ever be enough.

I'm enclosing the Contract (Draft) with York. The actual contract arrived today, and I have signed it and will return it tomorrow. The terms are $40,000, to be paid in instalments of $8,000 over 5 years, beginning in January 1982. I have not told anyone else the actual financial terms – I dunno why, but I just don't think it is most people's business. There is a lot of query about whether the sale of papers is Capital Gains Tax, or whether the total sum must be declared as income. I have a lot of stuff on that subject, from my accountant, from Hart[9] at York, from Revenue Canada, and will send you copies when the time comes that you need them. It seems to me that what will ultimately transpire is that the sale of papers will have to be declared as income, as this way Revenue Canada can tax the seller on the total amount received, rather than Capital Gains, under which only half the amount received, minus $1000 deductible, can be taxed as income. However, this remains to be seen.

The good news is that JASON'S QUEST has now come out (will not be out in bookshops until about Mar or April) in the paperback, with the new pics. I enclose a copy for Tamara. The pics are really nice, although on what amounts to newsprint they don't look as good as they should.

The bad news is that my books in Bantam paperback are all now going out of print in America. Actually, I think that only THE STONE ANGEL and THE DIVINERS were ever *in* print in Bantam paperbacks ... I had thought that all the Manawaka books were, and that the royalty reports included America, but now I realize none of them, except those 2, were *ever* in print in USA, and will now not be available there at all. The old story.

Much love to all,

M

MARGARET LAURENCE'S PAPERS ... DEPOSITED AT YORK UNIVERSITY, TORONTO.
TENTATIVE LIST OF CONDITIONS ... TO BE FINALIZED UPON SALE OF PAPERS

1. These papers are not to be accessible until such time as they are sold.

2. Should they remain unsold at the time of my death, my heirs and executors, Jocelyn Laurence and David Laurence, will sell them with such of the conditions as still pertain.

3. Upon decision to sell, York University shall at its expense have these papers evaluated and shall have the first opportunity to buy.

4. Future papers, comprising business correspondence, personal letters from other writers, letters from readers, desk calendars, shall be included in the York University collection, with no further payment, and shall be deposited there from time to time. Any such papers left in my effects at the time of my death shall also be added to the York collection, with no further payment.*

5. When the papers are sold, the business correspondence, the memo-rabilia, the original manuscripts, and everything else, *unless specified herein*, will be immediately accessible, with the usual copyright conditions that nothing can be quoted or published without the permission of the writer of the letter or the firm involved, or, in the case of material originating with me, my permission.

6. When the papers are sold, personal letters to me from other writers or critics, etc (in the separate files) will be accessible after my death. Copyright conditions will of course pertain, and no one may quote from these letters without the permission of the writers, or, in the event of their deaths, their heirs. In the case of persons who are

medically judged to be mentally incapable at that time, permission will be sought from their nearest relative or legal guardian.

7. Both before and after the sale of these papers, I will have access to them. I agree not to remove such papers from York University, but may make notes or copy portions for purposes of memoirs, etc, it being understood that I may publish or broadcast such portions only with the permission of the writers of same, or their heirs.

8. Both before and after the sale of these papers, in the case of personal letters from other writers to me, each writer shall have access to her or his own file of letters, provided that each writer agrees not to remove these letters from York University. After their death, their heirs shall have access.

Margaret Laurence
Lakefield, Ont.
18 July 80

Adele –[10]

* *Note* – I do *not* include future manuscripts of my own work, as I think these should be sold separately. Actually, McMaster has all my previous manuscripts of *novels*, at least the ones that are still in existence – I threw away some in Vancouver & England, before I knew better!!

1 Laurence's letter was full of typos.
2 Richard Rohmer (b. 1924), lawyer, soldier, and author of popular fiction dealing with national and international affairs. He was chancellor of the University of Windsor from 1980 to 1990. Laurence's reply was sent on 22 January.
3 Robert Kroetsch (b. 1927), Canadian novelist and poet
4 Michael Peterman was a member of Trent's Department of English.
5 Joyce Marshall (b. 1913), writer, translator, and editor, was writer-in-residence at Trent in 1980–1.
6 John Frick was the son of Alice Frick. His uncle and aunt, Dave and Vi Frick, were living in Lakefield.
7 Harold Horwood (b. 1923), writer, and chair of Writers' Union of Canada, 1980–1.
8 Ren and Michiel Duinker were Lakefield friends involved in the peace movement.
9 Hartwell Bowsfield was at this time York University archivist.
10 This was a handwritten note.

[324 Rushton Road]
early 6 April 1981

Dear Margaret,

It is very late; I've just finished a note to Dmitry's parents, & it occurred to me that a note to you too, on this self-destruct paper, might be a way to beat the problem, which I can't take too seriously at the moment anyway, of posterity's putative prurient poring over our correspondence. With the kind of paper they're publishing on now, we'll be spared any pouring over our books as well, since even we will likely outlast *that* paper.

At the moment I'm sitting in the living room. Dmitry & Tamara are long asleep. But I slug-a-bedded all morning, for the Sunday hell of it, so am of course all wired-up for half the night. The living room is nearly empty, still, but is now basically finished & ready for its furniture. It's the only totally completed room in the house. Tomorrow we'll probably get its furniture in. And then we can do the woodwork in the dining room & hall. Eventually we'll even get pictures up.

How is the work going? Your new regime is a good example to all of us, & what's more important, is going to be great for you, (not to speak of for Canlit). I have already peeled off a few lbs., under the aegis of my dragon lady, & feel a lot better for it. I'm swimming every chance I get,– over a mile the other day, – & my shot sinuses can prove it. But so too can the renewed spring in my tread, the increased energy, etc. While there is yet life, let's live, baby! I'm glad I set this up before my op., & have stuck to it since. I'm glad you too have decided to look after your health more. And I've decided this time to stick to the regimen, if I possibly can, through thick & progressively thinner.

The other evening Marian[1] invited me over for some wine. Arlene[2] happened by after dinner, so in the evening the two of us went over & spent a very pleasant couple of hours with Marian. She's back on chemo, & it seems to be working all right, though she still has a bit of fever. Her book seems to be selling well.[3] I had dropped in at the Longhouse to get a few copies for her to sign, to send to Tillie, & etc., & they had run out, but they've re-ordered. She's had more pictures framed & put up, & she's thinking of getting parquet down on the floors, which will look very good. Wouldn't it be nice to see a film of *Lunatic Villas*? If only some smart filmmaker would latch on!

We're planning to go to Montreal for the Passover-Easter weekend. Want to come? Seriously, my sister wondered if you might be interested when I called her today. I said you probably wouldn't, but I'd extend the invitation, anyway.

How is it coming? Everything? Anything? I was delighted to read that Helen Lucas' book of prints, which Eleanor Sniderman[4] is bringing out, will be ready soon. Apparently it's a very limited edition, but beautiful. And expensive. *But beautiful*; it can still be done.

I think it's probably past two. My record will soon be finished. I had better get to bed. Oh, the librarian at Tamara's school, whom I hadn't met before, told me on Friday how much she was enjoying Tamara; she's in charge of the 'Anne of Green Gables' production Tamara has a part in. She asked me if I'd noticed how the child has blossomed this year, was delightfully enthusiastic, & warmed utterly the cockles of this mother's heart.

love from us all three,

Adele

1 Marian Engel, who at this time was battling cancer
2 Arlene Lampert, a Toronto friend
3 Engel had just published her novel *Lunatic Villas*.
4 *This is My Beloved – Sometimes* (1981) is a series of charcoal drawings on themes of romance and sexuality. It was printed in a limited edition by Proclaim Publications of Willowdale, Ontario, whose president was Eleanor Koldofsky Sniderman.

[324 Rushton Road]
22 April 1981

Dear Margaret,

Thought I'd drop you a note. It's several hours since your call this afternoon, and I've just had a call from Joyce,[1] to say that she had just unexpectedly sat down & sketched out the first draft of a short story. So I'm thinking of arranging some trips for some of the writers here in tight-arsed Hog's Town. We'll go & breathe the air of Lakefield & Peterborough, & come back here & spread the *Renaissance* of *Literary Canada*. I'll promise not to let anyone disturb you or Joyce. We'll just tippee toesy around energetically divining wells of inspiration. Don't be fussed if strangely semi-familiar faces suddenly appear at & disappear from your windows. I'm thinking of offering sacred glimpses. Seriously, isn't it wonderful? It's such a gift, you ranging about with a headful of Ukrainians rampant, & Joyce snatching a story whole. Viva the spring out your way! I spent my day trying to get near my typewriter. I had it open three times. Well, at least I had it open, & caught a glimpse of some writing on a page. Mustn't be ungrateful. All in all I'm feeling very cheerful about all our respective stirrings.

Swam today again. Saw the dragon lady, & was encouraged. Did a shop which we needed. Walked the Osk. And have been up since 5:30 this morning. Strange how the days slip by. There's something wonderful about all us women writing, – making worlds. Hooray!

Tamara & Dmitry are both fine. It was lovely seeing you, & feasting with you, & really good of you to look after the Prince & Osker. It really enabled us to spend a pleasant, untroubled weekend in Montreal.

Keep working luv; these are the good times; they hold the bad at bay at least for a large little time.

See you soon.

love,

Adele

1 Joyce Marshall

[8 Regent Street]
17 May 1981

Dear Adele:

I was going to phone, then I thought I would write instead (halo). Eat your heart out, Ma Bell. I have been having a really fun time this weekend, and thought all of youse would like to hear. It is Lakefield's 'Victoria Days' celebration! Began yesterday (Saturday) and goes until tomorrow eve. Craft displays, hot dog stands on main street, which is closed to cars, people wandering around in genuine and pseudo Victorian costumes! I have a long printed dress, slightly Vic in appearance, on which last year, for the same event, I sewed a bunch of lace I once bought from an English gypsy, plus a long black cape lined with scarlet – a girl in Eng once made it for me, and I hardly ever wear it, but it's dandy for such an occasion as this. Makes me look like Meg Merrilies ('Old Meg she was a gypsy, and lived upon the moor ...').[1] Last evening I was one of the *five* judges in a Queen Victoria Look-Alike Contest. There were *three* contestants!! It was great fun. One of the contestants turned up in a pony-drawn carriage, complete with 'John

Brown' in kilt! (No whiskey in sight, however). After the proceedings, I was talking to a local woman who said 'If you'll wear your fancy dress to church tomorrow, Margaret, I will, too.' I said, 'Done.' So this morn I set off feeling like an idiot. However, she was as good as her word, and had even phoned another woman, a Grade 6 teacher who is a terrific gal, so there were three of us looking like idiots! Our young minister, who is really a good guy, delivered a sermon with which I disagreed about 75%. Maybe I should set him right?! Actually, I think it is more that he hasn't yet learned to say what he intends to say ... i.e. he knows what he wants to convey but he doesn't actually convey it. Anyway, today I ambled down at 2 p.m. for the Olde Tyme Fiddle Contest (yep, that is how it was spelled in the program). It, however, turned out to be 2 hours late; the folk dancers from T.O. didn't show; a local gal with a lovely clear light voice was pinch-hitting with a guitar and some of the good old *mournful* cowboy songs ('When ah die, I may not go to Heaven / 'Cause I'm not sure they let *in* cowboys There ...'); our Reeve, resplendent in dove-grey Victorian suit and top hat, was grimly calm and obviously on the verge of a nervous breakdown ('I tell you straight Margaret, I could write a *book* on what's gone wrong with this schedule here today ...'); kids were laughing and skipping ropes and everyone was munching hotdogs and hamburgers (me included). Finally I gave up and came home, but went down again about an hour ago (4 p.m.) to find that the Old Tyme had at last begun. It'll go on until about 8 p.m., but I don't have that kind of staying power. What I really wanted to hear was the 'Under 12 years old' category. Oh, Wow! Those kids! Both girls and boys, and so solemn and excited, dressed in their Sunday best, and amazingly good on the fiddle. I don't know if they read music or not, but they don't play with any music in front of them, as of course no real fiddler ever does. Accompanied by a pianist, sometimes a child, sometimes a parent or fiddle teacher. You would have loved two of the little guys ... brothers, both with bright red hair, dressed in identical navy blue suits (long pants), white shirts, scarlet waistcoats. One was 8 and the other 6 years old. The tiny one was hardly bigger than the fiddle he played! And he was good! Sure, a few notes went askew, but they do even with the adult fiddlers. I could hardly look at him, with his pants slipping a trifle and revealing his undershirt, and his face with snub nose and a small frown of total concentration – I thought I'd start weeping, as I remember always doing when my kids were little, at the Sunday school Christmas concerts. Each contestant is allowed to play 2 tunes – 1 slow, 1 fast. For his fast

number, the little tad played 'The Irish Washerwoman,' which I remember playing myself on *my* fiddle as a kid of about 12 or 13 (did I
ever tell you about my violin-lesson days? I hated the whole thing, as
I was not musical at all, but my beloved Mum, recalling my own pianist
mother, thought I should be given the opportunity). Of course, tunes
like that are so much a part of my past, and when I recall the words
now, I am appalled, but didn't even notice, way back then. ('Have you
ever been into / an Irishman's shanty / Where water is scarce / but
whiskey is plenty ...' Such are the opening words of the Irish Washerwoman). With this audience, here in L'field, the old familiar tunes,
especially the fast ones, cause people to begin clapping softly but
rhythmically. Well, this is one side of the coin of a small town; the other
side, as I know awfully well, isn't so cheery. But such events do give a
certain lift to the heart.

Remember the dire thesis and the gal we talked about? Well, a few
days after her fulsomely apologetic letter (maybe she was angry, Adele,
and maybe not – it seemed to me she was, and I could hardly blame
her, in a way), what do I receive in the mail but a calendar from her
(mailed *after* her 'apologetic' letter ... I checked on that) ... a 1981
Calendar with ... wait for it ... a great deal of stuff about the religion of
the Native Peoples of N. Amer., specifically the Six Nations (Iroquois).
This is her latest religious kick. No letter. Obviously a peace pipe, ho
ho. If someone sends you a gift, you have to write and thank them,
n'est pas? I will think about this when I feel stronger re: that problem.
It isn't that I am uninterested in N. Amer indigenous religions ... *I am*.
But I am not an Indian and have this strong feeling that it is a kind of
insult to *them* to be a make-believe one – I have known a number of
whites who have tried to become make-believe Indians or Africans. Trying to understand and respect is one thing; trying to change one's own
background is quite another. Of course, the lady in question may not be
trying to do that at all; I must not jump to conclusions.

Which brings me to another thing, a really good thing that happened.
Yesterday in the mail I got from Andy Suknaski[2] his latest book of
poems, entitled, IN THE NAME OF NARID. He said he'd seen you at the
book table at League Of Can Poets meeting. Then he and his lady a few
days ago saw the NFB film on me at the Regina Public Library,[3] and
there you were, and this seemed to please him a lot! Maybe he hadn't
realized we were long time friends? I dunno. He said in his letter that
he had seen this NFB film before, but saw more in it now. Interesting.
His book of poems has confirmed in my own mind what I have always

known, have fought against innumerable times but have always had to accept, finally – I cannot *ever* write about another cultural and ethnic background from the inside. It cannot be done, or not by me, anyway. I can write about my own, with *its* many variations. The others have to come in, but in ways other than *from the inside*. This was a problem I had with *The Diviners*, and the Metis, obviously, and it is one I have again now. Only worse. This is not an insuperable problem – it just takes one hell of a lot of working out. I think *this*, really, more than just the forthcoming Convocation,[4] is what has halted me. Temporarily. I think it was Graham Greene who once said that writers quite early on discover their individual limitations, and their ways around these are called Style. I think they are also called Form, or, more accurately, Voice. Whose voice, and from what background of information and feeling and *real* knowledge does it speak; also, from what *lack* of another kind of background does it speak? That can be telling, too. I think I'm going to learn how to go on with this story, but as always, it's not very simple. (Actually, it was much more simple years ago when I didn't know as much as I ... maybe ... do now).

I now discover that the Chairman of the Bd of Govs of Trent[5] will be having a very small (thank god) dinner on the 28th, on the night of Norma Edwards' performance at the Wenjack Theatre at Trent.[6] I will have to go, and will go to the beginning of the performance, at which time (about 8 p.m.), the President[7] will present me with a something ... piece of paper ... which says that there will be established a Margaret Laurence Scholarship at Trent, to which kindly people can ... hem hem ... contribute, and that it is M.L.'s wish (true) that this financial help (even if very minimal) be given to a student specializing in Canlit or Canadian Studies. After that, I will quietly slip away, because I have got to retire v. early that night, in order to get up v. early and get a purchase on the next day, convocation. Therefore, dear friends, I think it will be best if I leave in the fuse box, on my front porch, a duplicate key to the house. That will mean that if you are able to get here on the Thurs, fine, and you'll have the key. Also, during the next day, you'll be able to get in and out. I have to go on the 29th to the President's Lunch at noon, and thence to Convocation at 2:30 p.m., for the robing; the ceremony begins at 3 p.m. Everyone is going to have to look after themselves, which will be oke with all of youse, as I know. I wish it was over. They are going to have a piper! At Convocation, I mean. I only learned it last night. Jean Cole and I talked on the phone, and her husband, Alf, is the Registrar, as well as being a member of the History

Dept, so he is actually the guy who orchestrates Convocation. Jean said 'I didn't know if you'd be pleased or not, because you know, Margaret, what the pipes can do to us ...' She meant that either it would be like a shot of adrenalin or I'd dissolve into tears. I said I thought it would be the former. Well, it *will* be because it *has* got to be.

I tell you, on the morning of May 30, whatever the ceremony was like, I am going to be one happy and relieved lady! David and Nina may be coming here that day for the weekend ... that would be nice. I got 2 cards from Joc ... 1 from Eng and 1 from France; her and Karen's holiday seems to be v. good, thank heavens. She really needed a holiday.

Much love to all,

Margaret

P.S. My hair looks terrible. I have written to Bruce, explaining. Still, there are 2 weeks, and in that time it may grow out enough to look presentable after a shampoo. Ye gods ... the nonsensical things that plague us.

1 'Old Meg,' a poem by John Keats (1795–1821). It is quoted by Hagar in *The Stone Angel*.
2 Andrew Suknaski (b. 1942), Canadian poet
3 *The First Lady of Manawaka* (1978)
4 Laurence was being installed as chancellor at a special convocation on 29 May.
5 Erica Cherney was chair from 1980 to 1984.
6 As part of ceremonies marking Laurence's installation as chancellor of Trent, the actress Norma Edwards gave a benefit performance of her critically acclaimed *The Women of Margaret Laurence*.
7 Donald F. Theall, president from 1980 to 1987

[8 Regent Street]
22 January 1982
1:30 p.m.

Dear Adele:

Woe is me and me is woe! Why did I not take up a *simple* profession such as brain surgery, translating poetry from the ancient Persian, or becoming an ice hockey star? Have stuck to my realistic schedule this week, and have re-written (for the 100th time) the first part of Ch. 1.

Now I'm stuck again. Have just sat at that damn desk for about 2 hours. Nothing. Zilch. I know what I want to do but am scared to begin. The next bit has to be totally re-shaped in every way from the first way I did it – I must not even look at the some 75 pp (handwritten) I did before. I think of a sign that used to be on a local shop (shoppe?) ... Antiques & Junque. Those 75 pp are Junque. But contain the thread of the narrative I want. I don't know why I experience more crises of confidence these past few years than I ever did before. Yes, I guess I do know, and I know the way out, too – jump in and swim; nobody's looking. It ain't easy. However, we will overcome.

Mona arrives Feb 1. This house is filthy. My vacuum cleaner stands in the livingroom, a silent reproach to me. I must clean the house. I keep putting it off. Do I ever *hate* housecleaning!

This letter is by way of (a) sounding off in my state of self-pity; (b) avoiding cleaning the house (how come I made the same typing error twice in a row?);[1] (c) trying to fulfil in some tiny part our long-ago decision to write sometimes rather than always phoning.

I got a nice letter from Tiff[2] this morning, expressing thanks for my letters, and apologizing for his phone call. He doesn't need to apologize, but I suppose he needed to. He mentioned the 29th ... first I'd heard. I really wish I could go – I'd love to.[3] But I can't. I have to go to a Can Studies lecture that day. Mike Peterman always gives a lecture at this time of year on Canlit of the west, and I always go, and we meet the students afterwards in the Jr. Comm. Rm., where they always ask the same questions and Mike and I always make the same replies. Well, no, it's not really that dismal – they're good kids, always. Jocelyn is coming the next day (Sat), so I really can't go to Cannington on the Fri.

Can't remember when we last talked on phone. When I am thinking about the work, I get terribly absent-minded about everything else. Do you? The only exception, when my kids were young, was that I wasn't absent-minded about them. I think it was when you were so embarrassed about the abstract of yr James article, the 'female heroine' bit![4] Not to worry, kid, what's a redundancy here and there! I sometimes get the feeling, with myself, that my vocabulary is really quite small, as I constantly encounter words that baffle me. How did Shakespeare ever manage to acquire that huge vocabulary? Not through doing Readers' Digest 'Test Your Word Power' things, to be sure. So traumatized was I by my one error in their childish test that I forgot which word, but I think it was 'concomitant,' which according to the Concise Oxford, means 'going together ...,' and no, it doesn't mean what Hugh MacLennan once expressed as people's reaction to Can writing ... 'Boy meets girl in Winnipeg, and who cares?'[5] My parting gift is a typo that appeared a few days ago in The Peterborough Examiner, that haven of typos. The story was describing the plight of bus travellers in a recent snowstorm, somewhere north of here. It said that when the road became impassable, the passengers 'sought refuse in a nearby restaurant.' I bet they had no trouble in finding same, either!

Love to you all,

Margaret

P.S. Your lovely note cards have already drawn admiring comments from several lucky people to whom I've sent same.

P.S. 2. These 'A' stamps are abominable! Not only do I fear that the govt is going to raise the price from 30¢ to some much higher sum, but also I'm outraged that the perforations are shoddily done & the glue doesn't stick. If the Post Office has a motto, it should be – 'Pay More, Get Less.'

P.S. 3. Just received from Doug Killam (U of Guelph) a copy of an article on my work by some Englishman,[6] for one of the many publications with which Killam is involved. Among many other boring things it said that such is the nature of my 'style' that readers might think I had no 'style' at all, & might (*wrongly*, it said!) mistake me for a 'naive realist.' Well, heck, & gosh almighty, says the hayseed, me. When people tell me they're Post-Modernists, *now* I know what to say – '*I'm* a Naive Realist!' Me & Granma Moses.[7] Should we start a *Naive Realist Movement*? Did you see the recent issue of Books In Can? I was so angry I threw mine out, unfortunately. A long article quoted many of the visiting writers at the 'Amnesty' Conference in T.O.[8] The question, of course, was – 'How much is Can writing known *internationally*?' As expected, most of the writers from all over said 'Not at all.' With qualifications. Atwood, of course, was mentioned by writers from the many countries she has visited – Australia, W. Germany, Britain, Amer, etc. Soyinka, God bless him, but of course _damn_ him all the same, said that M.L. was known, but *only* because she had 'interested herself in Africa.' Ye gods! Achebe would *never* have said that; he knows better. But of course, he decided *not* to attend the conference, as I did myself. Some of the writers said – 'Yeh, well, I know about Richler, but I didn't know he was a Canadian.' I think Mordecai will probably be as cross about *that* as I am. No one mentioned the fact that many writers in many countries *simply do not read books by other writers*. Most of those persons seemed to be a case in point. I could tell B-in-Can an awful lot about our writing & its (admittedly gradual) impact abroad, but why bother? Translations; teaching of our books in courses in many countries; etc. I could even say some things about my own books. But what the hell? The drive of the article was to say – 'look, here are all these SUPER INTERNATIONAL guys who don't know Canadian writers even exist.' The knockdown, once again, & from a publication that still purports to be a Canadian magazine.

1 Laurence had typed 'clearn' and 'clearning.'
2 Timothy Findley (b. 1930), novelist, playwright, and short-story writer. Laurence had written Findley a letter after his father's death.
3 Findley had written on 19 January to thank Laurence for the letter and to invite her to dinner with Adele, Dmitry, and Canadian literature critic David Staines.
4 'What Price the Heroine?' *International Journal of Women's Studies* 4, 5 (Nov./Dec. 1981): 459–71
5 Hugh MacLennan (1907–90), Canadian novelist. 'A Boy Meets a Girl in Winnipeg and Who Cares?' was first published in the *Montrealer*, February 1959, 18–20, and then collected in *Scotchman's Return and other Essays* (1960).
6 Douglas Killam (b. 1930) was chair, Department of English, University of Guelph.
7 Anna Mary Robertson ('Grandma') Moses (1860–1961), self-taught American primitive painter
8 Barbara Wade, 'To See Ourselves,' *Books in Canada*, January 1982, 3–6

[8 Regent Street]
5 April 1982

Dear Adele:

Am going to begin sorting my 2 yrs papers tomorrow, and have been thinking about yours. Also thinking about your possibly taking the job in Montreal,[1] and other things. I think it's better that I write rather than phone, because maybe I can get my thoughts together in the printed word rather than the spoken. Please understand – as I know you will – this is NOT advice. This is just some of my thoughts.

As you know, I would really in some ways like to see my letters to you at York U, as all my other corresp with Can writers, especially you, is there. I'd also like to see my letters plus all your other papers, in a safe place. I'm not suggesting yr house isn't safe – but when one begins to think of papers in terms of a) archives and b) money, then I'm reminded of Ann Phelps, who apparently was approached by York, or so

Clara once told me a long time ago, re: her father's papers ... Arthur Phelps[2] had, of course, had correspondence with a huge number of writers, including F.P. Grove.[3] Apparently someone from York went out to The Mill, the old Phelps home near Kingston, and looked at the lot, but since then Ann hasn't done anything about the papers ... the person from York, maybe Anne Woodsworth,[4] I dunno, noted that much of Grove's letters had been eaten by mice! Well, your papers ain't gonna be eaten by mice, Oskie, Smoggins, etc, but still, me having been totally casual about all this stuff for yea these many years, I now feel it would be good if yr papers could be in safekeeping.

I also have been thinking about your having paid off the mortgage ... I mean, all of youse. Hurrah! But it occurs to me that a needed chunk of dough might be forthcoming with your papers, and that might even make it not too necessary for you to take an external job.

Two things occur to me. One is that you might sell my letters to York as a separate collection and get some money fairly quickly. This would, I think, probably be possible. I'll be seeing Anne W sometime within the next month, & could sound her out on this *if* you think that might be in any way helpful. On the other hand, of course, if you removed that lot from your total papers, the value of the total thing would be diminished by something, in terms of bucks, who knows. So it would seem that the total sale would be the best, naturally. But I've been looking up in my files, and I now see that Hugh Anson Cartwright, acknowledged the 'expert' assessor in terms of writers' papers, set the sum for *my* papers to be sold to York U, 2 years ago, at *9,000. That is all.* York whomped up some more, as you know, and I sold them for $40,000. Hart did not tell me of Cartwright's assessment, and I only found out later what it had been. Apparently, and from my knowledge of universities these days (e.g. Trent), the universities are undergoing cutbacks like you wouldn't believe. This is true. So money for acquiring papers from writers will probably not be all that great for some years to come. I think York offered you $25,000 ... they would probably still have that available; I think they would also probably be able to offer you a matching sum in tax write-offs ... i.e. you might get half in dough and half in tax write-offs, a total of $50,000. York is one of the few remaining universities that do have some actual dough for acquisitions.

On the other hand, there is the U of Calgary. I see from my files that the deal with the U of Calgary is that, unlike any other university in this country (at least, as far as I know), they have a deal with the Alberta government, whereby the U of Calgary gets writers' papers as a *gift*, and gives a tax thing, and the provincial government puts up dollar for dollar, so that what actually happens is that a writer *gives* her papers to the U, ostensibly, and is given a tax write-off (i.e. is able to deduct this 'gift' from her taxable income for that year, or spread out over x-number of years) for half the amount, and is given cash for the other half, which is of course declarable as income for however many years it is paid to the writer, but the money actually comes from the prov govt, so the U of Calgary actually acquires all this stuff and it doesn't cost them one cent. That is, apparently, what Mordecai did, half of the sum (whatever it was) in cash, and half in tax-write-off. I enquired, re: Richler, at M & S, & J.G. McC sent me a bunch of info – not, of course, the actual *sum*, but the terms. This was when I was drawing up a contract with York.

This is, mainly, FYI. It would appear that (a) not too many universities are into collecting writers' papers; (b) the U of Calgary seems to have a great deal going with the Alberta govt; (c) York U is probably one of the few universities around, nowadays, that actually itself can raise some dough for acquisitions; (d) times are getting really tough, re: universities' funding, and, like the post of w-in-r, the acquiring of writers' papers may be the first thing to go; (e) time, in terms of selling these things, is probably now *of the essence*. I think you are absolutely right to deal with universities not yourself, but through your lawyer, but I also think that not many lawyers know all that much about the university situation and the acquiring of papers for cold hard dough. Thinking of the shrinking finances of the universities, I wonder if you wouldn't be well advised to: a) list, roughly, what you have ... it wouldn't need to be listed in terrific detail; b) get your lawyer to approach both Calgary and York, because those two seem to be the best bets going these days. I think I told you that I sold, some years ago, some of my remaining manuscripts to McMaster. They bought the original manuscript of The Diviners plus a lot of work notes, etc etc, for $500. That's not much. But I don't regret it, actually. It was $500 bucks more than I would otherwise have made. I'm *not* saying we should, any of us, sell ourselves short. I'm just saying that I don't think many universities, in the near future, are going to have a whole lot of money for acquisitions of our kind. As I say, the only 2 universities that I know about right now that are still in the game are York and Calgary. Both are worth trying, but I really do doubt that many others are. I'd just like to see you get a chunk of dough from some university for all your papers, but my sense of the situation is that the sooner the better because time seems to be running out, at least for now, for that whole thing.

If this seems like ADVICE, please forgive. I just don't think that things are going to improve, economically, in a hurry.

Love to you all,

Margaret

P.S. See you Wed., with Oskie!

P.S.2 I now remember that *Queen's Univ* is also in the game – they bought Purdy's papers. The U of T does some acquiring, too, but is *not* well known for enthusiasm for Can writing. Au contraire, in fact.

YET ANOTHER P.S. I'm enclosing an article from Q & Q on Arthur Gelgoot,[5] who, if I am not mistaken, is Marian's accountant. She's told me for years that 'Arthur the Magic Accountant' would love to handle my income tax, etc. Well, he seems to me to be a really great guy! I won't, of course, change accountants, as I've been quite happy with my present one for years and years, and his stance is much the same as Arthur's. I was so delighted to read this article, though, and see that Gelgoot believes in the same things as I do – i.e. pay off the mortgage if you can; try to keep out of debt; put away your acorns; the old-fashioned values that we were brought up with, the reverse of the Credit Card never-never psychology that seems to predominate now. If you ever had any doubts, which you and Dmitry *didn't*, about the wisdom of paying off ye olde mortgage, here is magnificent vindication. Also, for many years, I've had the same philosophy re: money coming in and going out – I reckon that in any given year, my incoming money is about ⅔ mine and the rest goes to Revenue Can. I do make instalment payments, of course, and have for years. The problem he doesn't touch on, however, is that the instalment payments are based on the *previous* year's income, so I now make the minimum payments every 3 months, because it is easier to pay more at the end of April than it is to over-pay, if one's income this year should be much *less* than the previous year, because it takes forever to get the over-paid money back from Revenue Can, as I discovered about three years ago, as I've told you. Anyway, I think this article is interesting, and Gelgoot has a lot of sensible ideas, in my view. What amused me, tho, was that some of his clients hit a good year and 'start to make up for all the good things they never had.' I guess I have been especially fortunate, having travelled etc etc, in bygone days, and also now not being in a situation where I *want* a whole lot of stuff! I may spend over $2,000 a year on the phone bill, but by heck, I spend about 95 cents on makeup and damn little on clothes. This is not virtuous; it is just that people do tend to spend money on very different things. I was thinking of what you and I discussed, re: the *constant* expenses when the mortgage is paid off ... i.e. property taxes, heat and light, water, a reserve fund for essential repairs, etc, and the other expenses over which we *have* some control ... i.e. food, booze, cigs, phone, clothes, travel, etc. I read this interview and thought to myself that I wasn't a bad business person at all! I've known that for years, tho. Says she, with (maybe) spiritual pride. No, just plain ordinary pride, I think.

1 Wiseman was writer-in-residence at Concordia University in 1983–4.
2 Arthur Phelps (1887–1970), professor of English at United College (1921–45) and McGill University (1947–53). He had been one of Laurence's teachers.
3 Frederick Philip Grove (1879–1948), novelist and essayist
4 Director of libraries, York University (1978–83)
5 'Arthur Gelgoot: Writers Aren't Spectacular Money Managers,' *Quill and Quire*, April 1982, 8–10

[8 Regent Street]
10 February 1984

Dear Friends and Loving Hearts –

Have tried to phone you in the last few days but don't seem to phone when you are home. Did get Tamara the other day, and talked her ear off, telling her about the BC trip, as no doubt she told you.

So much to tell you – probably better I should do it in a letter rather than a phone call. This letter will probably save me about a hundred bucks!

Will tell you about the BC junket in a moment. Right now, re: David and Soña ... Dave phoned two days ago. They are fine and working like the dickens. His show in Mex City starts on March 6, and Soña's show, at the Punchinello Gallery in Toronto, starts on March 17. They plan to come up together about March 12 or 13. As maybe I told you, I came into some unexpected $$$ ... a Winnipeg dance group has done a dance based on A JEST OF GOD ... yes, it sounds weird, but there it is; a Wpg TV guy, Al Bleichert, came up about a month ago and did an interview with me because the dance thing is going to be filmed and shown on

TV[1] and it will include the interview with me ... my agent[2] very cleverly said '$2000 American bucks,' so last week I received my share, $1800 American which translated into over $2000 Canadian. I thought ... what is this nonsense and why wouldn't I try to get some pleasure out of it while I'm still here in this vale of tears? So I sent the kids some Amer bucks which hopefully will help with their air fares up here in March. Anyway, David told me that Dmitry had very very kindly offered to help out when Soña's show is on in Toronto. So what they are going to do is to phone Dmitry about the middle of Feb, when they have air-freighted the posters and invitations to him. (Dmitry, maybe you will have to pick up same at airport, or maybe they can be delivered to your place). David said that they would send some money with the invites and posters, to cover expenses for you. What they would like you to do (and they will phone you when they send the stuff) is to take it all to the Punchinello Gallery, but to keep out some posters and invites to be sent to special people ... me, Joc, Helen Lucas, and also the people that Jocelyn will draw up a list of (gosh, this sentence seems a bit ungrammatical). I phoned Joc two days ago and she'll get the list to Dmitry. Also phoned Helen Lucas and she, too, will do what she can. I gather that what they would appreciate much Dmitry doing is to pick up the posters and invites at the airport, take most of them to the gallery, and distribute a few with Joc's list in mind. Soña probably doesn't stand the chance of a snowflake in hell of selling any of the pics, but still, it is a foot in the door, so to speak. David was quite apologetic about asking for help from you guys, Joc, me, etc, but I said ... 'Forget it ... we will all be glad to try.' Anyway, Dmitry, they'll phone you when they send the posters and invites, probably mid-Feb. Gosh, how much they do appreciate your offer of help.

They are going to bring Soña's paintings up with them on the plane ... about 16 paintings. Joc is going to find out about any possible Customs difficulties. Adele, the Loons[3] may prove to be VERY HELPFUL. David said that he was going to see Reva and Leonard Brooks[4] in a couple of days ... well, both of them must know about bringing up photographs and paintings for shows in Toronto. He will have to be in Mex City for the opening of his show on March 6 but won't have to stay more than a week. He hopes to be able to arrange for his show to be put on in Toronto ... that remains to be seen. Believe it or not, he has *fifty-five photographs* for his show. That's a lot. He's working like a son of a gun, to get them printed and mounted. He sounded great! The adrenalin is pouring into the blood-stream, I guess! His show will be in the North-American Cultural Institute Gallery in Mex City, and will be there for some 3 weeks.

I'll give you their phone number ... San Miguel de Allende – 2 – 09 – 79 (They are 2 hours *earlier*) (phone in the name of Soña Holman).

A time of excitement! We pray a lot.

The B.C. trip went absolutely splendidly![5] Of course, I was nervous, because it really meant so much, and Hubert is so old and so frail and we all just prayed everything would be all right, and it was. I arrived on Wed eve, Feb 1, and Gordon Elliott met me at the airport and we had dinner. [...] Next day, Thursday, a woman from the book page of the Vancouver Sun came to my hotel room and interviewed me,[6] and then I went out to SFU and did a reading, had lunch with a few members of the Eng Dept at what they call the 'University Club.'..Jack Diamond, the previous Chancellor, funded it, and I think it is a bit amusing ... it is really the Faculty Club; it's open to everyone but students couldn't afford to join it. After that, I had a two hour session with some graduate students and some members of the Eng faculty. Afterwards, Sandra Djwa (sp?)[7] drove me back to the hotel, and that evening I had dinner with Rob and Peg Laurence, and Robin, my be-loved niece was there, and also Anne Laurence, with her new husband David, who is ... gasp ... a stockbroker ... I know John, Karen and Robin so well but actually had never met Anne before. She's a honey. Of course, everyone expected me to be anti-David on account of his being a stock-broker but I wasn't. Rob, of course, is just as right-wing as ever, and at dinner, Robin kept taking exception to Rob's statements, and rightly so ... I was very diplomatic and a bit quiet. They are good people, in many ways – our views just do not coincide. Rob was so pleased to learn that I hated Trudeau ... not so pleased to learn that I vote NDP.

Friday was THE DAY. I was picked up at my hotel by the Chancellor, Paul Coté, and his wife. We went to Horseshoe Bay to get the ferry to Gibson's Landing. We met up with the other people from SFU ... the President Bill Saywell, the V-Pres Academic, the Registrar, and the terrific lady, Donna Laws, who is the Director of Ceremonies and with whom I had instant rapport because she is just as much a worrier as I am. We had hardly got on the ferry when Paul Coté said ... 'This looks like the Queen of the fleet ... can this be the ferry to Gibson's Landing, and are we on the right ferry?' Imagine me. I shot out of my seat and began running around in little circles, yelling 'Who can we ask? We

gotta find out IMMEDIATELY!' It turned out we were on the right ferry.
But ... about 20 minutes out of Horseshoe Bay, there came an announcement over the loud-speaker ... 'The ferry has not picked up the bus. We
are returning to Horseshoe Bay.' OH WOE! Donna Laws, who had organized the whole thing, nearly had a heart attack and so did I. There
went the carefully planned schedule. We were to have lunch at a little
sea-side restaurant before proceeding to Hubert Evans' and the ceremony at 2:30 p.m. Donna, with masterful control, phoned ship-to-shore
to the restaurant and cancelled the soup and the dessert. We did
manage lunch; we did get to the Evans' house at the right time. And
from then on, it was wonderful.

I met Hubert, who had been resting most of the day, before the
ceremony began. He wanted that. He is a frail old man with a shock of
white hair, nearly 92 years old. It was very moving for me, and for him,
also, to meet at long last, having corresponded for about 9 years and
talked on the phone. My God, what a hero he is. Nearly blind, but
thank heavens his hearing is okay and his mind is as sharp as a tack
and very wise. The ceremony was moving ... it went exactly by the way
SFU presents honorary degrees. The academic party was in full regalia.
The livingroom was small, and apart from the SFU party, there were
only a few of Hubert's family ... his son and two daughters ... and a few
old friends. It was very moving. The President, Wm Saywell, read the
citation that I had written, and as part of the ceremony, I presented
Hubert with a cassette tape of myself reading it. When the citation was
being read by Bill Saywell, Hubert's eyes were filled with tears, and
looking at him, so were mine, to tell you the truth. I had a chance to
talk with him after the ceremony, and he talked about ... wait for it! ...
the way writers are being screwed by publishers and the percentages on
paperbacks! At one point, he said to me, 'Do you notice that I'm
wearing my gold wedding ring?' I said, yes, I'd noticed. He told me that
he has arthritis and cannot wear the wedding band all the time, but he
said, 'I wanted to wear it today ... I wanted her to be here with us.'
Anna, his wife, died in 1960. They were married for 40 years. I was
sitting beside him, after the ceremony, and he was holding the cassette
of my reading of the citation, and the leather case containing the
honorary degree and the fancily inscribed citation. I said to him, 'Is it
awkward for you to be holding those things, Hubert? Would you like
me to put them up on the piano?' He replied, very gently, 'No, I think
I'll just hold onto them for awhile.'

It was one of the most moving days of my entire life.

Howie White, Hubert's publisher,[8] was of course there, and I talked with him later. I gave him Dmitry's greetings. Howie then extended an open invitation to the Stone family to visit him and his family at any time. He spoke so warmly about Dmitry and about the work Dmitry is doing in terms of BC history. The guy is a good publisher ... and he is very very interested in Dmitry's book.[9]

Back to the hotel, myself exhausted and not wanting to do anything that evening except order up dinner from Room Service because I had to get up at 5 a.m. the next day, as I was being picked up at 7 a.m. to get my flight back to T.O. Only when I got into my hotel room did I realize what had happened ... the Van Sun had printed an article on me that morning, saying, 'from her hotel room in the Sylvia Hotel, Margaret Laurence said ...' etc. Everyone who knew me and many who didn't, in Vancouver, knew where I was. The phone rang incessantly for two hours. Most were old friends, including oh gulp Mona's mother ('Lila,' I said, 'I was just intending to phone you!'). But one call was very wonderful and strange ... from an old lady who said 'I'm a distant relative of yours ...' turned out she was the daughter of my grand-mother Weymss' half-brother George ... she was a Margaret Harrison as was my grandmother.

Next morn I got up at 5 a.m. Room service in the Sylvia doesn't start until 7:30 a.m. but I was smart. I'd ordered dinner the night before and had kept the coffee and warmed it up the next morning ... SFU had got me a suite in the hotel, with a kitchen. Not only a view over English Bay, which was what *they* were thinking of, but a suite with a fridge and a stove.

At the Van airport, at about 8 a.m., I picked up a Globe & Mail, and there was the article Bill French had done on me.[10] Actually, I think it is a good article and I am pleased and grateful. I scrunched down behind my who-dun-it on the plane, but to no avail. I was even wearing the same clothes as in the pic in the Globe. It turned out that a number of people in my immediate vicinity in the plane, and also some of the stewardesses, had also seen the Globe, so I found myself bizarrely autographing copies of French's article! Actually, I didn't mind – I was quite touched by the fact that all of the people who asked for my auto-graph were quite hesitant.

So – back home. Yesterday I wrote 32 letters. I am now caught up, for at least a day or so. I am resolved not to answer them all any more. We will see how that goes.

Adele, I sent you the stuff re: the Women's Calendar ... I hope it's okay. If not, let me know. Can you guys phone me, briefly, please, to let me know you've received this?

Much much love to all,

Margaret

CITATION – FOR HUBERT EVANS – SIMON FRASER UNIVERSITY – FEB 3/84 – ROBERTS CREEK, B.C:

HUBERT EVANS is known to Canadian writers as 'the elder of the tribe,' a tribute both to the man and to his work, carried out over a great many years, sometimes under conditions of adversity such as his near-blindness. Milton's poem, *On His Blindness*, spoke of 'that one talent which is death to hide.' Hubert Evans, by will and by faith, has not hidden that talent but has continued to develop it. Some of his best work has been done in his later years. He has grown in wisdom, tough-mindedness, compassion and the saving grace of humour. Born in Ontario in 1892, he is nonetheless a truly British Columbia person. As a young man, he and his wife Anna Winter settled in Roberts Creek. They later lived in northern B.C. for a time, and out of the experience came the novel, MIST ON THE RIVER, 1954, now rightly regarded as a Canadian classic. His first novel, THE NEW FRONT LINE, 1927, came out of his World War One experiences. He has written three novels, books for young people, a biography, many plays, serials and short stories, and three books of poetry. He has also been a union organizer, commercial fisherman, prospector and salmon hatchery superintendent. Writing, however, has always been both his trade and his true vocation. His autobiographical novel, O TIME IN YOUR FLIGHT, 1979, is unique in our literature, in its re-creation of a past era seen through the eyes of a nine-year-old boy in 1899, the year the century turned. In his 80's, Hubert Evans began to write poetry, and he has now given us three books of poems filled with his love of the west coast and its people. He has been a long-time and honourable writer, a partner in a long and loving marriage with his wife Anna, who died in 1960, a father, a grandfather, a great-grandfather, a builder of boats and of his own home in Roberts Creek. In a profound sense, he has been a builder all his life, a builder *for* life. He has called himself 'The Old Journeyman.' The name expresses his view of his writing as his trade, and his sense of journeying, not as an observer only but as a deeply committed participant in our journey here on earth. 'Journeyman' also means 'a qualified artisan who works for another.' Hubert Evans is a Quaker, and his work has been illuminated by his faith, a fighting faith that struggles for social justice, a meditative faith that mourns suffering even as it jubilates life, a faith that recognizes laughter as a gift of God. He has worked for himself and his need to communicate, as all serious writers do, but in so doing he has worked for 'another' – for his beloved family, for the people of his land, and for the holy spirit that has moved him and given him grace.

Mr. Chancellor, I present to you HUBERT REGINALD EVANS for the degree of Doctor of Laws, Honoris Causa.

(Citation written by Margaret Laurence)

1 Winnipeg's Contemporary Dancers had presented an adaptation at the Warehouse Theatre on 14–17 September 1983. Al Bleichert, production director for CKND Television in Winnipeg had interviewed Laurence on 7 December 1983. The interview and production were televised.
2 John Cushman (1927–84) of JCA Literary Agency had worked for Willis Wing. In the spring of 1966, he established his own agency and Laurence became one of his first clients.
3 The Loons was the name of a small, unofficial Toronto club of writers, artists, and members of the arts community.
4 Leonard Brooks (b. 1911), the artist, and his photographer wife Reva Brooks (b. 1913) were residents of San Miguel de Allende, where David Laurence was living.
5 Laurence had travelled to Vancouver because an honorary degree was to be presented by Simon Fraser University to the elderly Canadian writer Hubert Evans. Evans (1892–1986) had recently published his autobiographical novel *O Time in Your Flight* (1979).
6 Leslie Peterson, 'Laurence to Honor Her Hero,' *Vancouver Sun*, 3 February 1984, C1
7 A professor of English and Canadian literature at Simon Fraser University
8 Howard White (b. 1945) was president and publisher of Harbour Publishing, which he had established in 1974.
9 The book was apparently never published.
10 'Margaret Laurence: These Days Peace Is One of Her Top Priorities,' *Globe and Mail*, 4 February 1984, E1
11 Wiseman edited *The Canadian Women Writers Engagement Calendar* for 1985, which included an entry on Laurence.

[324 Rushton Road]
24 February 1984

Dear Margaret,

I have just got off the phone. They called from the airport that Sonja's two parcels have arrived. Unfortunately, the customs is closed and so we won't be able to pick them up till Monday morning. But at least they are here. Sonja phoned twice today, the second time when she had traced their route. Apparently they were coming on one of the Mexican airlines, which has a once weekly direct flight to Toronto. They had been transferred from the other airline to this one and were waiting for the weekly flight. Shortly, I will call the number Sonja left and leave a message for her that all is well. The gallery also called, and tomorrow sometime I'll pop in and tell them (unless I can find the phone no.,) that they'll get the posters, etc ... on Monday. I'll be speaking to you on the phone so by the time you get this it will be old news; nevertheless I feel like telling you right now.

I am enclosing a copy of *The Sacrifice*; – funny how schooling sticks. We were taught to underline book titles or print them in block letters and here I dutifully backspace and give the book its honorific gesture (I suppose that's what it could be called). Anyway, it's for Ren as you requested. I am so pleased and flattered that she really likes (here we go again) *Crackpot*. I hope she will like this one too. As you know, positive feedback is so welcome, and especially from someone so bright, that it should be so positive, is very heartening; – particularly heartening is the fact that it speaks to someone of a younger generation, also. I can even take all that hyperbole; believing it isn't necessary. It's the response that counts, not the place of the book on a scale. It makes it possible to briefly shuck off the ever present doubts. Thank Ren for me.

It's good to know you're over the first hurdle, and that your Dr. is being supportive. He's perfectly right; as long as there's no pathology, it's great that you've lost weight. I know that part of the reason I don't diet is that when I begin to lose weight I begin to panic about cancer. Talk about the double bind. It will be a relief when your x-ray is over with. I'm keeping my fingers (if you'll excuse the expression) crossed all will be well. I hope that you continue to fight the tobacco war even though all is well. It's important.

Was ever anyone so disorganized? I can't seem to pull myself together until the day is almost gone. The reading chore dismays me; I've taken another couple of days off, but simply have to get back to it.

Problem is, ironically, it is so guilt inducing. I always associated reading with pleasure and leisure. Now things are so turned around that I don't look forward to it with pleasure, and when I'm doing it I don't feel as though I'm working, because after all it's only reading, and at the same time it's the most unrewarding chore much of the time, that interferes with both pleasure and leisure. I suppose it's related to HAVING to do something, with no choices all the way down the line. Well, there will be one or two pleasant experiences by the time I'm through. Better go now. Much love. Cheers!

Adele

[8 Regent Street
Lakefield, Ontario]
6 March 1984

Dear Adele:

Thanks a million for your letter and for sending THE SACRIFICE (yep ... either caps or underlined!) for Ren. I know she'll write to you when she gets it. I'll be seeing her this weekend, as we plan to drive to Port Hope to see a friend there. I know what you mean about feedback amid the present doubts, but let's try not to doubt ... Corragio, Avanti! Look who's talking! You know, I felt really put down by that damn woman's letter to the Globe, implying that a writer was worthless unless they published something every year. There were some letters of rebuttal, incidentally. There is a dear man (I don't know him, but he writes letters regularly to the Globe and I usually agree with his views) called Sheldon Goldfarb, of Winnipeg, who wrote and said, in effect, obviously Shakespeare isn't worth much as a playwright; the lazy slob hasn't published a word in 400 years!

If there are a lot of mistakes in typing, it is because I now have arthritis in my right hand and one finger is bent, damn it, so typing is a bit painful. Am seriously thinking of an electric typewriter. NOT a word processor! I phoned the doc yesterday ... blood sugar is normal, to my surprise, considering small amounts of food, because of teeth, but then my doc said that in the last 10 years it has been found that people can get along, with potentially or actually high blood sugar, on many fewer calories then was previously believed. I have to phone today to see what results of blood tests for thyroid are. Am sticking to 1 pkg a day cigs, the ultra light ones, 9 times less tar and 6 times less nicotine. Next phase will be more difficult. Budge says she did it by not smoking in the morning, then not in the aft, then – gulp ... not in the eve.

Adele, what I am about to reveal is not HIGHLY confidential, but sort of confidential. I have done two outrageously angry things and I am outrageously happy about them! Guilt may descend later. It began yesterday afternoon. I was putting the finishing touches (ahem) to a poem I have written for Jocelyn, called *Hi! It's me*. (She always says that when she phones me, and I find it so touching). I am taking it to her tomorrow when I go to T.O. (Unless there is another blizzard, God forbid), along with a little package of things including a 'Surprise Gift Certificate' ... for an old Victorian vase from Elmcot that she's always loved and which she will have to collect some time as I cannot take it on the bus, but it is a symbolic thing for her new abode. Anyway, happily was I doing this, plus jotting down some ideas for songs (?) and stuff, and thinking that I want to get back to the memoirs which I dropped several years ago, having got to Hiroshima in 1945 and being struck silent. I also was feeling ENORMOUS GUILT because there were about three dozen unanswered letters on my desk, plus the page proofs of a novel by Geoffrey Ursell, to be published by Macmillan's, which Doug Gibson[1] had sent me in hopes of my giving a Tender Message for the jacket. I had decided I just couldn't cope right now with yet another T.M., plus the fact that Geoff (whom I know slightly and whose songs I really like) has written a Tall Tale novel called PERDUE OR HOW THE WEST WAS LOST, a la Kroetsch, in fact very a la Kroetsch.

Anyway, the phone rang and it was Jocelyn. She said that someone from Macmillan's had phoned her and wanted her to find out whether or not I was going to do a T.M. for Ursell's novel. Adele, Joc was perfectly calm and not annoyed at all. She does that kind of thing all the time, she said, and not only re: me but other writers. I, however, was furiously angry at Macmillan's. She said she'd phone and tell them I couldn't do a T.M. I was very grateful to her. Afterwards, I thought about it and the more I pondered, the angrier I became. She may get requests to contact other writers and no doubt does, but more re: me than anyone else because the goddamn sods know she is my daughter, and how bloody dare they!!

Then I thought ... here I am, happily writing, and yet feeling guilty because of unanswered mail, virtually all of which was requests for this and that ... go here, go there, read a manuscript, give a talk, meet with students, bla bla bla. And none of them ever think that I might have my own work to do, or that I have a personal life and might wish to pursue that, or might have been worried about something, as I was, as you know, re: weight loss. No, no. I am expected to be at their beck and call, and if I don't respond quickly enough, some of them feel they have the right to intrude into my daughter's life.

Something snapped.

Calmly, I went upstairs and collected all the unanswered mail and all the manuscripts sent to me ... poems, short stories, etc, which I had not yet read. With perfect icy chillness, I proceeded downstairs and put the whole works in a garbage bag. As it was Monday, it was the day for putting out the garbage. I had already put mine out. I added this bag to the others. I then sat down at my trusty typewriter and wrote Doug Gibson at Macmillan's a scathing letter (that's the second angry thing I did), in which I said, among other equally awful things, 'How dare your firm intrude into my daughter's life with a business matter concerning me!' and 'What am I supposed to be, some kind of unpaid civil servant?' and 'To try to get at me through my daughter, whose professional life is *hers*, just as mine is my own, seems to me to be reprehensible.' (I did make clear, incidentally, that Jocelyn had been quite calm and not angry ... the anger was mine). I went on in this fashion for a bit, ending by saying 'I find it difficult to comprehend how anyone could be so goddamn stupid, thoughtless, discourteous and dim-witted as to do such a thing.' It wasn't Doug who phoned Joc, but it must have been with his cognizance. I do not blow my stack frequently, but when I do, I do it properly, or should I say improperly.[2]

I sent the letter this morning, Special Delivery. I hope Joc won't think it was ill-advised. Well, no, it's not up to her – it is my own business matter and anyway she knows how mad I was and am. Gosh, as I get older I think I get more bad-tempered; maybe, however, it is that I have less to lose by saying what I think. And I did make it clear that it was only myself, not Joc, who was upset by what I regard as an unconscionable intrusion on her life and work. I told Gibson that if my daughter had been a brain surgeon, the question would never have arisen ... and just because she is an editor is no reason to impose on her in that way, re: me.

As for the unanswered and now thrown-out mail ... I woke this morn at 7 a.m. and heard the garbage truck. For one moment I wondered if I should dash out in my nightie and say, 'Garbageman, spare that green bag!' Then I thought ... WHAT IS ALL THIS SHIT? WHY AM I SPENDING MY LIFE DOING ALL THIS DUMB STUFF? I don't blame the people who constantly request me to do things, to give them something. But there is a limit to my ability and it has now been reached. I got up this morning, posted the letter to Doug Gibson, did my shopping and felt light-hearted and happy.

(LATER ... 2 p.m.) I have just talked on the phone to Jocelyn, who phoned me a short while ago. I told her all this, natch. At first she was regretful that I had written to Gibson, because she said he wouldn't believe me that the anger was mine, not hers. But I said I really had made it clear and if he didn't believe me, what can one do except say what one knows to be true and expect to be believed. After a bit, Joc said she could see that I absolutely had to make my anger known to Gibson and also, when I told her some of the things I had said to him, she could see that it was my own unique (!) outrage that was being expressed. The Good News is ... I told her about throwing out the unanswered letters. None of them, naturally, were things I felt strongly about ... I just dreaded all that lot. Joc said ... oh joy ... 'I'm proud of you! It's the best thing you've done for years!' I told her, which of course she already knew, that I would continue to do what I can for younger writers (ironically, it was over that question that she phoned today, but a whole different ballgame ... something I really do want to support and help if I can).

I've written a few things recently and will send you a copy of my new poem for her, if she agrees, which of course she will, but I want her to see it first. I wrote and now have re-written a song for the Bag Ladies, incidentally, and have a tune ... but I'm so musically ignorant that I'm afraid all my tunes are sort of variations on the same one! My mum was right when she wanted me to take piano and then violin lessons ... is it possible that someone who took music lessons until Grade 9 and actually played violin in the Neepawa Collegiate 'orchestra,' cannot now read one note of music and haven't been able to for many years?!

I am so glad that Joc approves of my throwing out the mail!!!!!!!!!! Tra-la-la!

The young man's[3] show begins in Mexico City today. We are thinking of him. Joc said she had phoned you re : her friend who has a large Cadillac (is a Caddy anything except large?) and who might be willing to pick up D and S at the airport on the 12th, with the paintings and all. It turns out the friend is Carsten Stroud, who wrote a book on the police force, called THE BLUE WALL (caps), about a year ago, and I read two excerpts, one in *Toronto Life* and the other in *Saturday Night* (books get capital letters; magazines get underlined). I found the pieces very very interesting indeed. Joc says she has become quite good friends with Carsten and his wife and kids. Good. I never knew anyone who owned a Cadillac, but what the heck.

Adele, I think I really do have to throw out the mail. There are so many things I want to do, and I just cannot continue to spend my life running a business office. I'll answer the letters that pertain to income, and the ones I really want to do for younger writers, and that is IT.

See you all soon. God bless you all for all your incredible help to the kids.

Much love,

Margaret

P.S. What good news about J.J.! I am finding it more natural now to call him *Jacques*.[4]
P.S. Ken Adachi[5] just phoned. Ernest Buckler died today. He was about 75. '*The Mountain and the Valley*' is one of our best novels.[6] I corresponded with him for some years. A lonely, lonely person. I admired and loved him.

1 Douglas M. Gibson (b. 1943), publisher at Macmillan of Canada
2 Always the gentleman, Gibson replied with an apologetic note explaining why he had called Jocelyn.
3 David Laurence
4 Wiseman's nephew
5 Ken Adachi (1928–89) was literary editor of the *Toronto Star*.
6 Ernest Buckler's (1908–84) *The Mountain and the Valley* was published in 1952.

[8 Regent Street]
22 March 1984

A TALE OF TYPEWRITERS[1]

Once upon a time, long ago in 1940, there was a prairie flower named Peggy Wemyss. She was 14 years old and she had just acquired two things – her first boyfriend and a knowledge of touch-typing at the Neepawa Collegiate Institute. The first proved not to be of lasting value in her young life. The second proved to be one of the smartest things she ever did. Why? Because she was a writer. No one else, except maybe her mum and Miss Mildred Musgrove, English teacher, knew that young Peg was a writer, but she herself, knowing this interesting fact, thought it prudent to learn how to type. Which she did, take Typing in Grades 9 & 10 as an extra subject, from the aforementioned Miss M.M. Her first typewriter, a small Remington portable, was obtained for her by her dear Aunt Ruby, second-hand, in the city of Regina. It cost $14 and in those far-off days, fourteen bucks wasn't peanuts. Peggy saved half from her Saturday afternoon job at Leckie's Ladies' Wear, and her mum put up the other half. The aspiring kid named the typewriter Victoria, which, as she later liked to think, had more to do with her aspirations than with a starchy monarch of the same name.

The years passed, as they are wont to do. Since that long ago time, she has had, she estimates, five typewriters. All but one have had names. To her eternal shame, Margaret (as she is now called, resuming her true name upon publication of her first book) cannot remember all their names. She recalls, however, the faithful Felicity, upon whose hard-worked keyboard most of M's books were typed ... the final version in triplicate ... what a horrible job that was! She also recalls Monica, the one before the last, because the make of the typewriter was Monica Olympia. The last one, alas, was (in parlance of yore) kind of like a horse unbroken and unruly ... M.L. never did get on so swell with that beast, which kept breaking down and doing other obnoxious things such as demanding a touch that was heavier by far even than Margaret's considerably heavy touch on the keys.

Now, Margaret always considered herself a progressive thinker ... small 'l' liberal, a social democrat, you name it. Underneath all this, however, in strictly personal/business ways, lurked a – oh woe – conservative heart. She resisted CHANGE in some areas. She continued with manual typewriters until that species was damn near extinct.

... see p. 2 for next thrilling episode.

Then, nearly 44 years after learning how to type, M.L. took the plunge. Unbelievable! She bought an electric typewriter at the very moment in history when these, too, looked to be doomed to extinction and everyone was going in for Word Processors. She made this incredible leap into the age of High Tech for 2 reasons ... (a) she figured that in a few years no parts or repairs for manual typewriters would be available; (b) she developed arthritis in her hands and thought – correctly – that if she could develop a light touch, l (that extra l will be explained soon), typing would not be such a physical strain on her hands and wrists as it had become. She thought she would take weeks if not months to get used to the new typewriter.

NO! Within four days, she could work it almost without flaw.!!!! Some of the things were in different places on the keyboard. The light touch did not prove a problem, but lthe fact that there was no space bar (an antiquated term referring to manual typewriters, not to the place where the beer is in a space ship) was a mite tricky, as the left hand, after 44 years of typing, automatically reached up to move the lcarriage and space. On her new electric model, simplest on the market, there is a dinky little button marked RETURN, which one touches with the pinky finger. After several days, Margaret thought 'Hey, this is neat! No more need to swing up the old left arm ... a simple touch with the tiny finger does it.' She found she could do super things ...

A little extra pressure on some keys produces a continuous line of:
_____ or -------------------------------------- whee!
or xxxxxxxxxxxxxxxxxxxxxxxxxx whee!
The asterisk turned out to look like a daisy ✳✳✳✳✳✳✳✳✳✳✳✳✳✳
The ribbon is the cartridge type, and can be slid in and out and replaced with a flick ... no problem. No more cursing and swearing while getting inky fingers changing a ribbon.

The correction cartridge, white, can be slipped in and errors whited out in no time at all! Wow!! Terrific! (There still is, however, no way of correcting carbon copies, but probably one is meant to do only one copy and get xeroxes, which is swell if you work in an office with a xerox machine but not too swell if you have to march down to Millages Plumbing & Heating to get same) so carbons, as now, will continue to have errors x-d out, rather than classily corrected.

M.L.'s dear friend Adele, also a prairie flower and a writer (although like M not necessarily in that order) had gone electric some time ago, with notable success. She had told M that the only thing she didn't like about the electric typewriter was that it buzzed while she was not typing and was trying to think and dream up marvellous things. M did not find this too much of a problem. Her model has a subdued buzz but also a button marked OFF, that can switch the little charmer off without having to unplug it. Do I sound naive and as though I'm not great at understanding THE MACHINE PER SE WHATEVER THE MACHINE MAY BE? You're right. But I can work this tripewriter and am even getting (after only 4 days) so that I can type while looking out the window as I am doing now at the swirling flakes of YET ANOTHER snowstorm oh hell. I still have to glance down from time to time because some of the punctuation isn't where I expect it to be, but shoot, that's nothing.

As in any garden of roses, there is a THORN. An ironic thorn.

M.L. got this electric job, as you will recall, partly because of her arthritis. The touch, light, is really a help to the hands and wrists and I find I can do it really without any trouble because the fingers and wrists really don't want to pound the keys any longer. But ... ah irony! The third finger of my right hand is now slightly crooked, bent down and won't straighten up. I found it puzzling why I was striking the letter 'l' so often without meaning to. The answer is so obvious I am amazed I didn't see it right away. The bent finger is positioned at starting point, so to speak, over the letter 'l.' When the finger moves either up or down to hit other keys, it tends to brush the 'l,' thus causing the damn letter to print. However, now that I know this, I think I can overcome it. It is just that that finger is at a different angle from all my other fingers, but I'm doing better today than yesterday, so we may yet overcome this slight problem. Ironic though ... I buy the typewriter because of arthritis, and arthritis makes it difficult to type accurately.

Well, what a boring account. But this event is important in my fairly staid life. I have, however, named this lady. She has the most sensational name of all my typewriters.

PEARL CAVEWOMAN

... see page 4 for explanation

I thought of calling her something really CONTEMPORARY. I abandoned the idea instantly. She must be called something relevant to the fact that I recognize that she and I are going to get on well ... I can feel the rapport already. I also felt that the name should reflect a sense of the past and what could be more past than CAVEWOMAN, I ask you. And yes, Adele, I was recalling with some amusement Mary Warshaw's friend who changed her name, legally, her surname, to Riverwoman and I thought 'Oh shucks, what an embarrassment to her son!' But the name PEARL CAVEWOMAN is a different version of my own name, you see! Wow! How about that? *Margaret* means 'a pearl' and my family name 'Wemyss,' as I was told when a child, according to my paternal grandfather John Wemyss, means 'a cave dweller,' because it refers to the Picts from whom he always (apparently) said we were descended, and indeed, in my trusty book that I've referred to so often throughout the years, THE CLANS AND TARTANS OF SCOTLAND, the word in Gaelic, 'weem' means 'a Pictish earth house.'..they did live in caves and in quite complex earth dwellings dug into hillsides ... that was in the time of Roman Britain. So PEARL CAVEWOMAN is this one's name ... the latter word a laugh at High Tech, too, of course. The Pict connection is also a tribute to Chaika.[2]

As you can all see, I have been having enormous fun learning how to use this machine and if it were not for the fact that I am doing 2 carbons I would demonstrate how the correction cassette does indeed make correction of errors easy and simple.

This letter is for Jocelyn, for David and Sóna, and for Adele, Dmitry and Tamara.

The manual, which I have been studying as though it were Holy Writ, says a bunch of stuff about Safe Operation of this machine, making it sound like a potentially lethal weapon. Don't get it wet! Make sure it is plugged into a 3 point plug, etc. Well, heck, it would be the same for any electrical thing. I got my electrician, Karl Maskos, to come on Tuesday and instal 3-point plugs in my study.

Love to all from the person who now has a SOUND SYSTEM (not a record player) and an ELECTRIC TYPEWRITER WITH A NAME AND PERSONALITY.

Better late than never

M

1 This essay was sent by Laurence to Wiseman.
2 Adele Wiseman's mother, Chaika, on hearing that Wemyss was a name that went back to the ancient Picts, had been delighted to note that, like the Jews, Margaret's family had also been 'picked.' The anecdote was always treasured by Laurence and Wiseman.

[8 Regent Street]
18 April 1984

Dear Adele:

I'm writing this shortly after you all left this evening. I'm sorry you felt so terribly angry at me for suggesting that not all critics and reviewers might be all bad. I enclose a copy of what I had written for the occasion – obviously, it would be totally unsuitable for what purports to be a fun evening but is actually planned as a total attack upon the critics and reviewers and I don't see too much real fun in that, to speak the truth. I have phoned Helen Weinzweig[1] to say I will not be able to be there. I did send some money and I do wish you all well.

I am sending a copy of all this to Jocelyn; I hope you don't mind.

Love,

M

P.S.   Please try not to stay angry ... I just can't bear it all that much. But I cannot back down from my position ... I believe it and I hold to it ...

THE CRITIC ON THE HEARTH

***for The Second Hundred Party – 28 April 1984[2]
******* Margaret Laurence

THE CRITIC ON THE HEARTH

Like all writers, I have suffered from time to time from the slings and arrows of outrageous reviewers. Many are the tales I could tell, and indeed will, at the slightest encouragement. I was sent a publisher's reader's report on my first novel, THIS SIDE JORDAN, that said among other things 'I was only reasonably nauseated by this novel.' When that novel was published, a male reviewer in Canada wondered why there had to be in every female novel 'the obligatory and boring birth scene.' (Male masturbation was really acceptable in those times, but birth was *out*). Of my novel THE STONE ANGEL, a reviewer in England said 'This is the most telling argument for euthanasia that I have ever read,' which didn't exactly reflect my purpose. Of my novel THE FIRE-DWELLERS, published in 1969, a Toronto male reviewer said of Stacey ... 'dead at 39,' which seemed to me to be a poor reading of the novel. In the *Vancouver Sun*, a male reviewer said of the same novel, 'Our Vancouver housewives aren't like that.' The next day, in the same paper, a woman columnist said *'Oh yes they are!'* (Bless her!) When A JEST OF GOD was published in 1966, a reviewer in Toronto said that Rachel was no more interesting than anyone you might sit next to on a streetcar, and that wasn't very interesting. In a review of THE DIVINERS, 1974, a well known American woman novelist in the New York Times Book Review section said that Morag had grown up on the *bleak plains of southern Ontario*, and in damning the book, added that Morag had had an affair with a M E T I man, a term she apparently thought was the singular form of MÉTIS. My children's book, JASON'S QUEST, was described once by an authority on Canadian children's literature as 'probably the most disappointing book in all of Canadian children's literature.' She hated animal fantasies and assumed that kids also hated them, although since then I've had a lot of letters from kids saying quite the reverse.

So what? Some twenty years later, the reviewer who made that remark about Rachel was reminded of it because I mentioned it in a TV interview, and she wrote to me to say 'Did I really make that stupid remark all those years ago? I'm sorry.' I wrote back and said – don't worry; I did the same thing myself ... many years ago, when I was 21 and working for a newspaper in Winnipeg. I was writing a daily radio column, as well as covering the Labour beat and doing almost all the book reviews. I reviewed a radio play produced and acted in by a young woman called Helene Winston, and I panned the hell out of it, quite wrongly. To my astonishment, Helene Winston phoned me up and said in effect – how *dare* you do this about something you don't know anything about? I was speechless and shocked. But forever after, I wrote very careful reviews. And some thirty years later, when I met Helene Winston, I was able to say to her – fine actress and beloved person that she is – I'm sorry I did that, all those years ago, and you taught me something.

We are not infallible, as any of us who have written anything must know. I have to say I acknowledge the perceptions and help of many many reviewers and critics who have indeed read my books with care, attention, skill and love, and who have, whether in reviews in news-papers or in critical articles in academic journals, spoken about my work in ways that communicated what I was trying to do, what I was trying to say. I am grateful to those who have gotten some of my books onto high school and university courses and who have fought to keep them there, against the rednecks and non-readers who wanted to have my books assigned to perdition, without, of course, having read them properly or skilfully, or indeed without having read them at all. I owe a great debt of gratitude to the skilled readers among our reviewers and academic critics and it is my honour to acknowledge it now.

Reviewers and critics aren't always correct in their assessment of our work. They're not always wrong, either. In the long run, the work will speak for itself.

Yes, we disagree often – writers, publishers, booksellers, editors, critics, reviewers.

We have one thing in common, and I suggest that we should never forget it. We all care about writing, in all its multitudinous spoken and written forms. We care about the Word. In a world where a lot of people do not care about or value the Word, let us know that whatever our differences we are on the same side.

****

– Margaret Laurence
– Lakefield, Ontario, April 1984

1 Helen Weinzweig (b. 1915), short-story writer and novelist
2 To raise money for the Writers' Development Trust, a hundred writers had acted as hosts for the first Night of One Hundred Authors Dinner on 29 September 1982 in Toronto. Helen Weinzweig had not been included in the event and had decided to establish the 'Second Hundred Club' at a party she was organizing. Laurence's piece plays on the title of Charles Dickens's Christmas story 'The Cricket on the Hearth' (1845).

[324 Rushton Road]
18 June 1984

Dear Margaret,

I am so sorry about John Cushman.[1] It seems somehow such a dreadful way to go. I guess few ways aren't, but this almost random seeming aggregate of accidental factors ... Although I guess also that we can no longer count hospital carelessness and indifference as accidental. That has become a commonplace hazard. Anyway, an awful thing, and no way one can say anything but that one is sorry. And if you need us, we're here, D and I and Tamara too till Friday, when she leaves, with her troupe, for Montreal. Please don't hesitate to ask if you need us. You don't even have to ask, – just say, whistle, crook your finger, whatever. I didn't know him but feel as though I did somewhat, after all those years of hearing loving things about him. A loss.

I went out and ran off those poems.[2] I am so relieved at your positive reaction to them. I myself have a curious faith, – as one must always have, of course, – but other people's negative or equivocal reactions do niggle somewhat, till one gets them into perspective. In a way they're good, because they remind one that it is still the same world, after all, and when you've changed hats those who are used to the old are apt to find the new unbecoming. But ah those dear words of confirmation! Thank you! I'm enclosing the five I read you, plus the one I've just retyped for you, which I thought you'd appreciate, – and understand. I'm also enclosing the Broadfoot review.[3] On rereading it I find it somewhat repetitious. Had I given it one more go I would have polished it some, but I just wanted it out of the way, and it says essentially what I wanted it to say. I hope I have been even-handed. I said as many nice things as I could, but felt I couldn't pretend I didn't find it a sloppy, and in some ways boring, book. So, by and large I don't think it's a bad review. I certainly don't think, though, that I would want to review many others of that kind. Too much time wasted giving it more consideration and writing more carefully than I think matters. Well, never mind. It's done.

Excitement building re Tamara's trip. She and two other kids from CC[4] are out 'shopping' now, for last minute things. Your birthday gift has certainly come in handy. Yesterday a reporter and a photographer from The Star came to interview the company at the theatre. The kids were sitting in a circle. The photographer looked at them and pointed at Tamara. 'That one,' he said. So she got all dressed up and made herself up 'punk,' and he used three roles of film. So there will probably be a picture of her alone, as well as of some of the rest of the group, on the front page of the 'Life' section in the Saturday Star in a couple of weeks. (Ahem, ahem.) Ah, our kids, bless 'em and protect 'em, – somebody, somehow, always.

Will mail this when I go out next. Much love. See you soon.

Adele

1 Cushman had died on 17 June of cardiac failure after emergency surgery.
2 There are several Wiseman poems in the Laurence Papers, Accession 5, Box 2, File 78. A cluster of these is apparently dated 13 June 1984. The Wiseman Papers contain drafts of many poems written by Wiseman during this period.
3 Wiseman's review of Barry Broadfoot's *My Own Years* (1984), *Alumni Journal* [University of Manitoba] 45, 1 (Autumn 1984): 17–18
4 A feature article on the cross-Canada tour of the Children's Creations theatre group appeared in the *Toronto Star*, 30 June 1984, L1.

[8 Regent Street]
12 November [1986]

Dearest Adele:

Old friend, sister, colleague ... please forgive me for the fairly miserable trip I put on you last evening, talking about my memoirs. It is just that I fluctuate in my feelings towards the manuscript. Sometimes I *do* feel it should be published, with *much editing*, and sometimes I feel the hell with it ... it shouldn't be published. Mostly I feel that it *should* be, but also that I really should be able to do more editing, and more importantly, more adding of anecdotes, myself, and I just do not think I can. It certainly is not that I don't care about it (although sometimes I take false refuge in saying I don't), but rather, that the spirit is willing but the flesh is weak. I am so grateful to you for reading it, and I know, really, what needs to be done with it, in terms of editing and adding, but I don't think I can muster the necessary strength. If I can, I will, but right now I feel too sick to think about it in terms of writing more. I seem to want to keep on scribbling in my so-called Journal, however. This is because it is a help to me to set down what is happening NOW, both grim and wonderful ... grim physically; wonderful in terms of my dear ones, my kids, their mates, my amazing friends ... you and yours chief among them, I need hardly say. In due course, I think probably that my kids should read that Journal; you are the only other person that I would really like to read it, if someday you want to. This 'passage' (my situation now) is a humbling experience, like writing, I guess ... one realizes that some things cannot be done by an act of will. Naturally, we have always known this, but it comes home more clearly to me right now. I was able to get to the third draft of those memoirs; I don't feel like continuing. If I felt okay, I would look forward to about a year of re-writing, editing, adding ... it actually would be pleasurable. But I don't feel like entering the manuscript again. Bad luck, but who am I to complain, having been so fortunate in my life.

Much love to you all, as always,

Margaret

P.S. I will give back to Jocelyn the doll 'baby' that your mum gave her years ago, with your mum's hopes of Joc having a child, & embroidered in both pink & blue, 'so it wouldn't matter if she has a girl or a boy.' A soft toy meant for a little kid. I have looked after it, for Joc (& for your mum) all these years. It will be Chaika's wedding present to Jocelyn. Your mum would have approved – of that I am *sure*. Your mum said to me, 'Just to help the luck along a little.'
P.S.2. When I said you were the only other person I wanted to read my Journal, I meant *initially*. If you & Joc & Dave think some parts should be published at some time, that's okay with me. Or not published, as the case may be.
[P.S.] This is the first time I have typed anything in weeks! Am writing rather than phoning, for reasons that will be obvious to you. I've *always* done this, when I wanted very much to say something *clearly*, not 'bibble-babbling!' (your great phrase!)

Index

Achebe, Chinua 381
Adachi, Ken 398, 398n
Adam 351
Adamson, Leslie 303, 316
Agamemnon 172–3, 174n
Amis, Kingsley 95, 96, 96n; *That Uncertain Feeling* 95, 96n
Andrzejewski, Bogumil W. 23, 52, 53n, 62, 65, 82, 84, 161, 162n, 198, 199, 200n; *Somali Poetry* (with I.M. Lewis) 198, 199, 200n
Andrzejewski, Sheila 23, 52, 62, 198
Anne of Green Gables (Montgomery) 374
Appeldoorn, Beth 354n
Arden-Clarke, Sir Charles 77, 79n
Asante, Kojo 270, 271n
Asante, Nadine 23, 161, 162N, 167, 270, 271n, 288, 289n
Asante people 210n
Asanthene 208, 210n; Golden Stool 210n
Atlantic Monthly 72, 100, 103, 107, 111, 112
Atwood, Margaret 26, 327, 328n, 330, 338, 342, 381; *Survival* 327, 328n, 330
Austin American-Statesman 345, 346n

Baker, F. Sherman 158, 162n
Baron, Delores 23, 155, 156n, 161, 166, 186, 206, 252, 254, 305, 306, 309, 311, 328, 329
Baron, Joseph Alexander 23, 155, 156n, 161, 166, 186, 187, 206, 209, 223, 252, 254, 276, 305–6, 311, 328, 329; *King Dido* 311; *The Low Life* 156n, 166, 209; *Seeing Life* 156n; *Strip Jack Naked* 209
Baron, Nicholas 311, 329
BBC (British Broadcasting Corporation) 157, 158, 164, 165, 186; Hausa Section, African Service 158, 162n; Somali Service 165; Women's Hour 157; World of Books 164
Beat poets 107
Beatles, the 171
Bedouins 285n
Bellow, Saul 5, 195
Beowulf 280, 281n
Bergonzi, Bernardi 271n; ed. *Innovations* 271n
Berton, Pierre 331, 331n
Best, Marshall 100n, 259, 260n
Best Boy 364, 364n
Beta Sigma Phi Award 16, 18

Bevan, Allan Rees 232, 236n, 252
Bicycle Thief, The 36; Maggiorani,
    Lamberto 37
Birney, Earle 119, 120n, 133
Birney, Esther Bull 167
Bissell, Claude 230, 231n
Black, Ken 251
Black Chiffon 35
Bleichert, Al 386, 392n
Blixen, Karen Dinesen (pseud. Isak
    Dinesen) 138n; Shadows on the
    Grass 136, 138n
Blondal, Patricia Jenkins 121, 122,
    123n, 129, 130, 130n; A Candle to
    Light the Sun 121, 122, 123n, 129,
    130n; From Heaven with a Shout
    122, 123n
Board of Education, Peterborough,
    Ont. 349n, 352n; Kenner
    Collegiate and Vocational
    Institute 352n; Lakefield District
    Secondary School 349n; Textbook
    Review Committee 349n
Bolton, Frances 161, 163, 164
Bolton, Kay 163, 165n
Bolton, Tom 186, 206
Book of Common Prayer 219
Bookman 123
Books in Canada 348n, 381, 382, 382n
Boult, Douglas 367
Bowering, George 344, 346n
Bowsfield, Hartwell 153, 156n, 370,
    372n, 383
Branching Out 352, 354n
Bread Loaf Writers' School 224, 225,
    226n
British Council 157
Broadfoot, Barry 405–6, 406n; My
    Own Years 405–6, 406n
Brooks, Leonard 387, 392n

Brooks, Reva 387, 392n
Buchanan, Robert J. 351, 352n
Bucholzer, John 136–7, 138n; The
    Horn of Africa 136, 138n
Buckler, Ernest 216n, 393, 398n; The
    Mountain and the Valley 216n, 398,
    398n
Bull, Donald 167
Burgess, Anthony 325n; A Clockwork
    Orange 324, 325n
Burnett, Whit 79, 80, 81, 81n, 82
Burton, Sir Richard 69, 70n; First
    Footsteps in East Africa 69, 70n

Calder (publisher) 263
Callaghan, Barry 209, 210n, 342
Callwood, June 355, 357n
Cambridge University 100n
Cameron, Donald 232, 236n, 341,
    343n; Conversations with Canadian
    Novelists 341, 343n
Cameron, Ian 306, 307n, 329
Cameron, Sandy 306, 307n, 329
Campaign for Nuclear Disarmament
    152, 153n
Canada Council 16, 107, 111, 113n,
    114, 120, 144, 145n, 147, 148, 149,
    152, 173, 174, 189, 219, 228, 230,
    251, 317, 317n, 333, 335, 336
Canadian Labour Congress 207n
Canadian Literature 27n, 138n, 346n,
    355n
Canadian National Railway 40
Canadian Pacific Railway 40
Canadian Tribune 5, 10, 34, 37n
Canadian Universities Society 160;
    Literary Supper 160
Carey, Elaine 348n
Cartwright, Hugh Anson 383
Cary, Joyce 4, 108, 109n; The African

Witch 109n; *Aissa Saved* 109n; *An American Visitor* 109n; *Mr Johnson* 108, 109n
Catch 22 (Heller) 250
CBC (Canadian Broadcasting Corporation) 14, 21, 23, 79, 81n, 83, 85, 87, 89, 92, 93n, 111, 128, 153, 156n, 158, 162, 162n, 165n, 171, 179n, 181, 226n, 238n, 251n, 340, 346; *Anthology* 114n; *Making It* 340; *Prairie Talks* 162n
CCF (Co-operative Commonwealth Federation) 206, 207n
Cecil, C.D. 271n
Chatelaine 224, 226n, 231
Cherney, Erica 378, 379n
Children's Creations 406, 406n
Chinada: Memoirs of the Gang of Seven 130n
Chinese Writers' Association 26
Church, Richard 123
CKND Television 392n
Clark, John Pepper 287, 288n
Clarke Irwin 336n
Clerk, Rev. Archibald 248
Cleveland Plain Dealer 300, 301n
Clytemnestra 174n
Cochrane, Elspeth 226n
Cohen, Max Charles 74, 74n, 79
Cole, Alf 378–9
Cole, Desmond 223, 224n, 236, 270, 291, 303
Cole, Jean 378, 379
Collier, F.C. 90
Collins (publisher) 276
Compton, Neil 282
Concordia University 382, 386n
Contemporary Dancers 386–7, 392n
Conton, William 120n, 123n; *The African* 120n, 123n

Coté, Paul 388
Coulter, John 153, 155n; *Riel* 153, 155n
Count Dracula 364, 365, 366, 366n
Coward, Noel 126
Cowley, Malcolm 109, 110n; *Exile's Return* 110n
Cromie, Donald Cameron 133, 134n
Crossley-Holland, Kevin 280, 281n
Cushman, Jane 18
Cushman, John 5, 18, 387, 392n, 405, 406n

Daiches, David 96, 100n
Daily Telegraph 168, 168n
Daily Worker 37
Dalhousie University 232, 235, 236nn, 238, 239n, 252, 260
Daniels, Roy 218, 220n
Davies, Robertson 230, 231n
De Bruyn, Jan 106, 107, 109n
De Lampedusa, Giuseppe 123n; *The Leopard* 123n
Diamond, Jack 388
Dickens, Charles 403, 405n; *Bleak House* 253; 'The Cricket on the Hearth' 403, 405n
Dickson, Horatio Lovat 5, 18–19, 23, 160, 162n
Dinesen, Isak. *See* Blixen, Karen Dinesen
Distler, Arnold 239n, 253, 260
Distler, Jacques J. 238, 239n, 253, 398, 398n
Distler, Miriam Wiseman 8, 15, 23, 33, 34, 34n, 37, 51, 53, 58, 70, 71, 79, 174, 216, 229, 231, 238, 239n, 253, 260, 303, 373
Distler, Vivian Bliss 238, 239n, 253
Djwa, Sandra 388

Dobbs, Kildare 5, 15, 102n, 136, 138n; 'Outside Africa' 136, 138n
Donadio, Candida 239, 245, 250, 251, 259, 269, 273, 274, 276, 289, 291, 303, 309
Dorn, Harold 226n
Dostoyevsky, Feodor 47; *The Brothers Karamazov* 46
Doubleday (publisher) 239n
Doughty, Charles Montagu 285n; *Travels in Arabia Deserta* 284, 285n
D.S. Brewer Ltd. 281n
Duinker, Hilary 369
Duinker, Michiel 369, 372n
Duinker, Ren 369, 372n
Duncan, Chester 350, 352n; *Wanna Fight, Kid?* 350, 352n

Eagle Press 81n
Edgar, Luella 345, 346n
Edwards, Norma 378, 379n; *The Women of Margaret Laurence* 378, 379n
Eliot, T.S. (Thomas Stearns) 52, 53n
Elliott, Gordon 106n, 110, 126, 153–4, 388
Emma (Austen) 253
Engel, Marian 26, 352, 354n, 355, 357n, 373, 374nn, 385; *Lunatic Villas* 373, 374n
Esquire 195
Evans, Anna Winter 389, 391
Evans, Hubert Reginald 25, 388, 389, 390, 391–2, 392n; *Mist on the River* 391; *The New Front Line* 391; *O Time in Your Flight* 391, 392n
Eve 351
Expo '67 215, 216n, 217, 223, 224, 231

Faulkner, William 299
Feltham, Velma Simpson 7, 102, 104n
Ferns, Henry Stanley 311, 312n
Fiedler, Leslie 14, 195–6, 197n
Findley, Timothy 380, 382nn
Fingal 244n
Finlay, Carol 345, 346n
First Jewish Relief Unit 11
First Lady of Manawaka, The 379n
First World War 8, 391
Foley, Martha 81n
Forer, Marion 313, 327
Forer, Mort 313, 314, 327; *The Humback* 313n, 314
Forster, Donald Frederick 230, 231n
Fortnightly Club 369; Ladies' Night 369
Fraser, Blair 160, 162n
Freedman, Jim 34
French, William 300, 301n, 390, 392n
Frick, Alice 23, 163, 165n, 167, 169, 202, 226n, 324, 372n
Frick, David 369, 372n
Frick, John 369, 372n
Frick, Vi 369, 372n
Frye, Northrop 185, 187n, 352
Fulford, Robert 341, 343n

Gadd, Jane 346, 347n
Gardner, Isabella Stewart 225, 226n
Gelgoot, Arthur 385, 386n
Gerson, Phyllis 11, 40, 41, 42, 42n, 51, 84, 223, 231
Gerussi, Bruno 155n
Gibson, Douglas M. 395, 396, 397, 398nn
Gibson, Shirley 335, 336, 336n
Globe and Mail 300, 301n, 347n, 390, 392n, 394; *Magazine* 215n

GM Presents 155n
Goddard, John 352n
Godden, Rumer. *See* Haynes-Dixon, Margaret Rumer Godden
Godfrey, Dave 278, 279n, 303, 304n, 307n, 333; *Death Goes Better with Coca Cola* 279n
Goering, Hermann 47n, 351, 352n
Golden Bough, The (Frazer) 169
Goldfarb, Sheldon 394
Goldman, Alvin 53, 57n, 216, 216n, 217, 223, 226, 238
Gollancz, Victor 5, 16, 92, 93n, 96, 263
Good Housekeeping 159
Gottlieb, David 17, 141n, 224, 226n
Governor General's Award 4, 16, 213, 214, 215, 215n, 218, 220nn, 324, 325n
Graham, Angela 369
Graham, John 369
Gray, John Morgan 21, 102n, 128, 136, 143, 229, 230, 250, 259, 270, 289, 291, 296, 297, 302, 304, 305, 307–8
Great Depression 7, 8–9
Green, Hannah 224, 225, 226n, 239, 250; *The Dead of the House* 239n
Greene, Graham 82, 133, 378; *The Power and the Glory* 82
Grosskurth, Phyllis 214, 215n, 347, 348n; *John Addington Symons* 215n
Grove, Frederick Philip 383, 386n
Guardian 168, 168n, 271n
Guggenheim Fellowship 16, 108n

Hackney Juvenile Court 11
Hallstead, Robert Nathaniel 71, 84, 144

Hansberry, Lorraine 110n; *A Raisin in the Sun* 110, 100n
Harbour Publishing 390, 392n
Harper and Row 148, 265, 273, 276
Harrison, Margaret 390
Hasan, Mohammed 'Abdille 198–9, 200n
Haskell, Max 70n
Haynes-Dixon, Margaret Rumer Godden (pseud. Rumer Godden) 160, 162n
Hebrew University 196, 197n
Heinemann (publisher) 263
Heiress, The 35
Helwig, David 355n; ed. *The Human Elements* 355n
Hemingway, Ernest 126
Heorte Music 330n, 335
Hickman, Mona Spratt 306, 307n
Hiebert, Paul 221, 222n; *Sarah Binks* 221, 222n; *Willows Revisited* 221, 222n
Hiroshima 395
Hirsch, John 136, 138n
Hodgetts, John Edwin 112, 113n
Holiday 213n, 214
Holloway, David 168n
Holman, Soña 386, 387, 388, 393, 397, 402
Holocaust 4, 9, 195
Homer 174n; *The Iliad* 173, 174nn
Hood, Stuart 301n
Hope, Bob 180, 182n
Horwood, Harold 369, 372n
House of Anansi Press 279n, 303, 333n, 335, 336, 336nn, 338
Howard, Joseph Kinsey 156n; *Strange Empire* 154, 156n

I.L. Peretz School 9

International Journal of Women's Studies 382n

'The Irish Washerwoman' 377

Jacobson, Dan 123n; *Evidence of Love* 123n

James, Henry 35, 380; *Washington Square* 35

Jardine, Douglas J. 199, 200nn; *The Mad Mullah of Somaliland*, 199, 200nn; Hasan, Mohammed 'Abdille, 198–9, 200nn

JCA Literary Agency 392n

Jewish Public Library, Montreal 246

Jewish Social Work in Great Britain 38

Jensen, Christian 212, 213n

John of Patmos 307

Johnson, Samuel 243, 244n, 248; *Journey to the Western Isles* 243, 244n

Jones, James 195

Jones, Joseph 14

Jones, Judith 264, 264n, 330–1, 331n, 332, 336

Jude the Obscure (Hardy) 253

Kaballah 246, 248, 344

Kattan, Naim 317, 317n

Keats, John 375, 379n; 'Old Meg' 375, 379n

Kenyetta, Jomo 280, 281n

Killam, Douglas 381, 382n

King, Martin Luther 239, 240, 240n

Knopf, Alfred 5, 205, 205n

Knopf (publisher) 26, 145n, 162n, 164, 165, 167, 249N, 256, 263, 264, 264n, 265, 266, 266n, 334, 336, 368

Kramer, Victor 79

Kreisel, Henry 4; *The Rich Man* 4

Kroetsch, Robert 368, 369, 372n, 395

Kroitor, Roman 217, 218n, 226; Labyrinth 217, 218n, 226

Kubly, Herbert 109, 110n

Kubrick, Stanley 325n

Kulesza, Severyn R. 157, 162n; *Modern Riding* 157, 162n

Kushner, Sylvia 79, 84

Ladies' Home Journal 122, 159, 165n, 169, 292, 294n; Book Bonus 294n

Lakefield Leader 348

Lamming, George 144, 145n, 223, 287; *In the Castle of My Skin* 144

Lampert, Arlene 373, 374n

Lantz, Robert 251

Laurence, Anne 388

Laurence, David 15, 16, 20, 21, 22, 24, 30, 89, 90, 91n, 92, 93, 94, 96, 102, 102n, 103, 104, 108, 112, 113, 116, 117, 118, 123, 126, 134, 138, 140, 141, 144, 147, 148, 148n, 150, 151, 152, 157, 158, 161–2, 165, 166, 167, 169, 170, 171, 174, 181, 184, 186, 187, 189, 194, 197, 198, 200–1, 202, 205, 207, 221, 226, 227, 227n, 231, 232, 233, 234, 235, 238, 243, 244, 246, 248, 251, 254, 255, 256, 258, 260, 266, 274, 275, 276, 277, 278, 279, 280, 281, 283, 285, 288, 289n, 292, 293, 294, 310, 315, 317, 318, 322, 323, 324, 325, 328, 329, 332, 337, 338, 346, 355, 367, 371, 379, 380, 386, 387–8, 392n, 397, 398n, 402, 406, 407

Laurence, Elsie Fry 353, 355n

Laurence, Jack 4, 5, 10–11, 12, 14, 15, 16, 18, 19, 20–1, 22, 24, 33, 34n, 36, 37n, 38, 39, 40, 42, 43, 45, 46, 49, 50, 52, 53, 53n, 55, 56, 58, 60,

61, 62, 66, 67, 70, 71, 72, 73, 74,
75, 77, 78, 79, 81, 81n, 83, 85, 86,
87, 88, 89, 91, 94, 101, 102, 102n,
103, 104, 104n, 105, 109, 113, 116,
118, 121, 125, 129, 138, 140, 143,
144, 146–7, 148n, 149, 151, 155,
156n, 158, 161, 164, 167, 171, 172,
173, 174, 181, 182–3, 184, 186–7,
187n, 194, 197–8, 200, 212, 213n,
227, 228, 233, 234–5, 237, 238, 239,
241, 244, 246, 248, 249, 251, 254,
255, 258, 260, 266, 268, 274, 275,
276, 277, 278, 280, 301, 319, 352

Laurence, Jocelyn 14, 16, 20, 21, 22,
24, 30, 75, 76, 78, 80, 82, 83, 85,
86, 87, 89, 91, 92, 93, 94, 96, 102,
102n, 103, 104, 108, 112, 113, 116,
117, 123, 126, 138, 140, 141, 147,
148, 148n, 150, 151, 152, 157, 158,
161, 162, 165, 166, 167, 170, 171,
181, 184, 186, 187, 189, 191, 197,
198, 200–1, 202, 205, 207, 214, 215,
221, 227, 231, 232, 233, 234, 235,
238, 241, 243, 244, 246, 248, 251,
254–6, 258, 260, 262, 266, 267, 269,
274, 275, 276, 277, 278, 279, 280,
281, 288, 289n, 292, 293, 294, 296,
298, 302n, 310, 311, 314, 315, 317,
318, 320, 321, 322, 323, 324, 328,
329, 331, 332, 334–5, 334n, 337–8,
347, 348n, 352, 353, 354n, 355,
369, 371, 379, 380, 387, 395, 396,
397, 398, 398n, 402, 406, 407

Laurence, Margaret Wemyss: A Bird
in the House 329; The Christmas
Birthday Story 205n, 365, 366n,
367; Dance on the Earth 7, 20,
27nn, 34n, 357n, 406–7; The
Diviners 22, 26, 310, 314, 317,
319–20, 329–30, 331–2, 334, 335,
336, 338, 338n, 339, 341–2, 345,
348, 348–9n, 351, 352n, 371, 378,
384, 403; The Fire-Dwellers 233,
237, 239, 240, 241, 242, 242n, 245,
247, 250, 256, 257, 261, 263, 280,
290, 292, 293, 294, 294nn, 295,
298–9, 300, 317, 329, 354, 403;
Heart of a Stranger 174n, 200n,
213n; Jason's Quest 205n, 228,
229n, 237, 248, 276, 280, 284,
285n, 340, 343n, 370, 403; A Jest of
God 22, 190–1, 192, 197, 199, 200,
201, 202, 202n, 204–5, 211n, 213n,
215n, 219, 229n, 242, 247, 248,
252, 262, 264n, 269, 270, 283n,
293, 343, 344, 344n, 354, 386, 403;
—, Now I Lay Me Down 248,
249n; —, Rachel, Rachel 249n, 274,
280; Long Drums and Cannons 210,
211, 212n, 216, 237, 242, 248, 276,
280, 282, 287; The Prophet's Camel
Bell 4, 18, 20, 21, 132–3, 134n, 141,
142, 145n, 149, 158, 162n, 165,
167, 168, 192; —, New Wind in a
Dry Land 145n, 167; The Stone
Angel 4, 16, 17, 19, 20, 21, 22, 24,
135–6, 140, 142, 145n, 148n, 151,
152n, 154–5, 156, 158, 162n, 164,
167, 169, 171, 172n, 173, 182–3,
192, 194, 220, 228, 242, 243, 248,
264n, 269, 292–3, 329, 365, 371,
379n, 403; This Side Jordan 4,
15–16, 18, 19, 92, 93n, 96–100,
103, 105, 106, 109n, 114, 114n,
141, 162n, 242, 403; The Tomorrow-Tamer 353; A Tree for
Poverty 4, 15, 65n, 74n, 81n;
'Amiina' 84, 87, 88, 89n; 'Captain
Pilot Shawkat and Kipling's
Ghost' 212, 213n; 'The Crying of

the Loons' 158, 162n; 'The Drummer of All the World' 15, 89n,
91n, 115; 'The Exiles' 125, 127n;
'Godman's Master' 109n, 115;
'Good Morning to the Grandson
of Ramesses the Second' 212,
213n; 'A Gourdful of Glory' 115,
120, 123n; 'Horses of the Night'
226n, 231; 'Let My Voice Live'
37n; 'Mask of Beaten Gold' 171,
172n; 'The Mask of the Bear'
114n; 'The Merchant of Heaven'
109n, 115; 'Mrs Stephens and Her
Adopted Family' 184, 184n; 'The
Perfume Sea' 114n, 115, 127n,
150, 152n; 'The Poem and the
Spear' 198–9, 200n; 'The Pure
Diamond Man' 142, 145n; 'The
Rain Child' 114n, 150, 152n;
'Sayonara, Agamemnon' 174n;
'The Sound of the Singing' 114n,
142, 145n; 'The Spell of the
Distant Drum' 130; 'To Set Our
House in Order' 165n; 'The To-
morrow-Tamer' 109n, 145nn, 150,
152n, 159, 162n, 169n; 'Uncertain
Flowering' 15, 80, 81n; 'The
Voices of Adamo' 130n; 'What's
Novel about Canadian Novelists'
181, 182n
Laurence, Peg 388
Laurence, Rob 388
Laurence, Robin 388
Laurie, Eileen 128
Lawrence, D.H. (David Herbert) 253;
   The Rainbow 253
Laws, Donna 388, 389
Layton, Irving 186, 187n
Leacock Award for Humour 222n
League of Canadian Poets 377

Learned Societies 245, 247n, 250, 258
Leckie's Ladies' Wear 399
Lee, Dennis 279n, 346, 347n; Alligator
   Pie 346, 347n; Nicholas Knock and
   other People: Poems 346, 347n
Legate, David 289, 289n, 294n, 295,
   298
Lessing, Doris 193, 195n; African
   Stories 195n; The Golden Notebook
   195n
Levine, Norman 235, 236n
Liberty Temple School 9
Listener 300, 301n
Little Drummer Boy, The 325
Ljungh, Esse 175, 179n, 182n
London Philharmonic Orchestra 35
London School of Economics 11
Long, Elizabeth 81n, 87
Longhouse Bookshop 352, 353, 354n,
   373
Longman (publisher) 309, 310n, 314
Loons, the (club) 387, 392n
Lowry, Malcolm 133, 134n
Lucas, Alec 303, 304n; Hugh
   MacLennan 304n
Lucas, Helen 365, 366n, 374, 374n,
   387; This Is My Beloved –
   Sometimes 374, 374n
Ludwig, Jack 223, 224n, 225, 227,
   229n, 230, 274, 295; Above Ground
   223, 224n; Confusions 224n
Luther, Martin 155, 156n

MacDowell, Edward A. 110n
MacDowell Colony 17, 109, 110nn,
   114, 225, 226n
MacGibbon and Kee (publisher) 263
Maclean, Alan Duart 5, 19, 22, 23,
   150, 152n, 156, 157, 160, 161, 169,
   198, 201, 205, 216, 267, 270, 273,

300; ed. *Winter's Tales* 18, 19, 112,
114n, 119n, 120, 125, 142, 145n,
150, 152n, 188
Maclean's magazine 125, 127, 127n,
162n, 167, 168n, 198, 300, 302n,
342, 343n
MacLennan, Hugh 380–1, 382n;
*Scotchman's Return and other
Essays* 382n; 'A Boy Meets a Girl
in Winnipeg and Who Cares?'
381, 382n
Macmillan Company of Canada 5,
15, 17, 21, 100, 102n, 110, 112,
128, 136, 138n, 188, 194, 250, 270,
302, 303, 304, 305, 395, 396, 398n
Macmillan, London 18, 19, 22, 93n,
111, 112, 114, 114n, 128, 134n,
141, 142, 145n, 150, 152n, 154,
155, 156, 159, 160, 161, 162nn,
164, 165n, 167, 169, 186, 256, 257,
259, 263, 267, 276, 284, 287, 296,
300, 305, 334, 335, 336
Macmillan, New York 128
Macpherson, James (pseud. Ossian)
243, 244, 244n, 246, 248; *Fingal*
244n; *Temora* 244n; *Works of
Ossian* 244n
Mailer, Norman 5, 195, 225, 227n;
Why Are We in Vietnam? 227n
Mandel, Eli 349
Manitoba Festival of the Arts
Committee 213n
Manitoba Theatre Centre 136, 138n
Marshall, Christine 78, 79n, 230,
231
Marshall, John 78, 79n, 230, 231,
232n
Marshall, Joyce 368, 369, 372n, 374,
375n
Martin, C.J. (Bob) 149, 150n

Martin, Claire 218–19; *La joue droite*
220n
Martineau, Jean 219, 220n
Maugham, Somerset 95
McClelland, John Gordon (Jack) 5,
18, 110, 110n, 121, 126, 128, 131,
149, 158, 164, 165, 169, 205, 211,
256, 257, 296, 345, 346n, 384
McClelland and Stewart Publishers
10, 21, 22–3, 27n, 110n, 111, 112,
113n, 114n, 126, 129, 134n, 141,
145n, 149, 248, 256, 271, 271n,
299n, 304n, 330n, 334, 339n, 340,
341, 343n, 345, 346n, 384; New
Canadian Library 10, 248; —, Ca-
nadian Writers Series 299n, 304n
McGill University 21, 165n, 211, 250,
303, 304n, 349, 386n; Macdonald
College 21, 165n, 224n, 238, 252,
269, 349
McMaster University 372, 384
McPherson, Hugo 223, 224n, 226,
230, 282, 316, 317n
McPherson, Louise 223, 226, 282,
316, 317n
Metalious, Grace 123n; *Peyton Place*
122, 123n
Metcalfe, Marion 144
Methodism 14
Métis 342, 360, 378, 403
Michener, Roland 218, 220n
Milton, John 391; *On His Blindness*
391
Mindess, Bill 155n, 251
Mindess, Mary Turnbull 153, 156n,
251; *City of the Rivers* 153
Miner-Johnson, Valerie 341, 342, 343
Mitchell, Adrian 210n
Mitchell, W.O. (William Orm) 216n;
Who Has Seen the Wind 216n

Montreal Star 130n, 181, 182n, 224n, 271, 271n, 289, 289n, 292, 294n, 295, 298; *Weekend Magazine* 162n, 238n

Montrealer 289n, 382n

Morris, William 244

Morton, W.L. 27n; *Manitoba: A History* 27n

Moses, Anna Mary Robertson ('Grandma') 381, 382n

Munro, Alice 26, 351, 352n, 354; *Lives of Girls and Women* 351, 352n

Muraire, Jules Auguste César (pseud. Raimu) 45, 47n; *Fanny* 47n; *Un carnet de bal* 47n

Musgrove, Mildred 398, 399

Mutton, Paul 318

Mycenae 172, 174n; Lion Gate 172

Naipaul, V.S. (Vidiadhar Surajprasad) 276, 279n

National Conference of Christians and Jews Brotherhood Award 16

National Film Board of Canada 218n, 224n, 377

NDP (New Democratic Party) 206, 207n, 388

Neepawa Collegiate Institute 232n, 397, 398

NeWest ReView 362

Newfeld, Frank 347n

Newman, Paul 249n, 270

New Statesman and Nation 96, 100n, 123, 127n

New York Times 133; *Book Review* 403

Night of One Hundred Authors Dinner 405n

Nkrumah, Kwame 77, 79n, 82, 95, 96n; Convention People's Party 79n, 95, 96n

Observer 96, 100n, 133

Oedipus 173

Olsen, Tillie 354, 355n, 364, 365, 366, 366nn, 367, 369, 373; *Silences* 354, 355n, 369; *Tell Me a Riddle* 364–5, 366n, 367

Ontario Arts Council 347

Order of Canada 323

Ossian. *See* Macpherson, James

Overseas School of Rome 12, 65n

Oxford University 221, 222n, 223, 268, 279

Panther Books 248, 249n

Papas, William 271n; Theodore 269, 271n

Parker, Dorothy 108, 109n

Parr, Joan 340, ed. *Winnipeg Stories* 343n

Parr, John 343n; ed. *Speaking of Winnipeg* 343n

Pater, Walter Horatio 238

Patterson, Jack 357

Pavlov 289

Penguin Books 282, 283n, 310

Penner, Addie 37, 38n, 205, 222, 223, 251, 327, 330

Penner, Roland 37, 38n, 205, 222, 223, 251, 327, 330

Pennsylvania State University 321

Pentecostal Church 350

Peterborough Examiner 343, 344n, 350, 352n, 381

Peterman, Michael 368, 372n, 380

Peterson, Leslie 388, 392n

Phelps, Ann 382–3

Phelps, Arthur 383, 386n

Picts 89n, 359, 363, 401, 402n
Piller, Ted 366n
Polk, James 335, 336n
Porter, Anna 340, 343n
Powers, Jean 318
Powers, Lyall 318, 319, 320n;
    Faulkner's Yoknapatawpha Comedy
    319, 320n
Pratt, Claire 21, 112, 113n
Pratt, E.J. (Edwin John) 112, 113n
Presbyterians 162, 184
Price, Mac 100
Prism International 18, 19, 106–7,
    109n, 112, 115, 116, 119nn
Proclaim Publications 374n
Punchinello Gallery 386, 387
Purdy, Al 5–6, 23, 219, 220n, 294,
    294n, 317, 346, 385; *The Cariboo
    Horses* 220n; *In Search of Owen
    Roblin* 346
Purdy, Eurithe 294, 294n

Quakers, 392
Quebec Ministry of Cultural Affairs
    165n
Queen's Quarterly 10, 15, 84, 86n,
    91n, 112, 119n
Queen's University 15, 86n, 113n,
    230, 385; Canadian Writers'
    Conference 15
Quill and Quire 345, 346n, 385, 386n

Radio Uganda 158
Raimu. *See* Muraire, Jules Auguste
    César
Random House 239
Reaney, Colleen 224, 226, 226n, 332
Reaney, James 224, 226, 226n, 332,
    333, 333n
Regina Public Library 377

Renault, Mary 125
Richardson, Boyce 224n
Richler, Florence 167, 168n
Richler, Mordecai 4, 92, 96, 167, 168n,
    216n, 282, 283n, 310, 381, 384; *The
    Apprenticeship of Duddy Kravitz*
    183, 216n; *Son of a Smaller Hero* 4,
    92, 93n; 'The Social Side of the
    Cold War' 167, 168n; ed. *Canadian
    Writing Today* 282, 283n, 310
Richter, Conrad 123n; *The Waters of
    Kronos* 123n
Riel, Louis David 153, 154, 155nn,
    329, 360
Riverwoman, Mary Warshaw 401
Rohmer, Richard 367, 372n
Rosenthal, Joe 188, 189n, 344, 345,
    346nn
Ross, Malcolm 9–10, 15, 84, 86n, 87,
    88, 89n, 90, 105, 112, 180, 182,
    182n, 183, 226, 230, 232, 235, 238,
    239n, 241, 252, 287, 289
Ross, Sinclair 216, 216nn, 217, 248,
    259; *As For Me and My House* 216,
    216n; *The Lamp at Noon and other
    Stories* 248, 249n
Rothe, Billee 309
Roy, Gabrielle 345, 346n
Royal Air Force 10
Royal Winnipeg Ballet 14
Rule, Jane 347, 348n; *Lesbian Images*
    348n; *Theme for Diverse
    Instruments* 348n
Ruskin, John 44, 47n, 238; *The Stones
    of Venice* 47n; 'The Nature of
    Gothic' 47n
Russian Revolution 8

Sahl, Mort 134, 134n
Sandler, Susan 354n

Sargent, Sir Malcolm 35
Saturday Evening Post 125, 127n, 130,
  130n, 133, 159, 164, 169
Saturday Night 341, 343n, 344n, 397
Saturday Review 125, 127n
Saywell, William 388, 389
Schultz, Audrey 364, 364n, 368
Scott, Jack 300
Second Hundred Club 403, 405n
Second World War 9, 47n
Selchen-Dorn, Miriam 224, 226n
Sherman, Kenneth 344, 346n
Sifton, Clifford 8
Simon Fraser University 388, 389,
  390, 392nn; University Club 388
Simpson, John 7
Simpson, Ruby 7, 102, 194n, 399
Sir George Williams University 21,
  165n, 282
Six Nations 377
Slater, Clare 225, 226n, 284
Sniderman, Eleanor Koldofsky 374,
  374n
Social Gospel 9, 14
Soyinka, Wole 251, 252n, 287, 297,
  381; Kongi's Harvest 251, 252n,
  287; The Strong Breed 297; The
  Trials of Brother Jero 297
Spark, Muriel 160–1, 162n; The Prime
  of Miss Jean Brodie 162n
Spock, Benjamin 118, 120n; Baby and
  Child Care 120n
St Martin's Press 93n, 114n, 115, 125,
  141, 158, 162nn
Stafford, Fiona J. 244n; The Sublime
  Savage 244n
Staines, David 382n
Stainsby, Donald 116, 120n, 341
Stanislawski Method 24, 193, 195n;

Alekseyer, Konstantin
  Sergeyevich 195n
State University of New York: at
  Buffalo 197n; at Stony Brook
  224n
Stepney Jewish Girls (B'nai B'rith)
  Club and Settlement 11, 12, 15,
  40, 41, 42, 42n, 51, 309
Stern, Stuart 219–20, 220n; Rebel
  without a Cause 220n; The Ugly
  American 220n
Stobie, John 15, 83, 84n, 88
Stobie, Margaret 15, 83, 84n, 88, 154,
  156n
Stone, Dmitry 22, 25, 223, 224, 224n,
  225, 229, 231, 235, 236, 237, 238,
  239, 242, 244, 245, 246, 247, 248,
  249, 250, 251, 253, 254, 258, 259,
  260, 265, 269, 270, 272, 273, 273n,
  275, 282, 283, 285, 288, 291, 292,
  297, 298, 299, 302, 303, 305, 306,
  307, 308, 309, 312, 313n, 316, 320,
  321, 326, 327, 328, 328n, 332, 333,
  334, 338, 339, 347, 362, 365, 373,
  375, 382n, 385, 387, 390, 402, 405
Stone, Marshall 25, 253, 260, 266,
  268, 272, 273, 273n, 274, 275, 282,
  283, 285, 286, 291, 292, 296, 303,
  309, 335
Stone, Michael 25, 253, 260, 266, 268,
  272, 273, 273n, 274, 275, 282, 283,
  285, 286, 290, 291, 292, 296, 303,
  335
Stone, Noel 223, 251, 270
Stone, Sergei 25, 223, 224, 224n, 225,
  265–6, 268, 269, 270, 274, 275, 282,
  283, 285, 286, 291, 292, 296, 303,
  308, 309, 312, 313, 316, 320, 321,
  326, 328, 328n, 333, 335, 339

Stone, Tamara 22, 23, 25, 30, 283n, 288, 295, 297, 303, 305, 306, 307, 308, 309, 311, 312, 313, 314, 316, 317, 320, 321, 325, 326, 328, 328n, 332, 333, 339, 343, 362, 365, 366, 370, 373, 374, 375, 386, 402, 405, 406
Story Press 81
Story: The Magazine of the Short Story in Book Form 15, 79, 81n
Stroud, Carsten 397–8; The Blue Wall 397
Styron, William 5, 195
Suknaski, Andrew 377, 379n; In the Name of Narid 377
Sunday Times 96, 100n
Sword, Constance 230, 232n
Sword, John 232n, 241
Sykes, Philip 300

Tallman, Warren 216, 216n; 'Wolf in the Snow' 216, 216n
Talmud Torah 9
Tamarack Review 112, 114n, 119n, 120, 125, 136, 138nn, 142, 145n, 171, 172n, 188, 314, 316n
Tanner, Margaret 348
Tate, Allan 225, 226n
Taylor, Winnifred 51, 51n
Tecumseh Press 27n
Telford, James 350, 351
Tennyson, Alfred Lord 74, 74n; In Memoriam A.H.H. 74n
Theall, Donald F. 378, 379n
Theatre 77, 138n
Thomas, Clara 25, 27n, 299, 299n, 323, 336, 344, 383; All My Sisters 27n; Margaret Laurence 298, 299n
Thomas, Morley 25

Thomas of Celano 219; Dies Irae 219
Thornton, Eugenia 300, 301n
Time magazine 290, 292, 292n, 293, 295
Times Literary Supplement 123, 127n, 300, 301n
Torell, Staffan 285n
Toronto Life 397
Toronto Star 348, 398n, 406, 406n
Toronto Telegram 130n, 210n
Trent University 25, 26, 331, 340, 343, 356, 357n, 363, 364nn, 366, 367, 368, 369, 372nn, 378, 379nn, 383; Margaret Laurence Scholarship 378; Wenjack Theatre 378
Tristan and Isolde 95, 96n
Tristram Shandy (Sterne) 253
Trojan War 174n
Trudeau, Pierre Elliott 388
Tupper, Margaret 100
Tutuola, Amos 280, 281n; My Life in the Bush of Ghosts 281n
Twayne World Authors Series 14

Ukrainian Labour Temple 10
Unitarian Church 140, 152
United Church 332
United College 8, 156n, 311, 312n, 320n, 386n
University of Birmingham 311, 312n, 314, 315
University of Bologna 197n
University of British Columbia 18, 104, 105, 106, 106n, 109nn, 111, 115, 120n, 153, 154, 216n, 220n
University of Calgary 383–4
University of Guelph 381, 382n
University of Iowa 11
University of London 200n, 236n;

School of African and Oriental Studies 53n, 200n
University of Manitoba 10, 14, 15, 21, 38n, 81nn, 84n, 86n, 156n, 213nn, 222n, 226, 252, 312n, 352n, 406n; *Alumni Journal* 406n; Chancellor's Prize 10
University of Michigan 320n
University of New Brunswick 235, 236n
University of Rome 197n
University of Texas 14
University of Toronto 23, 215n, 223, 227, 229, 230, 231nn, 232, 232n, 239, 241, 242, 258, 260, 274, 278, 279n, 282, 295, 307n, 310n, 323, 347, 385; Massey College 23, 25, 231n, 347; School of Library Science 230, 232n; Trinity College 230, 232, 238, 279n; Victoria College 323
University of Toronto Press 27n, 29
University of Western Ontario 226n, 331, 332, 369
University of Windsor 367, 372n
Ursell, Geoffrey 395; *Perdue or How the West Was Lost* 395

van Meegeren, Hans 44, 47n; *Christ in the House of Martha and Mary* 44, 47n
Vancouver Sun 116, 121, 127, 130, 130nn, 133, 134n, 300, 302n, 388, 390, 392n, 403
Vanity Fair (Thackeray) 237
Veale, Steve 343, 344n
Vermeer, Jan 44, 47n
Viking Press 5, 15, 26, 96, 100n, 259, 260n, 261, 262, 265, 266, 266n, 273, 276, 368

Vikings 368
Volkening, Russell 239

W. Boyd and Company 81n
Waddington, Miriam 327, 328n; *Driving Home* 327
Wade, Barbara 381, 382n
Waisman, Chaika Rosenberg 8, 9, 12, 21, 23, 34, 71, 210, 211, 222, 231, 250, 251, 253, 268, 272, 273, 275, 302, 305, 312, 338, 347, 356, 357n, 401, 402n, 407
Waisman, Pesach 8, 9, 12, 21, 23, 34, 71, 222, 231, 250, 251, 253, 268, 272, 273, 302, 305, 338, 347
Wakefield, Linda 343
Wakefield, Mrs 343
Wakefield, Susan 343
Warehouse Theatre 392n
Warhaft, Sid 79, 212, 213n
Waves 344, 345, 346n
Weaver, Robert 21, 112, 113n, 158, 161, 171, 174, 175, 181, 182n, 219, 220n, 244
Weinzweig, Helen 402, 405nn
Weiss, Peter 210n; *Marat/Sade* 209, 210n
Wemyss, John 7, 8, 401
Wemyss, Margaret Harrison 390
Wemyss, Margaret Simpson 7, 8, 16, 89, 96, 102–3, 102n, 104n
Wemyss, Robert 103, 104n, 346, 347n
Wemyss, Robert Harrison 7
Wemyss, Verna Simpson 7
Westerner 10
Wheeler, Lloyd 252
White, Howard 390, 392n
Whitelaw, Marjory 238, 238n, 243, 246, 251

Wiesel, Elie 357; *A Beggar in Jerusalem* 357
Wilson, Alan 356, 357n
Wilson, Budge 356, 357n, 395
Wilson, Colin 150, 152n; *The Outsider* 150, 152n
Wilson, Ethel 19, 130, 130n, 198
Wilson, Michael 106, 108n, 111
Wing, Willis Kingsley 5, 17, 18, 20, 130, 131, 133, 134–5, 141, 148, 158, 159, 162n, 164, 392n
Winnipeg Citizen Co-operative Publishing Company 10, 311, 312n, 404
Winnipeg General Strike 8
Winnipeg Little Theatre Centre 138n
Winnipeg Tribune 130n
Winston, Helene 404
Wiseman, Adele: *Crackpot* 4, 23, 26, 189, 194, 201, 202n, 203–4, 205–6, 214, 217, 222, 224–5, 236–7, 239, 241, 243, 245, 246, 247, 247n, 250, 253, 257, 258, 259, 265, 268, 273, 274, 283n, 287, 296, 297, 302, 304, 305, 307, 308, 309, 310, 310n, 314, 335, 336, 338, 339n, 344–5, 346, 349, 393; *The Lovebound: A Tragi-Comedy* 4, 16, 17, 134, 138–9, 163, 174–9, 179n, 180–1, 182, 182n, 183, 187, 194, 195–6, 202, 203–4, 262, 299, 305–6, 333; *Memoirs of a Book-Molesting Childhood and Other Essays* 4, 130n; *Old Markets, New World* 25, 188, 189, 189n, 194, 346n; *Old Woman at Play* 4, 25–6, 335, 336n, 338, 348, 352, 356; *The Sacrifice* 3–4, 5, 12, 13, 15, 16, 57n, 93n, 100n, 125, 128, 160, 177, 260n, 262, 269, 349, 393, 394; *Testimonial Dinner* 155n; 'A Duel in the Kitchen' 125, 127–8, 130n; —, 'On Wings of Tongue' 130n; 'How to Go to China' 130n; 'Junk Hunting at Home and Abroad' 162, 162n; 'My Burglar' 157, 162n; 'Nor Youth Nor Age' 10; 'On Food and Eating' 162, 162n; 'What Price the Heroine?' 380, 382n; 'Where Learning Means Hope' 157, 162n; ed. *The Canadian Women Writers Engagement Calendar* 391, 392n
Wiseman, Arnold 81n, 82, 210, 211, 211n, 222, 223, 231, 252, 260, 264, 321
Wiseman, Esther 54, 57n, 71, 78, 81, 81n, 82, 181, 182, 187, 191, 211n
Wiseman, Harry 34n, 81n, 82, 181, 211, 211n, 222, 230, 231, 244, 253, 260, 264, 268, 272, 279, 321
Wiseman, Morris 33, 34n, 51, 222, 231
Wohl, Ira 364n
Woman's Mirror 184, 184n, 187, 188
Woodcock, George 24, 17n, 216n, 354, 355n; ed. *A Choice of Critics* 216n, 217
The Wooden Horse 277
Woodman, Ross 144
Woodsworth, Anne 383, 386n
Woodward, Joanne 249n, 280
Woolf, Virginia 368; *To the Lighthouse* 253
Wordsworth, Christopher 168n
Wright, Richard 95, 96n; *Black Boy* 95, 96n
Writers' Development Trust 405n
Writers' Union of Canada 22, 25, 336n, 338, 339n, 340, 355, 357nn, 372n

Yaddo Artists' Colony 17
Yeatman, Robert 160, 164
Yeo, Gren 144
York University 230, 299n, 328n,
    346, 348, 348n, 349, 350, 364n,
    370, 371, 372, 372n, 382, 383, 384;
    Archives and Special Collections
    28; Scott Library 28

Young People's Theatre 364, 366n

Zahl, Amy 17, 130nn, 137, 141n, 224,
    226n, 231
Zilber, Jake 106, 109n, 115